Southern Biography Series
William J. Cooper, Jr., Editor

Earl K. Long

Earl K. Long

*The Saga of Uncle Earl
and Louisiana Politics*

———————◆———————

Michael L. Kurtz and
Morgan D. Peoples

Louisiana State University Press
Baton Rouge and London

Louisiana Paperback Edition, 1992

01 00 99 98 97 96 95 94 93 92   5 4 3 2 1

Designer: Diane Batten Didier
Typeface: Galliard
Typesetter: G&S Typesetters, Inc.
Printer and Binder: Thomson-Shore, Inc.

Library of Congress Cataloging-in-Publication Data

Kurtz, Michael L., 1941–
    Earl K. Long : the saga of Uncle Earl and Louisiana politics /
Michael L. Kurtz and Morgan D. Peoples.
        p. cm. — (Southern biography series)
    Includes bibliographical references.
    ISBN 0-8071-1577-0 (cloth); ISBN 0-8071-1765-X (paper)
    1. Long, Earl Kemp, 1895–1960. 2. Louisiana—Politics and
government—1865–1950. 3. Louisiana—Governors—Biography.
I. Peoples, Morgan. II. Title. III. Series.
F376.3.L67K87 1990
976.3'06'092—dc20
    [B]   89-37883
                                                                  CIP

AAT 5033.

Contents

Illustrations

Preface

During one of his campaigns for governor, Earl Long made a stump appearance before a crowd of farmers in rural St. Tammany Parish. In typical fashion, he promised that if elected, he would have a local road, heavily traveled and full of potholes, widened and paved. Long won the election and carried the rural district, but when the legislature convened, he failed to include the promised road work in his agenda of bills. Astonished and furious at this display of gubernatorial duplicity, a large contingent of irate citizens journeyed to Baton Rouge to see Governor Long. Earl would not see them, and they subjected his administrative aide to a barrage of threats and insults. Refusing to leave, they stood their ground and demanded that Long see them. Equally adamant, Earl turned down the impassioned pleas by his aide. The fist-shaking mob gave the aide one last chance, and out of sheer exasperation, he said to Long, "After all, governor, you did promise to have their road paved. What should I tell those people?" With a shrug, Earl replied, "Tell 'em I lied!"

Whether this or one of the two dozen other versions of the "Tell 'em I lied!" tale the authors have read and heard is the accurate one, it does illustrate one aspect of the complex personality of Earl Kemp Long. Almost everyone in Louisiana knows, or at least has heard, an Earl Long story, for he has become one of the legendary figures in the state's political history, remembered as much for his eccentric mannerisms as for his political accomplishments. There still exists a large body of politicians, journalists, and others who can regale their listeners for hours with amusing stories about Long's personal foibles and political exploits. Blessed with a gregarious personality, graced with a consummate wit, the old stumper could instantly transform a serious occasion into a frivolous one by injecting a liberal dose of unrestrained humor or displaying one of his many personal quirks. In the middle of a stump speech, he would pause, douse his sweat-beaded brow with a cup of iced cola, and resume speaking. On the floor of the legislature, he would stroll down the aisle, press the "aye" or "nay" button at the desk of a legislator, hand him a wad of cash, and continue on his way. At the Governor's Mansion, he would every morning carefully peruse the *Daily Racing Form* and check the local newspapers for grocery bargains. He could be found in giant Schwegmann's supermarket in New Orleans purchasing large quantities of Mogen David wine, or in a general store in tiny Montpelier haggling over the price of seed, or spending thirty minutes in a long-distance telephone conversation cursing out an associate who failed to get him a reduced price for potatoes.

He could achieve heights of eloquence when he spoke of the needs of Louisiana's poor masses, whose causes he championed throughout his career, and at the same time, he would infuriate his rural supporters by hurling insults at them. No other governor could point to as lengthy a list of positive achievements: old-age pensions; charity hospitals; welfare prescriptions; roads, bridges, and highways; hot school lunches; hefty pay raises for schoolteachers; enormous increases in state spending for health, education, and welfare programs. Yet none of these produced real, tangible improvements in the lives of the poor citizens for whom they were intended.

Like most human beings, Earl Long was a paradoxical individual. He could outpolitick even the most experienced professionals, and he possessed an uncanny sixth sense—he knew precisely the means necessary to win votes or get bills passed. Yet several times during his career, he lost touch with political reality and made mistakes that the rankest amateur would have avoided. He was a master campaigner, but he lost as many elections as he won. He could be scrupulously honest, yet he gained a reputation as a legendary wheeler and dealer. He could be overly generous, often taking money out of his own pocket to help a family in need, or hiring a man with a large family. Yet he could be niggardly in the extreme, making friends pay a nickel for a newspaper he simply took from a newsstand. And when the mood struck him, he did not hesitate to fire people for such reasons as "political halitosis."

A fascinating individual whose career spanned four of the most tumultuous and controversial decades in Louisiana history, Earl Kemp Long has attracted the attention of scholars, journalists, and others; their collective works provide a bonanza of information about him. Yet he remains the subject of much misinformation, and like the "Tell 'em I lied!" story, the more time passes, the wider grows the gap between Earl Long the man and Earl Long the legend. This work attempts to bridge that gap by presenting the first full biography of this remarkable man. It is a personal biography, but one that emphasizes Long's political career, for Earl Long was a political animal. Politics flowed in his blood, and he spent all his adult life and quite literally died politicking. All who knew him, both friendly and hostile, agreed that no one, not even his more famous brother Huey, had a more profound grasp of the byzantine world of Louisiana politics or proved more adept at wheeling and dealing. He was a trooper of the old school who manipulated the courthouse rings and the legislature with the skills that mark the great masters and who had no peer in his ability to communicate with the poor masses. It is also a personal biography that delves beneath the stereotyped depiction of Earl Long as a tragicomic, avuncular figure whose being committed to mental asylums in 1959 demonstrated his flawed and unbalanced personality. To be sure, Long had more than his share of faults and shortcomings, but he deserves an objective portrayal.

In describing the secret of his political success, Earl Long once said: "Don't write anything you can phone. Don't phone anything you can talk. Don't talk anything you can whisper. Don't whisper anything you can smile. Don't smile anything you can nod. Don't nod anything you can wink." Earl apparently adhered to that code, for the most formidable obstacle we encountered in our research was the almost total lack of manuscript materials. His innumerable whispers, smiles, nods, and winks went unrecorded, and the few surviving pieces of his correspondence consist primarily of typical gubernatorial messages to his constituents and official addresses and proclamations. We consulted official state records of the governor's office, the legislature, and the boards and agencies, and they do contain valuable factual information. But they offer no insight into the behind-the-scenes politicking that was crucial to Earl Long's success.

The published accounts about Earl Long range from the extremely useful to the virtually useless. Louisiana newspapers proved especially helpful. Despite the anti-Long prejudices of their publishers, such reporters as Maggie Dixon, Edgar Poe, Ed Clinton, Jim McLean, and James Gillis gave Long ample and balanced coverage. The national press, however, almost universally portrayed Earl as a clown and a buffoon, as yet another in an apparently unending list of southern demagogues whose only claim to fame rested on personal corruption and an inordinate lust for power. One exception deserves mention. A. J. Liebling of the *New Yorker* came to Louisiana in 1959 to find out what happens after the governor of a state goes mad. His conclusions, subsequently published in a book, *The Earl of Louisiana,* provide an amusing and penetrating analysis of Long and Louisiana politics.

Over a period of two decades, we have conducted hundreds of oral interviews with Long's family members, personal friends, and political allies and foes. Those interviews made us keenly aware of the hazards of oral history. In many, people displayed singularly convenient memories, recounting only those episodes they wished to reveal, often in unique versions of the actual events. They often showed a disregard for names, dates, places, and other sorts of information. There clearly were personal or political axes to grind. Several family members, for instance, appeared quite anxious to describe Earl Long in the most favorable light possible and either ignored or evaded questions that touched upon the seamy side of his career. A number of his political associates informed us at the outset that they would not say anything "bad" about him; some of his opponents proved all too eager to tell all the "dirt" they could. In some interviews, we heard stories that contained a grain of truth and a bushel of exaggeration.

Despite these obstacles, the oral interviews gave us a priceless storehouse of information unavailable elsewhere. From them, we have gleaned a considerable amount of previously unrevealed material about Long's life and political career. Following the accepted practices of both journalists and historians, we have used only those data from the interviews that could be corroborated by independent sources. In some instances, however, we did use information that accorded with known facts and appeared, in our judgment, to be reasonably accurate.

The most valuable single collection of source materials we used was the Governor Earl Kemp Long files of the Federal Bureau of Investigation (FBI). Between 1939 and 1960, the bureau's longtime director, J. Edgar Hoover, maintained more than a passing interest in Earl Long, and the hundreds of pages of declassified FBI files, employed here for the first time, provide a wealth of documentation about the seamier aspects of Long's political career. Although we had read and heard stories about

Long's connection with organized crime, we had seen virtually no sub-stantiation for the allegations made. The FBI files describe in explicit detail the names, dates, places, and even the actual amounts of money exchanged during the close relationship Long had with organized crime figures. As with all other sources, we have used the FBI files with caution, for some of them simply contain allegations and no proof. Those FBI materials we did use offered, in our judgment, sufficient facts to give them credibility. Obviously, we ourselves had no direct personal knowledge of the alleged connection between Earl Long and organized crime, nor do we make personal accusations against Earl Long either of such ties or of acts of political corruption. But we mention a number of specific instances of both, using information from the FBI files and, whenever possible, from other sources.

While a considerable amount of information is available about Earl Long's early life, comparatively little exists about his personal life during adulthood, especially regarding his relationship with his wife, Blanche. In numerous interviews, we found that those persons who knew Long intimately provided few details other than those already widely known, and they merely said such things as "He was a thoughtful, considerate man," "He and Blanche had a close, happy marriage," "He was a good man." In other words, we found little of value about his personal life, and most of what we did uncover centered on his activities at the pea patch farm in Winnfield. In the absence of accurate information, we decided that we would be remiss in our responsibilities as biographers simply to fill a chapter with meaningless discussions regarding Long's marriage and certain other aspects of his personal life.

The one exception to this dearth of material about Long's personal life concerns the most heavily publicized phase of his career—his "mental collapse" and confinement to mental institutions in Texas and Louisiana in the late spring and early summer of 1959. Because so much sensationalist writing surrounds these episodes, we give a detailed narrative of the actual events. We have also attempted a new explanation for Long's behavior, an explanation rooted in psychiatry. Aware of the dangers of "psycho-history," we nevertheless believe that sufficient information about Long's life is available to permit a plausible hypothesis. That Earl Long suffered from bipolar disorder, or, as it used to be called, manic depression, accords with all his known traits of personality and with all his peculiar personal habits. We consulted the relevant psychiatric literature, and an eminent psychiatrist reviewed the manuscript of our chapter on Long's mental illness to ensure that the material therein was both accurate and credible.

What emerges from these pages is a portrait of a man who was, as Huey Long described himself, sui generis, and Huey's younger brother Earl certainly was one of a kind. No one who ever met or saw Earl Long has ever forgotten his raspy voice, unpredictable mannerisms, and unique, colorful political style. He had more than his share of devoted admirers and of equally devoted opponents. He was one of those individuals who, by force of personality and by effectiveness of action, leave a lasting impression on their field. For over forty years, Earl K. Long brushed the panorama of Louisiana politics with his distinctive campaigns and programs, and he left a legacy that still exercises a profound influence, both beneficial and detrimental, on the state political system.

Earl K. Long

Introduction

Longism and Louisiana Politics

In Louisiana on October 22, 1983, former governor Edwin W. Edwards defeated David C. Treen in the gubernatorial election by a margin of nearly two to one, turning out of office an incumbent elected governor for the first time in the state's history. To those familiar with Louisiana politics, it came as no surprise that many people voted for Edwards mainly because they considered him a master political manipulator. For four years Treen had labored to demonstrate that it was possible for a politician to accomplish his goals in Louisiana without resorting to the unrestrained spoils politics of the past, but those efforts did not produce many of the tangible results by which the state's voters judge their leaders. Edwards, by contrast, had served as governor for eight years, and although numerous allegations of corruption had touched his administrations, no one questioned his political skill or achievements. His flamboyant life-style entertained more voters than it offended, for Louisianians have long reveled in colorful anecdotes about their leaders' activities and have traditionally looked to politics not only for the satisfaction of civil needs but for high drama and entertainment. More important, whatever polls revealed about the voters' estimation of Edwards' personal integrity, many people believed that he was more capable than his rival of dealing with the state's economic and social problems. Edwards far more than Treen typified Louisiana's unique political heritage and style.[1]

Many natives believe that in Louisiana dishonesty and corruption accompany the political process in as integral a manner as does humidity the weather. Some would call this attitude cynical, but others would label it realistic, an accurate appraisal of the experience of Louisianians with a political system unlike that in any other state. Editorial writers and political analysts have often compared Louisiana's brand of politics with that of the "banana republics" in Central America or with that of the Mediter-

ranean states, where the dispensation of favors comes in direct proportion to the amount of money distributed to officeholders. Throughout its
history, Louisiana has witnessed almost continuous political corruption
in all its many guises, an experience that derives largely from its citizens'
cosmopolitan heritage of European, Caribbean, African, and American
cultures. The state's political history comes replete with so many instances of fraud, graft, bribery, vote stealing, and other corrupt practices
that an investigation of vote fraud in a congressional election prompted
Time magazine to entitle its article on the case "Shaking the Money Tree:
Old-Fashioned Vote-Selling in Louisiana." No other state has elected
two governors simultaneously, but Louisiana has accomplished the dubious feat twice, in 1872 and 1876, the ultimate victor on both occasions
assuming office not through a legitimate count of the ballots but by force
of arms. In the last third of the nineteenth century, corruption had become so pervasive, as historian Joe Gray Taylor lamented, that "nobody
can say with certainty who legally won any Louisiana election between
1868 and 1900, nor can anyone say with certainty who would have won if
the elections had been honest, which none were."[2]

No one contributed more to this commonly held perception of the innate corruption of Louisiana politics than did Huey Long. During his
brief, eight-year regime, Long became a dictator, disdaining the ordinary
processes of constitutional government and flouting the principles of
separation of powers. The political machine he created came to be widely
identified with spoils politics of the most uninhibited kind. After Long's
death, his successors engaged in outrageous acts of personal enrichment,
stealing an estimated $100 million from the state. Huey's younger brother,
Earl, gave added weight to the common association of Longism with
corruption by openly practicing spoils politics. He wrecked the state civil
service system, fired civil servants for "political halitosis," and openly accepted "campaign contributions" from gamblers and mobsters. The
Longs did not invent corruption in Louisiana, but they certainly added
to the state's reputation as the most dishonest in the nation. To understand their impact on Louisiana politics, it is necessary to review briefly
the state's political history before 1928.[3]

Post-Reconstruction Louisiana was dominated by a coalition of rural
planters, parish courthouse rings, corporations, and the New Orleans
political machine. This coalition operated with little regard for the needs
of the poor masses and did not make even rudimentary efforts at improv-

ing their economic and educational status. It ran a state government of balanced budgets and benign neglect, which the people greeted with universal apathy and with a cynical toleration for corruption. On those occasions when the extent of the corruption grew to excessive proportions, as occurred in the 1880s, when Major Edward A. Burke and his cronies bilked the state of millions, temporary reform groups gained power and threw the rascals out of office. But these reformers showed no enthusiasm for substantial change, and they quickly revived the policies of the past. To assuage the rural masses, they disfranchised black voters and engaged in racist appeals. The voters tolerated this system because they paid few taxes and were accustomed to privation and neglect. Shrouded by this ultraconservative oligarchy, Louisiana seemed not to notice the onset of the twentieth century. In other southern states, populism ignited a bonfire of participation in government, but in Louisiana, its flicker was rapidly extinguished by a torrent of racial demagoguery and ballot stuffing. In the first three decades of the twentieth century, many southern states witnessed an expansion of popular democracy—such leaders as James Stephen Hogg in Texas, James K. Vardaman and Theodore G. Bilbo in Mississippi, Coleman "Cole" Blease in South Carolina, and Jeff Davis in Arkansas rose to power by using flamboyant stump tactics and firebrand oratory to rouse the masses from their historical lethargy. These "demagogues" railed against the rich and the elite, and, once in office, most did reward their followers with programs of expanded state aid to public schools and state regulation of public carriers and utilities. But like ol' man river, Louisiana rolled along, and no spokesman for the masses rose to challenge the ruling coalition until 1928. Thus, when Huey Long arrived on the scene, his clash with the entrenched powers took an especially dramatic and explosive form.[4]

Such is the traditional interpretation of pre–Huey Long Louisiana politics. Recent scholarly studies have shown, however, that Long did not appear in a political vacuum created by the conservative aristocracy, but rather that he expanded and extended programs of social and educational reform instituted by many of his predecessors in the Governor's Mansion. Far from a group of "gentlemen in frock hats, string ties, and wide hats" who gave Louisiana a "backward-looking 'government by goatee,'" the men who controlled the state between 1900 and 1928 tried to cope with the complicated problems arising from the growth of industry and the mass movement of the population from the farm to the city.

Inspired by the national Populist and Progressive movements, Louisiana governors and legislatures from 1900 to 1928 enacted a series of reforms that served as a solid foundation upon which Huey Long built. Governor William W. Heard, for example, abolished the notorious convict lease system and had legislation enacted allowing municipalities to regulate utilities. Governor Newton C. Blanchard, during his 1904-to-1908 term, instituted the party primary system for choosing nominees for elective office; vastly increased state spending for public schools; established state boards of corrections, charities, and forestry; and effected a minimum wage and maximum hour law. Under Governor John M. Parker, in office from 1920 to 1924, the positions of commissioner of agriculture and commissioner of conservation were created; severance taxes on oil, gas, and lumber, automobile license taxes, and the personal income tax were imposed; the state university was moved to a new, larger location; and state construction of roads and highways was begun. Most significant, Louisiana during the entire period reduced its adult illiteracy rate by more than 50 percent and doubled state appropriations for public education. All in all, before Huey Long took office, the record of accomplishment was impressive for what certain historians have labeled a conservative, even reactionary hierarchy that cared only for its own selfish interests and nothing for the common people. Despite this record, much remained to be done for the people of Louisiana.[5]

Thus, by the time Huey Long came to power in Louisiana, his predecessors had set the stage for his programs. Long, then, can be considered not as a revolutionary but as a popular leader who advocated and implemented policies started by others. Huey Long, however, was not merely another in a series of reformers. With a charismatic personality and a driving ambition, he became Louisiana's "messiah of the rednecks," leading the poor masses to political and economic salvation. He could see clearly what his opponents only dimly perceived, that in the common people, there existed a political force of unusual potency, and he would harness it to his advantage. Capturing the hearts of the poor, Long became their champion by voicing their grievances and frustrations and promising to do something about them. He awakened the tenant farmer and the sharecropper and the common laborer from their traditional apathy and brought them to the polls in record numbers. Attacking the big corporations and the vested interests, he engendered a mass movement among the people, thus linking his power firmly to the bedrock of overwhelming popular support. Once in office, Long realized that to retain that support, he would have to live up to his campaign promises, and within a few years, the state abounded with physical monuments to his success: thousands of miles of new roads, many of them paved; bridges spanning broad rivers; a vastly expanded state university; a magnificent new state capitol. At last, state government seemed to care for the ordinary man and woman. That Long's programs did not substantially improve their standard of living hardly mattered to the people. What did matter was that in Huey Long, they had a deliverer. By a sudden transformation, Louisiana politics became based on popular support, and this had a magical effect on public opinion. By the time of his death, Long was revered and idolized as was no other figure in the state's history. To this day, many Louisianians give him credit for things he did not do—for example, state-funded old-age pensions and the new Charity Hospital in New Orleans.⁶

Even though he had the support of the people, Huey Long came increasingly to make a mockery of the democratic process. Bribery, intimidation, graft, and a wholesale disregard for the ethical principles of democratic government came to characterize his rule. Long brooked no opposition. He ruthlessly gerrymandered his opponents' electoral districts, ordered the kidnapping of a potential political threat, directed the National Guard to "supervise" elections, and tried to suppress the editorial freedom of newspapers critical of his policies. He appointed political hacks to head the state universities and the charity hospital system, ran "dummy" candidates in elections to take votes away from the opposition, and destroyed the municipal independence of the city of New Orleans. By 1935, Huey Long dominated Louisiana to an extent unrivaled in American history, but he retained the affection and support of the people. Not only did they tolerate his methods, Louisianians actually endorsed them. The only way Long could get things accomplished, people believed, was to ignore or violate customary legal procedures. What did it matter if he resorted to spoils politics of the most flagrant type? What did it matter if his handpicked candidates in 1932 received the votes of such individuals as Babe Ruth, Jack Dempsey, and Clara Bow? What did it matter if the state legislature and the courts were reduced to impotency? What did matter was that Huey Long promoted the cause of the people, and that excused him from blame for his abuse of office. Huey Long thus invigorated political democracy in Louisiana while simultaneously destroying its checks and balances.[7]

Long forged a new alliance of politicians and cemented that alliance through an ever-expanding distribution of state jobs and money. He catapulted into power men who had demonstrated their loyalty, rewarding them with the bountiful patronage resources of state government to construct a powerful machine, constantly extending its tentacles into parish and local government, grabbing more and more power and suffocating the opposition. Despite the assertions of Long apologists, he did not destroy the political power of the old planter–New Orleans Ring coalition. On the contrary, he welcomed into his fold anyone who would support him, regardless of past affiliations. Nor did Long, who waxed eloquent on the stump in his denunciations of the corporations, especially the big oil companies, hesitate to include titans of finance in his camp. Among his inner circle were such men of wealth and prominence as Robert S. Maestri, Seymour Weiss, and oilmen Louis Roussel, William O. Helis, and James A. Noe. Long's political organization existed for one purpose only, to serve his interests. His Share Our Wealth philosophy, which he intended as a platform for his attempt to gain the presidency, proved to be a clever ploy appealing to the impoverished masses during the depression. Even though he ran Louisiana with an iron hand, Huey did not implement a single part of the Share Our Wealth program in his native state. His entire coterie of most trusted advisors consisted of men of great means; they would hardly have supported his plan for radical redistribution of the wealth. Instead, they joined his cause because he provided them with the opportunity of further enriching themselves or of enhancing their power.[8]

Appreciating the economic potential of the state's most abundant natural resources, oil and gas, Long used them as the main source of new state revenues to fund his public works projects. He swelled the state's coffers through increased severance taxes, mineral leases, and royalties, which levies the energy companies simply passed on to consumers by raising prices. He also financed many of his projects through long-term bonds. The revenues generated enabled him to avoid directly taxing property, sales, and income, thereby placing himself in an impregnable political position. He could advertise his programs as "free," free bridges, roads, highways, school textbooks, and charity hospitals. The voters believed him because they saw the actual results of his policies without paying additional taxes to fund them. Huey Long thus fostered the delusion, still strongly held in Louisiana, that state services can be provided "free," instilling in the citizens of the state an aversion to sources of recurring revenue commonly used in other states—among them, property taxes and realistic automobile license fees. In reality, Long obligated future generations to pay for his projects, a fiscal policy that would become habitual with most Louisiana governors.[9]

With oil and gas money overflowing the treasury and with payrolls consisting of thousands of public works employees, the Louisiana state government under Long dominated local politics down to the level of justice of the peace. Long, of course, controlled the state, directly during his gubernatorial term and indirectly during the term of his figurehead successor, Oscar K. Allen. After he crushed his opponents in the impeachment crisis of 1929, the Kingfish brought all state agencies under his wing, dictated the annual budget, and, through his adroit use of patronage and of the line-item veto, turned the legislature into what one newspaper called a "bunch of trained seals." Even after Long's death and the end of the dictatorship, the office of Governor of Louisiana became the most powerful in the United States: in fact, not once in over seventy-five years has the legislature overridden a gubernatorial veto. Earl Long also graphically demonstrated the control over the legislature that an expert wheeler-dealer wields. In 1948, his health, education, and welfare bills received a combined vote of 1,620 for and 8 against.[10]

One of the most potent weapons at the governor's disposal came through his vast appointive authority. Through their control of the state, the Longs had thousands of jobs to dispense, many lucrative patronage positions requiring little work. In addition, the governor could fill vacancies in local government. During his last term, Earl Long appointed 803 local officials and filled 702 vacancies in parish and municipal offices. It need hardly be mentioned that these positions went to those who cooperated with the governor. The Longs combined patronage with absolute control over the state budget. To a far greater extent than in other states, the Louisiana state government provided the lion's share of the money for the functions of local government. The state paid most of the salaries of schoolteachers, sheriffs, judges, assessors, clerks of court, and numerous others. Local government depended on Baton Rouge for the funding for projects ranging from pothole repairs to the construction of bridges over creeks. Mayors and police jurors gladly acquiesced: the state's assumption of responsibility relieved them of the politically unpopular task of levying the taxes necessary to pay for such projects. In Louisiana under the Longs, a peculiar form of revenue sharing came into existence, with the state raising the revenue and sharing it with local government. And the amount of the revenue shared was naturally dependent on the degree of political cooperation by local officials.[11]

The Longs greased the machinery of Louisiana politics with the universal lubricant, patronage. Architects who proved generous with campaign contributions found themselves rewarded with state construction contracts paying a 10 percent architectural fee. Faithful contractors received inside information about precise fees and specifications so their bids would be accepted. Assessors who carried their constituents for the machine won gubernatorial connivance at their widespread practice of appraising property at ridiculously low levels, far below its true market value. Friendly sheriffs were allowed to keep a larger portion of the local taxes they collected than they were entitled to. Police jurors who placed a call to the governor obtained jobs for relatives or constituents.[12]

Such practices, of course, are not unique to Louisiana and indeed are endemic to American politics, but in Louisiana under the Longs, they pervaded every aspect of state government. Certain safeguards, minimal as they are, have been enacted in recent years. But under the Longs, there was not even the semblance of legal restraint. Both Huey and Earl Long regarded civil service with disdain, and Earl actually abolished the state merit system. Charity hospitals, mental institutions, colleges and universities, prisons, public schools, all fell victim to heavy politicization. Schoolteachers, for example, who did not back Huey Long quickly found themselves without jobs, since Huey rejected all efforts to enact a tenure law. To secure his release from the state mental asylum in 1959, Earl fired the institution's director and replaced him with an aged physician who had no expertise in the treatment of the insane. The brothers Long packed state regulatory boards and agencies with their supporters, and businesses desiring favorable treatment from the boards soon learned that they first had to see the governor. Department heads who administered large budgets became used to merely rubber-stamping gubernatorial dictates. The spoils system infested every part of the state's activities, and citizens grew accustomed to seeing political hacks running universities, hospitals, and prisons.[13]

The Longs devised ingenious methods of manipulating state government to their political advantage. A. J. Liebling described Earl Long's attempts to maneuver a loan-shark bill. Ostensibly designed to curb usury, the bill limited the interest on loans to 3.5 percent per month, but it also allowed loan sharks to make loans of more than $1,000, a privilege formerly limited to the banks. The loan sharks backed the bill, and the banks opposed it. The New York reporter did not comprehend the significance of the bill, since in his home state, loan sharks were not considered important sources of graft. A friend, versed in the Machiavellian world of Louisiana politics, explained that special bills had to be passed every time a new loan shark wanted to obtain a license. To get the bill through the legislature and signed by the governor, the shark would give a lobbyist $10,000. As the bill progressed through the legislature the shark would give "campaign contributions" to key legislators and to the governor, keeping the remaining money for himself. Earl's bill would have changed the fundamental statute itself, so both the banks and all the loan sharks had to cough up huge amounts of money. As governor, Earl would get the bulk of the cash, and he readily accepted "contributions" from both sides.[14]

In similar fashion, the state's regulation of the oil and gas industry offered untold opportunities for graft. One of the stalwarts of the Long–Old Regular machine in New Orleans, assessor James E. Comiskey, recalled that every time the legislature met, Earl would have bills introduced to raise severance taxes and to impose stricter regulation on the industry. Comiskey estimated that it cost the energy companies a quarter of a million dollars each legislative session to kill the bills. During the 1930s, Huey's henchman Bob Maestri served as conservation commissioner, in which capacity he allowed cooperative oilmen to produce huge amounts of "hot oil"—oil, that is, in excess of state quotas. Since hot oil was illegal, it was exempt from severance taxes, and Maestri's office determined the extent of the illegal practice. The state Mineral Board also provided imaginative politicians with new sources of income. In exchange for generous donations, the gubernatorially appointed board permitted extensions of past-due royalty payments, allowed exemptions from certain restrictive licensing requirements, and less than vigorously enforced state pipeline regulations. No wonder some of the staunchest political backers of the Longs and some of their successors came from the very industries they had promised to regulate.[15]

Decades before the rise of the professional fund-raising business, with its computerized mailing lists and staffed phone banks, the Longs raised millions. At a time when campaigning was relatively inexpensive, and with no public disclosure laws to hamper their activities, they became masters at innovative ways of keeping cash flowing steadily into their treasury. In 1928, Robert Maestri contributed over $40,000 to Huey's campaign chest, and Earl gave his brother over $12,000, unheard-of sums for that time. Huey's notorious treasure chest for his intended campaign against Franklin Roosevelt in 1936 reportedly contained over $1 million in cash. Earl put the touch on oil and gas magnates, politicians, bankers, lawyers, and even organized crime bosses. Both Frank Costello and Carlos Marcello gave hundreds of thousands of dollars to Earl during his career. The "deduct" system was probably the most imaginative of the Longs' fund-raising devices. State employees discovered their paychecks showed a mysterious deduction of 5 or 10 percent from their salaries. These deducts were directly deposited into the Long campaign chest by the state government. Since their jobs depended on the Longs, state employees dared not complain.[16]

Huey Long kept a tight rein on his followers and ensured that the graft did not reach scandalous proportions, but his successors, under Governor Richard W. Leche, proved unable to keep from succumbing to greed. They dipped into the trough of political corruption and personal enrichment so deeply that a popular revolt ensued. As the scandals of 1939 unfolded, revealed in all their sordid details by enterprising journalists, the Long machine lost much of its public support and a viable opposition developed rapidly. Rendered virtually extinct by the Kingfish, this opposition, commonly labeled the anti-Longs, revived by exploiting the public's growing repugnance at the flagrant corruption of the Leche regime. Soon the anti-Longs had constructed a machine as formidable as that of the Longs, and they successfully contested the statewide elections of 1940. Assuming the mantle of reform and pledging to institute "good government" in Louisiana, the anti-Longs did put an end to many of the most outrageous abuses of office that the Long machine had perpetrated, but in many respects, they continued politics as usual. Historically, American reform movements have incorporated demands for political change with sweeping revisions of the existing economic and social order, but in

Louisiana, the "reform" faction pointedly avoided proposing revolutionary social and economic upheaval. Instead, they merely wanted to replace one political faction with another.[17]

Many scholars believe that the division of Louisiana politics into the Long versus anti-Long rivalry compensated for the lack of a genuine two-party system. In this point of view, the sharp differences between the Longs and the anti-Longs gave the voters a clear choice in elections, a bifactional substitution for a Democratic versus Republican contest. In reality, the Louisiana political situation was far more complex than this argument assumes. The evidence shows that neither the Longs nor the anti-Longs advocated a program that could reasonably be distinguished from that of its opposition. Thus, when Sam H. Jones became governor in 1940, he actually expanded and improved many of the programs Huey Long had begun. Jones, for example, increased state funding for roads, schools, and hospitals. In its social, educational, and economic aspects, Sam Jones's legislative record fully accorded with those of the Longs. Some authorities contend that the real difference between the two sides lay in their approach to the principles of good government, that the anti-Longs observed commonly accepted ethics of government while the Longs scorned them. It is, of course, true that the anti-Longs did espouse a commitment to responsible government, advocating civil service, the appointment of qualified persons to responsible positions, and stringent fiscal accounting. In practice, however, the anti-Longs did not hesitate to employ many of the methods the Longs had used. Upon taking office, Sam Jones fired more state employees than did Huey Long, and he appointed more of his followers to state positions than did the Kingfish. In both programs and political methods, the Longs and the anti-Longs had far more similarities than differences.[18]

With little to distinguish between the Longs and the anti-Longs, Louisiana voters cast their ballots, as they always had, largely on the basis of the candidates' personalities. The intensely personal nature of state politics often resulted in shifting allegiances from one election to the next. Louisiana politicians have traditionally supported those candidates with the best chances of winning, regardless of nominal loyalties. Thus, in 1940, Sam Jones welcomed into his fold one of Huey Long's most fervent supporters, James A. Noe. In 1948, anti-Long kingpins Sam Jones and deLesseps Morrison vigorously backed Robert F. Kennon in his race for the United States Senate against Russell Long because Kennon stood a reasonable chance of winning. Yet in the same primary, both Jones and Morrison covertly backed the Long candidate for the other Senate seat, Allen Ellender, because Ellender was certain to win. In 1952, Russell Long strongly backed anti-Long T. Hale Boggs in the first gubernatorial primary, and in the second primary, he threw his support to anti-Long Robert Kennon against the handpicked candidate of his Uncle Earl, Carlos Spaht, because Spaht had no chance of winning. In name only (that of opposing factions) could Louisiana be said to have had a bifactional political system, and it is both inaccurate and unrealistic to appraise state politics during the era of the Longs as consisting of distinctive political organizations.[19]

Because of the immense rewards of being governor of Louisiana, gubernatorial elections have historically attracted large numbers of candidates. To win election, a contender must gain appreciable support from all components of the state's complex political demography. Experts usually divide the state into geographical regions, each comprising a unique electorate: the New Orleans metropolitan area, with about 25 percent of the statewide vote; north Louisiana, with about 25 percent; Acadiana, with about 20 percent; the central region, with about 15 percent; and the Florida Parishes, with about 15 percent. A successful candidate for governor must carry at least three of the regions by a majority and run reasonably well in the others. This presents a formidable obstacle: unlike other southern states, Louisiana has a quite heterogeneous population, and the diversity of racial, religious, ethnic, and cultural patterns can be bewildering. The fundamentalist Protestants in the north must be balanced against the free-living Catholics in the south. The white, Anglo-Saxon majority in the north and central regions must be balanced against the black, Cajun, Italian, Irish, and other ethnic groups in the south. Furthermore, the south is heavily industrialized and unionized, and the north is generally agrarian.[20]

It was the genius of the Longs to overcome these and many other racial, religious, cultural, and ethnic divisions by employing economic class distinctions as the basis of their appeals. By pitting the poor against the rich, Huey and Earl constructed a powerful voting bloc of the lower classes. They persuaded tenant farmers, rednecks, Cajun fishermen, and common laborers to join together in common cause. In the 1950s, Earl Long went so far as to actively court the growing black vote, thus adding a new element to the bloc. The Longs turned the traditionally apathetic, disfranchised poor into citizens who cast their ballots on election day and demanded that government take care of their needs.[21]

The Longs made political campaigns in Louisiana the most elaborate, exciting, and expensive in the nation. Masters of the art of political manipulation, they introduced innovative techniques of campaign organization and advertising. Well before such devices became common, they used sound trucks, radio broadcasts, bumper stickers, broadsides, and advance men. To attract crowds, they provided entertainment—free food and country music. Once in office, they never stopped campaigning for the next election and bombarded voters with political newspapers and other forms of propaganda. To win votes, they engaged in highly inflammatory stump tactics that invariably provoked charges of demagoguery from their opponents. Name-calling, invective, ribald humor, biblical references, and a host of other rhetorical tricks gave rural audiences refreshing, emotion-laden reprieves from their everyday routines. Huey was mesmerizing: he delivered typical harangues against the rich, he displayed the force and brilliance of his intellect, he flavored his speeches with allusions to classical mythology and to literature. Earl, too, won them over, by a combination of spicy humor, graphic language, and eccentric personal habits. Even more than Huey, he could communicate with poor farmers, white and black, in their own language and make them feel he was one of them. Respecting the ingrained cynicism of Louisiana voters about state politics, the Longs spoke freely and openly about exploiting the system through methods that could generously be termed questionable.[22]

In office, the Longs set the pattern for future administrations, that is, their policy was that government offer many benefits at minimal expense to the taxpayer. Because of the steadily increasing revenue from taxes on the oil and gas industries, they were able to finance a cornucopia of state services in health, education, and welfare. Standard means of raising revenue—state income taxes, property taxes, and reasonable fees for the public's use of state services—were avoided. As the years passed, people came to expect and demand those services at little or no cost to themselves. The ultimate result of these fiscal policies came in the 1980s, when the state government found itself continually short of revenues because of an economic depression in the energy industry. More than anyone else,

Huey and Earl Long perpetuated the myth that people could get something for nothing, and the politicians of the 1980s proved eminently incapable of coping with the economic crisis they inherited.[23]

Whatever their shortcomings, the Longs revolutionized Louisiana politics. They took the state political system off its aristocratic pedestal and placed it squarely on an egalitarian base. They made Louisiana politics the most exciting, and the most corrupt, in the nation. Like gumbo, state politics combines many ingredients, heavily spiced by the personalities of the men in power. None would prove more colorful than Huey's younger brother, Earl.

1

Country Boy

To get to Winnfield, you have to travel through some of the poorest land in Louisiana. Driving down a two-lane highway, you pass dilapidated, abandoned sharecroppers' shacks, tin roofs half off, huge tracts of cut-over pine forest, and everywhere you look, the tell-tale signs of deep erosion in the red clay soil. Even today, with all the trappings of modern society—paved roads, telephone and electric lines, air-conditioned combines, every now and then a satellite dish antenna—you can't help being overwhelmed by the impression that Winn Parish is a poor place. There are no booming industries, no "high-tech" businesses, no large cities. It is a rural area through and through, still rough and primitive and, in the countryside, still showing the signs of the tough environment that the first settlers must have faced. Those people in the 1850s came from hardy pioneer stock, for only the hardiest would have dared to tackle the rolling hills and pine forests in a land so desolate, a local saying goes, "a man would skin a flea for the hide and tallow." [1]

One of the pioneering families who did take up the challenge in Winn Parish bore what would become one of the best-known political surnames in American history, the Longs of Louisiana. In their campaigns, Huey and Earl Long often referred to their humble origins, but the Longs in fact had more than a touch of class in their ancestry. In the 1750s, a young resident of London, England, named John Long decided for unknown reasons to migrate to America, and he and his wife made the voyage across the Atlantic and settled in Maryland. In 1760, they had a son, James, who grew up in Maryland but, upon reaching adulthood, set out for the newly opened Northwest Territory. Like many pioneers, James wandered through several areas until he found a permanent place to settle. Known as the "preacher-doctor," James had received a medical education at a Baltimore college, and he was an ordained Methodist minister. After spending a number of years in Springfield, Ohio, James's religious duties took him to Mississippi, where he lived in Jones, Jasper, and Smith counties, preaching his faith, attending to the medical needs of the people, and becoming a planter of modest means.[2]

James had several children, one of whom, John Murphy Long, was sixteen when the family moved from Ohio to Mississippi. The year the Longs moved south, 1845, John Murphy decided to start a life on his own, and he married Elizabeth Smith Wingate, the daughter of a neighbor in Smith County. As part of the marriage agreement, John Murphy converted to his bride's Baptist faith. John and Elizabeth lived for fourteen years in the small town of Raleigh, where they started a family and began a life of farming. In late 1859, John and Elizabeth Long loaded their possessions into an ox wagon and, together with their six children, left Mississippi for Winn Parish, Louisiana. After crossing the Mississippi River, they traveled along the Harrisonburg Road, ending their two-month journey in a small community named Tunica, located a few miles from the parish seat of Winnfield. John's brothers, James, Michael, and George, had already settled there, along with several other families from Smith County, and Tunica became, like many other towns in the rural South at the time, one whose population consisted largely of migrants from a neighboring state. It is hard to imagine why John Murphy Long gave up his life in Mississippi to make the hazardous, nearly three-hundred-mile trek to north-central Louisiana. In Raleigh, John had acquired several hundred acres of land, and his family's life was relatively comfortable. Three of Earl Long's sisters, Olive, Clara, and Lucille, believe that John Murphy was an adventurous man, struck by the pioneering spirit, who moved to Winn Parish to join his brothers in seeking economic opportunity in a new, unsettled region. However, the Long sisters were zealous in genealogical matters, ever eager to attribute the most noble of motives to their ancestors. Another, perhaps more plausible reason for John Murphy's move came during one of Earl Long's tirades before the state legislature: "My old grandfather got run out of Mississippi for racing horses on a Sunday. He come over here to hunt, to run horses, and to fish. He wasn't worried about working. He cleared up about a four or five acre patch."[3]

Earl's remark about his grandfather touched on one aspect of his character, his failure to provide a decent living for his growing family. For a

decade after he moved to Tunica, John Murphy Long struggled for economic survival while he and Elizabeth added to the family. They had a
total of fourteen children, eleven of whom would live to adulthood. The
years from 1860 to 1869 proved harsh and brutal for the Longs. Like many
other small farmers in the South, they faced falling prices for land and
crops during the severe upheavals of the Civil War and Reconstruction. It
would be easy to blame the Longs' problems on these events, but it is
clear that John Murphy bore the main responsibility. Unlike his brothers,
who prospered, John Murphy did not have the desire to undertake the
back-breaking labor that was necessary for a farmer in Winn to make a
success. Instead, he preferred to breed horses and race them, usually
losing his bets. By 1869, he had sold off most of the family holdings to
pay his debts, and he retired from farming. Ostensibly, illness forced him
to retire, but that explanation, again offered by his granddaughters, does
not ring true. Only forty to forty-four years old in 1869—accounts differ
about the exact year of his birth—John Murphy's illness could not have
been too serious, for he lived until 1901. The real reason probably was
imminent bankruptcy. In any event, the management of the farm was
turned over to seventeen-year-old Huey Pierce Long, the eldest son still
at home. Huey shared his father's passion for fine horses, a trait Earl
would inherit in full measure, but he came gifted with a keen business
sense. Despite his youth, he quickly made the Long homestead into a
profitable enterprise, expanding it to 360 acres in just seven years. Aware
of the risks inherent in a one-crop agricultural system and knowing how
inhospitable the Winn soil was to staple crops, he diversified into animal
husbandry, gaining a reputation as one of the area's leading producers of
hogs, horses, cattle, and oxen.[4]

In 1875, when he was twenty-four and earning a steady income, Huey
married Caledonia "Callie" Tison, the fifteen-year-old daughter of a respected Winn family. Callie came from French Huguenot, Welsh, En-
glish, Scottish, and German stock. One of her ancestors had helped survey the Louisiana Purchase territory, and another, Dennis Mackie, had
plotted out the land, mapped the boundaries, and chosen the name of the
new parish of Winn in 1852. Her grandfather, William Tison, reportedly
owned a thousand acres and a large number of slaves, and her father had a
sizable holding at Albright's Prairie, located near Atlanta, a small town
some ten miles southwest of Winnfield. During the Civil War, Callie's
parents, Edward and Cornelia Tison, lost all their land, and their poverty-

stricken existence contributed to Cornelia's death in 1865, when Callie was only five, and to Edward's death seven years later. After her father died, Callie lived until her marriage with her older half-sister, Mary Woodruff, who had a large family of her own.[5]

After a brief honeymoon, Huey and Callie moved in with his parents and lived in the Long home for five years. By 1880, Huey had saved enough money to buy a small farm adjacent to his parents' place, and he began to raise livestock there while still managing John Murphy's farm. While Huey and Callie lived in Tunica, they had four children, Charlotte, Julius, George, and Helen, who died at the age of eighteen months. Huey's brother, George, already an established businessman, advised him to buy land. Recognizing the potential for growth in the tiny community of Winnfield, Huey bought a large tract there from two of the town's earliest settlers, Anson and Hanson Little. The land covered much of Winnfield's northern half, and fifty years later, Earl bought some of that land back and used it as his famous pea patch farm. In 1886, Huey bought a 320-acre farm in Winnfield and moved his family there. A log cabin stood on the property, known as the David Pipes place. Large, sturdy, with a twelve-foot-wide center hall flanked by two spacious rooms, with an L-shaped back wing that contained the dining room and kitchen, the cabin served as the Long home for seven years. There, three more children were born, Olive, Clara, and on August 30, 1893, Huey Pierce Long, Jr. Although big enough for the growing family, the cabin was drafty, and Callie constantly complained about the chill, so in late 1893, Huey built a new house on the property, smaller but sturdier and warmer than the cabin. For the next thirteen years, the Longs lived in this "salt-box house," as they called it. Although small, it accommodated the family, for the older children were beginning to leave home. The last three of the children were born in the salt-box house, Earl, Caledonia, and Lucille. In 1907, the family moved into a comfortable, sixteen-room, two-story house in Winnfield.[6]

The 1890s and 1900s proved boom years for Winnfield and for the Longs. During that time the lumber industry moved into Winn Parish, and the region soon became dotted with sawmills, labor camps, and railroad spurs. In typical fashion, the lumber companies remained for a couple of decades, and when they left, the parish had more than twelve million acres of cut-over wasteland and a depressed economy. While the boom lasted, Old Hu, as Huey Sr. was called, took advantage of the opportunity presented by the encroachment of the timber outfits. Hearing that the Arkansas Southern Railroad was going to build a spur line into Winnfield, he sold some of his holdings to the company for a handsome profit. To make Winnfield a more attractive place for business investment, he helped widen the streets, and he assisted in establishing the town's first newspaper, library, and public schools. As Winnfield's population grew rapidly, the name of Long became one of the most prominent in the community. Besides Huey, his brother George was a vice-president of the local bank, operated a mercantile store, and owned 2,300 acres of land.[7]

Six feet tall, wiry and slender, with small hands and feet, Huey P. Long, Sr., had a ruddy complexion and a powerful, booming voice, reminding one reporter of the pioneers who had settled the region. Old Hu, or Uncle Hu, as some longtime residents still refer to him, had little formal schooling and felt out of his element when it came to disciplining and educating the children, so he left these matters entirely in Callie's hands. Although he converted to Callie's Baptist faith when he married her, Old Hu lacked her intense religious devotion and rarely attended church. His greatest love was farming, breeding, and draying, and he spent most of his time at these outdoor activities. At home, he seemed more interested in politics than in any other subject, and he often led dinner-table discussions on current issues. In 1900, he ran as an independent candidate for the state senate on a platform endorsing free silver, opposing the expansion of the United States by the bayonet, and attacking "corporate control of the government." Without organized machine support, his first and only fling at political office ended in failure. Many years later, a northern newspaper reporter interviewed Old Hu, and he expounded on his political views: "There wants to be a revolution, I tell you. I seen this domination by capital, seen it for seventy years. What do these rich folks care for the poor man? They care nothing—not for his pains, nor his sickness, nor his death. Maybe you are surprised to hear talk like that. Well, it was just such talk that my boys was raised under." Often quoted as a reflection of the Longs' political philosophy, the statement appears contrived, a remark to give the reporter good copy. Old Hu certainly did not talk that way, but he could playact when he wanted.[8]

Little has been written about Huey P. Long, Sr., but he was "more colorful than Huey or Earl," according to a close friend. Like his sons, Old Hu was a drinking man, and a Winnfield old-timer said: "Uncle Hu liked a snort of whiskey every now and then. One day, we stopped at his cousin's house in Williana, and he asked for a swig. Tom gave him a bottle, and Uncle Hu took a drink. After one swallow, he spit it out. 'My God, Tom, that's pure creosote!' Tom said, 'Yeah, Uncle Hu, I keep that creosote for fellows like you. It makes them appreciate good whiskey once they've had a drink of that stuff.'" Until Callie died, Old Hu was a faithful and considerate husband, but after her death in 1913, when he was sixty-one, he began to turn an eager eye toward the opposite sex. In the mid-1920s, he married a considerably younger woman, and they lived in Dry Prong, a small town about twenty miles from Winnfield. The marriage lasted a few years, but in 1931, his wife successfully sued for divorce on grounds of desertion.[9]

Caledonia "Callie" Tison Long stood five feet, five inches tall and weighed less than a hundred pounds. She had an attractive, softly dignified face, large hazel eyes, and jet-black hair; she impressed everyone with her natural beauty. All her adult life, Callie was frail and sickly, and the strenuous life she led would contribute to her death at only fifty-three. A fiercely determined woman, Callie was deeply devoted to her husband and to her children, ingraining in them a strong sense of family solidarity. After Huey Jr. launched his spectacular political career, almost all his brothers and sisters actually campaigned against him because they believed that he placed political concerns above family interests. Callie also gave her children a sense of mission, a feeling that each of them had a better future than a life of farming in Winnfield. Eventually, all the Long children would leave home to pursue careers in teaching, politics, law, and dentistry. A firm disciplinarian, Callie did not hesitate to administer a severe thrashing with a hickory switch, but at the same time, she could be affectionate and caring with her children. A "Rock-ribbed Baptist," she required all the children to read the Bible daily and to attend church regularly. Near the end of his life, Earl reminisced about his mother awaking at five o'clock every morning to prepare breakfast for the six Catholic boarders so they could attend Mass. Like Huey's story about driving his Catholic grandparents to church, Earl's tale has no basis in fact, though all authorities agree on Callie's devotion to God and family and her genuine tolerance for all persons. Callie also instilled in her children a dedication to education, and she provided them with an abundance of reading material at home and kept careful track of their progress in the classroom.[10]

The Reverend Gerald L. K. Smith, the fiery evangelist who headed Huey's national Share Our Wealth movement, preached that "God had just a certain quota of brains for the Longs, and He gave it all to Huey." Besides reflecting Smith's doting adulation of Huey, his remark unfairly and inaccurately characterized the siblings, for by any standards, the nine children Huey and Callie Long raised were a remarkable lot. The oldest son, Julius, had a mind as quick and retentive as Huey's, and like Huey, he studied law for one year at Tulane University, absorbing enough information to enable him to pass the state bar examination on his first try. After serving as district attorney in Winn Parish, Julius moved to Shreveport, where he enjoyed a successful career as a civil lawyer. Another brother, George, became a dentist, served in the Oklahoma state legislature, and represented Louisiana's Eighth Congressional District in Washington for three terms. All five Long sisters obtained college degrees in teaching. One sister, Caledonia, spent much of her life in sanitoriums in Arizona and Colorado. The others, Olive, Clara, Charlotte, and Lucille, taught school at the elementary, secondary, and college levels.[11]

The eighth of the children and fourth son, Earl Kemp Long, was born in the salt-box house on August 26, 1895. His grandfather, John Murphy Long, gave him his first and middle names from close friends of his from Smith County, Mississippi. By all accounts, Earl had a happy childhood. As the youngest boy, he received pampering from his sisters, especially Lucille, who was one year younger. Callie Long also doted on Earl because from an early age, he displayed an enthusiasm for religion that was pointedly lacking in his brothers. Julius, George, and Huey all resisted their mother's efforts to foster their religious upbringing and attended church services only because she made them. In his autobiography, Huey remarked that "while at home I was under compulsion a regular attendant of all religious ceremonies." As a youngster, Earl loved to go to church, and he studied the Bible so assiduously and participated in church services so avidly that his schoolmates gave him the nickname "Preacher." When Earl left home at the age of seventeen, he quit going to church, but when he was sixty years old, he was baptized into the Baptist faith.[12]

Julius, George, and Huey detested farming, and they performed their regular chores in the fields only because Old Hu made them. But Earl again differed from his brothers in his genuine love for farming. Even as a toddler, he raced out into the fields early in the morning and stayed until lunchtime. More than anything, he loved to round up stray cattle and hogs. After catching a hog, he would try to wrestle it to the ground. The hog, of course, easily withstood the assault, but Earl persisted in his efforts to corral it. The youngster carefully observed his father slaughter the hogs and make sausage, ham, and bacon. He also often accompanied Old Hu on visits to neighboring farms and to the general store in Winnfield. Earl also liked to mount the family mare, Old Grey, and ride through the fields and into the woods. All relatives and friends agree that Earl Long was a country boy at heart. After he became governor, he made frequent trips to his pea patch farm near Winnfield to get away from Baton Rouge. On the campaign trail, he urged farmers to "vote for a man that looks like ye and works like ye and smells like ye on Saturday," describing himself as "just a country boy, born and raised in the country." Many writers attribute Earl's earthiness to precisely that agrarian background, but it should be noted that he never made a career of farming and spent his entire adult life in the urban environments of Shreveport, Baton Rouge, and New Orleans.[13]

Like his brothers, Earl had an innate sense of business. After Old Hu finished slaughtering the hogs, Earl gathered the discarded pork tongues and chitlings. Then he got Huey and Lucille to help him sell them to black sharecroppers for fifteen cents a tubful. Giving his brother and sister small commissions, Earl kept the rest for himself. He also loved to play, his favorite pursuits being baseball, marbles, and fishing. He and Huey often played with the children of black sharecroppers on the Long property, and they often fished at Black Creek. Earl also liked to collect hickory nuts for Callie to use in making cakes and pies, and he picked muscadine grapes, mayhaws, and blackberries for jams and jellies. Always a mischievous youth, he liked to sneak into the kitchen to grab an extra slice of pie or a piece of slab bacon fresh from the frying pan. When Earl was about five, he climbed onto the kitchen cupboard and swallowed some lye. Fortunately, Callie saved his life by inducing vomiting, but the lye permanently damaged Earl's vocal cords. For the rest of his life, he had a unique, distinctive, raspy voice, and his deep gravelly tones could range to a high-pitched crescendo.[14]

Over the years, many stories and tales about the early life of the Longs have appeared, many of them uncorroborated and obviously embellished. All authorities, however, agree that Earl and Huey became particularly close. Julius and George were considerably older and had left home by the time Huey and Earl started school, so as the only boys, the two younger brothers, Earl recalled, "slept together, played together, and ate together." Two years older and with a naturally domineering personality, Huey became Earl's role model. He idolized Huey and followed him around everywhere. Earl remembered how Huey "sold papers, and I was his understudy. He had the *Saturday Evening Post*, the *Country Gentleman*, the old *Grit*, and the *Blade*. After we sold the papers, I helped him count the money." Some sources maintain that the young Huey was a physical coward and whenever he got into trouble, he left Earl to do his fighting for him. Julius wrote that Huey would call people "insulting names," then run away, leaving Earl to take the punishment. The older brother also recounted an episode that occurred when Huey was fourteen and Earl was twelve. Two boys had gotten the best of Huey in a fight. Broomstick in hand, Earl jumped into the melee to help his brother. When he called for Huey to help him, he saw Huey "fast disappearing down the road in a cloud of dust." These stories, it should be noted, come from a highly prejudiced magazine article Julius wrote in 1933, after he and Huey had broken all ties with each other. In the article, Julius colors the narrative with extremely biased material, invariably depicting Huey in the worst light possible, and the episodes he relates took place long after he had left home. It does appear that Earl sometimes did intervene on his brother's behalf, but that can be attributed to his natural desire to help Huey, rather than to cowardice on Huey's part.[15]

Several scholars believe that Earl had a belligerent streak, leading to his involvement in numerous fights. One historian wrote that "Earl fought for the sheer pleasure of combat, with savage and joyful passion. He delighted in the clash of bodies, and he battled with every weapon at his disposal, including his teeth." Another writer considered Earl's tendency to fisticuffs a "basic flaw in his emotional character and self-control," evidence of his "emotional inadequacy" and of a "low frustration threshold." That Earl Long had a quick temper cannot be doubted. Virtually all who knew him attest to his vitriolic tongue, his frequent obscenity-laced outbursts, and his cantankerous nature. At least nine occasions on which he engaged in physical combat as an adult have been documented. Yet, Earl could be sensitive and caring. He often gave food and money to poor people, provided state jobs for unemployed men with large families, supported his sick sister and his aging father, and gave financial assistance to his brother's widow. "I was the one who saved the kittens," he proudly exclaimed, referring to the time he jumped into a creek to rescue several kittens that had been thrown there to drown. Earl's roughhouse nature got him into trouble more than once, but on balance, the amateur psychoanalyzing of him as a violence-prone individual is unwarranted.[16]

Earl's brothers and sisters were superior students, and Julius and Huey were truly precocious, but he did not take to the life of the classroom. In Winnfield's public schools, Earl's grades were generally mediocre—he barely passed arithmetic and grammar, and displayed an interest only in history. Encouraged by Old Hu, he frequently played hooky from school to stay home and work in the fields. Callie constantly tried to get him to study his lessons and do his homework, but he resisted, and often received stern reprimands for unruly behavior and poor attendance. Earl did not lack intellectual ability; he simply refused to study subjects that held little interest for him. Asserting that good "horse sense" mattered much more than "book learning," he rebelled against the structured discipline of the classroom. Earl Long had a sharp mind. After he decided to become a lawyer, he studied for two years in a non-degree legal curriculum at Loyola University, and he passed the state bar examination on his first attempt. During his terms as governor of Louisiana, he demonstrated his profound grasp of the intricacies of state and local government, often astounding associates with his knowledge of minute details of the huge state budget. But formal schooling was not to his liking at all, and as soon as he had the chance, he dropped out.[17]

In October, 1912, a little over a month after he reached the age of seventeen, Earl quit the eleventh grade at Winnfield High School to go to work for Huey, who was district manager of the Memphis, Tennessee, branch of the Faultless Starch Company. Accounts differ on his reasons for leaving school. One writer inaccurately states that he quit after Callie died in 1913, but the evidence clearly shows that he left home several months before her death. Another writer merely says that he went to Memphis "at Huey's request." Yet another author maintains that Earl left town after he got into legal trouble for cutting a classmate with a knife. In this version, Julius, the newly elected district attorney in Winn Parish, used his influence to avert a court hearing, but he advised his brother to leave town until the incident had been forgotten. In all probability, Earl quit school because he had grown tired of it. As the only boy still at home, he missed the companionship of other males. His idol, Huey, had done the same thing two years earlier, dropping out of the eleventh grade to begin a career of selling. Like his siblings, Earl had already decided to leave his hometown to seek opportunities elsewhere. He may have enjoyed farming, but he refused to be tied down to a life of drudgery in Winnfield. When Huey called him to join his sales force in Memphis, Earl jumped at his first chance to make real money and to break away from home.[18]

As soon as he started working for Huey, Earl demonstrated his innate talent for salesmanship. Originally hired to train salesmen, he proved so adept that less than a month after he joined Faultless, he won promotion to the sales force in Arkansas and Tennessee. When Callie died in 1913, Earl's sisters tried to persuade him to return home to complete his education, but he refused. Already earning handsome commissions, he could afford to pay all his expenses and live the way he wanted. In December, 1913, however, poor economic conditions forced Faultless to close down its Memphis operations, and Earl was laid off. Without a job, he accepted Julius' offer to finance his college education, and in January, 1914, he enrolled at Louisiana Industrial Institute (today, Louisiana Tech University) in Ruston. Lacking a high school diploma, he entered a two-year associate degree program in business, but once again, he refused to discipline himself to the rigors of academia, and he paid no attention to his studies. The eighteen-year-old did receive his introduction to one of his favorite pastimes, gambling, in Ruston. He joined a poker and craps club, among whose members were Paul and Raoul LeBlanc, that met every night. The LeBlancs introduced Earl to their older brother, Dudley, who had a sales route in north Louisiana. Dudley and Earl became close friends, sharing a passion for gambling and for the fast life. Dudley had already acquired a reputation for wooing members of the opposite sex, and he advised Earl to be aggressive in his approach to women. Earl apparently took the advice too literally, and one lady who knew him then remembered him as "too forward."[19]

After one trimester, Earl resigned from Louisiana Industrial. The school's records were destroyed by a fire in 1936, but it has been well established that Earl did not pass a single course. In May, 1914, he again turned to selling. Harley Bozeman, a close friend of the Long brothers from Winnfield, had called Huey to join him selling patent medicines for the Chattanooga Medicine Company in Arkansas and Louisiana. Huey and Harley made good money, and they asked Earl to start selling the medicine. Earl immediately took a job as drummer for such standards as Nature's Remedy, Black Draught, and Wine of Cardui. Again, Earl made a lot of money, but as happened with Faultless Starch, he lost his job when the Chattanooga company had to curtail its operations. After returning home to Winnfield, Earl succumbed to his sisters' pressure and made a final effort at obtaining a college education. In February, 1915, he enrolled in a non-credit curriculum at Louisiana State University (LSU). At that time, the LSU campus stood on the grounds of the present state capitol complex, and the Pentagon Barracks, currently an office and apartment building for politicians, served as a dormitory, where Earl lived in a $14-a-month room. Not surprisingly, he refused to study, preferring to spend his time raising hell. One of his lifelong friends, Ernest S. Clements, met Earl at LSU and remembers him getting into many fights. In less than a semester, Earl withdrew from LSU and returned home.[20]

After a few months at home, the twenty-year-old Earl Long grew restless, and when Huey invited him to work for him selling Never Fail kerosene cans, he eagerly accepted. Equipped with pumps, the cans made pouring kerosene for lamps and stoves easier and safer, and with his natural gift for gab, Huey had established a thriving business throughout north Louisiana. He became so swamped with orders that he called Earl to take over selling in small towns and in the countryside while he covered the larger towns and cities. The arrangement did not work. Earl was a hustler, traveling through the rural areas, stopping at countless farms, and his sales soon exceeded Huey's, but Huey kept most of the commissions for himself. Earl complained that he did not receive his fair share of the money, but Huey argued that as district manager for the company, he was entitled to a larger percentage. All the Long brothers had stubborn streaks in them, and neither brother could bring himself to admit that the other might be right. Earl quit Never Fail in November, 1915, and went to work as a salesman for the Calumet Baking Powder Company, a job he would hold for the next three years. His sales route included Louisiana and Texas, and he quickly demonstrated his capabilities, earning a handsome salary supplemented by commissions and bonuses. Calumet rewarded Earl's sales record by giving him a free trip to Chicago and promoting him to manager of the Louisiana-Texas region. In the summer of 1918, Earl began to neglect his duties with Calumet to assist Huey in his first political campaign. The company began charging him with "irregularities," including improperly completing order forms, failing to meet his sales quotas, and maintaining inaccurate financial records. When Earl failed to correct these matters, Calumet fired him in November, 1918. Earl sought employment with the rival Jack Frost Baking Powder Company, but he was turned down.[21]

That unsuccessful attempt to get a job turned out to be fortunate for Earl Long because in January, 1919, he became a salesman for Dyanshine, a leading manufacturer of shoe and boot polish. For the next eight years, Earl would be Dyanshine's star salesman. With a beginning salary of $3,000 a year, he set up his main office in Shreveport, and drove all over Louisiana and Texas selling the polish and hiring salesmen. Since he had such an affinity with them, he found no difficulty convincing farmers, housewives, artisans, and lumberjacks of the virtues of having brightly polished shoes and boots. Easily exceeding his sales quota, he rapidly advanced to district manager. By 1921, he earned an annual salary, plus commissions and bonuses, of over $10,000, a substantial income for the years following World War I. With his new affluence, Earl bought a car and a house, and he acquired a wardrobe that was the latest in men's fashions. Those who knew him at the time agree that Earl Long was a super salesman. "He could outsell anybody I ever saw," said Dudley LeBlanc, quite a compliment coming from the Hadacol promoter. Just as he would in his political career, Earl took his unique personal touch to the hustings of selling shoe polish. He spent countless hours on the road contacting farmers in remote areas, often helping the men plant crops and spending a lot of time with them. Instinctively, he knew that nothing appeals to people more than personal attention, and he gave it to his customers in abundance. Because of his genuine interest in and empathy for their way of life, many farmers bought products from him that they refused to buy from his rivals.[22]

During the early 1920s, traveling salesmen could be found all over the rural areas of Louisiana. Making their rounds from town to town, sometimes riding by train, often driving old jalopies over primitive country roads, these men formed a natural nomadic society of fierce business competitors who were close personal friends. Spending extended periods of time away from home, they sought refuge from their boredom in the traditional vices of alcohol, prostitution, and gambling. In his journeys through the country, Earl grew especially attracted to gambling. One plausible tale about his life as a traveling salesman dates from this era. In the 1920s, salesmen often stayed overnight at the Nakatosh Hotel in

Natchitoches, about thirty-five miles southwest of Winnfield. After spending the weekend with his family, Earl asked his cousin, Otho Long, to drive him to Natchitoches. Like Earl, Otho loved practical jokes and selected his cousin as his latest victim. Before Earl got into the car, Otho told him that another passenger, Bob O'Quinn, was a Baptist preacher, and he admonished Earl to watch his language, which was usually colorful and graphically profane. Previously, Otho had told O'Quinn, actually a salesman, the same story about Earl, so the drive to Natchitoches was unusually quiet and reserved. Later that night, O'Quinn entered the second floor of the Nakatosh and to his astonishment, he spotted the "Reverend" Earl Long on his knees taking his turn with the dice in a crap game.[23]

At the age of thirty, Earl Long was attractive and handsome, standing about five feet, ten inches tall, with a slender, muscular build. Like Huey, he had brown hair tinged with red, and his face featured a prominent, bulbous nose, but he did not have his brother's pronounced jowls. During the 1920s, he dressed in style, wearing fine Palm Beach suits, white shirts with stiff collars, wide ties, and black and white oxford shoes. All in all, he appealed to the opposite sex and dated sporadically. For a few weeks, he became engaged to Hazel Haynes, a Winnfield schoolteacher, but the engagement was broken off when he refused to follow her advice to settle down in the town and go into business there. In 1927, Earl met Blanche Revere, and he was so enamored of the young lady and her charms that he dated her exclusively until their marriage five years later.[24]

During his eight years as a traveling salesman, Earl picked up several habits that persisted through much of his adult life. He started smoking cigarettes, consuming two packs a day, which he continued to do until he suffered a heart attack in 1950. He also began drinking wine, whiskey, and beer, with no preferences in brands or types. Huey had a very low tolerance for alcoholic beverages and had great difficulty controlling his drinking; Earl did get drunk on occasion, but he always kept his drinking under control. Outside of politics, his greatest passion was gambling, particularly playing the horses, as his father and grandfather had done. Dudley LeBlanc related how he introduced Earl to pari-mutuel betting. One day in 1926 or 1927, LeBlanc took Earl to the Fair Grounds racetrack in New Orleans. "Earl bet one dollar, won ten, and was hooked on the horses ever since," LeBlanc stated. During racing season, he made regular trips to the track, and when the track was closed, he placed bets with bookies all across the country. An inveterate devotee of the racing sheets, he perused them every morning, made his selections, then got on the telephone to place his bets. After he moved to New Orleans in 1924, Earl became a regular patron of the 1-2-3 Club, located on Baronne Street directly across from the Roosevelt Hotel, where he made his bets with the bookmakers and anxiously awaited the results on the wires.[25]

Always an eccentric person, Earl was usually oblivious to the time of day. He possessed an extraordinary amount of restless energy, a characteristic of the males in the Long family. He could go without sleeping for forty-eight hours and, after a catnap, awaken refreshed and energetic. He seemed constantly on the go, needing to be doing something. Although he liked typical southern country food—cornbread, greens, ham—he usually wolfed down his meals and paid little attention to table manners. Many times he would conduct business in the middle of the night, and friends and political associates grew accustomed to being awakened at two o'clock in the morning by a telephone call from Earl. He had an amazing ability to recall names and faces and knew thousands of people by their first names. A naturally gregarious person, he loved to talk and, with an unexcelled talent for communicating with people, could captivate them for hours by delving into his endless storehouse of tales and anecdotes. Other than the daily racing sheets and grocery ads in newspapers, which he studied religiously, he read very little, considering reading books a waste of valuable time. One of his best-known habits was his passion for bargains. Earl Long simply could not resist a bargain whenever he came across one, and he reveled in trying to talk a merchant into lowering his prices. In 1938, he even persuaded the manager of the fashionable Marshall Field's department store in Chicago to give him a discount on the merchandise he wanted to buy. Earl became so legendary for his incessant bargaining that whenever general-store owners in rural Louisiana heard he was headed their way, they posted inflated prices on their items just so Earl could "talk them down." On numerous occasions, he delayed campaign appearances and press conferences to stop at a store. Once when he was governor, he was in a tiny country store owned by a black merchant in Richland Parish. He looked at the merchandise and did not see anything he wanted and was very disappointed. Earl went out back and returned several minutes later quite excited. "What's in them troughs?" he asked, referring to several wooden troughs filled with mud he had seen. "Earthworms, Governor," the man said. "I'll take three buckets full," Earl exclaimed, and departed from the place a happy man.[26]

Earl also consistently displayed earthiness, which often degenerated into crudeness. Although he could act with charm and grace when the occasion demanded, he frequently tried deliberately to cultivate an image as a crude, uninhibited hick. Once he was talking to reporters in the lobby of the Roosevelt Hotel in New Orleans, and he suddenly turned his back on them and urinated on the marble floor. He was often in his underwear when he entertained male visitors, and political aides still vividly describe him in his "union suit." In his later years, as a dinner guest at someone's house, he would remove his false teeth after a meal and immerse them in his water glass. "Got to clean them choppers," he would tell a startled hostess. At one campaign appearance, he kept a crowd waiting while he went into a local store to buy shoes. Earl used the men's room in the store, then left and climbed onto the platform, with his pants unzipped and his shirttail hanging out of his fly. When an aide discreetly called his attention to the problem, Earl nonchalantly put the shirttail back in, zipped up the trousers, and casually told the shocked audience: "If you elect me governor, I'm going to give you women folk back these fancy zippers if you'll give us back your buttons." [27]

Earl Long did not discard his country roots, and all his life, he would reflect his rural upbringing. Like his siblings, he left Winnfield as a young adult, never to return to settle there, but unlike Huey, he remained devoted to his family and to his boyhood home. Winn Parish old-timers still recall with fondness Earl's frequent visits there and his unfailing kindness and consideration for his numerous friends and neighbors. He may have been a country boy at heart, as he liked to tell his rural audiences, but politics increasingly became the consuming passion of his life.[28]

2

Political Baptism

Earl Long grew up in an environment in which farming and politics formed the main topics of discussion. Riddled with poverty, Winn Parish became a focal point for iconoclastic political movements almost from the time it was founded. Many parish residents refused to support the Confederacy during the Civil War, and in the hard times of the 1890s, populism swept the region. Attacking banks, railroads, and other large corporations for their exploitation of the poor, advocating national government control over key sectors of the economy, Populist politicians found in Winn Parish a receptive audience for their cause. In 1892, the Populist candidate for governor, himself a resident of the parish, carried Winn by a five-to-one margin, and until the party expired in 1900, Populist candidates won every election held in Winn. Some local politicians went so far as to advocate a socialist economic system, direct government ownership of the means of production, as a panacea for the region's ills.[1]

The Longs did not espouse populism. Old Hu rejected the party's rigid doctrinaire positions, an ideological stance that would contribute to its demise. A harsh realist, he knew enough about life and about people to see that compromise and concession were necessary to get things accomplished. Old Hu, however, did share the Populists' hostility toward the dominant interests in society. Although he had achieved material success, he harbored a deep resentment toward the social elite that controlled Louisiana, an elite based on old family names and connections with the corporate interests in the cities. At the dinner table, Old Hu often railed against the rich and demanded that government assume the responsibility of taking care of the common people.[2]

It is impossible to ascertain whether these dinner-table remarks had any impact on the Long brothers. In their careers, both Huey and Earl championed the needs of the masses, but neither developed a systematic political ideology. On the contrary, the Longs became known as hard-nosed, realistic politicians, readily discarding their stated positions on issues in the name of expediency. Of far greater significance to their future careers was their exposure during their youth to the practical side of politics. Because of their wealth and influence, the Longs entertained a stream of local politicians seeking favors. As boys, Huey and Earl heard their father and their uncle George talking with police jurors, assessors, and sheriffs on local issues. One sister recalled Earl listening intently as Old Hu talked the parish assessor into lowering the assessed value of his property in return for a promise of support in the next election. She also stated that as a teenager, Earl loved to hang around the parish courthouse watching the politicians come and go and listening to their conversations. In 1906, when he was eleven, Earl received his first education in campaign politics—his oldest brother, Julius, ran for district attorney of the parish. Together with Huey, Earl went all over the countryside tacking up Julius Long circulars to trees and fence posts, and they even tried to persuade their classmates to talk their fathers into voting for Julius. The brothers also accompanied him on his swings around the parish.[3]

As an adult, Earl first became actively involved in Louisiana politics in 1918, when Huey ran for the Third District (north Louisiana) seat on the state Railroad Commission, which regulated common carriers and public utilities. A twenty-five-year-old lawyer practicing in Shreveport, Huey challenged the incumbent, Burk A. Bridges, and Earl enthusiastically supported his brother, paying the $125 filing fee and covering the whole district soliciting votes. Since Bridges was an entrenched incumbent, Huey realized that his only chance for victory lay in outhustling him for votes. Following tradition, Bridges relied on a heavy vote in Shreveport, Monroe, Ruston, Minden, and other larger places, and he ignored the rural areas. Having observed firsthand the firebrand oratory and flamboyant stump tactics of the famous demagogues Jeff Davis of Arkansas and James K. Vardaman of Mississippi, Huey conducted an innovative, exciting campaign designed to rouse the poor farmers into voting for him. To assist him in planning and managing the campaign, Huey called on a trio of Winn Parish natives that would play a major role in all his early campaigns, brother Earl, his close friend Harley Bozeman, and the parish assessor, Oscar "O. K." Allen.[4]

In the campaign, Huey used Earl primarily to spread his message among the isolated farmhouses scattered around the region. As a traveling salesman, Earl had made numerous contacts throughout north Louisiana. He had gained innumerable friends by sharing farmers' dinner tables, helping them plow fields, and simply talking with them. One sales competitor marveled that "Earl would spend three hours with a farmer talking about the best way to grow watermelons just to sell him one can of shoe polish." But Earl knew that the three hours were well spent, for he had made a permanent friend and gained a permanent customer. Besides, Earl loved to chat with people, an enduring personal trait. One of the first men in Louisiana to campaign by automobile, Earl drove over rough gravel roads and through mud paths to reach voters. Many a farmer was both surprised and flattered to find a politician contacting him personally. The technique proved so successful that Earl persuaded Huey to start driving around the district himself. Earl also helped in lining up some of the local politicians for Huey. Years later, he discussed his contributions to Huey's first run for political office: "I put up the $125 qualifying fee for Huey Long to run for the Railroad Commission, and I wore out an old jitney working for him. I sold him more than the baking powder I was supposed to be selling." Earl's yeoman work contributed to Huey's upset second-primary victory over Bridges, as did the hard work of many others, including virtually the entire Long family. Of course, the main factor in the victory was Huey Long himself, particularly his inimitable campaign style and captivating personality.[5]

After the election, Earl resumed his sales career, but he closely followed Huey's spectacular success on the Railroad Commission (renamed the Public Service Commission by the state constitution of 1921). On his frequent sales rounds, Earl stopped in Baton Rouge to assist his brother in his growing dispute with Governor John M. Parker. Huey had supported Parker in the 1920 governor's race and originally backed Parker's legislative program that earned him a reputation as a reformer. He increased the severance tax on oil and gas, built roads and bridges, moved the campus of LSU to its present location, and provided increased funds for public schools. But Huey broke with the governor over what he considered Parker's capitulation to Standard Oil Company, and he soon became one of Parker's most vocal critics. The young public service commissioner also won widespread popular acclaim for his denunciations of the large corporations and for his struggle to obtain reductions in rates on telephone usage and gas consumption. In 1923, brash, thirty-year-old Huey P. Long decided to run for governor. Rejecting the advice of his family, who urged him to postpone such an important race until 1927,

Huey formally announced his candidacy. Once again, brother Earl contributed both money and labor. He donated over $5,000 to the campaign and joined Harley Bozeman and O. K. Allen in drumming up votes in north Louisiana. Huey's two opponents, Henry L. Fuqua, the general manager of the state penitentiary, and Hewitt Bouanchaud, the incumbent lieutenant governor, commanded much of the organized machine support, so Huey conducted yet another innovative campaign, featuring his rabble-rousing stump oratory and the mass mailing of political literature to over 400,000 voters. The results of the January 15, 1924, primary showed Fuqua and Bouanchaud qualifying for the second-primary runoff with over 80,000 votes apiece, but Huey a surprisingly close third with almost 74,000 votes. In the second primary, Huey threw his support to Fuqua, who easily won the race. The narrowness of his defeat in 1924 gave Huey Long great encouragement for the 1927–28 gubernatorial campaign, and he immediately began stumping the state to build up his organization and to corral votes. One of those he trusted most with these preparations was brother Earl.[6]

Earl Long followed Huey's rising star in Louisiana politics with a mixture of admiration and envy. He loved his brother and willingly helped him achieve political success, but he also began to develop the ambition for a political career of his own. Although he was making good money at selling, Earl found himself thinking more and more of holding office, and he decided to use his influence with Huey to obtain a patronage job after Huey won election as governor. Knowing that the traditional stepping-stone to a political career lay in law, the younger brother decided to become a lawyer. Without a high school diploma, he could not enter law school, so in 1924, he moved to New Orleans and enrolled in a two-year, non-degree legal curriculum at Loyola University. During the day, he managed his thriving Dyanshine business, and at night, he took courses to prepare for the state bar examination. It was not necessary at that time to graduate from college or to attend law school to become a lawyer. The only legal requirement was to pass the bar exam, and for two years, Earl studied law. He had a difficult time. Unlike Julius and Huey, he did not have a quick, retentive mind capable of absorbing information from books, but he managed to learn enough law to pass the bar exam in April, 1926. Earl K. Long, Attorney-at-Law, hung out the shingle in front of his newly opened law office in New Orleans, but he hardly had time to practice, for politics would occupy his full attention.[7]

In the 1923–24 campaign, Huey had run very strongly in north Louisiana, finishing third because of a meager showing in the southern half of the state, especially in Acadiana and in the New Orleans metropolitan area. Huey focused his efforts on southwestern Louisiana and charged Earl with building up support in the southeastern sector. Operating from New Orleans, Earl traveled all over the region trying to win backing for his brother. Because the assignment consumed all his time and because he relished politicking, early in 1927 he sold his Dyanshine route for $17,000, a very substantial sum for the era. The money, plus the amounts he had saved in previous years, enabled him to work full-time for his brother without having to hold another job. Earl failed to increase Huey's support in New Orleans because of the stranglehold the Old Regulars had on city politics, but in the surrounding areas, he helped to give Huey a dramatically larger vote than in 1924. In several parishes, Earl made deals with local leaders to swing their backing to Huey. In Lafourche Parish, for example, he won over Harvey Peltier, and in Terrebonne, Allen Ellender. He also put Huey in touch with Jules and Joseph Fisher of Jefferson Parish and with Leander Perez in Plaquemines. In New Orleans, Earl made initial contacts with several well-heeled people who would become some of Huey's most intimate associates. One such individual was Robert S. Maestri, a wealthy real estate investor, furniture-store owner, and reportedly one of the kingpins of New Orleans' flourishing vice trade. Through contacts, Earl learned that Maestri had fallen out with the Old Regulars, so he arranged to meet him in a New Orleans restaurant in July, 1927. Maestri informed Earl that he was willing to donate serious money to any candidate who would reward him with an appointive office. Recognizing a golden opportunity, Earl arranged for a meeting between Huey and Maestri, and with his own considerable powers of persuasion, Huey converted Maestri to his side. With the promise of a political appointment—Maestri became conservation commissioner—and with the assurance of regular access to the governor's office, Maestri shelled out over $40,000 to the Long campaign chest, probably a record amount in an American state campaign at that time.[8]

Earl also brought into the Long camp other men from New Orleans who would become key figures in the organization's hierarchy. One of these men, Seymour Weiss, worked as assistant manager of the Roosevelt Hotel. Earl had met Weiss at the 1-2-3 Club across the street from the hotel, where both men liked to play the horses. A shrewd manipulator of men and money, Weiss rose quickly to the position of Huey Long's financial director, controlling the vast sums that flowed into the Long machine treasury. Another wealthy New Orleanian Earl recruited was Abraham "Abe" Shushan, a clothing retailer, who contributed large sums to the campaign. In addition to his fund-raising activities, Earl also managed the sound trucks, yet another innovative vote-getting device. Decorated with pictures of Huey Long, loudspeakers attached to the roof, the trucks crisscrossed the state, blaring out the Long message to tens of thousands of people. When a sound truck arrived in a town, it played music, and Earl and other aides pleaded for votes. Invariably, the trucks attracted large crowds of curious onlookers. The trucks also served to advance Huey, notifying people of his personal appearances. In the campaign, Huey Long won over the voters through his oratory and his platform, which was designed to aid the poor people of the state. In the first primary, held January 17, 1928, Huey collected 126,842 votes, far more than his rivals, Congressman Riley J. Wilson of Ruston, with 81,747, and Oramel H. Simpson, who had become governor when Fuqua died in office, with 80,326. When Simpson threw his support to Long, Wilson realized that he had no chance in the second primary, so he withdrew from the runoff. At the age of thirty-four, Huey P. Long, Jr., won election as governor of Louisiana.[9]

In the interval between the election and his inauguration, which would take place on May 21, 1928. Huey faced the difficult task of building a cohesive majority in the legislature to pass his program of free school textbooks, free roads, bridges, and highways, and natural gas for New Orleans, which he had promised his thousands of constituents. Historically, incoming governors had little trouble gaining a legislative majority, since they themselves had won election with the support of the dominant interests in Louisiana. But Huey Long's was a largely personal victory, secured without the planter oligarchy and the New Orleans machine. Huey also had short shirttails in the race, carrying only two members of his statewide ticket to victory, and he had the support of but a few legislators. To build the legislative majority he needed, Huey decided to back Philip H. Gilbert for president pro tem of the senate and John B. Fournet for speaker of the house, though neither man had actively campaigned for him. To assist him, he again turned to his Winn Parish advisors, Earl, Harley Bozeman, and O. K. Allen. With promises of patronage and the liberal dispensation of money—according to Bozeman, the legislators "didn't come free"—Huey got the votes he needed for the selection of Gilbert and Fournet.[10]

Not long after Huey took the oath as governor, Earl called on him to fulfill his promise of appointing his brother as attorney for the inheritance tax collector, a choice patronage position entailing few responsibilities and paying annual commissions of $10,000 to $15,000, the highest-paying state job. For over a decade, Earl had performed unheralded but invaluable political work for his brother, and he believed that he was entitled to the position. Although Huey had indeed made the promise, he reneged. Fearing accusations of nepotism from his strongly entrenched opposition, he informed the legislature that he would abolish the position and spend the money on state hospitals. Naturally, Earl felt betrayed when he learned of Huey's change of heart. Enlisting family members and political associates, he pressured Huey into relenting and making the appointment. In his autobiography, Huey said: "This brother had at all times been a political supporter, a good and faithful worker. It was almost impossible with the forces which prevailed in his favor for me to decline any reasonable request by him or in his behalf." One scholar maintains that there were strings attached to the appointment—Earl had to agree to support their aging father and their convalescent sister, Caledonia. Another scholar argues that Huey continued to help pay their bills at least three years after the appointment. The evidence clearly demonstrates that neither position is accurate. Earl had been supporting Old Hu and Caledonia for over ten years, buying his father a house in Winn-field and paying for Callie's medical care in Arizona and Colorado. Once he left home, Huey did not exhibit any particular concern for his family, and several sisters and close friends of the Longs have stated emphatically that Huey never paid as much as "one dime" toward the support of his father and his sister. They contend that Earl had been helping other family members by giving them money as well.[11]

In his job as attorney for the inheritance tax collector, Earl opened a law office in New Orleans and hired a young lawyer, Nicolai Simoneaux, to run it. Simoneaux did all the leg work for the firm, investigating and closing estates, computing inheritance taxes, filing the necessary legal papers. Earl, who paid no attention to the details of the legal profession, simply signed the documents Simoneaux had prepared. Earl preferred the excitement of politics to the drudgery and paperwork of law, and he spent most of his time in Baton Rouge aiding his brother. As a new governor confronting a potentially hostile legislature, Huey needed Earl's help in getting his bills passed, and for three years, Earl would serve as one of the Kingfish's most capable and effective lieutenants. Huey used him in a variety of ways: as an unofficial legislative whip, garnering the votes needed for the administration's measures; as a liaison between the governor's office and local officials across Louisiana; as an organizer of Long machines in the parishes; and as a political "gofer," tackling the innumerable problems that arose every day. A shrewd judge of men, Huey once remarked of his brother: "You give Earl a few dollars and turn him loose on the road and he will make more contacts and better contacts than any ten men with a barrel of money." With an instinctive ability to sway people, Earl became an acknowledged master of the art of wheeling and dealing. Both friendly and hostile contemporaries of the Longs have unanimously attested to his acumen for politicking. In numerous interviews, T. Harry Williams found that "surviving politicians testify admiringly to Earl's skill in handling the assignments Huey gave him." Allen J. Ellender, one of the leading Long men in the house, observed: "He [Huey] was always looking ahead. He never had time to deal with day-to-day politicking, so he used Earl to take care of it. If a senator or a sheriff or a judge needed a relative on the payroll, Earl saw to it he got it. Earl knew a lot more people than Huey, and Huey sent him all over the state to take care of his business." Dudley LeBlanc claimed that he saw Huey instruct Earl to go to New Orleans to pick up $20,000 from Bob Maestri and Abe Shushan. After Earl left, Huey said that "Earl can spend the money better than I can." [12]

In Huey's first year as governor, there arose a firestorm of opposition to his proposal for a $30-million bond issue to finance the construction of state roads and highways. A radical departure from the traditional method of financing state projects directly from annual appropriations, the bond issue generated a solid front against it. Headed by nearly the entire Orleans Parish delegation, the opponents believed that defeat would be easy, since the proposal came in the form of an amendment to the state constitution, which required a two-thirds legislative majority for passage. But the Long brothers worked feverishly—Huey took his case directly to the people, and Earl won over uncommitted legislators—and secured passage of the amendment. The two also worked hard to get legislative approval of the bill to provide free school textbooks to all schoolchildren in Louisiana, including those attending parochial schools. [13]

Earl Long's legislative maneuverings at this time deserve exploring, for they illustrate the political methods that later made him famous. In dealing with individuals, he had no peer. A master of the art of persuasion, he possessed that innate flair for discerning strengths and weaknesses that marks the great political manipulators. With an encyclopedic memory for names and a profound grasp of the issues of greatest concern even in the smallest towns, he could use his personal touch to win politicians over to his side. Essentially, Earl applied the successful salesman's principles and practices to politics and sold his brother's programs as adeptly as he had sold boot polish. When asked his secret of politicking, how he could persuade a legislator to vote for a bill, Earl replied, "I find out where he itches so I'll know where to scratch him." Intuitively, he knew the precise location of the itches and the right type of scratching. Three of Louisiana's perennial members of Congress, Senator Allen Ellender and Congressmen Hale Boggs and Jimmy Morrison, who observed presidents from Franklin Roosevelt through Richard Nixon, agreed that in their experience of Capitol Hill politics, the only people comparable to Earl Long in wheeling and dealing were Sam Rayburn and Lyndon Johnson.[14]

In working the legislature for passage of the road construction bonds, Earl, as always, adopted a flexible approach. Some legislators, he knew, could be bought; other, more principled men had to be won over through persuasion. With some, he was polite and restrained; with others, overbearing and threatening. Before he talked to the legislators, he invariably did his homework, carefully studying their districts, their political backers, and other matters. One wavering senator voted for the bond issue because Earl advised him to invest in oyster shells. "Oyster shells?" asked the puzzled politico. "Yeah," Earl replied. "Those roads got to have a foundation, and we're going to give the contracts to the oyster shell companies recommended by our friends." He gained another critical vote when he found out that an uncommitted senator had a relative who sold automobiles. Earl promised that in return for the senator's vote, the state would purchase a large number of vehicles from the dealership. One representative could not be moved by such approaches, so Earl told him in moving detail of the extreme difficulties farmers in his district experienced at harvest time when they tried to transport their crops to market over worn-out and washed-out mud paths.[15]

The aid Earl Long gave his brother in 1928 paled in comparison to what he gave the following year, when Huey faced the supreme crisis of his political career, his impeachment and the attempt to remove him from office. At a special session of the legislature in March, 1929, Huey's well-organized opposition struck back at him with a vengeance. Governor Long had called the special session to consider an occupational license tax of five cents on every barrel of crude oil refined in Louisiana. Earlier, the United States Supreme Court had temporarily suspended an increase in the oil severance tax that Huey had enacted in 1928, and without that revenue, he needed the occupational license tax to finance his free school textbook program. Unaware that he was facing disaster, Huey believed that the legislature would easily pass the tax. When the session opened, however, he ran into immediate trouble. By a large majority, the house voted to bar unauthorized visitors, a move clearly designed to prevent him from lobbying. During the next few days, his opposition gained strength, and Huey extended the session. But he failed to crack his opponents' growing front, so he decided to end the session. When House Speaker Fournet tried to adjourn, he was shouted down, and on March 26, the house passed a resolution calling for the impeachment of Governor Huey P. Long on nineteen charges. After lengthy deliberation, the house passed eight articles of impeachment and formally submitted them to the senate. Under the state constitution, the senate would hold a trial on the impeachment articles, and if Long were found guilty on any of them, he would be removed from office. Fifteen senators, however, produced a document, the famous round robin, which stated: "The undersigned, constituting more than one-third the membership of the Senate, sitting as a court of impeachment, do now officially announce that by reason of the unconstitutionality and invalidity of all impeachment charges against Huey P. Long, Governor, they will not vote to convict thereon." Since conviction on the impeachment charges required a two-thirds vote of the entire senate, or twenty-six senators out of a total of thirty-nine, the round robin meant that Huey had fifteen senators firmly committed to vote for acquittal, two more than necessary. Faced with the inevitable, the senate voted to adjourn *sine die,* thus averting a lengthy trial and keeping Huey in office.[16]

Huey Long's victory in the struggle against this concentrated effort to remove him from office resulted from the work of many individuals. Huey himself stumped the entire state and masterminded the operation to get the fifteen signatures on the round robin. Three lawyers, Lewis L. Morgan of Covington, John H. Overton of Alexandria, and Leander H.

Perez of Belle Chasse, devised the ingenious legal defense that since the special session technically lasted until April 6, any impeachment charges filed after that date were illegal. Bob Maestri, Seymour Weiss, and Abe Shushan raised large sums of money for Huey's defense. Many politicians used their muscle to help Huey. All sources agree that no one besides Huey played a more instrumental role in the successful fight than did Earl Long. Huey's son, United States Senator Russell B. Long, stated that without his uncle's help, his father would have been convicted. Huey's biographer wrote that Earl proved "tireless in Huey's defense. He worked all day and most of the night. 'Earl never slept during the impeachment,' a legislator recalled admiringly." Earl himself said that he "went broke keeping him out of trouble when the legislature was full of men trying to impeach him." [17]

All accounts of the impeachment and attempted removal agree that Earl gave his brother invaluable assistance throughout the ordeal, but the specific details of his contributions remain fragmentary at best. The reason is simple. The outcome of the issue was decided not on its merits, but on Huey Long's ability to outpolitick his opponents. None of the innumerable deals made were recorded on paper, but huge sums of money changed hands, and more than a few senators went along with the side that paid them the most. One legislator's statement that "you could pick up $15,000 or $20,000 any evening then" could be termed an exaggeration only in the amount of money in question, and certainly not in the wide-open bribery that occurred. In his study of legislative politics under the Longs, Edward F. Renwick estimated that it cost $54,000 for Huey to obtain only four signatures on the round robin, with one senator holding out for $23,000 and the others splitting $31,000. Both sides were well financed, with Huey receiving most of his money from Bob Maestri and Seymour Weiss, and his opposition receiving funds from Standard Oil and other corporations and wealthy individuals. Although the total amount of money spent by the opposing forces is unknown, it can reasonably be assumed to have easily exceeded a quarter of a million dollars. Although Earl claimed to have gone broke in helping Huey, how much he personally donated to the cause is not known. But he did serve as a "bagman" for his brother, journeying to New Orleans to collect money from Maestri and Weiss, then spending it on everything from printing Long circulars to buying signatures on the round robin. [18]

To get the vital signatures, according to Williams, Earl Long dealt with politicians in "whispered corner conferences in the capitol or in covert conversations behind hotel doors. This was the kind of negotiating in which he excelled, in which he was better than Huey." Some of the better-known Earl Long impeachment stories concern his unique methods of winning political support for his brother. Learning that an uncommitted senator was staying at the Istrouma Hotel, Earl went to his room and repeatedly knocked on the door. Knowing that the senator was in hiding, Earl crawled through the transom, awakened the sleeping politico, and dragged him to the capitol to sign the round robin. On another occasion, Earl and O. K. Allen visited Senator V. V. Whittington in a futile attempt to get his signature. Among other inducements, they offered him the state insurance contract, reportedly worth $50,000 a year. The most famous story recounts Earl's fight with Harney Bogan, an anti-Long leader from Shreveport, whom the men had known since 1918. One night Earl saw Bob Maestri chatting with Bogan in a capitol corridor, and he asked Maestri why he was talking to that "sonofabitch." Bogan struck Earl, and the two fell on the floor fighting. Later, Bogan claimed that Earl bit, clawed, and scratched him so severely that he got a shot of "lockjaw serum" just to be on the safe side. When told that Earl and Bogan had battled, Huey laughed and asked if Earl had bitten him.[19]

It is certain that Earl obtained several of the signatures on the round robin, but the exact number cannot be ascertained. Late in his life, he stated flatly that "Huey would have been impeached if it hadn't been for me," and he said that he got four people to sign. "Huey was pretty worried," he boasted, "but I really clinched that business." Aside from the inaccuracy—Huey *was* impeached—these claims, made to a television reporter in the midst of a tight election campaign, should not be taken literally, but they do contain some valdity. Cecil Morgan, an anti-Long legislator from Caddo Parish, said that Earl signed up Senators James Anderson, William Boone, and Lester Hughes, but Boone's own privately published account of the impeachment and round robin does not mention Earl. Even more than securing signatures, unswerving loyalty to his brother proved to be Earl Long's greatest contribution. At a time when many erstwhile political allies and close friends such as Harley Bozeman were deserting Huey, giving up his cause as hopeless, Earl remained steadfastly behind him. When the impeachment resolution first passed the house, Huey was stunned, and he fell into a deep depression for several days, even going so far as to talk of resigning. According to one account, Earl brought Huey back to his senses. "What the hell's the matter with you?" he screamed. "We can lick this thing if you stop your crying and acting like a baby!" In another version, Earl and Julius met privately with Huey and, after several hours of brotherly cajoling, helped Huey regain his self-confidence and fight the move to oust him from office. In an interview, T. Harry Williams acknowledged that throughout the entire crisis, Earl was Huey's "Rock of Gibraltar," remaining absolutely loyal and spending money out of his own pocket to win the battle. That is why, according to Williams, Huey never held a grudge against Earl and gladly welcomed him back after a temporary defection.[20]

Having survived the impeachment and removal attempt by his enemies, Huey Long extended his political control over Louisiana until, as political scientist Allan Sindler remarked, "the Kingfish swallowed the pelican." After his landslide victory in the 1930 election for a seat in the U.S. Senate, Long became increasingly obsessed by his ambition for a national political career, and he devoted less time and attention to state politics than he had previously. To maintain and expand his domination over the state, he relied heavily on his political machine. Long would use it for the necessary functions of state and local government and for the distribution of patronage and the winning of votes. In the absence of a scholarly analysis, one can plausibly argue that the Long machine changed the course of Louisiana politics for over half a century.[21]

The origins of the Long machine may be traced to Huey's campaigns for the Railroad Commission in 1918, the governorship in 1923–24, the Public Service Commission in 1924, and, of course, the governorship in 1927–28. Ignoring the considerable support he received from other family members, Huey wrote of his first campaign, "We had only two votes when we started, Earl's and mine." From that modest base, Huey built the nucleus of a political organization in the small rural parishes of north Louisiana. Beginning in his native parish of Winn, he enlisted local politicians in Grant, Lincoln, Jackson, Webster, Richland, and Natchitoches parishes. Because of the numerous contacts he had made as a traveling salesman and because of his own talent for organization, Earl helped enlist sheriffs, assessors, police jurors, and other politicians. By the time Huey became governor in 1928, he and Earl, along with their allies, had built a loose political organization. It had backed him in the campaign, but could hardly be called a machine. When Huey observed how his tightly organized foes, especially the Old Regulars, had tried to cripple his legislative program, he decided to forge his own machine, more powerful and effective than those of his opponents, and he assigned brother Earl the task of supervising the construction. Earl handled the assignment with skill and agility. Appreciating the fundamental dictum that patronage forms the cement that binds all political organizations, Earl doled out state jobs and construction contracts to those individuals and companies willing to commit themselves to Huey Long. To an extent greater than virtually any other politician in southern history, Huey Long could win over the masses through personal charisma, and many politicians flocked to his side solely out of loyalty and adulation. But he and Earl also realized that most politicians survived on patronage, which was used to keep them in his camp. Through his public works projects, Huey added thousands of new supporters to the state payroll, and the state budget mushroomed during his regime. Eager for a share of this inviting booty, politicians requested that some be spent within their local jurisdictions. In return, Earl, the administration's main patronage dispenser, demanded absolute loyalty to his brother, and he brought many influential local leaders into the organization.[22]

As Huey's chief political advisor, Earl supervised the details of political patronage, but his only official position with the state was attorney for the inheritance tax collector. Since most of the jobs and money would be channeled through certain state agencies, he and Huey saw to it that trusted friends headed those agencies. Bob Maestri, for example, served as conservation commissioner, in which capacity he regulated the oil and gas industry. As public demand for oil and gas rose dramatically, so did state revenues from severance taxes, mineral leases, and royalties on energy extracted from state land. Conservation Commissioner Maestri quickly reached an accommodation with Huey's erstwhile enemies, the energy companies. In exchange for lax enforcement of state regulatory policies, the industry would pump millions into the Long treasury. Since many of the Kingfish's public works projects entailed the construction of roads, bridges, and highways, he appointed his old Winnfield ally, O. K. Allen, to head the critical Highway Commission. Not an astute politician, Allen readily took orders from Earl, who ensured that pro-Long contractors were hired. For example, State Senator Jules Fisher and his nephew, Representative Joseph Fisher, the political kingpins of Jefferson Parish, received huge state contracts to purchase shell for road construction. Colonel Harry Nelson and his brother John owned a large construction company that supplied the state highway program with guardrails and asphalt at immense profits, in return for which the company made generous donations to the Long machine treasury. When they made appointments or spent money, Maestri, Allen, and other state agency heads reported to Earl, and Earl reported to Huey on developments.[23]

Any political organization needs money, and in the days before direct mail solicitations and professional fund-raising companies, Earl Long devised ingenious ways of filling the machine's coffers. None proved more notorious than the deduct policy, whereby state employees "contributed" a certain percentage of their paychecks to the Long machine. According to Seymour Weiss, who served as the machine's treasurer, Earl conceived the deduct system because, as a legal means of raising money, it would not attract unwelcome federal investigations into Long finances. Many low-paid state employees were exempt from the deducts, except during campaigns, but higher-paid employees regularly coughed up 5 to 10 percent of their salaries. The money was actually deducted directly from their paychecks by the state government, which sent the proceeds to Seymour Weiss. After Huey started his propaganda newspaper, the *Louisiana Progress,* Earl ordered state agencies to purchase expensive advertisements in the paper. Distributed free to hundreds of thousands of Louisianians, the *Progress* brought the Long message to the people, many of whom could not afford to subscribe to daily newspapers. Since state agencies paid for the advertisements, Huey Long in effect had the taxpayers foot the bill for his own political propaganda. Later, when the *Progress* was renamed the *American Progress,* Earl talked Huey into requiring contractors, architects, and others wishing to do business with the state to purchase the costly ads.[24]

The Longs raised huge sums in other ways. Kickbacks became commonplace. Any individual or company that received a state contract kicked back 10 percent of the profit to the Long machine. Seymour Weiss's brother, Leon, got most of the state's architectural work during the 1930s, and his firm kicked back 15 to 20 percent of the price. But the oil and gas industry proved the best source of funds. The Longs made the energy companies pay handsomely for the privilege of increasing production quotas, and individual wildcatters contributed huge sums. Despite Huey's public denunciations of the oil and gas corporations, his close friends and backers included oilmen William O. Helis and William C. Feazel, and the chief lobbyist for the hated Standard Oil Company of

Baton Rouge, Louis Lesage, was one of Seymour Weiss's closest friends.
In 1934, James A. Noe bought a substantial interest in state-owned land
rich with oil. One month later, he founded the Win or Lose Corporation,
to which he transferred the mineral rights on the land. Seymour Weiss
and Earle Christenberry, Huey's private secretary, each put up $200 for
one share of Win or Lose stock, the only actual money exchanged in the
formation of the corporation. One year later, Win or Lose declared a
dividend of $2,000 a share, with Weiss and Christenberry each making a
profit of $1,800, and Huey, to whom Noe "donated" thirty-one shares,
receiving $62,000. Noe sold the biggest block of the state oil land to the
Texas Company in return for annual payments for the mineral leases. The
deal transformed the fledgling company into Texaco, and the original
stockholders of Win or Lose, all of whom were major figures in the Long
machine, made immense profits. Through the various methods of fund
raising, the Longs in 1935 had unquestionably the richest political organization in the country, and the coffers overflowed with an estimated one
million dollars in cash.[25]

In New Orleans, Earl assisted in founding a Long machine that would
eventually crush the Old Regulars. Together with Seymour Weiss and
Bob Maestri, he served as the Long patronage dispenser in the city,
lavishly doling out jobs and money to those agreeing to join the organization there. Called the Louisiana Democratic Association, that organization grew quickly, and by 1930, it threatened to replace the Old
Regulars. In that year, Huey came within five thousand votes in New Orleans of his opponent in the Senate race, and two of his candidates
defeated Old Regular men for seats in Congress. Alarmed by Huey's
strength in the city, Mayor T. Semmes Walmsley, the leader of the Old
Regulars, sought an accommodation with Huey. Distrusting Walmsley,
Earl urged his brother to reject the approach, but Huey made a deal with
the mayor. In the rural parishes, Earl helped to build individual Long
machines. As statewide coordinator, Earl allowed the parish organizations considerable autonomy in local affairs, provided they went along
with Huey in state matters. By telephone and in person, the younger
brother maintained regular contact with local politicians and influential
citizens. In his dealings with the parish machines, Earl was in his element. Numerous associates recall how he seemed to know the location of
every road that needed blacktopping, every town that needed a new public school or a new courthouse, every clerk of court with an unemployed

relative. He also traveled the state extensively to keep in touch with local happenings and to meet personally with local leaders. When critical bills came up before the legislature and during crucial campaigns, he person- ally organized the towns and parishes into formidable machines capable of getting out the vote. All in all, by 1930, Earl Long had played a signifi- cant role in the construction of the vaunted Long political machine.[26]

The Long machine represented a variety of diverse interests and politi- cal beliefs, and its ranks contained small farmers devoted to Huey and his programs, as well as affluent businessmen who saw in Long an oppor- tunity to enrich themselves. Those who joined the organization or at least voted for its candidates were called Longites because they banded together under Huey Long's aegis, but it would be misleading to at- tribute to them a political ideology. Most of the Kingfish's inner circle of political and personal associates made no secret of their disdain for his avowed policy of helping the poor people of Louisiana. Such men as Seymour Weiss, Bob Maestri, Abe Shushan, and Richard Leche had little use for his Share Our Wealth program, and after his assassination, they abandoned it. Concerned with power and the opportunities it presented, they joined because Huey's team was a victorious one. Such political leaders of the Long machine as Leander Perez, Allen Ellender, John Overton, and John Fournet also opposed many of Long's radical eco- nomic policies, siding with him because he had the support of the voters. The single element unifying the machine was absolute loyalty to Huey Long. Whatever their personal and political views, these men carried out the Kingfish's orders and supported him in his meteoric rise to power. Awed by his towering intellect and by his magnetic personality and po- litical genius, they added to his foundation of mass popular support the force of one of the most potent political machines in American history.[27]

Inevitably, a politician as controversial and revolutionary as Huey Long arouses determined opposition. Commonly called the anti-Longs, Huey's political opposition also defies concrete description. The anti-Longs in- cluded in their ranks idealistic crusaders for good government, conserv- atives anxious to return to low taxes and neglecting the legitimate needs of the people, members of the traditional ruling aristocracy shocked by Long's dictatorial methods, and hard-nosed politicians unable to strike acceptable bargains with the Longs. Their opposition to Huey Long came not from a differing philosophy of government, but from a struggle for political power. As Long grew more and more ruthless, the anti-Longs posed as reformers bent on instituting honesty in state government, but they proved far more concerned with gaining power themselves.[28]

A genuine two-party system had not existed in Louisiana since Reconstruction, and the Democratic party served as the only viable political organization. Technically, Louisiana elections were actually Democratic primaries, but with the Republicans reduced to impotency, those primaries determined the outcome of political contests. Factions of the same political party were therefore competing against each other, but it is inaccurate to describe, as have some historians and political scientists, competition between the Longs and anti-Longs as bifactional. In reality, Louisiana politics has always been characterized by a high degree of volatility, with frequent shifts in factional allegiance. From Huey Long's time to the present, state politics has featured no-holds-barred competition transcending factional loyalty and ideological purity. Candidates for election often joined the opposition, and few individuals could point to a consistent record of solid Longism or anti-Longism. Neither side espoused rigid philosophies of government, the main distinction being their desire to win elections. Thus, while Huey held power, his opponents constantly criticized his heavy taxing and spending policies, but when they gained power in 1940, they expanded his programs far beyond anything he had advocated. Individual politicians have been so likely to change factions during their careers that any effort to categorize them as Long or anti-Long would be futile. In the period of Long versus anti-Long "bifactionalism," the following are among the many who supported both sides at various times: James A. Noe, Russell B. Long, Leander H. Perez, Sam H. Jones, deLesseps S. Morrison, F. Edward Hebert, John H. Overton, and James H. Morrison. The most striking example of a politician who switched sides was Earl K. Long.[29]

3

"Feeling His Political Oats"

It was perhaps inevitable that two brothers as gifted, ambitious, and headstrong as Huey and Earl Long would clash. All the Longs had a stubborn, independent streak, and they refused to play second fiddle to anyone. By 1930, Earl felt that his brother had not given him the recognition he deserved. All his hard work during the past dozen years, he believed, had contributed mightily to Huey's political successes, but Huey took all the credit. Earl also found himself being subtly removed from the inner circle as such men as Seymour Weiss and Bob Maestri became the Kingfish's intimates. For his part, Huey appreciated Earl's great talent for politicking and used it to advantage, but he viewed his brother's awakening ambition with alarm. Recognizing in Earl a politician whose abilities nearly matched his own, Huey had no intention of allowing him to pursue a career. The Long organization had room for only one leader, and Huey kept Earl carefully confined within its middle echelons. As the statewide election campaign of 1931–32 approached, Earl began to feel the tug of political ambition, and he started a series of defiant maneuvers that would result in an open split with his brother.

The first phase of the sibling rivalry came in the New Orleans mayoral election of January, 1930, in which the Old Regular candidate, T. Semmes Walmsley, ran against Public Service Commissioner Francis Williams. As the Long machine organizer in the Crescent City, Earl viewed the election as a golden opportunity for Huey to crush the Old Regulars by actively intervening on Williams' behalf, but Huey decided to remain neutral in the race. Having already experienced Williams' stubborn attitude when he was a member of the Public Service Commission, Huey preferred to deal with Walmsley, a loyal machine man, who could turn the Old Regulars into a powerful Long ally. But Earl believed otherwise and publicly campaigned for Williams. In the election, Walmsley won, but Williams ran a close second and would almost certainly have won had Huey backed him. In any event, Walmsley's victory paved the way for the famous deal that brought the Old Regulars temporarily into the Long camp.[1]

In the 1930 session of the legislature, Earl again openly defied his brother by lobbying against passage of one of Huey's pet projects, a $5-million bond issue to finance the construction of a new state capitol. Huey wanted Louisiana to have the most magnificent state capitol in the nation, and he authorized a New Orleans architectural firm to draw up plans for a resplendent, luxuriously appointed skyscraper. The structure, which appealed to Huey's growing conceit, would be the tallest building in the South, and he pushed the measure with unusual vigor. When the bill reached the house floor, Earl informed key legislators that Huey secretly opposed it, and he swung several votes against it. Underestimating Earl's talent for legislative maneuvering, Huey was shocked to discover that the vote fell short of the two-thirds needed for passage, and only last-minute intensive personal lobbying on his part gained house approval. T. Harry Williams offered the most plausible explanation: "The younger brother was feeling his political oats. His ambition was to run for a high state office in 1932, and he thought, strangely, that he would further his chances if he demonstrated that he could defeat one of Huey's measures and thereby show his independence of Huey."[2]

When Huey ran for the U.S. Senate in September, 1930, Earl supported him, but the race gave him added incentive to set off on his own. The campaign showed that Huey no longer needed him; in fact, with his enormous personal popularity and his powerful political machine, Huey could easily have won without any assistance at all from Earl. During the race, an incident occurred that solidified Earl's determination to make the break with Huey. A Highway Commission employee named Sam Irby threatened to disclose evidence of corruption in the agency, thereby damaging Huey's chances in the election. At a meeting of Long strategists, Huey authorized a bizarre plan to kidnap Irby until after the election. During the meeting, Earl jokingly suggested that they "take the sonofabitch and kill him." One witness said that when Huey heard the remark, he "wheeled Earl around and I never kicked a nigger in the ass harder than he kicked Earl." Humiliated, Earl made up his mind to run for state office in the 1931–32 campaign.[3]

Several months after Huey's victory in the Senate race, Earl decided to run for lieutenant governor. Accounts differ about the circumstances. Julius wrote that Earl made the decision "with Huey's knowledge and without any objection from Huey." Like almost all his other writings about his brothers, Julius' story is inaccurate. Huey objected vehemently to Earl's making the race, and since Earl eventually ran on an anti–Huey Long platform, he could hardly have had Huey's consent. The Kingfish gave a different version: "My young brother began to announce his ambition to run either for Governor or Lieutenant Governor. I sought to discourage him, stating that it would be disastrous for a brother to undertake to have a brother succeed him in the office or to have him elected Lieutenant Governor." Huey's version is accurate as far as it goes, but it omits many of the underlying reasons why he refused to back his brother. Other writers attribute Earl's decision to run for lieutenant governor to his financial independence and to his thirst for revenge against Huey. What really happened was more complex.[4]

Since his inauguration as governor, Huey had pointedly ignored his family, except, of course, Earl. Although in his campaigns, Huey often proclaimed his country roots, once in office, he shunned them. Only once since 1928 had he visited his aging father in Winnfield, and he did so primarily to be photographed chopping wood and planting crops. Old Hu's affinity for women, alcohol, and gambling alarmed Huey, who considered him a political albatross. Huey also came to enjoy life in the big cities, spending most of his time in his suites in the Heidelberg Hotel in Baton Rouge and in the Roosevelt Hotel in New Orleans. And he wore expensive, flashy clothes and relished the company of wealthy men. By 1930, he had virtually broken all ties with the rural way of life he so eloquently praised on the stump, and he had even shunned most of his brothers and sisters. By way of contrast, Earl remained close with his family and boyhood friends and made frequent visits to his hometown. Unlike Huey, he tolerated his father's passion for the fast life, and on occasion, he took Old Hu to the racetrack and to the French Quarter. Julius, Lucille, and the other Long brothers and sisters were infuriated by Huey's behavior, for they considered family obligations paramount, and for several months they pressured Earl to run for office as a way of striking back at Huey.[5]

In the meantime, Huey spent the latter half of 1930 vacillating about several possible candidates to head his ticket in the 1931–32 statewide campaign. Even though he had been elected to the U.S. Senate in 1930, Huey dared not assume his seat in Washington because if he resigned as governor, his determined enemy, Lieutenant Governor Paul N. Cyr, would take over the state. Eager to launch his career in national politics, Huey intended to take his seat in the Senate as soon as his handpicked candidate took the oath of office as governor in May, 1932. In Washington, Long would not exercise the same direct control as he could in Baton Rouge. Therefore, he had to ensure that the new governor would be a loyal, docile individual, readily carrying out his orders. Three men seemed to meet these criteria: House Speaker Fournet; Alexandria attorney John Overton; and Highway Commission chairman O. K. Allen. Long's ultimate choice of Allen reflected his intuitive ability to judge men. Although all three men had proven their loyalty, Fournet had bungled the impeachment proceedings in 1929, and he lacked neither ambition nor ability. Overton had never held elective office, and he did not have extensive experience in Baton Rouge politics. Allen, however, was ideal. The Winn Parish native was an old friend and political supporter of Huey's who had demonstrated his loyalty since 1918. As a member of the legislature and as head of the Highway Commission, he had displayed a remarkable lack of both intelligence and ambition, and more significantly, he had always executed Huey's orders without question. With Allen in the governor's chair, Huey would have no fear of a coup. So in the spring of 1931, Huey decided on his ticket: O. K. Allen for governor and John Fournet for lieutenant governor.[6]

Earl Long had made desperate attempts to get on the ticket. At first, he entertained the thought of running for governor, but he realized that Huey would never permit such a thing, so he decided to talk his brother into allowing him into the race for lieutenant governor, as Allen's running mate. The more Earl thought about the idea, the better he liked it. Knowing O. K. Allen as well as Huey did, Earl was sure that he would be a figurehead, and with Huey away in Washington, Lieutenant Governor Earl Long would dictate to Governor Allen. In effect, Earl would dominate state politics while Huey pursued his national career. He therefore approached Huey and asked for his endorsement, but to his astonishment, Huey rejected the proposal immediately and shortly afterwards informed Earl that he had selected John Fournet as Allen's running mate. Angrily, Earl demanded that Huey reconsider. If Huey could not endorse an O. K. Allen–Earl Long ticket, he would not object—after all, both men were from Winnfield. So he asked Huey to simply forgo endorsing anyone for lieutenant governor, thus giving him the chance to win the election on his own. As the Kingfish's brother, Earl knew that he could easily capitalize on the magic of the Long name and win. But Huey remained adamant, telling Earl that he had no intention of allowing him to hold elective office at that time. Earl would have to wait until 1936 before he could run as a Huey Long candidate. Earl was furious and told Huey that he would run against Fournet in the race.[7]

Earl Long failed to credit his brother with the same perception of the political situation he himself held. As T. Harry Williams succinctly summarized: "Earl as lieutenant-governor would dominate Allen; the wrong Long would be running the state." Huey, of course, instantly saw this. With a better appreciation of his brother's political abilities and ambition than even Earl possessed, Huey clearly saw the danger in placing his younger brother so close to the highest state office, especially with the docile Allen in it. Although no evidence exists to even suggest an Earl Long plot to take over Louisiana after Huey went to Washington, the possibility remained. Unlike most of the Kingfish's inner circle, consisting as it did of men who carried out his wishes without hesitation and without argument, Earl had often refused to submit meekly to Huey. He was in fact one of the few men who would disagree with him. On several occasions, he had openly quarreled with his brother, and his public campaigning for Francis Williams in the New Orleans mayor's race and his active opposition to the capitol bond issue provided concrete evidence of his determination not to become yet another in the Kingfish's coterie of yes men. In the past, Huey had trusted Earl with many important political assignments, but he always harbored reservations about him. "You have to watch Earl," he told a friend. "If you live long enough, he'll double-cross you. He'd double-cross Jesus Christ if he was down here on earth." Earl's adeptness at wheeling and dealing, his vast knowledge of state and local politics, and his domineering personality reminded Huey of too many of his own qualities. Knowing that Earl could talk O. K. Allen into almost anything, he could easily envision his brother trying to become a new Kingfish. Years later, Earl acknowledged that the primary reason for his brother's refusal to back him in the 1931–32 campaign was "not the possibility of 'too much Long' in state politics," but that "there might not be 'enough Huey Long.'"[8]

Lacking Huey's support and facing the formidable opposition of the political machine he helped create, Earl must have known that he stood no chance of winning. Nevertheless, he entered the race as an "independ-

ent" candidate for lieutenant governor on a ticket headed by George Seth
Guion, a New Orleans lawyer who had no formal machine backing. His
main opponents were John B. Fournet, the Huey Long candidate, and
Ruvian J. Hendrick, a Caddo Parish politician who ran on an anti-Long
slate headed by Public Service Commissioner Dudley J. LeBlanc. The decision to run for lieutenant governor in defiance of Huey Long at the
height of his popularity reflected some of the flaws in character and political judgment that would plague Earl Long the rest of his life. The
first was a stubborn insistence on getting his own way, regardless of the
obstacles he faced. "Earl was the most bull-headed man I ever knew,"
opined Clem H. Sehrt, a longtime political associate. "He could make a
deal and stick to it better than any other politician I ever saw, but sometimes he just had to get his own way, and he didn't care if it meant losing
an election to get it." The second flaw was vindictiveness. Earl saw in the
campaign a chance to get even with Huey for past slights, both real and
imagined, and his public denunciations of his brother from the stump,
many of them viciously personal, gave him a deep sense of both satisfaction and vengeance. The third, most damaging flaw was an inability to
comprehend political reality. Despite his renown as a master politician,
Earl Long at various times in his career engaged in actions that are in-
comprehensible. He would go out of his way to antagonize voters or to
arouse the hostility of powerful voting blocs and influential political
bosses. His strong personal feelings seemed to overwhelm his usual perceptive analysis of a political situation, allowing him to succumb to passion, prejudice, and jealousy. His active opposition to his brother in the
1931–32 campaign clearly demonstrated that he had temporarily lost his
ordinarily reliable political instincts.[9]

Earl Long's campaign for the lieutenant governorship in 1931–32 has
not received the attention it deserves. In fact, it set the tone for all his
later campaigns. Typically, he plunged into the campaign with enthusiasm and vigor and, actively assisted by brother Julius and sister Lucille,
stumped the state for the Guion-Long ticket. Even by Louisiana standards, the campaign was a lively one, featuring name-calling, invective,
and innuendo in abundance. Enraged by Huey's betrayal of Earl, Julius
denounced him with bitterness and hatred. In one speech, he proclaimed
that Earl had more principle in his little toe than did Huey in his entire
body. In another, he asserted that Huey was the only member of the
Long family—"right down to the fourth cousins"—to have engaged in

unethical practices. After the election, Huey wrote that his brothers and sisters were angry at him for his refusal to give Earl's candidacy his blessing, and things got worse when "well-defined and displayed articles of the press fanned their anger into flame and then into a madness." Actually, press stories had nothing to do with his family's opposition, and for the rest of Huey Long's life, some of his most vocal critics would be his own brothers and sisters.[10]

Since the election represented a mandate on his record as governor, Huey did most of the campaigning for the Allen-Fournet ticket. Aware that Earl posed no threat, Huey ignored him and focused his attacks on the anti-Longs. In early January, 1932, during a speech Huey gave at Downsville, Earl sat in the audience heckling him, but he paid no attention. On occasion, Huey could not resist the temptation to ridicule his brother. One of his stories concerned a church supper in Winnfield. During the meal, the women had laid their babies on a pallet under a tree, and when a violent thunderstorm suddenly erupted, they rushed to get the babies. When they left, one infant remained under the tree, "an ugly, squalling brat." Callie Long took pity on the helpless baby and took him home to raise him. "That was Earl," Huey exclaimed, to the crowd's great delight.[11]

In Louisiana political campaigns, candidates who fail to obtain organized machine support usually run as "independents," loudly proclaiming their lack of commitment to political bosses. In the 1931–32 campaign, Earl did likewise. Carefully avoiding mention of his own strenuous efforts to get Huey's backing, he emphasized his independence of the machine that ran the state. In fact, Earl had great difficulty obtaining any endorsements, even from minor parish officials. They realized that he was certain to lose. Without the organizational support he had hoped for, he took his case directly to the people in a rip-roaring campaign, a style that would become his trademark. Because Huey's public works programs had touched people's hearts, Earl promised to outdo anything his brother had accomplished. The Earl Long campaign platform of 1931–32 is instructive: there are certain planks, ones that would mark his political credo throughout his career, incorporated into a program of heavy state spending for the needs of the poor people of Louisiana. It called for expanding the road and highway construction program, building new schools, and creating a comprehensive charity hospital system. It advocated old-age pensions, an idea first promoted by Dudley LeBlanc, but one that Earl Long would champion as his own. It also proposed pay raises for schoolteachers, free hot lunches for schoolchildren, an increase in the homestead tax exemption, and a variety of other benefits.[12]

In one sense, Earl Long's campaign platform of 1931–32 was a typical political device to sway the voters by outpromising his opponents. One of its planks, for example, called for a state civil service system, the first such proposal in Louisiana history. In light of Earl's later destruction of civil service and his widespread practice of spoils politics, this plank appears as little more than an unsubtle, insincere attack on Huey's unrestrained use of patronage. Yet all other parts of the platform proved more than mere vote-getting gimmicks, for in his administrations as governor, Earl had all of them enacted. His platform was far more ambitious and comprehensive than anything Huey had achieved. Despite the claims of such scholars as T. Harry Williams that Huey Long produced enormous benefits for the state's poor masses, his record of actual accomplishment in that regard pales in comparison to that of his younger brother. Huey, for example, refused to endorse old-age pensions, opposed a tenure law for schoolteachers, and did not build new charity hospitals. To a far greater extent than his brother, Earl never forgot his roots in poverty-ridden Winn Parish, and one of the consistent threads in his future administrations would be his vast expansion of social benefits for the poor.[13]

On the stump, Earl focused his attacks on Huey and his ticket, for he knew that the election would turn on the question of whether the people were behind Huey Long. At campaign appearances, he directed personal attacks against his opponents. In name-calling and invective, he had no peer, and he had imaginative ways of characterizing his rivals. John Fournet, who liked flashy clothes and jewelry, "wears a diamond-studded wristwatch and rolls his socks." At various campaign stops, he called Fournet a "gourd-head," a "wife-beater," and a snake-charmer," and he told one crowd that the literal translation of Fournet was "someone who sticks his nose in everybody else's business." He berated O. K. Allen as nothing but a figurehead, a man who would be a surrogate governor while Huey ran the state from Washington. This, of course, was an entirely accurate description of Huey's intentions, and later, after Allen became governor, Earl made one of his classic remarks about Allen's subservience to Huey: the wind blew a leaf into the governor's office, and Allen signed it into law. But Huey had made no secret of his scheme to dominate Allen, and he campaigned on the stated position that if the people wanted him to continue his programs, they would elect the Allen-Fournet ticket. Earl also launched attacks against Huey, calling him a "yellow coward" and challenging him to meet "at the Roosevelt Hotel or anywhere else that he wants to meet me."[14]

In his first campaign, Earl Long established patterns that would characterize all his races for elective office. Both before and after he spoke, he sat on the platform drinking Cokes, swatting flies, crossing and uncrossing his legs, and engaging in other mannerisms to catch the audience's attention. After the speeches had ended, he would mingle with the crowd, shaking hands and swapping tales. A young *Times-Picayune* reporter assigned to cover Earl's campaign, Edgar A. Poe, remembered him introducing a gimmick that would become an Earl Long trademark later, the "giveaways." During the week before one of his appearances, sound trucks would announce the time and date of his arrival and invite people to come receive free gifts. Upon his arrival, Earl and his helpers would distribute hams, turkeys, watermelons, loaves of bread, and assorted other items. After he spoke, he gave peppermint candy and money to the children. His speeches followed no logical pattern. In the middle of a discussion of the merits of the old-age pension, he would suddenly engage in diatribe and ridicule, always holding people's attention with his repertoire of hilarious anecdotes.[15]

Campaigning in Louisiana in 1931 entailed a combination of adventure, hardship, and excitement. Many rural roads were still mud paths, primitive and dangerous. Once, on the way from Winnsboro to Mangham, Earl and his entourage had to walk the last three miles into town, for a hard rain had rendered the road impassable for automobiles. Comprising about twenty people riding in five or six cars, his campaign caravan included the candidate, his brothers and sisters, and several aides and reporters. Invariably, they fell behind schedule, for Earl stopped at farmhouses and general stores, only to emerge loaded down with bushels of corn, coops of chickens, rakes, shovels, ropes, and whatever else struck his fancy. When the impulse to barter hit him, Earl became completely oblivious to campaign schedules and any other pressing business. Usually the merchandise he procured would be used for his "giveaways." Once, he and Huey campaigned in the same town, and while Huey spoke Earl pilfered everything he could from Huey's black limousine and the next day, he distributed the goods to poor farmers in Grant Parish. On another occasion, Earl and his team spent the night at the same hotel as

Huey and his entourage. The following morning, Huey's men discovered that all the tires on their sound truck were flat, and they blamed Earl.[16]

The Longs introduced a unique Louisiana political phenomenon. Opposing candidates frequently spoke at joint stump meetings, giving the voters the opportunity to contrast the men. Naturally, these joint appearances often degenerated into name-calling contests, and, at times, candidates lost their tempers. Always hot-headed, Earl succumbed to his temper and sometimes tried to assault his opponents. At one such meeting in Dry Prong, Julius opened with a series of vicious personal attacks on John Fournet. When Fournet's turn came, he retaliated with insinuations about the circumstances of Julius' and Earl's birth. After listening to the harangues for several minutes, Earl, unable to tolerate the insults any longer, charged toward the platform, shouting, "I'll clean your plow!" A group of farmers managed to restrain him from doing bodily harm to Fournet. Years later, Fournet recalled the incident and remarked that "the son of a bitch would have killed me."[17]

Despite his flamboyant campaign style, Earl Long attracted little attention during the race, and one observer at a speech in Jennings remembered him as a "lonely, dejected figure." Earl must have known that he could not win. The election was a mandate on Huey Long, and the King-fish's personality and record clearly dominated the issues. Since Huey had captured the support of most of the common people, the results of the election were a foregone conclusion. Huey and his machine produced a heavy majority for his slate, which swept the state. In the lieutenant governor's race, Earl finished a poor third, with only 65,209 votes to Fournet's 184,392 and Hendrick's 109,269. It was his worst showing in a Louisiana election. Earl's only strength was in some small rural parishes in west and north Louisiana. He carried West Carroll Parish with a majority, and he won pluralities in Winn, Sabine, Richland, Red River, Madison, East Carroll, and Concordia parishes.[18]

As devastating as was his defeat in the lieutenant governor's election, Earl failed to learn his political lesson, and he continued his struggle against Huey. In 1932, he endorsed and actively supported, with both personal campaigning and money, the bid of U.S. Senator Edwin S. Broussard for reelection. Because Huey had backed him in his 1926 campaign, Broussard had supported Huey for the governorship in 1928, but since that time, the two had broken all ties, and Broussard became one of Long's most outspoken critics. Determined to defeat Broussard in 1932,

Huey threw the full weight of his personal popularity and his machine behind the candidacy of his handpicked man, Alexandria attorney John Overton. Although Overton's victory was thus virtually assured, Earl stumped the state for Broussard, raised money for him, and even tried to enter a dummy candidate, the Reverend R. L. Cox, a Baptist minister from West Monroe, to draw votes away from Overton in north Louisiana. The tactic failed. When Huey learned of Earl's scheme, he persuaded Cox not to file. The results of the September, 1932, election provided further evidence of Huey Long's political strength. Overton won nearly 60 percent of the vote, and most Long candidates for Congress won their races.[19]

In early August, Earl left the Broussard campaign to join his sister Lucille and his fiancée, Blanche Revere, in Estes Park, Colorado, a western resort town that Earl had visited before. There, on August 17, 1932, they were married by a Methodist minister. Until their famous separation twenty-seven years later, Earl and Blanche had a close and congenial marriage. Born in rural St. Tammany Parish in 1902, Blanche moved with her parents to New Orleans when she was two. After finishing high school, she completed the stenographic curriculum at Soulé Business College and went to work. In 1927, Earl and Blanche met while they were both working in Huey's gubernatorial campaign. For several years they dated and became engaged in 1931. Then in 1932, after a brief honeymoon, they set up housekeeping in a fashionable apartment Earl owned in New Orleans. Later, they moved into a house on Napoleon Avenue, where they lived until Earl became governor in 1948. Blanche Long provided Earl with a measure of stability decidedly lacking during his bachelor days. She helped him manage his financial affairs, to which he paid little attention, and she helped to restrain him during his periodic indulgence in alcohol. Tall, attractive, with a quick and retentive mind, Blanche became one of her husband's most trusted and capable political advisors. In a political system dominated by men, she would join two of Earl's protégées, Lucille May Grace and Mary Evelyn Parker, as the most influential women in Louisiana politics. And she retained that status for over a decade after Earl's death.[20]

No longer part of Huey's team, Earl devoted some of his time to making money. Acting on the advice of his friend Bob Maestri, who had made a fortune in real estate, Earl bought several apartments in New Orleans, and he also purchased a number of empty lots in the newly developing Lakeview section of the city. The income from these investments gave him a comfortable existence. Earl also was apparently lucky at gambling, for he kept on doing it without any detrimental effects. One gambling buddy of his still marvels at Earl's ability to "pick the horses" accurately. Sometimes, Earl placed his bets according to the usual "scientific" methods—studying breeding, track conditions, length of races, etc. More often than not, he simply played his hunches. In his betting on horse races, he became acquainted with a number of people involved in the New Orleans gambling establishment, which shortly would fall under the control of organized crime.[21]

After his defeat, Senator Broussard filed a complaint with the U.S. Senate's Special Committee on Investigations of Campaign Expenditures. Specifically, Broussard charged the Long machine with using dummy candidates to produce an inflated, illegal vote for Overton. Since Louisiana law allowed every candidate for elective office to be represented by a voting commissioner in every precinct, Huey Long typically entered a large number of dummies. These people would formally pay their filing fee and enter their names for office and then, on the last day to withdraw, leave the race. Even though they were no longer running, the dummies were still entitled to commissioners. Huey saw to it that his henchmen acted as commissioners in those polling places where his opposition was expected to show strength. Under the law, a commissioner could assist an illiterate voter, or any other voter who asked for help, in marking his ballot. Long did not invent the dummy ploy; the Old Regulars had used it for years in New Orleans. But he did expand it to the entire state, thereby offering an opportunity for fraud. The Senate committee sent an investigating team to Louisiana, and the team reported that the systematic use of dummies had indeed resulted in fraudulent votes for Overton. The committee, therefore, held public hearings in New Orleans during the first two weeks in February, 1933. Altogether, seventy-five witnesses testified.[22]

Earl Long's testimony highlighted the hearings. He began by telling the committee that he did not intend to attack his brother, but that is precisely what he did. The accusations he leveled at Huey ranged from physical cowardice to political corruption. His most serious charge, which Julius confirmed in his testimony, was that during the 1927–28 gubernatorial campaign, Huey had accepted a $10,000 bribe from a utility company for a promise to reduce its taxes. He asserted that graft permeated the construction of the new state capitol: there was "graft in the cement, graft in the architecture, graft in the land, and God knows what else." He accused the Long machine of levying a $10,000 surcharge on every mile of asphalt highway in the state, and he claimed that the toll bridge interests promised Overton $200,000 if he would persuade Huey to impose tolls on state bridges. He denounced Governor Allen as a puppet, saying that Allen dared not even put on his pants or speak to his wife without first asking the Kingfish's permission. Earl's testimony enraged Huey, who interrupted his brother several times with such remarks as "That's a goddamn lie!" Calling Earl a liar, Huey said that lying was a sin. Earl retorted that "you must have committed a million sins during your lifetime." Serving as counsel for his side, Huey got Earl to admit that he knew of no specific instances of vote fraud, and since Earl himself had tried to use dummy candidates, he pointedly avoided mentioning the practice. The hearings produced clear evidence of fraud in Louisiana elections, but the conclusion was that Overton's victory was so overwhelming, he would have easily defeated Broussard in a completely honest race. The committee therefore recommended, and the Senate concurred in, seating John Overton as the new senator from Louisiana.[23]

Earl Long's testimony against his brother convinced the anti-Long faction that he would be a powerful addition to their side, so they secured a job for him as an attorney for the Home Owners Loan Corporation, a New Deal agency assisting needy homeowners by refinancing mortgages, purchasing delinquent mortgages, and lending money to pay home repair bills and property taxes. The job was a political plum designed to bring Earl into the anti-Long camp. By mid-1933, Senator Huey Long and President Franklin Roosevelt had split, and Long rapidly became the most prominent and vocal Democratic critic of the New Deal. Roosevelt retaliated: all federal patronage in Louisiana would be channeled through the anti-Longs. Postmaster General James A. Farley, Roosevelt's chief patronage dispenser, began funneling New Deal jobs and money through Louisiana's anti-Long congressmen. When Farley learned of Earl's overtures to the anti-Longs he personally ordered that Earl be hired as attorney for the corporation.[24]

The year 1933 marked the lowest point in Huey Long's political fortunes since the impeachment crisis of 1929. Cut off from federal patronage, Long found his political base in Louisiana weakening. In July, his strong ally Congressman Bolivar Kemp, Sr., died, and it appeared certain that his bitter enemy J. Y. Sanders, Jr., a son of the former governor and a leading anti-Long, would capture the vacant seat. Huey tried various illegal maneuvers to prevent an election to fill the seat, but Sanders eventually did become the Sixth District congressman from Louisiana. That year also witnessed the rupture of the Long–Old Regular alliance because of patronage disputes and because of personality conflicts between Senator Long and Mayor Walmsley. In the fall, crowds in former Long strongholds jeered the Kingfish during a speaking tour. In early 1934, Huey suffered further reverses when Walmsley and the Old Regulars easily defeated a Long slate in the citywide elections.[25]

Hoping to capitalize on Huey's apparent decline, the anti-Longs concocted a plot to wrest control of the state from him. When the legislature convened in May, 1934, they planned to oust Huey's man, Allen Ellender, as speaker of the house and replace him with Representative George Perrault, an anti-Longite from St. Landry Parish. In the senate, they also planned to have an anti-Long chosen president pro tem. After gaining control of the legislature, Huey's opponents then intended to impeach, convict, and remove Governor Allen and Lieutenant Governor Fournet; the president pro tem would become acting governor. Such a fantastic and complicated scheme probably had little chance of success, but the anti-Longs persisted. By April, 1934, they had obtained the signatures of forty-seven house members on a round robin to vote for Ellender's removal. Earl Long played a key role in the conspiracy, for he had promised to get the additional six signatures necessary for a house majority. Confident of success, the anti-Longs eagerly looked forward to the convening of the legislative session.[26]

Huey's opponents did not know that the man they counted on for the success of their scheme, Earl Long, had returned to his brother's fold. During the first week of April, 1934, the U.S. Senate held hearings to confirm the appointment of two anti-Longs to federal positions in Louisiana. Earl and Julius went to Washington ostensibly to testify on behalf of the two men, and Julius, still on the outs with Huey, did testify. But Earl began meeting regularly with Robert Brothers, one of Huey's aides. After one meeting, Earl returned to his hotel room quite drunk, and Julius accused him of selling out to Huey. On Huey's instructions, Brothers had given Earl $400 to cover his expenses, and Earl agreed to rejoin the Long camp. The next day, Earl and Huey met, shared a tear-filled embrace, and agreed to set aside their differences. They remained close, politically and personally, until Huey's death. There are conflicting versions of the circumstances of their reunion. In 1939, Huey's secretary, Earle A. Christenberry, said that Huey initiated the reconciliation because he needed Earl's help in foiling the anti-Long plot. "Huey could get along without Earl when riding high," Christenberry said, "but he would look Earl up when he got his back to the wall." Christenberry made this statement when he was running for state office on a ticket headed by Earl Long, and he was obviously trying to exaggerate Huey's reliance on Earl. In another version, Gerald L. K. Smith, the evangelist who headed the Share Our Wealth movement, claims that he brought the brothers back together, but Smith's memoirs contain so many inaccuracies and distortions that no serious credence should be placed in that work. In yet another version, Bob Maestri said that he reunited the brothers. Still another account maintains that the Long brothers and sisters made Huey and Earl reconcile in the interests of family solidarity, but that explanation hardly suffices, since Julius and Lucille continued to oppose Huey until his death. In all probability, Huey and Earl came to understand that the quarrel made no sense. Earl realized that he would have to play second fiddle to Huey, and Huey recognized Earl's help in his political career.[27]

One prominent anti-Long offered a unique explanation of the fraternal break. He claimed that Earl's defection was part of Huey's elaborate scheme to insinuate a spy into the anti-Long ranks. To gain their confidence, Earl would publicly criticize Huey and campaign against him. After being recruited by the anti-Longs, Earl would obtain inside information about their political machinations and pass it along to Huey. Thus, despite exhaustive efforts at secrecy, the anti-Longs could not keep Huey from learning the details of their plot to remove Ellender, and Earl's bolting their cause just before the opening of the legislative session enabled Huey to crush the plan. This startling version of the estrangement does not accord with traditional historical accounts, but it cannot be dismissed. Such an ingenious plan to cripple his opposition was not beyond Huey—indeed, it was consistent with his methods. Like all the other versions, this one is not corroborated by documentary evidence, but it remains plausible and intriguing.[28]

One of Earl's rewards for his return to the Long side was an appointment as attorney for the Louisiana Tax Commission, another patronage position paying lucrative commissions and demanding little work. Relishing his new prominence in the Long hierarchy, Earl stumped for Huey's candidates in the fall, 1934, elections, and he served as one of his brother's leading lobbyists in the legislature during the notorious seven special sessions held between August, 1934, and September, 1935. On the night of September 8, 1935, as he walked along a capitol corridor, Huey was shot. He underwent emergency abdominal surgery at a nearby hospital, but he grew steadily weaker from internal hemorrhaging. Huey Long died early in the morning of September 10, with Earl and other family members at his bedside.[29]

Inevitably, writers have made comparisons between Huey and Earl Long, and nearly all agree that Huey emerges as much more influential. Obviously, Huey had a far greater impact on state and national politics. He made Long one of the most famous surnames in American political history. He revolutionized the Louisiana political system, influenced the leftward direction of the New Deal, and posed a threat to Franklin Roosevelt's chances for reelection in 1936. Huey's ambition drove him to seek higher and higher goals, his ultimate objective being the White House itself. Huey Long was a larger-than-life figure; people stood in awe of him. They blindly followed the paths he blazed and ignored the means he employed to accomplish his ends. He became all-powerful in Louisiana, scorning the orderly processes of constitutional democracy and inspiring comparisons between him and his European contemporaries, Benito Mussolini and Adolf Hitler. He so alarmed novelist Sinclair Lewis that the author wrote *It Can't Happen Here*, a frightening story of a Long-type dictator becoming president and using his private militia to eradicate civil rights and liberties in America. Through his Share Our Wealth program and his dynamic personality, he won millions of admirers all across the country. Both friend and foe feared him, and at the crest of his popularity and power, Franklin Roosevelt considered him one of the two most dangerous men in America (the other was Army Chief of Staff Douglas MacArthur). Beneath Long's public facade of buffoonery lurked a sinister, paranoiac individual who came to identify himself and his policies with moral righteousness and his enemies with evil incarnate. He fostered an atmosphere of intimidation and repression and created a dictatorship, in which free speech and open dialogue, academic freedom, honest elections, and republican government were counted among the casualties.[30]

Long's programs for roads and bridges, free school textbooks, an expanded state university, and an adult literacy campaign provided the people of Louisiana with certain benefits badly needed and certainly overdue. A brilliant and original thinker, Huey Long could be boldly imaginative. His policy of curtailing cotton production to raise prices anticipated Roosevelt's Agricultural Adjustment Act by three years, and his public works programs served as models for the PWA and the WPA. Unlike other southern demagogues, Long did not invoke the Lost Cause of the Confederacy, enshrine the flower of southern femininity, or raise the specter of the "nigger" to win popular support. Instead, he possessed a rare, mystical personal quality that cemented a bond between himself and his audiences. Long campaigned in the language of the common people, but he always remained above them. When he took to the stump, a curious phenomenon occurred. Shunning the typical demagogic tactics of sporting outlandish attire, kissing babies, shaking hands, and engaging in "good ol' boy" chatter, he would stroll slowly through the crowd, allowing the people to touch him, almost as if he carried not just a political message but spiritual salvation. He inspired awe and reverence in his followers, for somehow they knew that even though he championed their cause, he towered above them.[31]

However hard he may have tried, Earl Long never became a second Kingfish. "Earl is trying mighty hard to wear Huey's shoes," one reporter observed, "but he sort of rattles around in them." When asked to compare the Long brothers, a contemporary remarked that "it's like comparing a university graduate and a grade schooler." Another associate of the two described their relationship with the people: "Huey drove 'em to water; Earl had to lead 'em." But it is unfair to argue, as did T. Harry Williams, that Huey was the greater because his vision extended beyond Louisiana. Except for his last campaign, when he won election to Congress, Earl's ambition remained completely rooted within his native state, and even in that last campaign, his real intention was to make yet another successful race for the governorship. His political career obviously rested on the foundation Huey laid, but in his own right, he modified and extended the domain of the Kingfish. Earl certainly played raw-boned politics, but he never resorted to the police state, as did Huey. Once in office, Earl could point to accomplishments that far outshone those of his more famous brother.[32]

There were some stark differences in their personalities. With a photographic memory and a genius for instantly discerning the essence of a problem, Huey impressed virtually everyone with the force and brilliance of his intellect. He enjoyed intellectual discourse and in his speeches alluded to mythology, literature, and philosophy. Earl gave the opposite impression, that of earthiness and, to those who did not know him, of ignorance. A. J. Liebling pointed out another difference in the two. One day, Huey arrived at a friend's house and asked for a drink. The friend went to his cellar and returned with a bottle of fine Jack Daniel's. When the friend started to open the bottle, Huey put it in his pocket and left. "Earl would have given him a drink out of the bottle." Harnett Kane observed that "where Huey damned and roared and flew about like a whirling dervish, Earl narrows his eyes, pauses and calculates." Earl himself remarked that "I ain't like Huey. He could go a chomping around and get away with it. I've gotta go slower—I might get my head knocked off. Maybe I ain't as great a genius, but I got more horse sense."[33]

The differences between Huey and Earl Long should not obscure the similarities. In political philosophy and policy, both men espoused government's responsibility for the needs of the people. Both directed their appeals to the common man, but neither emphasized the vicious racism so characteristic of their southern political contemporaries. Both possessed a keen awareness of human nature and exploited it to political advantage. Both fostered the illusion that the benefits they provided came at no cost to the citizens of Louisiana. Both used political office for personal gain, a notion that all too many Louisiana politicians have applauded. They turned a state political system into one that was flagrantly corrupt. There was a marked lack of respect for the checks and balances of democratic government. What made Huey both the more famous and the more dangerous of the two brothers was his lack of moral inhibition. He did not hesitate to attempt things that Earl would have refused.[34]

4

Lieutenant Governor

The death of Huey Long left his political machine leaderless and badly divided. Although he had carefully selected his inner circle of political advisors and confidants, the Kingfish had made no provision for a successor. Loyalty, subservience, and lack of ambition were his criteria for associates entrusted with positions of power. He gave political office to such figurehead politicians as O. K. Allen and positions of real authority to such businessmen as Seymour Weiss and Robert Maestri. Men of ability and ambition, such as brother Earl, he relegated to innocuous positions with no patronage or money, thus ensuring that he would have no rivals within the machine hierarchy. A Texas state legislator succinctly summarized Huey Long's political heritage: "Long stands politically like a mule—without pride of ancestry or hope of posterity."[1]

Despite genuine affection for Long, many viewed his death as an opportunity for furthering their own careers. The Kingfish had hardly drawn his last breath when Longite leaders began jockeying for power. On the very day Huey died, September 10, 1935, Governor Allen convened a meeting of the Long power brokers to assert his own hegemony, but few accepted that. As a puppet dancing to the strings Long pulled, Allen was hardly in a position to dominate the machine, and he faced several direct challenges. The Long leaders' public display of unity at Huey's funeral masked a fierce struggle for internal control. One faction was composed of Seymour Weiss, Bob Maestri, and Abe Shushan, its claim resting on its control of the machine's purse strings. One story that rings true but that, naturally, has never been documented tells of a secret trip Weiss made to New York within hours of Long's death. There, he found and took the notorious "deduct box," Huey's campaign fund for his planned 1936 race against Franklin Roosevelt. Containing over a mil-

Earl's father, Huey P. Long, Sr.,
ca. 1880.
Courtesy of Charlotte Davis Parrott

Earl's mother, Caledonia Tison
Long, *ca.* 1880.
Courtesy of Charlotte Davis Parrott

Earl K. Long (right), Huey P. Long, Jr. (left), and Lucille Long (center),
ca. 1902.
Courtesy of William Davis Green

U.S. senator Huey P. Long (right) and state senator James A. Noe (left)
State Library of Louisiana

New governor Earl K. Long (second from left) moments after his
swearing-in, June, 1939. At left is Mrs. Long. At right of Long are former
governor Richard W. Leche and Mrs. Leche.
State Library of Louisiana

Governor Earl K. Long in 1940
Authors' collection

Governor Earl K. Long (third from right) listening while state senator Dudley J. LeBlanc (at microphone) discusses the mailing of the first group of $50 old-age pension checks, 1948.
State Library of Louisiana

Earl Long stumping for governor, 1955
State Library of Louisiana

Long (seated, center) receiving congratulatory handshake from Old Regular leader Captain Billy Bisso for winning the 1956 governor's election in the first primary. To Long's left is U.S. senator Russell B. Long.
State Library of Louisiana

Three Louisiana governors: Earl K. Long (right), Jimmie H. Davis (left), Robert F. Kennon (center), Baton Rouge, 1956.
Langston McEachern for Shreveport Times

Leander H. Perez, political boss
of Plaquemines Parish.
State Library of Louisiana

Governor Earl K. Long (center) with Leander H. Perez (left) and Louisiana
National Guard Adjutant General Raymond A. Hufft, 1958.
State Library of Louisiana

Governor Long with political allies, Ruston, 1958
Shreveport Times

Blanche Revere Long
Earl K. Long Papers, Louisiana and Lower Mississippi
Valley Collections, Louisiana State University Libraries

Governor Long (center), Mrs. Blanche Long (third from left), state senator
B. B. "Sixty" Rayburn (third from right), and friends, 1957.
Earl K. Long Papers, Louisiana and Lower Mississippi Valley Collections,
Louisiana State University Libraries

Governor Long (seated) and sisters Olive Long Cooper (to Earl's left), Clara
Long Knott (to Earl's right), and Lucille Long Hunt (standing directly behind
Earl). Also in the photo are some of his sisters' children and other relatives, and
Mary "Doc" Allen, mayor of Winnfield and also a relative (seated, far right).
Winnfield, 1958 or 1959.
Courtesy of Raymond Carpenter

lion dollars in cash, the box provided the Weiss-Maestri-Shushan faction with a powerful argument for its domination of the Long machine. House speaker Allen J. Ellender headed another faction. Only moments before he was shot, Huey had said, according to Ellender, that "the boy from down in the bayou would be the next governor." State senator and acting lieutenant governor James A. Noe also put in his bid, asserting that on his deathbed Huey had named him as Allen's successor. The Reverend Gerald L. K. Smith led a group of dedicated Share Our Wealthers whose primary interest lay in implementing Huey's national program, but the professional politicians in the Long camp quickly got rid of them.[2]

Weiss and Maestri used their financial muscle to swing the politicians into line behind them. The New Orleans businessmen wanted to unite the machine behind a slate of candidates in the January, 1936, statewide primaries for local, state, and national office. On September 20, Weiss, Maestri, and Shushan met in the Roosevelt Hotel with O. K. Allen, Allen Ellender, and Earl Long to decide on the Long machine's ticket and campaign strategy. Agreeing that unity was essential to victory, they decided to name an "official Huey Long ticket," capitalizing on public sympathy for the fallen Kingfish. They also agreed that the most powerful position on the ticket, that of governor, should be filled by another figurehead, and they selected a judge of the Orleans Parish Court of Appeals, Richard W. Leche. Before becoming a judge, Leche had served as an advisor to Allen and to Huey, and Huey had mentioned him as a possible choice for governor in 1936. As an obscure politician with no solid base of power, Leche made the ideal compromise candidate and, as governor, would become another O. K. Allen, complaisant and docile. The Long leaders agreed to run Earl Long for lieutenant governor. Although none of them trusted Earl, they believed that in that office he would have no opportunity to exercise real power, but would give the ticket added popular appeal because of the magic of the Long name. To fill Huey's unexpired Senate terms, they chose O. K. Allen, and to fill his six-year term in the Senate, they named Allen Ellender. Not surprisingly, these arrangements were strongly opposed by Longites excluded from the deliberations. Some disaffected politicos offered a ticket of Lewis L. Morgan, the district attorney of St. Tammany Parish, for governor and O. K. Allen for senator. James A. Noe publicly declared that he should be Leche's running mate because Huey had planned for Leche to resign in 1938 to run for the state supreme court, with Noe filling the rest of the term. These efforts at rebellion proved short-lived, and the Long leaders used their influence to persuade all machine members to rally behind the Leche-Long ticket.[3]

For Earl Long, Huey's death had been a great personal tragedy—he genuinely loved his brother. But the political vacuum created in the aftermath of Huey's assassination provided him with an unanticipated chance to further his own career. Unlike Noe, Earl cleverly suppressed his gubernatorial ambitions and cooperated fully with the machine, publicly announcing that his loyalty lay with the organization. With Weiss and Maestri controlling the patronage and the money, Earl knew that any attempt on his part to challenge their authority would result in his speedy removal from the machine hierarchy. Earl, of course, realized precisely what Weiss and Maestri intended by running Leche for governor and him for lieutenant governor, but he also saw more deeply. As governor, Dick Leche would play the same figurehead role for Weiss and Maestri that Allen had played for Huey. Earl saw this as a great opportunity to lay the foundation for his capturing the governor's chair in 1940. With his usual instinctive ability to judge men, Earl knew that Leche and Weiss would prove unable to resist the temptations that political power offers, and he predicted to Maestri that Leche and his cohort would engage in wholesale graft, a completely accurate prognostication. Because it was entirely possible that such actions would become public knowledge, Earl and Maestri decided to remain outside the administration's inner circle so they could exploit the predicted Leche scandals and wrest control of the machine for the 1940 campaign.[4]

In the 1935–36 statewide campaign, the anti-Longs felt confident of winning, since Huey was no longer around. Their slate of candidates included Congressman Cleveland Dear for governor, State Senator Clement Moss for lieutenant governor, and Congressman John Sandlin for senator. Their platform called for a full-scale investigation of the Kingfish's assassination, the repeal of many of Huey's dictatorial laws, a $3 automobile license fee, homestead exemptions, and old-age pensions. In many respects, the anti-Longs proposed a broader range of government services than those Huey had enacted. The Long team stressed its role as Huey's anointed heirs, and Leche campaigned as the "Huey Long candidate" for governor. A widely distributed Leche campaign booklet featured a front-page cartoon in which Huey's ghost, its hand resting on Leche's shoulder, proudly proclaimed, "As I lay dying, I expressed the wish that I might live to complete my work! Now I know that it will go on." Leche pledged to continue Huey's programs, and toward the end of the campaign, Earl Long persuaded Leche to promise that he would en-act old-age pensions. Typically, the campaign produced plenty of name-calling. The Leche forces branded their opposition as the "assassination ticket," unsubtly hinting that the anti-Longs had had Huey murdered. Dick Leche confined his campaigning to reading prepared addresses, leaving Earl Long to serve as the ticket's hatchet man. With Huey's widow and children at his side, Earl stumped the state, denouncing and attacking the anti-Longs. He called Cleveland Dear "Dodo Dear," Clement Moss "Dear Sweet Little Ol' Clementine," John Sandlin "Slippery Sandlin," and two of the anti-Longs' chief political supporters, T. Semmes Walmsley and J. Y. Sanders, Jr., "Old Hooked Nose" and "Old Buzzard Back." He also charged the Home Rulers, as the anti-Longs termed themselves, with pressuring WPA workers to support their ticket, obviously neglecting to add that the Long machine did precisely the same with state employees. The anti-Longs fought back. Clement Moss called Earl Long a "liar and a demagogue," and Hodding Carter, Jr., the vehemently anti-Long editor of the Hammond *Daily Courier,* wrote that "Earl Long is a foul-mouthed contemptable [*sic*] scoundrel who runs true to his breed." But the anti-Longs could not stem the tide of public support for the Long machine, and the entire Leche-Long statewide ticket, as well as the vast majority of their candidates for local, state, and national office, swept to victory by margins of two to one. In a remarkable display of straight-ticket voting, the Louisiana electorate gave Leche 362,502 votes, Long 360,815, Allen 368,115, and Ellender 364, 931.[5]

On January 18, 1936, Governor Oscar K. Allen died unexpectedly, and Acting Lieutenant Governor James A. Noe became governor for the three months that remained before Leche's inauguration. Upset by his exclusion from the Long ticket, Noe saw his chance to get revenge on Weiss, Maestri, and Earl Long. Allen's death meant Huey's Senate term still had a year to run, and the Long leaders pressured Noe to appoint Ellender. Since Ellender had already won election to the full six-year Sen-ate term, which would begin in January, 1937, the early appointment would give him an edge in seniority. But, out of spite, Noe refused and instead appointed Huey's widow, Rose. Noe also declared Huey's birth-day, August 30, a state holiday, a move that Leche had intended to make. Noe formally abolished the deduct system, thereby depriving the ma-

chine of a major source of revenue. Made in defiance of machine man-
dates, these maneuvers convinced the Long leaders that Noe had to be
cut off from power, and they entrusted the task to Earl Long. Earl denounced Noe publicly as "the only governor of Louisiana by accident,"
and he campaigned, unsuccessfully, against a Noe-endorsed candidate for
the house. When the legislature convened in May, 1936, Long thwarted
Noe's plan of getting himself elected president pro tem of the senate by
having Senator Coleman Lindsay of Webster Parish selected for the post.
Also, as presiding officer of the senate, Lieutenant Governor Earl Long
appointed Noe, now a state senator, to the innocuous library committee,
and Earl funneled state jobs and money away from Noe.[6]

The administration of Governor Richard W. Leche has the quite deserved reputation as the most corrupt political regime in Louisiana history. Leche's oft-quoted remark, "When I took the oath of office, I didn't
take any vows of poverty," aptly characterized the attitude he and his political cronies had toward government. So flagrant were the abuses of
office during Leche's tenure and so numerous were the acts of bribery,
graft, and outright thievery that the voters of Louisiana, who had displayed remarkable tolerance toward political chicanery, finally rebelled.
Leche and many of his closest associates wound up in federal penitenti-
aries, their political careers ruined. Huey had maintained a close watch
on the graft, but Governor Dick and the boys simply could not restrain
themselves. Despite the corruption, Leche's administration proved significant in the development of modern Louisiana politics, and it bears on
Earl Long's career. Thus we will examine its more important aspects in
detail.[7]

Shortly after their sweeping victory in January, 1936, the Long leaders
held a conference at the Roosevelt Hotel. Bob Maestri, Seymour Weiss,
Dick Leche, Allen Ellender, and Earl Long attended the meeting, and
they quickly decided to put an end to the hostility that existed between
the state government and the FDR administration. Huey's Share Our
Wealth program, his relentless public criticism of the New Deal, and his
stated intention to oppose the president in 1936 had provoked the federal
government into cutting the Long machine off from all federal patronage
in Louisiana and into investigating the financial dealings of such Long
stalwarts as Seymour Weiss, Abe Shushan, and Joseph and Jules Fisher.
Now that Huey was gone from the scene, his political heirs saw no purpose in continuing his battle with Roosevelt. None of them had any na-

tional ambitions, and they looked with eager anticipation at the chance of grabbing some New Deal money for themselves. Nor did Franklin Roosevelt desire to continue the struggle, which had largely been a personal one between himself and the Kingfish. With a presidential election approaching, he wanted nothing more than a united South behind him, so he ordered his people to strike a bargain with the Longs. In early February, 1936, Earl Long, Bob Maestri, and Congressman Paul Maloney met in Washington with emissaries of Postmaster General Farley and worked out a deal. In exchange for the Long machine's supporting Roosevelt in the presidential race and cooperating with the New Deal, the federal government would drop its prosecution of Longites on income tax evasion charges, and it would pump large amounts of WPA and PWA money into Louisiana through the Leche administration.[8]

To fulfill their part of the bargain, the Long leaders purged Reverend Smith and other zealous Share Our Wealthers who insisted on the radical redistribution of the wealth Huey had called for. According to Maestri: "Share Our Wealth was a lot of bullshit! Hell, Huey only used it to get attention, but Smith wanted to take *my money* and give it to the poor!" The Long leaders also had the legislature repeal Huey's anti–New Deal legislation, and in June all Louisiana legislators journeyed to Texas, where they attended a celebration of the state's centennial that featured a personal appearance by the president. Later that month, Seymour Weiss and Earl Long led the Louisiana delegation to the Democratic National Convention, where they unanimously backed Roosevelt's renomination and voted to abolish the two-thirds rule. In return, Roosevelt began appointing Long people to federal positions, visited New Orleans in 1937, and shared generous amounts of public works funds with the state government. It also appears that U.S. attorney Rene Viosca was ordered to pursue the federal indictments of several Longites with a minimum of diligence, and after a federal jury acquitted Abe Shushan of income tax evasion, Viosca dropped all charges against the others.[9]

On good terms with the federal government, Leche, Long, Weiss, and Maestri now turned their attention to fulfilling their campaign promise of continuing the work Huey had begun. In the legislative session of 1936, they enacted a series of far-reaching laws that vastly expanded state services in transportation, health, education, and welfare. The laws included a $35-million bond issue for roads and bridges, a constitutional amendment for free school textbooks, a tax exemption for new businesses locating in Louisiana, and an increase in the homestead exemption to $2,000 (which effectively relieved almost all homeowners of paying property taxes). Earl Long personally pushed several measures, including a $5-million appropriation to begin construction of a giant new Charity Hospital in New Orleans. Long had visited Harold Ickes, the PWA administrator, and received assurance that the PWA would put up two-thirds of the money for the new hospital if the state appropriated the $5-million, one-third share first. Another bill Earl successfully steered through to passage was Louisiana's first old-age pension. Under the national Social Security Act of 1935, individual states could supplement social security with their own pensions. Originally, Governor Leche opposed the state pension, arguing that Huey himself had refused to enact one in Louisiana, but Earl talked him into supporting it. The old-age pension paid elderly citizens $10 a month, keeping a campaign promise Earl had made five years earlier, an accomplishment of which he remained proud.[10]

In the field of education, Earl lobbied for several bills that effected improvements in the public schools. One was a teacher tenure law, under which teachers would complete a three-year probationary period and would then retain their jobs for life. Because of Huey's gross interference in the public schools, including the wholesale firing of schoolteachers who opposed him politically, the Southern Association for Colleges and Schools had threatened to deny accreditation to Louisiana's public schools. The tenure law effectively eliminated the threat of political reprisal against schoolteachers, though it did not, of course, end the heavy politicization of all levels of education in Louisiana. A second bill Earl sponsored returned control of the public schools to the individual parish school boards. Under Huey, the state government had superseded local school boards in all parishes that had decidedly anti-Long leanings. The local control bill, vigorously backed by Superintendent of Education Thomas H. Harris, reduced the amount of damage state officials could inflict on the schools. Earl also pushed through a bill providing for a teachers' retirement system as an alternative to Social Security. Since the benefits were far greater than those of Social Security, Louisiana teachers had some compensation for their low salaries. Finally, Earl used his connections with such federal officials as the WPA administrator, Harry L. Hopkins, to obtain federal funds for the construction of hundreds of new public school and college buildings across the state. Because of the cordial relations between Washington and Baton Rouge, Long leaders were permitted to award the architectural and construction contracts to their allies.[11]

Historians have neglected Earl Long's role in the enactment of these programs in 1936, but such legislation formed a consistent theme in his political career. In interviews, personal friends and political contemporaries unanimously credit Earl with the passage of those historic laws in 1936. Dick Leche and his cronies paid little attention to the details of politicking, preferring instead to devise ways of bilking the state out of millions. One politician remembered that "Dick Leche was on the golf course most of the time, while Earl was on the floor of the legislature pushing his bills." As lieutenant governor, Earl had direct access to the legislative floor and to the committee hearings, and to get his bills passed, he employed the same techniques that contributed to his reputation as one of the most effective wheeler-dealers in Louisiana history. The huge sums of federal and state money appropriated for public works projects offered untold opportunities for politicking, and Earl used them to advantage. "When a courthouse needed repair, or a new school was built, or a new road was laid," one sheriff recalled, "Earl would call us up and find out who we wanted to handle the plumbing and the brick-laying and the paving. He must have gotten two hundred jobs for my men." Another local leader recounted his experiences with Long: "Earl got construction jobs for sixty-two of my people on just one job. Dick was stealing the state blind. Earl took some for himself, but at least, he got jobs for people. Remember, it was the depression back then, so there was plenty of people who were glad to get a job." One politician stated the case frankly: "You can call it graft, but that's what makes the game work." In the legislature, Earl helped to stifle the attempts by Noe and other anti-administration spokesmen to embarrass the Long machine. When a bill to lower the occupational license tax on oil from five cents to one cent a barrel came up for a vote, Noe tried to leave the senate floor in protest because, he asserted, the bill "violated Huey's memory." Earl had the sergeant at arms escort Noe back to his desk. In another maneuver, Earl got a house committee to table a bill appropriating $100,000 for a thorough investigation into the circumstances of Huey's assassination. Because an investigation might lead into areas potentially damaging to the Long political machine, the administration hardly encouraged such a probe.[12]

Earl Long also actively intervened in New Orleans politics. After

Mayor Walmsley and the Old Regulars broke with Huey in early 1934, the Kingfish had the legislature enact a series of laws that effectively emasculated the city government's municipal autonomy and fiscal stability. The state assumed direct authority over the city police and fire departments, cut city revenues in half, destroyed the mayor's political power, and controlled all elections in the city. By the time of Long's death, the city government of New Orleans was virtually nonexistent. Powerless as mayor, his Old Regular machine decimated by the loss of patronage, Walmsley stood ready to concede defeat, but not to his hated rival, Huey Long. Now that Long was dead, the mayor was eager for an accommodation with the state, and the Long machine leaders also wanted to bury the hatchet. So the two sides reached an agreement that brought the Old Regulars back into the Long camp.[13]

The most common version of the settlement holds that in March, 1936, Leche informed Walmsley that he would have to resign as mayor before the agreement would be finalized. A few days later, Leche, Maestri, and Weiss went to Hot Springs, Arkansas, and worked out a scheme whereby Maestri would, after Walmsley's resignation, become mayor and take control of the Old Regulars. The Hot Springs meeting, however, had another purpose that will be discussed shortly. The real settlement occurred at the Roosevelt Hotel in October, 1935. Dick Leche, Seymour Weiss, Bob Maestri, and Earl Long represented the state machine, and T. Semmes Walmsley, assessor James E. Comiskey, ward leader William Bisso, and Police Chief George Reyer the city machine. The two sides agreed that after Leche's inauguration in May, 1936, Walmsley would announce his intention to resign, Maestri would run unopposed for mayor in a special election, and the Old Regulars would back the state administration in return for the repeal of Huey's anti–New Orleans laws and for state patronage. That the deal was consummated before the Hot Springs meeting is evidenced by the overwhelming New Orleans vote for the Leche ticket in the January, 1936, election: it carried the city by margins of three to one. Had the Old Regulars still been opposed to the Long machine at that time, the Leche slate could hardly have done so spectacularly well. In the summer of 1936, the plan was implemented. Walmsley resigned; in July, Maestri gained the Democratic nomination for mayor without opposition. When no Republican filed to challenge him in a general election, Maestri became mayor of New Orleans on August 17, 1936, without having been elected to the office. In a raw display of machine power, the legislature postponed the next mayoral election until 1942, thus giving Maestri an unprecedented six-year term.[14]

Both political scientist Allan Sindler and journalist Harnett Kane denounced the manipulation of New Orleans politics as a typical Longite travesty of the democratic process. Sindler concluded that "the city government had been raped and its voters scorned." Maestri did indeed serve a six-year term as the unelected mayor of the city, and the political deals involved did indeed mock the model urban governments so neatly outlined in political science textbooks. Yet a deeper analysis shows that the city of New Orleans unquestionably benefited. Under Maestri's rule, the city regained its fiscal integrity and municipal independence, and Maestri used his political muscle to obtain massive state and federal funding for such projects as the new Charity Hospital, low-income housing projects, and a citywide sewerage and drainage program. When Maestri ran for election in 1942, the city's voters rewarded him with an easy first-primary victory over his opponents. No doubt Maestri's regime was heavily politicized, but Walmsley's hardly served as a paragon of urban democracy, and even the vehemently anti-Long New Orleans press praised the deal as serving the city's best interests.[15]

For Earl Long, Maestri's ascendancy in New Orleans offered the opportunity to link the Long machine in the city's metropolitan area firmly to the organized criminal syndicate headed by Frank Costello. In August, 1933, Costello had met Huey Long in Sands Point, New York, where Costello lived. The Kingfish and the mobster became close friends and frequently met in Long's suite at the Roosevelt Hotel. After the reformer Fiorello La Guardia became mayor of New York in 1934 and began closing Costello's slot machine and handbook operations in the city, Long invited Costello to move his illegal activities to southern Louisiana. Long promised that the city and state authorities would not interfere with the slot machines, in return for which the syndicate would pay the Longites a certain percentage of its profits from illegal gambling. In early 1935, the mob had begun to set up slot machines in New Orleans and to operate gambling casinos in the neighboring parishes of Jefferson and St. Bernard.[16]

Huey Long's death did not affect this arrangement. After Weiss and Maestri had solidified their control over the Long machine, Earl Long proposed that they meet with Costello to seek a mutually acceptable agreement. Newly declassified documents from the files of the FBI confirm the details of Earl's involvement. With an extensive background in vice—both Weiss and Maestri had been closely connected with prostitution and gambling even before they met Huey Long—the two men agreed with Earl's proposal. In February, 1936, after the political manipulations by which Maestri would take over control of New Orleans politics had been finalized, a meeting took place at Hot Springs, Arkansas. There, Seymour Weiss, Bob Maestri, and Earl Long met Frank Costello, Philip "Dandy Phil" Kaistel (Costello's chief associate), and Meyer Lansky (financial genius of the national syndicate), and they quickly made a deal. Maestri's Old Regulars in New Orleans and the sheriffs in Jefferson and St. Bernard, Frank Clancy and L. A. Meraux, would refuse to enforce anti-gambling laws, allowing the mob to expand its gambling empire. The Longites, in return, would receive a substantial share of the profits from slot machines, casinos, and handbooks. In less than a year, the mob had installed over a thousand slot machines in New Orleans alone, and casinos in Jefferson and St. Bernard, as well as an extensive network of bookies throughout southern Louisiana, came under mob control. Kaistel administered the entire operation from his suite in the Roosevelt Hotel, and Earl Long served as his contact with the political machine. Long would collect the payoffs from the mob and distribute the money to key individuals. In turn, his supervision ensured political cooperation with the mob. For example, one FBI memorandum of 1937 reported that the New Orleans police were inspecting bars to see that Costello's newly installed pinball machines did not compete with his slot machines. The same memorandum also quoted the New Orleans police chief of detectives: "I know better than to touch the slot machines." [17]

The FBI files on Earl Long contain extensive documentation of his direct involvement in the political aspects of organized crime's expansion in the New Orleans area during the time he served as lieutenant governor. One of the deals the Long leaders had made entailed the mob's control over the gambling casinos. During Huey Long's regime, local businessmen operated the establishments. For example, Courtney Kenny owned the Arabi Club in St. Bernard while Manasse and Marks Karger operated horse-racing handbooks and nightclubs where gambling flourished. George and Rudy O'Dwyer opened a fashionable casino in Jefferson, just past the Orleans Parish line. These men were friends of Huey's, but they were small, local operators with no close connections to organized crime. Costello and Lansky ordered them out of the business so their own people could move in. Earl Long administered the takeover. By 1938, the FBI reported that Dandy Phil Kaistel controlled the four casinos near New Orleans and that the Costello organization dominated the handbook operations centered in the city. Together with Weiss and Maestri, Long helped to expand the domain of organized crime in many ways. The three men, for example, ousted the owners of the Fair Grounds racetrack and took over its operations through dummy stockholders. Maestri's close friend, Placide Frigerio, became the largest stockholder in the track, which the FBI pronounced the most "crooked" in the United States, with at least one race each day being fixed. A frequent visitor, Earl won large sums by betting on key races. In a sensational trial in New York in 1938, testimony was presented about the Fair Grounds, which was directly connected to the numbers racket in New York City. Those with inside knowledge stood to win substantial amounts on the fixed races, and Earl, who usually sat with Weiss and Kaistel in a special box at the track, became one of the most consistent winners. Earl also, according to the FBI, devised the ingenious notion that during racing season, all handbook operations in Louisiana would cease, so the gamblers would have to place their bets in person at the track. In this manner, the mob would collect from track betting during racing season and from the bookies when the track was closed. Earl even went so far as to assist the bookies in collecting unemployment compensation during racing season.[18]

From FBI records, it also appears that Earl was responsible for the rise of James Brocato as one of the kingpins of organized criminal enterprises in New Orleans. Commonly known as "Diamond Jimmy Moran" because of his penchant for wearing flashy, expensive clothing adorned with diamond stickpins, Brocato had been a bodyguard for Huey Long. After Long's death, he grew quite close to Earl and Maestri. The two politicos decided that Brocato would be a perfect middleman for their activities, and they persuaded Kaistel to use Brocato as one of the chieftains of his expanding and lucrative pinball business. Located in bars, restaurants, nightclubs, and many other establishments, the pinball machines "paid off," *i.e.*, those who made high scores would receive cash from the proprietors. Naturally, few people scored high enough, and the machines made a lot of money. Kaistel owned 40 percent of the pinball machine business in New Orleans, and when his income taxes were in arrears, the IRS confiscated the money put into 40 percent of the pinball machines in the city. It collected $3,500 in one day. On an annual basis, Kaistel's share of the pinball machine business came to over $1 million, with an estimated net profit of $500,000. Brocato, who owned 60 percent, shared his annual $600,000 net profit with Maestri, Weiss, Long, and he made substantial payments to policemen, bartenders, etc. He personally netted almost a quarter of a million dollars a year.[19]

Until the release of the FBI files, none of these connections between Lieutenant Governor Earl Long and organized crime were known, and we shall review substantially more of them. To supplement his $2,400 annual salary as lieutenant governor, Earl formed a law partnership with two of the machine's most influential men in New Orleans, Clem H. Sehrt and Shirley G. Wimberley, both of whom had joined the Long organization in the city during Huey's governorship. As usual, Earl did not practice law, but through the firm's political connections, he brought in a large amount of business with the city and state governments, and he earned commissions for doing so. His reported legal income for the 1930s was considerably higher than that of the average American during the depression. Between 1930 and 1932, he earned $10,000 to $15,000 a year as attorney for the inheritance tax collector. In 1933, after he broke with Huey and lost that patronage job, his income from his law practice and from real estate investments was $5,388.72. In 1934, he made $6,121.22, mainly through his job as an attorney for the Home Owners Loan Corporation. In 1935, he made $5,999.72, and in 1936, he earned $6,124.80. For the rest of his lieutenant governorship, his income jumped significantly because of his legal commissions: in 1937, he made $14,185.38; in 1938, his income was $14,975.22; and in 1939, it was $14,010.17. The figures for these years included his salary as lieutenant governor, rental income from property in New Orleans, legal commissions, and profits from his pea patch farm in Winnfield, which he purchased from the Federal Home Land Bank in 1937 for $3,000.

These were the income figures Earl Long disclosed during the 1948 gubernatorial campaign, and apparently they were what he reported to the IRS. His real income, however, was substantially higher. None of the listed amounts included any of his gambling winnings, which, according to racetrack associates, were quite large. Nor did they include any of the payoffs he received through his organized crime connections. Earl also made extra money by consulting for various state agencies, a common means in Louisiana of rewarding political friends. By far the most lucrative of these consulting jobs was with the Louisiana Public Service Commission, an agency Huey had used to earn vast sums. The text of the largest check Earl received from the commission reads: "Louisiana Public Service Commission to Earl K. Long: For professional services rendered in Statewide investigation of the Rates, charges, and Practices of the Southern Bell Telephone and Telegraph Company, Inc., in Case No. 2428, $10,000." The files of the Public Service Commission show that the case entailed merely a routine request for a rate increase, and there is no record of the "professional services" Long rendered to earn his $10,000. According to associates, Earl was a consultant to other state agencies and earned fees of $500 to $2,500 during the period from 1936 to 1939. In addition, he used his political influence to sell to the state pork, beef, and other foodstuffs he produced on his farm, though the lack of adequate financial records from state agencies makes it impossible to ascertain his net profit. All in all, as lieutenant governor, Earl Long probably had an annual income of $25,000 to $50,000.[20]

From the time he became lieutenant governor, Earl Long began laying the foundation for his own campaign for the governor's office in 1939–40. With some justification, he regarded himself as his brother's legitimate political heir, and given his personal ambition to become governor, he felt that he should head the Long machine ticket in 1940. He viewed Dick Leche as an outsider, a compromise choice to head the ticket in 1936. Further, Leche could not succeed himself. But Earl knew that he had to remain cautious and not betray his ambition to Leche, who had grown quite attached to the office, especially to the fringe benefits. A popular governor still in possession of many of the dictatorial powers Huey had employed, Leche sloughed off the figurehead role he was supposed to play and began acting like another Kingfish. In addition to his connivance in and personal profiteering from the widespread corruption infecting his inner circle, Leche started to lay plans for a personal dynasty, intending to run his own figurehead candidate in the 1939–40 race to keep the real power in his own hands.[21]

Aware of Leche's scheme, Earl decided to bide his time, covertly making deals with such trusted politicians as Bob Maestri but remaining an ostensibly loyal administration supporter. Earl also started to build a favorable public image, and he availed himself of some of the ceremonial functions of his office. Throughout 1937 and 1938, he traveled extensively, cutting ribbons and giving talks to Rotary clubs and other organizations and ingratiating himself with local citizens in small towns by dedicating their new public school buildings and town halls. In public speeches, Earl always invoked Huey's memory and cleverly associated himself with his brother's programs. Before private, all-male audiences, he won countless friends by reciting from his repertoire of ribald stories. One of his favorites was about a man who attended a national convention of the American Legion. After the banquet, a well-endowed young woman appeared out of a cake and began shedding her clothes. By the time she had stripped down to her underwear, all the Legionnaires were whooping and hollering. Then, Earl sadly announced, the man suddenly died. "What happened?" a member of his audience would invariably ask. "Was it a heart attack?" "That's what his widow thinks," Earl would respond with a wink, "but he was really trampled to death by all the drunken fools running up to the platform trying to reach the girl!" Another of his favorite stories described how a lonely, elderly widow went to a pet shop and bought a parrot for companionship. When she took the bird home, it suddenly let loose a torrent of obscenity. The pet-shop owner informed the lady that the parrot had belonged to a sailor and had acquired its graphic vocabulary from him. The upset widow did not know what to do, so she consulted her parish priest, who took the bird and kept it for a week. When he returned the parrot to the widow, she noticed that it had a string tied around each leg. The priest proudly announced that he had solved the problem and instructed the lady to tug the string tied to the bird's right leg. When she did so, the parrot reverently recited the Lord's Prayer. When she pulled the string around the left leg, it recited a Hail Mary. The old lady was delighted. Then she asked the priest what would happen if she pulled both strings at the same time. The priest replied, "I hadn't thought about that. I don't know what would happen if you pulled both strings at the same time." The parrot then squawked, "I'll fall on my ass, you stupid sonofabitch!"[22]

On his travels around the state, Earl always left plenty of time for discussions with local politicians. In New Orleans, for example, he had persuaded Mayor Maestri to throw the support of the Old Regulars behind his candidacy in the 1939–40 race. In Plaquemines and St. Bernard, he spent time with Leander Perez and Sheriff L. A. Meraux to get their backing. Although Jimmie Noe had been talking of running for governor, Earl did not consider him a serious threat, correctly perceiving that Dick Leche was in effect the most formidable obstacle to his plans. With the enormous patronage at the governor's disposal, Leche began groom-ing his personal secretary, David Ellison, as his successor. Using his con-nections with the Roosevelt administration, Leche obtained a presi-dential appointment for Attorney General Gaston L. Poterie to a newly created federal judgeship in Louisiana, and he appointed Ellison to serve the rest of Poterie's term as attorney general, a virtual guarantee of pub-licity for Ellison.[23]

Aware of Leche's scheme, Earl decided to wait for the opportune mo-ment to thwart it. In the meantime, he continued his faithful support of the administration. In the 1938 legislative session, he again used his politi-cal skills to win passage of an extensive program of public benefits: new roads; much higher state supplements for schools, hospitals, and old-age pensions; a central railroad station for New Orleans; and a one-cent sales tax. Governor Leche, of course, claimed credit for the popular program, and Earl grew increasingly frustrated by Leche's stranglehold on state politics. But the month of June, 1939, witnessed a dramatic reversal, for on June 21, Governor Richard Webster Leche astonished the state by an-nouncing his intention to resign his office within a week. A couple of days later, a pajama-clad Leche held a press conference while lying in his bed in the Governor's Mansion, and he told reporters that his decision would make "Mrs. Richard W. Leche and Mrs. Earl K. Long the most profoundly happy ladies in Louisiana today." In apparently robust health, the governor attributed his impending resignation to illness, primarily arthritis, and to "general complications." As it turned out, those "com-plications" had nothing to do with the state of Leche's health. The prob-lem was a growing torrent of publicity about political corruption within his administration. Leche knew better than anyone that the newspapers in June barely touched the extent of the corruption. When he learned that federal investigators were considering a probe into Louisiana politi-cal misdeeds, he knew that his career had come to an end.[24]

On June 9, 1939, a reporter for the New Orleans *States,* F. Edward Hebert, wrote a story about LSU employees performing millwork on a private home in New Orleans, with university trucks used to deliver the building materials. Hebert's source was Jimmie Noe, who had been studying the corrupt activities of Leche and his people since 1936. Know-ing that his only chance of winning the governorship in 1940 lay in de-stroying Leche, Noe began leaking the information he had compiled, thereby violating a cardinal rule of politics, Never reveal what goes on behind closed doors. Initially, Leche promised to investigate, but Attorney General Ellison stated that the newspaper had simply misrepresented a common practice of state colleges' selling products manufactured by students to raise money. Unconvinced, the *States* published a scathing editorial, asking, among other questions, "Have any other persons besides politicians and their friends been given the opportunity to 'do business' with L.S.U.?" Leche's reply, "I deny the allegations and I defy the alligators," suggested that he considered the LSU millwork issue a minor annoyance that would quickly fade from the front page.[25]

The political damage might indeed have proved minimal had not another, more sensational revelation appeared in the nationally syndicated "Washington Merry-Go-Round" column by Drew Pearson and Robert S. Allen on June 17. The columnists possessed six affidavits from WPA employees that they had been forced to work on the construction of private homes owned by the governor and other state officials and that the building materials they used had been stolen from WPA stockpiles. The column provoked a storm of criticism in Louisiana. Although the state's voters were not naïve about political corruption, they considered certain matters above spoils politics, and the New Deal was one of them. The WPA employed thousands of hungry people in public works projects to help get them through the depression, and people all over the state were shocked by the revelation. James A. Crutcher, the WPA administrator for Louisiana, naturally denied the charges, but he did admit that one of the men had actually worked for the WPA and that certain WPA materials had been used to build Leche's mansion in Mandeville. Crutcher's denials of wrongdoing—he claimed that all the materials had been paid for—fell on deaf ears, and he and his close friend Dick Leche came under increasing criticism.[26]

The Pearson-Allen column pushed Leche along the road to resignation, but the event that finalized his decision came on June 21, when Dr. James Monroe Smith, the president of LSU, informed him that he had squandered over half a million dollars in university funds in speculation in stocks and bonds and in commodities futures. Smith also astonished Leche when he told him that he had lost an additional half a million dollars of his own money. It did not take long for Leche to realize the implications of Smith's actions. The building of LSU into a major regional university had been one of Huey Long's proudest accomplishments, and the Kingfish had led the people of Louisiana in their admiration for the institution. That the president of their beloved university would actually steal its own money would infuriate the voters, as Leche well knew. "Where the hell did that bastard get half a million dollars?" Leche asked. A few quick phone calls convinced Leche that Smith was not the only person to profit off LSU. That in fact dozens of leading figures in his administration had used the university to enrich themselves solidified his decision to resign.[27]

Privately delighted with the prospect of becoming governor, Earl Long maintained a public posture of caution, telling the press that he was not governor yet, and that Leche might change his mind. To avoid prying reporters, Earl stole off to his pea patch farm in Winnfield, where he spent the next three days. On June 25, he returned to Baton Rouge and was surprised to learn that Leche had decided to remain governor. In a private meeting in the Governor's Mansion, Leche told Long about Smith's theft of LSU funds, and Leche told him that Smith had suddenly departed the state, and he wanted to allow Smith a few days to make his escape from the authorities. Earl exploded, telling Leche that he had to resign and that Smith had to be captured and returned to Louisiana to stand trial. Earl called Seymour Weiss and Bob Maestri, who rushed to Baton Rouge, and the three men talked Leche into following through on his promise to resign. Leche caved in to the pressure, and an inaugural ceremony was hurriedly arranged. At about 6:30 P.M. on June 26, 1939, Richard Leche entered the East Room of the Governor's Mansion and said, "Take it, Earl, it's all yours." About forty minutes later, with the room packed with family members, politicians, and reporters, an old Long family friend, Associate Justice John R. Land of the state supreme court, administered the oath of office to Earl Kemp Long as the new governor of Louisiana.[28]

5

Louisiana Hayride

Less than a month before Earl Long succeeded Richard Leche as governor of Louisiana, Long attended the annual convention of the Louisiana Peace Officers in Baton Rouge. There he had occasion to speak with B. E. Sackett, the special agent in charge of the New Orleans Field Office of the FBI. After the convention, Sackett wrote a lengthy letter to the FBI director, J. Edgar Hoover, in which he described Earl Long: "Long impressed me as being about the 'dumbest white man' I have ever talked to, has very little intelligence, no tact, and not very much common sense. He has an over-abundance of confidence in himself, speaks authoritatively about matters he quite evidently knows nothing about, and generally makes a very poor impression. He is quite stubborn, egotistical, and is the type of man who would not listen to reason or advice from any source." Sackett also informed Hoover that F. Edward Hebert told him that Long was "extremely and rabidly anti-Semitic," and that if Long became governor, "the Jews in Louisiana would just about have to leave the state." Therefore, Sackett continued, Seymour Weiss and other leading Jews were not only opposing Earl's bid for the governorship in 1940, they were also demanding an impartial investigation into Huey Long's assassination because they felt certain that Earl had masterminded the murder.[1]

On the night of Leche's resignation and Long's inauguration, the FBI agent sent a telegram to Hoover in which he offered a unique reason for Leche's abdication: "so that Long would be put in office now in order that he would make a fool of himself . . . so that the party leaders would not back him. The party leaders fear Long, do not want him in office, as Long [is] allegedly vindictive and vicious and can not be controlled." In subsequent communications with Hoover in late June and early July,

1939, Sackett pursued this interpretation, branding Long "utterly unpredictable" and repeating his earlier contention that Leche resigned to let Long "make a damn fool of himself." The reason, Sackett explained, lay in Leche's scheme to have acting attorney general David Ellison become governor in 1940. Since Earl was sure to be Ellison's main opponent in the governor's race, Leche resigned before his term had expired to allow Long to so disgrace himself in office that the Long machine leaders would turn to Ellison as their candidate.[2]

Whether FBI agent Sackett's version of Leche's motivation for resigning was accurate, Governor Earl K. Long did not disgrace himself or "make a damn fool of himself," and in fact came extremely close to winning the 1940 election. With over two decades' experience in Louisiana politics, dating back to Huey's first campaign, Earl Long easily adapted to his new office and exercised its powers with aplomb. In January, 1940, only seven months after he took the oath of office, the first gubernatorial primary would take place, and Earl intended to use the full powers and patronage resources now at his disposal to ensure his election to a four-year term. The scandal involving LSU, which persuaded Leche to resign, Earl regarded as eminently forgettable. The persistent rumors of corruption throughout the administration he sloughed off as inconsequential, for he knew through experience that chicanery traditionally accompanied the political process in Louisiana. At worst, a few people might go to jail and a few politicians might lose their jobs, but the all-powerful Long machine would carry him to victory. Earl knew that he would not be personally implicated in any of the scandals, for he had taken care to have no close ties with Leche. Back in 1936, he had correctly predicted that Leche would get into trouble for not knowing how to control the graft. Deducts, kickbacks from contractors, consulting jobs, nepotism—these were the practices the public was accustomed to and would not cause any problems. But Governor Dick and the boys had stolen millions and had not even the sense to leave such sacred cows as the WPA and LSU alone. So Earl, Bob Maestri, and other smart politicos had kept their distance. Now that Leche had removed himself from the political scene, Earl thought that he had won a free ride in the next election.[3]

Earl Long badly misread the political situation in Louisiana. From the beginning of his administration, he faced almost daily revelations of scandal and corruption and, despite his repeated efforts to minimize their significance, found himself continually harassed by a growing body of investigative reporters bent on publicizing every instance of wrongdoing in state government. Less than an hour after he took office, Long held a press conference, and to his surprise, the reporters showed no interest in his plans for the new administration, focusing all their questions on Smith's disappearance. "What I am going to do as governor, I don't know," Earl stated, adding that he felt "bewildered" and could not "think clearly" about the scandals, but he did promise to "get to the bottom of this thing" and to "let the chips fall where they may." To counterbalance the heavy newspaper publicity about the Leche scandals, Earl enlisted the propaganda organ of the Long machine, the *Progress,* which he had purchased from Leche, to publicize himself as the reincarnation of his brother. One issue of the paper, which was handed out to people all over the state, depicted Earl Long as the champion of free roads, charity hospitals, and old-age pensions, and another issue announced his plans for increased funding for state colleges in Natchitoches, Ruston, Lafayette, Baton Rouge, and Hammond. The new governor also took his case directly to the people. On July 4, he informally announced for governor and, in his opening campaign address, told a large crowd that he should not be blamed for Leche's misdeeds: "The Baptists tried to raise $75 million, and before they had got halfway, they found the secretary had stolen half that." As for Smith's trying to line his pockets with LSU's money, he told an audience in Opelousas that "it's a terrible thing when a man shows up crooked, but when Christ was on earth, he picked twelve men and got a son-of-a-gun among them."[4]

These unsubtle attempts to excuse the scandals failed to stifle reporters' curiosity, which was already stimulated by persistent rumors of corruption throughout state government. By the middle of July, 1939, reporters, using information supplied them by Jimmie Noe and that they had discovered, had uncovered evidence of the systematic theft of state funds, the private use of state property and of state employees, and the abuse of public office by most of the leading figures of the Leche administration. Daily newspapers clamored for a thorough, impartial investigation by the new governor. For the rest of the year, Earl Long faced an almost daily barrage of editorial criticism for his failure to use the full resources of state government to bring the rascals to justice. Despite certain gestures Long made in the direction of reform, the press criticism proved justified.[5]

As Harnett T. Kane so effectively recounted in his *Louisiana Hayride,* Leche and many of his closest associates exploited, in unfettered fashion, the powers and purse strings of the Louisiana state government for their own financial enrichment. Not only did Leche not take a vow of poverty when he took the oath of office, he must have taken one of affluence, for he profited immensely from his three years as the state's chief executive. One method he used involved the *Progress*. Not long after he became governor, Leche bought the *Progress* for $38,000, and he passed the word that anyone desiring to do business with the state would enhance his prospects by purchasing expensive advertising space in the paper. Those businessmen who refused found themselves denied state contracts, with sudden huge increases in their property tax assessments, their licenses suspended, and their places of business subject to "surprise inspections" by state fire and health officials, who invariably discovered numerous violations of state codes. One merchant who did not take out a subscription discovered the sidewalk in front of his shop splattered with tar. During his trial in federal court, Leche testified to the profits the newspaper brought him. Leche "invited" politicians to buy stock in the *Progress,* and he sold a total of $187,000 worth. After deducting the initial purchase price of $38,000, Leche made $149,000 off the sale of stock, plus $36,000 in dividends. In addition, Leche claimed that he sold the paper to Earl Long for $200,000, which meant that his total gain from the *Progress* alone was $385,000, plus the normal profits the paper earned from the sale of advertising space and the practice of forcing state employees to purchase five subscriptions apiece.[6]

Leche's problems began when the federal government decided to probe the LSU scandals. O. John Rogge, the thirty-five-year-old head of the special Criminal Investigation Unit of the Justice Department, took charge of the federal inquiry, which quickly branched out from its original focus on LSU to virtually every part of state government. Assisted by Elmer Irey, the crack IRS investigator, and by Rufus Fontenot, the collector of internal revenue for Louisiana, Rogge had planned to prosecute the Leche gang for income tax evasion, the charge on which Al Capone had been convicted. But the Louisiana boys proved smarter than the mob, for they actually had the audacity to report their illegal income from graft on their federal income tax returns. For example, Seymour Weiss listed $134,000 he made off an illegal hot oil scheme, and Leche reported a 1937 income of $90,000, only $6,000 of which was his salary as governor, the rest being his profits from the *Progress* and from kickbacks. Rogge was astonished that these politicians would go so far as to report illegal income to the IRS, but since they did, he had to look for another federal charge to use. After consulting with federal attorneys, he decided that his best chance to prosecute lay in the charge of using the mails to defraud, and most of the culprits in the Louisiana scandals of 1939 were convicted on that charge.[7]

Most of the leading members of the Leche administration and their political associates were implicated in the scandals. Typically, these corrupt politicians used their influence to extract huge profits from state contracts and from the failure of key officials to enforce state laws. With the connivance of the conservation commissioner William Rankin, Leche, Weiss, and certain oil wildcatters made immense sums selling oil produced in excess of state quotas without paying the severance taxes, mineral leases, and royalties on it. Leche was convicted of defrauding the Highway Commission of $31,000 in a typical kickback operation, and he received a ten-year sentence, by far the stiffest penalty meted out to any of the culprits. The Caldwell Brothers and Hart Construction Company, a favorite contractor, joined with Seymour Weiss in defrauding LSU of over $150,000 in the sale of the Bienville Hotel to the university for use as a nurses' dormitory. Abe Shushan was convicted of mail fraud in bilking the Orleans Levee Board of nearly half a million dollars. The list of the scandals could continue almost endlessly. Altogether, two hundred fifty indictments were issued against politicians and businessmen; several prominent businessmen committed suicide. Many state officials went to jail. The estimates of the amount of money Governor Dick and the boys stole from the state range from $25 million to over $100 million. It was indeed the "second Louisiana Purchase."[8]

As governor of Louisiana during the latter half of 1939, when the scandals were publicized and many of the trials held, Earl Long tried desperately to ignore his responsibility to enforce the laws of the state. The bulk of the crimes committed fell under state law, and as governor, he had to ensure that the wrongdoers were prosecuted. Instead, Long used his position to interfere, and he tried to obstruct parish grand juries in their investigations. Publicly, Earl made repeated statements of his commitment to justice, honesty, and integrity, and he made several gestures toward reform to give the appearance of honesty. Upon close examination, those measures gave the appearance of reform while continuing politics as usual. For example, Governor Long did formally abolish the deduct system, but he authorized "voluntary" contributions from state employees to the Long campaign chest. As a former Highway Commission employee stated, "It was 'voluntary,' all right. If you didn't 'volunteer' 5 percent of your paycheck, you got a pink slip on payday." As lieutenant governor, Earl had actually justified the deduct system as a "legitimate and honorable way of raising funds from people who owe their jobs to the state and would have nothing otherwise." Another practice he formally ended was double-dipping by state legislators, but in reality many of their jobs were simply filled by relatives. Long also padded the state payroll by adding over five thousand new employees in the last six months of 1939, people who were told in no uncertain terms that their jobs depended on their actively supporting Long in the campaign. As Earl's ally, Bob Maestri, who also added over five thousand new names to the city payroll in the same period, frankly acknowledged, "Five thousand new workers meant at least 10,000 votes on election day."[9]

One scholar believes that Earl Long made sincere and genuine attempts to investigate the scandals and to prosecute the guilty. The main evidence for this thesis was Long's appointing a special team of lawyers to probe the LSU issue, a team headed by the prominent attorney J. Fair Hardin. In fact, this unit proved yet another public relations gesture. To ensure that the lawyers did not touch too close to home, Long appointed Lewis L. Morgan, a leading Longite, to the team, and Morgan used his influence to divert the investigation from the most serious matters. The special team never recommended the prosecution of a single individual, even though one of the leading culprits in the scandals was George Caldwell, the LSU building superintendent. To a group of inquiring reporters, Governor Long said, "I am determined to remove from the seat of authority every man who in any degree worships Mammon rather than God." But for three years, Bob Maestri had served as conservation commissioner, and during his tenure, numerous oil companies, including one in which Maestri owned stock, exceeded their monthly production quotas. Rogge claimed that Maestri and such prominent Long campaign contributors as William O. Helis, Louis Roussel, and William C. Feazel each made over $1 million from hot oil schemes, but Long adamantly refused to open the books of the Conservation Commission to public inspection, and he refused to prosecute Maestri and the others. When the Orleans Parish Grand Jury began its investigation, Earl ordered the district attorney, Old Regular stalwart Charles A. Byrne, to proceed with considerable caution. When acting attorney general David Ellison appointed his assistant, James P. O'Connor, to replace Byrne, Earl responded with fury. In a maneuver reminiscent of the Kingfish, he called out the National Guard for a "drill" and threatened to declare martial law in New Orleans. Then he fired Ellison and O'Connor, and in the resulting public furor, Byrne was forced to resign his office.[10]

Earl Long desired above all to win the 1940 gubernatorial election, and he knew that a legitimate, impartial investigation of the scandals would destroy his chances for victory. The reason was simple. Although Long was never indicted, he had a great deal to hide. During his eleven-month tenure as governor, he engaged in many practices that placed him in the forefront of the corrupt politicians of the era. The recent declassification of the Earl K. Long files of the FBI now make it possible to reveal for the first time how deeply implicated Long was in political corruption in the period from 1936 to 1940. The FBI documented several specific instances of Earl Long's involvement in graft operations. In one such, Long and his New Orleans law partners, Clem H. Sehrt and Shirley G. Wimberley, together with Mayor Maestri, received handsome payoffs from a prostitution and gambling ring in New Orleans. Long and his partners sent an agent, code-named "Faulkner," to the Marine Bar Room in the French Quarter to receive payoff money from a person named "Mabel." In a letter to U.S. Attorney Rene Viosca, Sackett explained that the Marine Bar Room was actually a front for gambling and prostitution and that Mabel was the madam of the establishment. Sackett stated that Earl Long and Bob Maestri and their partners received weekly payoffs of $8,000 from Mabel, and that Faulkner, the bagman in the operation, was in reality an employee of the Maestri-dominated Orleans Levee Board. The FBI also uncovered evidence that both Governor Long and Maestri obtained a "considerable amount of graft" from WPA and FHA funds in the construction of a low-income housing project in the Irish Channel. Long also, in another FBI report, forced Civilian Conservation Corps (CCC) workers to construct a fence around his pea patch farm in Winnfield.[11]

These FBI reports offer convincing evidence that Earl Long used his office as governor for personal gain and that he received graft from federal funds. In all previous studies of the scandals, Long was never implicated in the abuse of WPA money, as were Leche and other politicians, but the FBI records clearly show that Long shared his predecessor's contempt for honesty in public office. Long went so far as to pressure WPA employees to give him active political support in his election campaign. On February 20, 1940, the Long machine threatened to fire any WPA employees who failed to vote for Earl Long in the second gubernatorial primary. The FBI obtained affidavits from three former WPA employees who lost their jobs after they refused to campaign for Long and to allow Earl Long signs to be put in their front yards. After further investigation, the FBI reported that James A. Crutcher, the WPA administrator for Louisiana, was a golf partner and close friend of Dick Leche's and that he was also close to many leading members of the Earl Long administration. Although the FBI did not state so specifically, the clear implication was that Crutcher had made deals with Leche, Long, Maestri, and other Louisiana political powers to allow them to rake off WPA funds.[12]

The most serious evidence of political corruption that the FBI discovered during Earl Long's first gubernatorial administration had to do with a hot oil scam. In a lengthy memorandum to Edward A. Tamm, Hoover's chief deputy, agent David M. Ladd of the New Orleans Field Office detailed Long's purchase of the *Progress* from Leche for $200,000. According to Ladd, Long got the money from an unidentified "group" in exchange for allowing the members to pilfer 100,000 barrels of hot oil from the state and to obtain drilling leases exempt from royalty payments to the state, even though the leases covered oil extracted from state-owned land. Ladd said that the deal netted the oil cartel over $250,000 a year, and that Long's ownership of the *Progress* would earn him profis of over $100,000 a year. A final FBI investigative report disclosed that Frank Costello agreed to contribute a very large sum of money to Long's campaign, in return for Long's promise that the Costello organization could expand its gambling empire in south Louisiana. It is little wonder that Earl Long tried so strenuously to conceal the extent of the scandals.[13]

Despite his efforts, the continual revelations about the Leche administration aroused public indignation, giving rise to the most concerted and organized campaign against Longism since the impeachment issue in 1929. Most Louisiana politicians have exhibited a real flair for discerning the prevailing political winds, and as the scandals continued to unfold, the number of Earl Long's political enemies increased in direct proportion to the decline in his public popularity. Like the Republicans after Lyndon Johnson's landslide defeat of Barry Goldwater in 1964, the anti-Longs had suffered a crushing loss in 1936, but they revived quickly as public confidence in the Longs dropped dramatically. The genesis of the anti-Longs' resurgence was the numerous citizens' committees that had sprung up to investigate the scandals. Some committee members were sincere about instituting honesty and integrity in state government, but most were ready to exploit the troubles of the Long machine for their own political advantage. One such committee was the People's League of New Orleans. Ostensibly founded to pressure district attorney Byrne into an exhaustive grand-jury probe of the city scandals, this committee actually served as a front for the anti-Long movement in the Crescent City, and its membership included young, ambitious anti-Longs ready to replace the Longs in public office. Two law partners, T. Hale Boggs and deLesseps S. Morrison, headed the league, and they used it as a convenient means for raising campaign money and for running candidates. Earl Long correctly perceived the committees for what they were, and he refused to knuckle under to their demands for a thorough investigation. When one citizens' group urged Governor Long to conduct a "Louisiana Seabury probe," similar to Judge Seabury's investigation of the New York City political scandals of the early 1930s, Long turned down their suggestion that he appoint a special prosecutor, stating that he had "no right to shirk or in anywise delegate to other persons the fulfillment of my duties." In reality, of course, Long blocked any serious attempt to use his office to get to the bottom of the scandals. The *Progress* neatly summarized Long's real attitude toward the citizens' committees: "Citizens' Gang Kicked in the Pants!"[14]

On September 22, 1939, Governor Earl K. Long officially announced his candidacy for election to a full term as governor. On that same day, the Louisiana Democratic Association, the legal name of the state Long machine, endorsed its ticket: Earl Long for Governor; State Senator Harvey A. Peltier for Lieutenant Governor; Earle Christenberry for State Treasurer; Francis Burns for Attorney General; and incumbents E. A. Conway for Secretary of State; Harry D. Wilson for Commissioner of Agriculture; L. B. Baynard for State Auditor; and Lucille May Grace for Register of the State Land Office. It was a typical balanced ticket containing candidates from all sectors of the state and including people who had been very close to Huey Long. Despite the scandals, Earl Long believed that he and his ticket would win the election, for they had the formidable support of the heretofore invincible Long machine.[15]

But Long faced serious opposition. In Louisiana, gubernatorial fever has proven highly contagious, and in the fall of 1939, it infected a large number of politicians. Some, like Dudley LeBlanc, A. P. "Pat" Tugwell, and Wade O. Martin, Sr., briefly floated trial balloons but, finding little machine support and money, decided to withdraw. Four candidates formally filed to oppose Earl Long in the race: Lake Charles attorney Sam H. Jones, State Senator James A. Noe, Hammond attorney James H. Morrison, and New Orleans attorney Vincent Moseley. Of these men, Jones and Noe posed the most formidable challenges. Moseley had no political backing, and no one took him seriously in the campaign. Morrison had support in the Florida Parishes, where he had gained popularity by trying to organize strawberry farmers into a union. Although he stood no chance of winning, Morrison did provide comic relief in a campaign characterized by bitterness and animosity. Traveling around the state, he led a "convict parade" featuring men dressed in prison stripes, all of them roped together, and branded "Dick Leche," "Earl Long," "Bob Maestri," etc. At a huge rally in New Orleans on January 11, 1940, Morrison paraded thirty-five Mardi Gras floats down Canal Street, each decorated to illustrate one facet of the scandals. One float was entitled "Thievery Company" and a sign on it read: "We steal from the churches, taxpayers, schools, hospitals, anywhere." Another float depicted Earl Long pedaling a bicycle to nowhere, since, a sign explained, he was nothing but a messenger boy for Mayor Maestri. Throughout his campaign, Morrison had as his regular stump companion a monkey named Earl Long, which he would introduce to the crowd and then apologize before delighted audiences for giving it such a notorious name. When the primate escaped, Earl Long retorted that Morrison was too cheap to buy it peanuts. Claiming to be the "genuine Huey Long candidate," Jimmie Noe cut heavily into Earl's main source of strength, the small farmers. Noe attracted Longites dismayed by the scandals, and in growing numbers, many who traditionally voted for Long became disgruntled with the corruption under Leche and Long. Although few expected Noe to survive the first primary, he was very popular in north Louisiana, and his endorsement would prove crucial to anyone hoping to win the runoff.[16]

Long's most dangerous opponent by far was Sam Jones, who had strong machine support and an overflowing campaign chest. The public outrage at the scandals generated an explosion in the number of good government advocates in Louisiana. Politicians who had fed plentifully at the trough of spoils politics during the heyday of the Longs now became vocal advocates of honesty, ethics, and reform. They were joined by sincere, dedicated citizens wanting nothing more than to clean up the mess in Baton Rouge, by crusading journalists eager to embellish their reputations for investigative reporting and anxious to settle old scores with the Longs, by traditional conservatives ready to turn the clock back to the pre-Long era, and by diehard anti-Longs seeking to regain control of the state. In Sam Houston Jones, they found an ideal candidate around whom they could unite. Unlike many of his supporters, Jones had never held elective office and was therefore untouched by connections with state politics. In his campaign, Jones took the high road, posing as a champion of good government, denouncing the scandals and offering specific remedies—state civil service; fiscal and administrative reorganization; reduction of gubernatorial powers; honest and fair elections; the opening of state books to public inspection; and the abolition of deducts, double-dipping, and deadheadism. A fresh young candidate untainted by previous political dealings, Jones quickly captured the imagination and support of many of Louisiana's leading newspapers, who portrayed him more as a crusader for righteousness than as someone running for office. Jones became cast as the man who would purge the state of fraud and corruption, and his campaign assumed the aura of a moral crusade.[17]

In reality, Sam Jones was neither a naïve evangelist for truth and justice nor a political novice. As a realist, he knew that to have a chance of defeating Earl Long, he would have to make the deals necessary to gain support. Furthermore, the public image of an idealistic crusade for good government would have to be tempered by heavy employment of traditional political methods in the campaign. The press lambasted Earl Long for his backing by such politicos as Bob Maestri, Allen Ellender, and Joseph Fisher, yet Sam Jones did not hesitate to enlist the support of such experienced political infighters as Dudley LeBlanc and Pat Tugwell, whose records were not entirely unblemished. Jones also reached out to sheriffs, police jurors, assessors, mayors, and other officeholders for their machine support. He took great care not to campaign solely as an anti-Long. Aware of the Kingfish's continuing hold on the public imagination, he emphasized that "I am not running against a dead man. I am running against a gang of rascals as live as any gang that ever lived, and I'm running to clean out every one of them." To the disappointment of some of his followers, Jones promised to expand some of Huey's programs, for he realized how popular they had become, and he pledged to work for $3 automobile license plate fees, teachers' salary increases, and $30 monthly old-age pensions. In an interview, Jones said that "it would have been political suicide for me to run as an anti-Long. In 1940, people still revered Huey Long as a saint. I had to make sure that people understood that I was against corruption, but for Huey Long." [18]

Historically, the cost of campaigning in Louisiana has far exceeded that in every other state, and the 1939–40 campaign certainly fit the pattern, with both the Long and the Jones forces spending huge amounts of money. Since there were no campaign finance disclosure laws at the time, it is impossible to ascertain the total that was spent, but several million dollars is not unlikely. Jones received the bulk of his contributions from well-heeled individuals—businessmen, lawyers, rural landlords, and members of the state's pre-Long ruling hierarchy. By his own admission, Chep Morrison alone raised $65,000 for Jones just from people in New Orleans' upper-class Twelfth Ward. Especially vulnerable to having their pocketbooks tapped were the "goo-goos" (for "good government"), the wealthy who saw in the Jones candidacy the opportunity to create a political utopia in Louisiana. In addition, Jones raised large sums from the more cynical observers of state politics, who bet their money on him in the expectation of favors after his election. Earl Long's funds came from a variety of sources. The bulging coffers of the Long machine, swollen from four years of kickbacks and deducts, provided an untold amount. Established energy companies and independent oil and gas wildcatters donated lavishly because they expected Long to continue the benevolent regulatory policies of the past. Organized crime also proved a lucrative source of funds. Frank Costello and "Dandy Phil" Kaistel, as well as casino operators, bookies, pimps, and bartenders, proved generous. Entrenched politicians, their jobs dependent on a Long victory, also gave considerable amounts. Both Jones and Long received many contributions from the same people, those who followed the time-honored tradition of backing both sides. After his second-primary defeat, Earl Long accused the Jones forces of buying the election: "Never in the history of this state was money used during an election as it was by my opponents in this one. Around the polls they had fistfuls of it. It dangled from the hands of some of their supporters like apples on trees." While the charge carried more than a little truth, Earl did not mention that his own followers employed precisely the same tactics. [19]

The gubernatorial campaign of 1939–40 was one of the rowdiest and dirtiest in Louisiana history, with both sides pulling out all the stops. Long and his opponents engaged in name-calling, invective, innuendo, and character assassination on a broad scale. Jobs and money bought political endorsements and votes, which plenty of individuals were willing to sell to the highest bidder. As governor, Earl used the propaganda resources of the state to great effect. One issue of the *Progress* lambasted his editorial critics in the metropolitan press. A political cartoon captioned "Under the Vulture's Wings" showed two vultures labeled the *Times-Picayune* and the *States* dropping bombs called "calumny," "abuse," "slander," and "lies" on the state of Louisiana. Earl also had the *Louisiana Conservation Review,* a state agency publication mailed free to tens of thousands of rural citizens, publish a laudatory article about himself. Entitled "The Career of Earl K. Long: From Farm Boy to Governor," it depicted Earl in the Horatio Alger rags-to-riches mold. "Scratch beneath the surface," it suggested, "and you will find a keen intellect, a direct method of approach and tenacity of purpose—a combination that is apt to overcome great obstacles and seldom accepts defeat." The Long propaganda machine also covered the state with broadsides and circulars praising Long and defaming Jones.[20]

As the first primary approached, Earl crisscrossed the state, giving speeches in almost every community. Typically, he posed as a friend of the common man and spoke with his customary frankness. He told one fundamentalist audience that both sides "have crap shooters, preachers, and church people. My side has more because we have more voters. The other side has more liars and hypocrites." Appealing to rural prejudice, he denounced the mass-circulation newspapers that backed Jones. "The *Picayune* is like a girl in love: loves a boy, and doesn't love the boy." He accused the New Orleans *States,* the Baton Rouge *Morning Advocate,* and the Shreveport *Times* of "scandal mongering," and he attacked the "lying newspapers," declaring that "they can't control me. I can stand all the lies they print about me." Sam Jones received the full brunt of Earl's imaginative tongue. Calling Jones a tool of the large corporations, Earl predicted to a crowd of farmers that Jones "would tax everything you got—your bedsprings, your bedbugs, your jackasses, your billy goats, and your nanny goats," and he branded Jones a "skin-game artist trying to win votes." Other examples of Earl's attacks on Jones provide substance to the opinion that no one could better him at name-calling: "Sam Jones is like a gnat in a bowl of milk. He's all messed up." "Sam Jones is the biggest smart alec that God ever let live. He is so out of touch with the common people that he sprinkles himself with perfume every morning just to keep from smelling like you and me." "He's High Hat Sam, the high society kid—the high-kicking, high and mighty snide Sam, the guy that pumps the perfume under the arms." To emphasize Jones's upper-class way of life, Earl bet the two apartment houses he owned in New Orleans against $10,000 of Jones's "corporate money" that he would lead Jones in the first primary, and he challenged the *Picayune* to publish a photograph of "my modest shack in Winnfield along with a picture of Mr. Jones's mansion in Lake Charles that he made out of the corporations he represented." Although he did not attempt to match Long in name-calling, Jones did get in a few good barbs of his own: "Anyone who says he served as lieutenant governor under Dick Leche and remained honest is either lying or too stupid to be governor." "When we bury Earl Long, we're going to bury him face down, so the more he tries to grab, the closer he'll get to home." Jones even went so far as to inject the race issue into the campaign by accusing Long of appealing to the minuscule black vote.[21]

The day of the first primary, January 16, 1940, was marked by violence, drunkenness, and innumerable accusations of vote buying and other fraudulent electoral practices. The Tensas *Gazette* reported that in some precincts, "whiskey flowed freely at the court house. Some men got so drunk that they fell down and were carried away. . . . Also, one old woman was so full that she keeled over in the voting place." In one precinct in New Orleans, fifteen people charged into the voting booths and poured ink into the ballot boxes. Fraud undoubtedly accompanied the balloting, but with Rogge and other federal officials remaining in Louisiana to supervise the vote tabulations, the certified count probably was an accurate reflection of the ballots honestly cast. The results showed Earl Long with 226,385 votes, Sam Jones with 154,936, Jimmie Noe with 116,564, Jimmy Morrison with 48,243, and Vincent Moseley with 7,595. A superficial glance at the results gave the impression that with 41 percent of the first-primary vote, Earl Long was in a very strong position to win the runoff against Jones, but a closer examination reveals that Long was in deep trouble. For the first time since 1928, a Long candidate for governor had failed to secure a convincing majority in the first primary. In 1940, the vaunted Long machine had simply failed to deliver. Even in New Orleans, Maestri's Old Regulars had managed to give him only a bare majority of the citywide vote. Jones had rolled up impressive totals not just in anti-Long strongholds but also in areas of historic Long strength, and Jimmie Noe had cut deeply into Earl's potential vote in many rural areas. If Sam Jones could obtain Noe's endorsement for the second primary, Earl knew that Jones would be a formidable opponent.[22]

Only three days after the first primary, Sam Jones announced to a large rally in New Orleans that Jimmie Noe had endorsed him, and he praised Noe as "the greatest man in Louisiana today." Earl's comment on the Noe-Jones alliance came in the usual sarcastic fashion: "In the first primary, Sam Jones told the people that Jimmie Noe was unfit and unworthy to be governor, and Jimmie Noe was telling the people that Sam Jones was owned by the corporations. . . . Now Sam Jones and Jimmie Noe are bedfellows, as close as two peas in a pod, and the love-making act they are staging is the most disgusting I have ever seen." The political rhetoric masked a real concern within the Long camp that Noe would deliver the bulk of his votes to Jones. Extremely popular in north Louisiana, Noe used his radio stations in Monroe and New Orleans to remind voters of Earl's split with Huey, and he read excerpts from Earl's testimony against Huey at the Overton hearings. Noe mailed thousands of copies of a photograph of him and Huey, with the Kingfish's personal inscription praising Noe as the finest man he ever met, and he managed to convince many voters that he, rather than Earl, was Huey's legitimate political heir. In addition, Noe doled out lavish sums of money from his personal fortune to help line up sheriffs and other local officials behind Jones. Noe had both personal and political reasons for backing Jones. He saw the election as a chance to get even with Earl and his chief political supporter, Bob Maestri, for their role in bumping him from the machine ticket in 1936, and he believed that he would gain entrance to Sam Jones's inner circle in the new administration. But Noe's main motivation had an old-fashioned political basis: he made a deal with Jones, claiming that Jones offered him 50 percent of the state patronage for his support. Noe had made the same overture to Earl, but Earl refused to give away so much power to the unreliable Noe. Thus, Sam Jones, who based his public campaign on denunciations of political wheeling and dealing, privately resorted to such tactics to win the election.[23]

To curry favor with the public, Earl called a special session of the legislature on January 20. Eager to appease voters, legislators easily passed Long's package of sops for all large voting blocs: $1-million increases in funding for school lunches and old-age pensions; the repeal of the one-cent sales tax; and an exemption from the gasoline tax on farm machinery fuel. The legislature also made several gestures toward reform by repealing some of Huey's dictatorial laws, returning home rule to Baton Rouge, and prohibiting dual office holding by legislators. The obviously political purpose of the special session backfired on Earl Long. His sudden conversion to the cause of good government failed to convince anyone, and the repeal of the one-cent sales tax combined with the funding increases reduced state revenues and produced a $10-million deficit. The special session was highlighted by a shouting match between Jimmie Noe and Earl Long. To embarrass Earl, Noe introduced a host of bills incorporating the entire Sam Jones platform, and Earl had them killed in committee. When Noe accused Earl of betraying his brother's legacy, Earl shot back that Noe "knew Huey P. Long just three years. He put twenty-six deadheads on the payroll of the Bureau of Criminal Identification when he was governor and seventy-four on the Highway Commission." When Noe demanded that Long allow him to inspect the records of the Conservation Commission, Long replied that "you wouldn't know how to read them if I showed them to you." [24]

The special legislative session was another of those occasions when Earl Long inexplicably seemed to lose his mastery of state politics. When Governor Long announced the calling of the session, the powerful teachers' lobby petitioned him to include a teachers' pay raise in the agenda, but with an uncharacteristic devotion to fiscal integrity, Long stated that there was no money available to fund the raise. Instead of trying to explain this in a diplomatic manner, he lost his temper and publicly berated the teachers, telling the press that he was "not ready to turn the affairs of the state over to the teachers—not by a devil of a lot." When the teachers threatened to endorse Jones, Long wrote a public response that seemed calculated to lose votes. The pro-Jones press gave it front-page coverage: "I understand that a few teachers in this state had failed to cooperate with the school lunch program and they tried to give the impression that it was just a temporary vote-getting scheme, and that I expected to make an investigation after the election, and if the charges are proven true, I wanted them removed from the teaching profession as they are unworthy of being in it. To be brief, no one can put a pistol to my head because the election is a few days off." The letter's suggestion of political reprisal against teachers renewed public concern about a revival of the Kingfish's strongarm tactics, and teachers all over the state turned away from Long. In a cliff-hanger campaign, their united opposition to Earl Long cost him the most tightly organized voting bloc in the state, clearly contributing to his defeat. [25]

In the three weeks between the end of the special session and the second primary, Louisiana voters were treated to a campaign that exceeded the typical mud-slinging and outright fraud. Political propaganda blanketed the state. One leaflet distributed throughout the Florida Parishes accused "Deceiving Sam" Jones and "Sneaky Little J.Y." Sanders, Jr., of conspiring to cheat and defraud the voters. The *Progress* stepped up its smear campaign against Jones. One issue predicted that "Sam Jones Would Be A Dictator!" The article was signed by a group calling itself the Committee for Democratic Government in Louisiana, an unsubtle Longite version of the numerous citizens' committees backing Jones. On the stump, Earl lambasted Noe and Jones, accusing Noe of selling worthless stock in oil companies to "widder women" and Jones of being the candidate of "forty-three corporations." Earl also tried his hand at campaigning over the radio, but he got into trouble. Radio station KWKH in Shreveport cut him off the air for using too many "hells" and "damns" in his address, and he was widely criticized for his profane language. Forced to apologize, Earl said that he promised "some preacher friends and some good ladies" that he would refrain from using profanity, even though it would reduce his vocabulary "by a considerable amount."[26]

As election day approached, both sides resorted to desperate tactics to win votes. In a flagrant appeal to racial prejudice, Sam Jones publicly accused Long of "consorting with Negroes," and he said that Earl had gone to Michigan to enlist the oratorical talents of Reverend Gerald L. K. Smith, so Smith could "put into operation some tactics he learned while dealing with that Negro, Father Divine of New York, working in a religious racket." The Jones camp also spread the word among voters that Long planned to register thousands of blacks and to replace white state workers with blacks. In north Louisiana, some of Noe's people started a rumor that Earl Long was "sleeping with a nigger." Earl Long responded in kind. To guarantee an honest election, he informed the press that he would use the National Guard and the State Police "armed with machine guns and bombs" to "supervise" counting the ballots. This belligerent threat to resurrect one of Huey's most reprehensible maneuvers aroused a storm of public criticism, and Earl backed down. The Long machine put the muscle on municipal, parish, and state employees to go all-out to get votes for Earl Long. In New Orleans, policemen, firemen, and other government employees who refused to put Long signs on their lawns were "persuaded" to change their minds. Both sides spent many thousands of dollars on everything from the outright buying of votes to transporting voters to the polling places. On election day, every precinct in the state contained one Long and one Jones supporter, each carefully eyeing the other to ensure that no ballot tampering occurred.[27]

In one of the closest gubernatorial elections in Louisiana history, Sam Jones defeated Earl Long by 284,437 votes to 265,403, a margin of 51.8 percent to 48.2 percent. Earl carried New Orleans by 15,000, but he lost heavily in all other urban areas, and Jones had cut deeply into the usually solid Long vote in the country. Increasing his first-primary vote total by over 130,000, Sam Jones clearly captured almost the entire Noe and Morrison vote; Earl had increased his first-primary total by only 39,000. By far the strongest factor in Long's defeat was the voters' revulsion against the scandals. Try as he might, Earl never succeeded in dissociating himself from that corruption, and he never appreciated the intensity of public demands that certain reforms be instituted in Louisiana state government. Although Sam Jones was not a dynamic public speaker, he had organized support throughout the state, and his campaign did not hurt for money. For his part, Earl failed to rouse the voters to become an irresistible force, as Huey had, and he relied too heavily on traditional Longite tactics. In any event, the gubernatorial election of 1940 marked the end of the most explosive era in state political history.[28]

Allan Sindler remarked that "Earl Long proved to be a graceless loser," an entirely accurate observation. Refusing to concede to Jones, Earl emerged from two days' seclusion at the Jung Hotel in New Orleans with one comment to the press: "I don't owe the newspapers a goddamn thing!" Furious that he had lost, Long resorted to a desperate maneuver. On February 19, E. A. Conway, the incumbent secretary of state, who had won a first-primary reelection victory, died suddenly. Earl forced the State Central Committee of the Democratic party to declare him the party's nominee. Since there would be no second primary for the position of secretary of state, Earl thought that the position was thus guaranteed him. But the Jones forces applied their muscle to the committee, which reversed its earlier decision. Earl also tried to call a lame duck special session of the legislature, but it did not materialize. On the day before Sam Jones's inauguration, Earl conspicuously left town to avoid attending the ceremonies. It was indeed a graceless end to Earl Long's first term as governor of Louisiana.[29]

6

Political Phoenix

Earl Long's defeat in the 1940 gubernatorial election prompted his numerous enemies among the metropolitan press to proclaim his political demise. The New Orleans *States* was delighted that Long had sung "his swan song. The good people of Louisiana will never see Earl Long as a serious threat against peace and decency again." The New Orleans *Item* gloated that "as a politician, he is dead and doesn't know it. And the more the political corpse kicks, squirms, and blusters, the deeper it digs the grave in which it lies." When Sam Jones took the oath of office on May 14, 1940, the Baton Rouge *State-Times* proudly announced to its readers that the "last vestige of the twelve year old dictatorship ended at noon today with the inauguration of Sam H. Jones." Four years later, the press repeated these sentiments when Long lost an election for the lieutenant governorship. But the predictions of Long's political death proved premature, for in 1948, Earl Long emerged phoenix-like from the ashes of his political career to score a spectacular victory over Sam Jones in the gubernatorial election.[1]

In his inaugural address, Governor Jones promised to clean up state government by purging the political arena of dishonesty and corruption. In making this promise, Jones was fulfilling the popular mandate that had put him and the anti-Long forces in office. The people of Louisiana had demanded an end to the scandals and to the excesses of Longism, and they had given Jones and his followers a clear electoral indication that they were expected to straighten up the mess in Baton Rouge. Jones did not disappoint the people: under his direction, the 1940 regular session of the legislature enacted the most sweeping series of reform measures in Louisiana history. Most of Huey's oppressive dictatorial laws were repealed, including those empowering the state to arrest citizens without bond, permitting the National Guard to ignore the orders of civil court judges, and allowing judges hand-selected by the governor to circumvent the investigative functions of parish grand juries. Such abuses as deducts, payroll padding, double-dipping, and nepotism were formally abolished. All state agencies were required to open their records for public inspection. Voter registration rolls were opened for public review, and safeguards were enacted against such fraudulent voting practices as falsified voter registration, the use of dummy candidates, and the employment of multiple commissioners at the polls. The governing board of LSU and the Orleans Dock Board were reorganized, giving their members a large degree of freedom from political reprisal. The state's management of its fiscal affairs was modernized, and sophisticated accounting procedures for tighter control over expenditures were implemented.[2]

Of all the reform measures, none elicited as much support as the enactment of state civil service. The Longs' wholesale exploitation of the spoils system became a key feature of their political methods. Both Huey and Earl had loaded the state government employment rolls with their own supporters, and they had passed the word that any state worker who wished to retain his job would be well advised to campaign for the Long machine. Public schools, charity hospitals, mental institutions, and all other state functions were infested with political cronyism of the most blatant kind. For the more idealistic supporters of Sam Jones, civil service would cure Louisiana's political ills. Under the ideal civil service system so neatly outlined in civics texts, all government employees would be hired strictly on the basis of qualifications, regardless of their political leanings—those who scored highest on competitive examinations would get the jobs, and once hired, they would have job security, protecting them against political reprisal. All civil service employees would earn promotions and pay raises according to a carefully graduated scale of seniority to eliminate favoritism. The Sam Jones civil service program incorporated many of these features. A five-member Civil Service Commission, appointed by the governor from a list of nominees submitted by college presidents, would supervise the system, and the commission's members were protected against being dismissed by the governor. All classified (*i.e.*, civil service) state employees would have job tenure, and an accompanying act prohibited them from engaging in such partisan activities as campaigning for candidates. The new civil service law could be repealed only by a two-thirds vote of the legislature.[3]

The legislative session of 1940 produced an impressive list of political reforms and gave Sam Jones a reputation as the man who returned honesty and ethics to state government. In many respects, this depiction of Jones was deserved, for in comparison with the abuse of power under the Longs and Leche, the Jones administration became a model of morality and integrity, just as Jones's ardent admirers portrayed him. In reality, as Jones himself would later admit, "not all the good guys were on one side and all the bad guys on the other side." Once he took office, Jones quickly discovered that he had to temper his commitment to reform with a heavy dose of politics as usual. Unlike some of his doctrinaire supporters, Sam Jones knew that the game of politics must be played according to certain rules, the most significant of which taught that to govern effectively, an officeholder had to make deals. Many of his most influential backers, men like Dudley LeBlanc and Jimmie Noe, could hardly be considered champions of reform politics. They and the other politicians who backed Jones did so not from an altruistic devotion to the principles of good government, but in the expectation of political rewards, old-fashioned jobs and money. Jimmie Noe, for example, stated publicly that for his endorsement, Jones had promised him 50 percent of the state jobs in his administration. Jones vehemently denied the claim, and he and Noe soon parted company, but in an interview, Jones acknowledged that he had indeed promised to give Noe a leading voice in patronage decisions. Another Jones supporter, Dudley LeBlanc, denied accusations that Jones had paid him $75,000 to withdraw from the race: "They never gave me nothin'. I mean, what the hell, I didn't *want* nothin' from Jones. I figured that after he was elected I would be rewarded and taken into consideration—that was my pay, if you can call that pay. And if *that* was my pay, Sam Jones cheated me out of it. He never gave me a comma on a letter!"[4]

Sam Jones received very sympathetic coverage from the press, and such Long opponents as Harnett Kane and Douglas Manship, Sr., wrote numerous columns and editorials praising Jones for his reforms in state government. But beneath the good government surface lurked spoils politics in the Louisiana tradition. The much-heralded civil service program, for example, turned out to be an ingenious device for strengthening the anti-Longs politically. Endorsed by the voters in November, 1940, the civil service system did not take effect until 1942. The two-year gap, need it be said, gave Sam Jones more than enough time to weed out the Long people from state government and replace them with his own followers.

During that period, the governor fired thousands of Earl Long backers and put Jones backers in their places. He fired the presidents of all the state colleges, the heads of the charity hospitals and the mental institutions, and numerous agency directors. Once the anti-Longs were firmly entrenched in their positions, Jones began implementing the civil service system, for the law stipulated that state workers employed when the merit system took effect had to pass "non-competitive" examinations to retain their jobs. Those persons wishing to obtain state jobs under Jones's successors would have to pass much more rigorous competitive examinations. Thus, Sam Jones's vaunted civil service program actually became a tool for perpetuating the anti-Longs' political strength. The Jones civil service law also exempted thousands of state employees from the system. These "unclassified" employees, whose ranks included schoolteachers, members of state boards, hospital workers, and highway workers, found their jobs dependent on the continuing favor of the politician who originally gained them their employment.[5]

Despite his disclaimers of partisanship, Sam Jones did attempt to exact political revenge against his enemies. He had the legislature establish a special Crime Commission to investigate the scandals and to prosecute the guilty. Composed of Governor Jones, his executive counsel, and the attorney general, the commission quickly degenerated into a vehicle for the political persecution of leading Longites. Earl Long became its first victim. After a cursory investigation, the Crime Commission filed criminal charges against Long for embezzling state funds and for employing deadhead workers on the New Orleans docks while he was governor. The blatant political motivation behind the charges made Sam Jones seem another Kingfish trying to destroy his enemies. No substantial evidence of embezzlement of state funds by Earl Long was ever uncovered. Earl was too clever to do anything so stupid as to embezzle money. "Earl never stole any money," a friend said. "Hell, when he needed money, all he did was to send a 'bagman' out to collect it, or he would pass the word to the lobbyists, and he would get it right away." Another lucrative source of funds was deducts, a perfectly legal means of raising money. The deadhead charge against Earl, of course, contained a great deal of truth. Under the Longs, the state payroll burgeoned with thousands of employees, many of them holding political patronage positions with few duties. When Chep Morrison became mayor of New Orleans in 1946, he claimed that he discovered three thousand "rat-catchers" whom Maestri and the Old Regulars had hired. Legally, the deadhead charge simply would not stand up in court, since the practice did not violate any laws. In 1940, a state grand jury in Baton Rouge conducted an investigation into the charges against Earl, and it concluded that no evidence of criminal activity existed to warrant the issuing of an indictment, and all charges against him were dismissed. Sam Jones also tried to prosecute another leading Longite, Leander Perez. Despite his campaign promises to revoke Huey's dictatorial powers, Jones conveniently retained one of Long's measures that gave the governor and the attorney general the right to intervene in local governmental affairs. In actions that revived memories of the Kingfish, Jones unsuccessfully tried to use the Crime Commission to prosecute Perez, and he tried to use the National Guard and other state offices to wrest control of the Plaquemines Police Jury and Sheriff's Department from Perez. These and other actions tainted Jones's aura of respectability, and many of his crusading followers became disillusioned with him.[6]

For his part, Earl Long maintained a generally low profile during the first two years of the Jones administration. He did lobby the legislature against the Jones reform package, but he attended more to personal rather than political matters. In 1940 and 1941, he managed his real estate holdings in New Orleans and operated a cattle auction business in Alexandria. He also spent a lot of time at his pea patch farm in Winnfield, where he raised crops and animals, and he visited with family members and friends. By 1942, Earl again began to feel the tug of politics, and with his ambition for high office as active as ever, he began making preparations for a run for governor in 1944, traveling around the state lining up politicians and money. Since Sam Jones could not succeed himself, Earl believed that he could make a comeback in 1944, and nearly eleven months before the first primary, he announced his candidacy for governor on March 27, 1943. His platform included the repeal of the state property tax, highway improvements, teacher pay raises (he learned his lesson from 1940!), new trade schools, and a $30 monthly old-age pension. Although Earl gained the endorsement of the Louisiana Democratic Organization, a group he founded to counteract Maestri's growing influence with the statewide Long machine, he failed to secure Maestri's backing and was forced to withdraw from the governor's race and run instead for lieutenant governor.[7]

Bob Maestri decided that the Long ticket for 1944 should be headed by Lewis L. Morgan of Covington, with Earl Long as his running mate. The reasons for Maestri's refusal to back Earl for governor remain unclear. Allan Sindler stated that Maestri believed that Earl had lost the 1940 governor's election to Sam Jones because of his "erratic temperament," and he did not want to risk having Earl suddenly lose his temper again and blow the 1944 election. But this is not a very convincing argument. If Maestri truly wanted to win in 1944, he could hardly have chosen a less appealing candidate than the elderly, obscure Morgan, whose dreary stump appearances failed to excite the voters. In an interview, Maestri said that he and Earl had had a "misunderstanding," but he refused to elaborate. Allen Ellender, whom Maestri courted before Ellender decided to remain in the Senate, said that Maestri did not trust Earl. If Earl became governor, Ellender said, Maestri was afraid that he would try to take over the Old Regulars, so Maestri went with Morgan. In a private memorandum, C. J. "Bobbie" Dugas wrote that Pat Tugwell was trying to form a ticket, so Earl got the jump on him by announcing very early for governor. Through an emissary, Adlie Stuckey, Earl invited Dugas to a meeting at the Roosevelt Hotel. There, Earl, Bob Maestri, and Old Regular assessor Jimmie Comiskey advised Dugas to announce for lieutenant governor on Earl's ticket, but a couple of weeks later, they decided on the Morgan-Long slate. It does not seem that Dugas' recollection is accurate. No other politician recalls the meeting, and it does not appear likely that the leaders of the Long machine would select a political novice as their candidate for lieutenant governor. Nor is there any evidence that Maestri had ever seriously considered backing Earl for governor in 1944.[8]

Earl's close friend and political supporter Clem Sehrt gave a plausible explanation for the Maestri-Long rift. Sehrt believed that the reason for their falling out was the gambling money flowing into the machine coffers. Although gambling was wide open and widespread throughout southern Louisiana in the early 1940s, the focus of operations was New Orleans. Personally opposed to gambling, Maestri tolerated it in New Orleans because, as Martin Behrman said, "You can make it illegal, but you can't make it unpopular." During World War II, the large numbers of servicemen passing through the city provided a steady source of customers for the lotto dealers, pinball and slot machine operators, and bookies. Under orders from the mayor's office, Police Chief George Reyer refused to enforce anti-gambling ordinances, and in return, the gamblers paid kickbacks to the Old Regulars. In neighboring parishes such as St. Bernard and Jefferson, the sheriffs and other politicians also received payoffs from the gambling interests, but they shared the take with the state Long machine. In New Orleans, however, Maestri and the Old Regulars retained all the money for themselves. "Why should they have a cut?" Maestri asked. "We were the ones taking the risks." Earl and his rural people, of course, felt differently, and they demanded that Maestri give them their share, but the mayor refused to consider doing so.[9]

Here was a classic clash of personalities and political interests. Above all, Bob Maestri was a loyal machine politician, and when he took over the Old Regulars in 1936, he transferred his loyalty from the state machine to the city organization. When it served the interests of the Old Regulars, Maestri went along with the state Long machine, but on occasion, he did not hesitate to make deals with the anti-Longs. For example, in the 1940 legislative session, Maestri and Sam Jones reached an arrangement: voting machines would be installed in New Orleans and Maestri's Old Regular delegation would vote for many of Jones's bills; and Jones would continue to allow Maestri to have a free hand in running the city's affairs. When Earl Long approached Maestri about the governor's race in 1944, he was turned down immediately. Although they had been close friends and political allies for many years, Maestri and Long never attained the degree of trust that marks a genuinely intimate association. Furthermore, Maestri preferred to lose the governor's election with Morgan rather than win with Long and risk having Earl destroy his domination of the city in the same manner in which Huey had destroyed Walmsley.[10]

The anti-Longs originally intended to run State Treasurer A. P. "Pat" Tugwell as their candidate for governor in 1944, but when someone, possibly Earl Long, leaked a story about Tugwell's acceptance of a $5,000 "donation" in 1936, he dropped out of the race. The anti-Longs then lined up behind Public Service Commissioner James H. "Jimmie" Davis of Shreveport. A former schoolteacher, clerk of court, and city commissioner in Shreveport, Davis had gained a national reputation as a country and western singer. The other candidates included Jimmy Morrison and Vincent Moseley, both trying again despite their decisive defeats in 1940, Dudley LeBlanc, Shreveport mayor Sam Caldwell, and State Senator Ernest Clements. By Louisiana standards, the 1944 campaign was one of the dullest and quietest in recent memory, with the usual raucous stump techniques tempered by the national mood of wartime self-sacrifice.

Davis stumped the state on a "Peace and Harmony" theme, winning voters through his renditions of "You Are My Sunshine" and other songs. Earl Long complained: "How you gonna debate a clown like that? All he gives them is music." Apparently, Davis' tactics paid off, for he led Lewis Morgan in the first primary by a wide margin. In the lieutenant governor's race, Earl Long led Davis' running mate, Emile J. Verrett, by a substantial margin. But Long realized that Verrett would probably win in the runoff because Davis was certain to defeat Morgan, and voters usually vote straight tickets. That is exactly what happened. In the second primary, Jimmie Davis easily defeated Morgan, 251,228 votes to 217,915, while Verrett beat Long by the much smaller count of 237,452 to 226,649.[11]

Earl Long claimed, and many authorities agreed, that he could have defeated Jimmie Davis in 1944, had he headed the Long ticket. Morgan, with his bland personality and lackluster campaign style, certainly contributed little, and Earl Long gave the ticket whatever excitement it generated among voters. But whether he could have beaten Jimmie Davis remains questionable. Davis captured many votes in traditional Long areas, and the temper of the times did not favor the kind of flamboyant stumping that suited Earl. In the second primary, Earl managed to increase his first-primary vote by only 32,000; his opponent added 109,000—a clear indication that the Long machine no longer possessed its legendary vote-getting prowess. Jimmie Davis' easy victory over Lewis Morgan suggested that the Louisiana electorate preferred to continue the reform movement begun by Sam Jones. Earl Long would undoubtedly have made the governor's race much closer, but Davis would in all probability still have won.[12]

After the first primary, Earl Long pulled a maneuver that reminded people of some of the underhanded methods that the Longs made famous. According to the peculiar rules of the Democratic party in Louisiana, if there would be no second primary for governor, either because someone captured a majority in the first primary or because his opponent withdrew from the second primary, no second primaries would be held for any statewide office, and those candidates who led in the first primary would automatically gain the Democratic nomination. For example, in 1928, when Riley Wilson withdrew from the second primary, thus giving the gubernatorial election to Huey Long, all candidates for statewide office who led in the first primary were also thereby elected. In 1944, Earl Long was ahead in the first primary for lieutenant governor, as was State Senator Joseph T. Cawthorn, the Long candidate for attorney general, in the first primary for that office. If Morgan could be persuaded to with-draw from the second-primary race for governor, not only Jimmie Davis but also Earl Long and Joe Cawthorn would be elected. So Earl put a lot of pressure on Morgan, telling him, quite accurately, that he had no chance to defeat Davis, and that therefore he should step down, to allow Earl and Cawthorn to win their races. But Bob Maestri forced Morgan to remain in the race because he did not want Earl to become lieutenant governor. Dudley LeBlanc, who backed Davis in the runoff, said that an-other reason was that Morgan hated Earl and told him that he would resign for "that little s.o.b. under no circumstances." With his usual flair for embellishing a story, LeBlanc also told Floyd Martin Clay that had the Morgan-Long ticket won, Earl would have murdered Morgan or had him murdered to take over as governor.[13]

In his first administration, Governor Jimmie Davis combined a Longite commitment to heavy state spending on social programs with an anti-Long respect for governmental ethics. With the state treasury overflow-ing with revenues from oil and gas severance taxes, Davis substantially increased spending on health and education, as well as on drainage. He also pushed passage of a state employees' retirement system and vetoed a highly controversial right-to-work bill that organized labor strongly op-posed. Davis proved a more adept fiscal manager than his predecessors, Sam Jones and Earl Long, not only balancing the budget but leaving a $45-million surplus. Despite these accomplishments, Davis became known as a "do nothing governor." His refusal to align with either the Longs or the anti-Longs irritated both sides, and his excessive absen-teeism generated a popular mood of boredom.[14]

Probably the most significant political development during Davis' ad-ministration was the upset victory of deLesseps Morrison over Robert Maestri in the January, 1946, New Orleans mayoral election. Early in 1945, former governor Sam Jones organized an Independent Citizens Committee to find a candidate to oppose Maestri in the race. The com-mittee, whose ranks included Governor Jimmie Davis, Congressman Hale Boggs, *Times-Picayune* president John F. Tims, and many of the city's social elite, wanted to break the Old Regulars' stranglehold on the New Orleans city government. At first, the committee turned to former Longite congressman Joachim "Bathtub Joe" Fernandez, but in De-cember, 1945, came Fernandez's betrayal—he withdrew from the race and publicly endorsed Maestri. Desperate for a candidate, the committee drafted Chep Morrison, who had just returned from wartime service in Europe. In a six-week, fourteen-hour-a-day whirlwind campaign, Morrison carried his case to the people, promising to "sweep the city clean" of organized crime and vice, with a housewives' "broomstick brigade" rallying citizens behind him. Maestri paid little attention to what he considered an amateurish campaign, and he failed to mobilize the Old Regular machine until it was too late. Lavishly financed, young, handsome, and energetic, the thirty-four-year-old Morrison scored a narrow upset victory over Maestri, ending a half century of Old Regular rule in New Orleans.[15]

As mayor of New Orleans, Chep Morrison quickly earned a national reputation as an effective, progressive urban leader. Within a year of taking office, he launched a program of modernizing city services, a citywide overpass network, a model city recreation department, and revitalizing the port of New Orleans. Beneath the veneer of a polished, urbane reformer, an image cultivated by a slickly operating public relations department, Morrison proved to be a political manipulator every bit as effective as Bob Maestri and Earl Long. He constructed a personal political machine, the Crescent City Democratic Association (CCDA), which he employed with ruthless efficiency to destroy the Old Regulars. Purging the city payroll of Old Regulars and replacing them with CCDA people, Morrison by 1948 had built a formidable political base in New Orleans, which he and his close friend, Sam Jones, hoped to use as the foundation for another Jones victory in the 1948 gubernatorial election.[16]

Neither Chep Morrison nor Sam Jones had counted on a revival of Earl Long's political fortunes, but as Earl would remark later in his career, he had "plenty of snap left in my garters." After his loss in 1944, Earl spent three years preparing for the 1947–48 campaign for governor. Visiting practically every town in the state, he lined up support from politicians and raised money from wealthy contributors. Promising to abolish civil service and to double state spending, Earl had little trouble recruiting local politicians eager for a share of the loot. When Earl made his official announcement for governor in March, 1947, he stated that "practically every politician in the state gave me the cold shoulder," but, in fact, he had done his political homework. His ticket included William J. "Bill" Dodd for Lieutenant Governor; Wade O. Martin, Jr., for Secretary of State; Bolivar Kemp for Attorney General; Shelby M. Jackson for Superintendent of Education; L. B. Baynard for State Auditor; and William E. Anderson for Commissioner of Agriculture. Besides these candidates for statewide office, the Earl Long ticket for 1948 included candidates for the legislature, sheriff, clerk of court, assessor, judges, police jurors, and practically every other office in the state. His platform promised something for everyone: $50 monthly old-age pensions; free hot school lunches; new charity hospitals and mental asylums; $2,400 annual teachers' salaries; $5,000 homestead tax exemption; a trade school in every parish; and a bonus for World War II veterans or their survivors.[17]

Long's main competition came from Sam Jones, again running as the leading anti-Long candidate. With the support of Jimmie Davis, Chep Morrison, John Overton, and many other influential politicians, and with a platform that promised nearly as much as did Earl Long's, Jones appeared to pose a serious challenge. But his use of traditional spoils politics had alienated many of his original crusading supporters. They turned to Judge Robert F. Kennon of Minden. Relatively unknown outside his north Louisiana base, Kennon appealed to those who believed that the cause of good government demanded a fresh candidate untainted by political experience in Baton Rouge. Sixth District congressman Jimmy Morrison of Hammond also entered the race, his third straight run for governor. Outside the Florida Parishes, Morrison counted on the backing of the Old Regulars to swing enough votes to him so he could make the second primary. Still on the outs with Earl Long, Bob Maestri and Jimmie Comiskey threw their weight behind Morrison mainly to keep their options open for the second primary. According to several sources, Earl had made a deal with Maestri and Comiskey to back Morrison in the first primary to draw votes away from Jones in New Orleans, and then swing their machine behind Earl in the runoff. Morrison vehemently denied the story, claiming that he was a serious candidate.[18]

Aware that after eight years of dull reform government, the voters were ready for a change, Earl Long in 1947–48 embarked on a rip-roaring campaign that exceeded even those of the Kingfish in theatrics. The fifty-two-year-old Long put in grueling sixteen-hour days, stumping nearly every town in the state. To attract crowds, his advance people used sound trucks to announce the day and time of his arrival. The unique entertainment of an Earl Long stump appearance offered people a refreshing break from their everyday burdens. The candidate and members of his state ticket would sit on the platform while local politicos made their appeals. After a series of brief speeches from the others, Earl would step up to the microphone and let loose one of his celebrated harangues. He never read from prepared addresses, and his diatribes followed no logical pattern. His colorful speeches were unique blends of humor, pathos, sarcasm, invective, and sermonizing. From a low-keyed discussion of state finances, he would suddenly switch to a graphic denunciation of an opponent. Often speaking for well over an hour, he had an instinctive ability to hold his audience's attention. With his gravelly voice and eye-catching mannerisms, he interspersed pie-in-the-sky promises with tales and anecdotes so hilarious that the crowd would overlook his neglect of the tax increases neccessary to pay for the promises. The master campaigner made diatribe and ridicule into art forms of the highest order. To illustrate his affinity with the poor, he often told the story of the rich old miser who died and tried to get into Heaven. At the pearly gates, St. Peter's clerk thumbed through hundreds of pages of records of his cheating, lying, and stealing from the poor. The miserable wretch replied that he had given a nickel each to a blind man, to a widow, and to the Red Cross, so the clerk took his appeal to St. Peter. "You know what St. Peter said?" Earl would ask the audience. After a long pause, he roared out the answer: "Give him back his fifteen cents and tell him to go to Hell!" Of all Earl's rhetorical tricks, the one that always delighted his audiences was his demolishing his opponents. Robert Kennon fell victim to three of Earl's best barbs: "The Army tested Kennon's blood and found it contained 65 percent champagne and 35 percent talcum powder." Mocking Kennon's prominent ears, Earl quipped that "they tested his ears, and the doctor said, 'Judge, your ears are perfect. You can hear an election coming two years off.'" "Judge Kennon's got the best ears around. He can stand in a court house in Ville Platte and hear a dollar bill drop in Opelousas."[19]

To counteract Earl's whirlwind campaign, Sam Jones tried to repeat his 1940 theme of honesty versus corruption. Calling the election a contest between "proud progress and depravity," and branding Earl Long another Richard Leche, Jones constantly reminded voters of the righteousness of his cause and of the evils of Longism. This time, the tactics did not work. Not only had Louisiana voters experienced eight years of reform government that had clearly failed to produce the promised political utopia, many of Jones's most prominent supporters engaged in political maneuverings that blurred the distinction between morality and venality. One of Jones's most avid political supporters, deLesseps Morrison, for example, secretly resorted to the same kind of wheeling and dealing that Jones so loudly condemned Earl Long for using. Unlike most Louisiana politicians, Morrison recorded many of his political deals, and his correspondence contains a gold mine of information about the internal political operations of the Jones forces. Several letters between Morrison and Jones illustrate the employment of Longite tactics to win the election, making the Jones campaign theme of "good government" ring hollow. In one letter, Morrison said that he had secured the support of Old Regulars Edward Haggerty, Charles Degan, and Henry deFraites in return for lucrative state jobs. In another letter, Morrison won a promise from Jones to increase state patronage in New Orleans and to allow the mayor to raise the city sales tax by 1 percent. Morrison also used his considerable influence with the national press to get local newspapers to endorse Jones. The mayor persuaded his friend Henry Luce to appoint Ashton Phelps, a member of the *Times-Picayune* board of directors, to the prestigious Time-Life International Forum Steering Committee, and he had Luce personally call the editors and publishers of newspapers all over Louisiana to endorse Jones. Morrison also talked his friends Elmer Irey and William Slocum, two of the crack investigators who had probed Long machine finances, into releasing an article in *Coronet* magazine two weeks before the first primary. In the article, Irey and Slocum accused Earl Long of receiving $46,000 in deduct money during his 1939–40 term as governor, and they suggested that Long had not paid his proper share of income taxes. In a letter to Morrison, Irey stated that *Coronet* had agreed to publish the story ahead of schedule because of its potential impact on the Louisiana election.[20]

Jones and Morrison also tried to brand Earl Long a tool of organized crime in Louisiana. Morrison alleged that the "gambling czars in Jefferson Parish supported Long and were his principal sources of funding." Jones claimed that Frank Costello was actively backing Long. Earl had little difficulty refuting the allegations. Remarking that "people who throw stones shouldn't live in glass houses," he pointed out that Monk Zelden, one of Costello's attorneys, was backing Jones. As we now know, the charges about the links between Earl Long and organized crime were indeed accurate. Several documents from the FBI files on Earl Long confirm the close relationship between Long and the Costello organization. One states that Costello contributed $500,000 to the Long campaign, and that "after Long is elected Governor, the syndicate (controlled by Costello) will have complete freedom to operate throughout the State of Louisiana to operate gambling activities." Another document states that the Long people in New Orleans promised cab drivers "a whore and a slot machine apiece" if they backed Long. Another lengthy document charged that Clem Sehrt, Earl's leading political associate in the New Orleans area, "collected very substantial sums of money from gambling syndicates in Jefferson Parish to support the gubernatorial campaign of Earl K. Long." Yet another FBI document, labeled "Political Tie-Ups With Organized Crime," alleged that Long "got all gamblers, pimps and prostitutes to vote for him" and to campaign for him. Despite the accuracy of the charges against him, Earl Long did not experience public opposition in the campaign.[21]

Another of the charges that Jones hurled against Long was that Long had engaged in old-fashioned wheeling and dealing to get elected. Certainly the charge was true, but Earl had never posed as a reformer, as had Jones. In behind-the-scenes politicking, Long proved a master at lining up numerous politicians. In mid-1947, he approached his erstwhile enemy Dudley LeBlanc to run for lieutenant governor on his ticket, but LeBlanc refused. Several weeks later, Earl returned with a promise to have LeBlanc's $50 monthly old-age pension program enacted and to have LeBlanc chosen president pro tem of the senate if LeBlanc would actively campaign for him. LeBlanc accepted—on condition that Earl give him $15,000 in campaign expenses. "I knew the s.o.b. had some money buried, you unnerstan'," LeBlanc said, "and I wasn't going to use *my* money to get *him* elected." Earl agreed, but instead of giving LeBlanc the lump sum, he gave him $5,000 every two months, to ensure that the Cajun politico was fulfilling his part of the agreement.[22]

Other politicians Earl recruited included Jimmie Noe, who had broken with Sam Jones over patronage disputes. A fervent Jones man in the 1940 second primary, Noe suddenly became a loyal Longite in 1948, yet another illustration of volatile political factionalism in Louisiana. Leander Perez also threw his support to Earl, supposedly in return for Earl's naming Perez's friend, Raymond Hufft, adjutant general of the National Guard. Earl joked that he gained Perez's backing when he promised to have the oleander named the state flower. Congressman F. Edward Hebert became a surprising convert to the Long camp. Until 1947, Hebert had been a leading anti-Longite, and he shocked many people when he endorsed Earl Long in the race. In his reminiscences, Hebert wrote: "Of all the people in the world for me to support, Earl Long. But being in the system, and being of the political system, I made the sign of the cross, said an act of contrition, and asked God to understand my

weakness and my necessity." Hebert did not mention that Earl threatened to run a strong candidate against him in the 1948 congressional elections, and since Hebert knew that Earl stood a good chance of winning
the governor's race, he decided to back him.[23]

Earl Long spent lavish amounts of money from a campaign chest that
was filled with funds from politicians, oil and gas interests, and organized
crime. As the campaign progressed, the public began to turn toward
Long, and numerous politicians lined up to join the Long bandwagon.
"Earl made them pay through the nose for the privilege of getting his
support," said William H. "Little Eva" Talbot. A giant of a man, Talbot
himself had switched sides, managing Jimmie Davis' gubernatorial campaign in 1944 and Earl Long's in 1948. Talbot elaborated: "Anybody who
wanted to run on Earl's ticket had to pay. It cost $2,000 to run for clerk
of court; $20,000 for assessor; and $25,000 for sheriff or legislator. Earl
would send me out to collect the cash, and as soon as I delivered it to
him, he added another name to the ticket. By the time of the second primary, Earl had so much money, he didn't know what to do with it. If he
liked a politician, he wouldn't charge him anything, but if he knew he
was holding out on him, he would charge him double." In the early summer of 1947, Earl called L. B. Baynard, the incumbent state treasurer, and
told him that it would cost $5,000 to run on his ticket. Baynard raised the
money and took it to Earl's home on Napoleon Avenue in New Orleans.
Earl was in the bathroom and told Baynard to put it in his back pocket,
and Baynard followed the instructions and left. "Hell, I didn't need that
five thousand dollars," Earl laughed. "But I knew old Baynard was tight,
and I wanted to make him squirm."[24]

Earl used most of the campaign money to get out the vote. He hired
Justin Wilson, the Cajun humorist, to travel around the state imitating
Sam Jones and promising to raise taxes. Long's people used funds to pay
for transportation to the polls on election day and to pay people to vote
for him. On the days of the first and second primaries, Long commissioners appeared at every precinct in the state, handing out Earl Long
tickets marked with the correct numbers of his candidates so the voters
could simply pull the levers in the voting machines or mark the ballots.
In many precincts, $5 would be paper clipped to the ballot. Earl kept
careful track of the money. Bill Dodd, his running mate in 1948, recalled
how Earl would give a politician nineteen $100 bills and say, "Here's
$2,000 to get out the vote." If the man asked for the extra $100, Earl gave

it to him without hesitation. Dodd asked Earl why he adopted this odd method, and Earl's reply provides an insight into his mastery of Louisiana politics: "If he don't ask for it, I know he's planning to pocket most of the money anyway, and that's the last money of mine he'll ever see. If he does ask for it, I figure he's got it budgeted pretty good."[25]

Held on January 20, 1948, the first primary showed Long with 267,253 votes, or 41.5 percent; Jones with 147,329, or 22.9 percent; Kennon with 129,569, or 19.8 percent; and Morrison with 101,754, or 15.8 percent. On the surface, these 1948 first-primary results appeared to be a close reflection of the 1940 first primary, when Long had 40.9 percent of the vote; Jones, 28.0 percent; Noe, 21.1 percent; and Morrison, 8.8 percent, with Jones scoring a narrow win in the second primary. In reality, 1948 proved entirely different. Robert Kennon's surprisingly strong showing suggested that the anti-Long reformist voters no longer held Jones in the same esteem they had in 1940. Fully aware of the implications of the first primary, Jones made desperate attempts to smear Long. First, he alleged that "between 75,000 and 100,000 votes tabulated that weren't cast" gave Long an artificially high total, an allegation that had no basis in fact. Then Jones accused Long of receiving illegal income, and he released his income tax returns for the period from 1936 through 1947 and challenged Long to do the same. Jones's returns showed that in the twelve-year period, he received a total of $178,000, with his highest income coming after he left the governor's office and earned an average of $23,000 a year from 1944 to 1947. Earl Long took up Jones's challenge. His income tax returns for the same period showed that Long made a total of $90,000, and that his income between 1940 and 1947, after he left the governor's office, averaged only $5,700 a year.[26]

On February 24, 1948, Earl Long scored an impressive victory in the second primary, capturing 432,528 votes, or 65.9 percent, to Sam Jones's 223,971, or 34.1 percent. Earl carried sixty-two of Louisiana's sixty-four parishes, and he even swept New Orleans, 94,316 to 56,146. His coattails proved so lengthy that the entire Long statewide ticket easily won election, as did 75 percent of all Long-endorsed candidates for the legislature and for local office. Earl Long, in the 1948 landslide, had a doubly sweet victory. He gained his revenge on Sam Jones, and the people of Louisiana had given him a popular mandate that exceeded even those the great Huey generated.[27]

7

"Back in the Saddle Again"

Writing for the Atlanta *Journal*, the noted newspaper editor Hodding Carter, Jr., expressed his opinion of Earl Long's victory in 1948: "And now with Governor Earl Long, Louisiana returns to 'normalcy.' Louisiana is a Caribbean republic again." *Time* magazine also commented on Earl's return to power: in the governor-elect's words, "the Longs are back in the saddle again." Indeed, Earl Long was riding high. Euphoric over his triumph, he set up a "temporary state capitol" in the Heidelberg Hotel in Baton Rouge and received an endless stream of lobbyists and politicians seeking favors. Constantly reminding people that his brother had never won an election as smashingly as he had, Earl prepared for his inauguration so he could enact his program. Perhaps nothing symbolized the mood of the incoming governor more than his decree to reilluminate the floodlights shining on Huey's grave across from the capitol. Extinguished by Governor Sam Jones as symbolic of the demise of Longism, the relighting signaled a revival of the hectic political atmosphere of the 1930s. Earl Long's inauguration on May 11, 1948, also indicated what was to come as well as celebrating the pinnacle of Earl's career. Instead of the usual formal ceremonies at the capitol, Earl's inauguration was held at the LSU football stadium. A gala affair attended by tens of thousands, it featured parades, song and dance, food and drink. The huge throng was treated to one hundred gallons of buttermilk, ten thousand cases of soft drinks, twenty thousand pounds of hot dogs, and, for those who knew where to look, numerous kegs of beer. Entertainment included country music, clowns, cowboys, a baseball game, and, after the swearing-in, an open house at the Governor's Mansion. All in all, everyone had a thoroughly enjoyable time.[1]

When the state legislature convened in May, Governor Earl K. Long used his considerable talents to push his entire program through to enactment. With the exception of a handful of hardcore anti-Longs, the senators and representatives passed everything Earl asked by thunderous majorities, with little debate or discussion. A couple of years later, the New Orleans *Item* would term the legislature "a bunch of trained seals," so amenable it proved to gubernatorial pressure. The analogy was accurate, for Earl Long exercised a degree of control over the legislature unmatched in recent Louisiana history. Even Huey had been unable to dominate the legislature during the notorious seven special sessions of 1934 and 1935. Earl's crushing win over Sam Jones had given him a genuine popular mandate, and his expertise at political manipulation resulted in his practically complete domination of state government. Every one of Long's most important bills for raising revenue and for spending money passed both houses by more than 90 percent, and his bills on health, education, and welfare had a total vote of 1,620 for and 8 against.[2]

In his campaign, Earl Long had promised to enact a $50 monthly old-age pension, and he gave top priority to it in the legislature. With a swiftness noticeably lacking in today's cumbersome bureaucracy, the governor got the $50 pension bill enacted into law and the first checks in the mail less than three months after he took office. In a bill-signing ceremony at the state capitol, Long graciously paid tribute to Senator Dudley LeBlanc as the "father of the old age pension," correctly crediting LeBlanc with originally sponsoring the idea. It was a rare occasion when two such headstrong men as Earl Long and Dudley LeBlanc could join together, and, not surprisingly, the two soon parted company. After the enactment of the pension, LeBlanc sent out tens of thousands of postcards to elderly Louisianians, one side advertising himself as the father of the old-age pension and the other promoting his Hadacol product. When he saw one of the cards, Earl was furious. "What the hell does that son of a bitch think he's doing?" he bellowed. "That bastard may have thought of the pension, but *I* got 'em passed!" Not only did Earl object to LeBlanc's trying to cash in on his program, he also thought that LeBlanc was trying to deceive people with the supposedly medicinal virtues of Hadacol. "Ain't nothing but a cheap way to get drunk," Earl said of the heavily advertised product, which indeed contained a few vitamins in a cherry-flavored liquid with a 12 percent alcohol content. To punish LeBlanc, Earl cut him off from all patronage, openly backed LeBlanc's bitter enemy, Wade O. Martin, Sr., for the Public Service Commission, and when the legislature met in 1950, he had LeBlanc removed as president pro tem of the senate.[3]

Next to the old-age pension, education was at the top of Earl's list. A fourfold increase in funding for school lunches financed a free hot lunch for all schoolchildren in Louisiana. Teachers at every level received hefty pay raises, and for the first time in history, the pay scale for white and black teachers was equalized. When Earl took office in 1948, white teachers earned average salaries of $2,512, and black teachers $1,547. By the time he left office in 1952, white teachers' salaries averaged $3,509, and black teachers' salaries averaged $2,837. Hundreds of new school buildings were constructed, and five new trade schools were established. State colleges and universities also received very large increases in appropriations. The 1948 legislative session was also significant for its work in other areas. Veterans received $5,000 homestead tax exemptions and a $1,000 bonus for serving in World War II. To provide assistance for the poor, Earl sharply increased state spending for aid to families with dependent children, disability assistance, aid to the needy blind, "welfare prescriptions," and "other assistance." Farmers came in for their share of state help, and organized labor was rewarded for its strong support of Earl in the election with the defeat of a proposed right-to-work bill and the repeal of the Goff Act of 1946, which prohibited unions from engaging in coercive tactics during strikes.[4]

To pay for these programs, the legislature passed the full complement of Earl Long's tax increases. The state sales tax was doubled and its coverage broadened. The beer tax was quintupled, and the gasoline tax raised by two cents a gallon. The tax on cigarettes rose by three cents a pack and that on liquor by five cents a fifth. The severance tax on crude oil was tripled, and the severance tax on all other natural resources except sulfur was doubled. Long was so eager to seek new sources of revenue that he had the legislature tax slot machines, even though the one-armed bandits were illegal in Louisiana. All in all, Earl Long and the legislature increased the total tax burden on Louisianians by 50 percent. In 1947, the per capita tax in Louisiana was $55.94, compared with the national average of $47.22. In 1949, the state per capita tax mushroomed to $86.10, compared with the national average of $50.81, giving Louisiana the dubious distinction of having the highest per capita tax in the nation.[5]

Little opposition to the new taxes developed. The general economic

prosperity made it possible for most people to pay the taxes without serious financial hardship. During Long's administration, Louisiana experienced an economic boom, as the enormous increase in national energy
consumption during the late 1940s and early 1950s precipitated a rapid
expansion in the state's oil and gas industry and the beginning of the
petrochemical industrial development that would continue into the
1970s. Even though many of the new taxes, such as that on sales, had a
direct impact on the ordinary citizen, most state taxes, such as severance
taxes, fell on industry. During the boom years, Louisiana came increasingly to rely on the energy industry as the major source of state revenues,
thus allowing political leaders to avoid imposing such unpopular taxes
as those on property. In election campaigns, Earl Long often boasted
that the people of Louisiana paid the lowest taxes in the nation and received the greatest benefits from state government. In reality, his policies,
adopted by his successors in the governor's office, fostered the commonly
held misapprehension that the many benefits the state bestowed "free" on
its citizens came at little or no cost to the taxpayers. During Long's administrations, the state experienced no problems because of the steadily
increasing revenues from severance taxes, but the fiscal and economic
policies he promoted would one day create the most serious economic
crisis in the state's history.[6]

Had Earl Long remained content with the enactment of his tax measures and his vast expansion of state social programs in 1948, he would
have retained his great popularity. But he mistakenly interpreted his victory as a mandate to revive spoils politics, and he proceeded to implement a series of measures that brought to the surface the most repugnant
aspects of Longism. Civil service, despite his campaign pledge, became
the first victim of Long's unbridled ambition. Since patronage was one of
the main rewards of political loyalty, he saw no reason to keep all the Sam
Jones and Jimmie Davis people in state government. In the regular legislative session, Earl pushed through to passage the Madden bill, which
stipulated that the governor appoint the members of the Civil Service
Commission, the body that had final authority over appeals from classified employees who had been dismissed. The Madden bill also provided
for the firing of all the Jones people who were under civil service but had
not taken competitive examinations. Although the Madden bill effectively
crippled state civil service, many of Earl's political backers complained that
it did not go far enough, so he called a special session of the legislature in
September, 1948, and state civil service was abolished altogether.[7]

In an address to the legislature in 1950, Governor Earl Long proclaimed that "there has been no wholesale firing of state employees during my administration." In fact, Long systematically purged the state employment rolls, getting rid of anti-Longs and replacing them with Long people, and he added an estimated four thousand persons to the state payroll. Within a year of Long's taking office, spoils politics infested state and local government as it had during the heyday of the Kingfish. In the New Orleans office of the state Board of Health, Long fired over two hundred political allies of Mayor Morrison for "political halitosis" and "incompatibility with the public." On the Orleans Levee Board, two dozen CCDA men lost their jobs to Old Regulars, and seventy-eight Long supporters were added to the board's payroll. When asked his criteria for hiring and firing, the secretary of the Levee Board bluntly answered, "It's simple. The ward leaders write me a little note saying, 'I want so-and-so fired and so-and-so to take his place.'" The president of the Levee Board proved even franker: "Some of the boys just voted the wrong way." Earl appointed his brother, Dr. George Long, a dentist, superintendent of the state training school at Pineville. Dr. Long acknowledged that by January, 1949, none of the school's employees who had supported Jones in the election still held their jobs. "I fired every one of them," Long declared.[8]

In addition to purging many of his opponents from the state payroll and adding thousands of his allies, Earl took other steps to augment his control over state government. In the interests of "efficiency," he had the legislature abolish the Department of Institutions, decentralize the Highway and Hospitals departments, and create the Division of Administration. These acts gave the governor considerably more power over the hiring and firing of state employees and much more direct control over the state budget. He also had the legislature pass several constitutional amendments that, if approved by the voters, would mean his absolute domination of the LSU Board of Supervisors and over the patronage-laden Orleans Dock Board. Another proposed amendment gave the Long-controlled Board of Liquidation of the State Debt increased authority to borrow money on the state's credit. These "power grab" actions, as Long's opponents labeled them, revived popular memories of the excesses of Longism and began to lose for Earl some of the public support with which he began his administration.[9]

In interviews, many of Earl Long's political allies vigorously defended his spoils politics of 1948. One politician asked, "Why shouldn't Earl put his own people in state jobs? They were the ones who backed him in the election. Sam Jones put his people in, and he was called an honest governor, but when Earl did the same thing, they called him a dictator." This argument does have a considerable degree of validity. It is a cardinal rule of politics that officeholders reward their followers with patronage, a rule obeyed even by presidents of the United States. Because of the lack of accurate records, it is not possible to present a comprehensive record of the extent to which Earl Long engaged in spoils politics during his 1948–52 administration, but a careful review of the records that are available substantiates the claim of Long's supporters that Sam Jones and Jimmie Davis did essentially the same as did Earl Long. During the period from 1940 to 1948, when Jones and Davis held office, state employment increased by 5,100, and the state payroll rose by 4,200 during Long's 1948–52 term. Considering that the state budget more than doubled under Long, the total number of state employees he hired is not out of line with the number hired under his predecessors. What did distinguish Long from his opponents was the manner in which he operated, for Earl never made any pretense of supporting the principles and practices of good government.[10]

In the giddy atmosphere of the spring and early summer of 1948, Earl tried to imitate Huey by regally receiving visitors in his suites at the Heidelberg and Roosevelt hotels. One legislator who visited Earl at the Heidelberg recalled that during their hour-long talk, he heard several "thumps," and each time he looked for the origin of the strange noise, he saw a roll of cash lying on the floor of the suite. Unable to suppress his curiosity, he asked Earl about the incidents. Earl nonchalantly replied, "That's transom money." "Transom money?" the legislator asked. "Yeah, those fellows who want favors throw the money through the transom." Earl went on to explain that he never accepted direct contributions, but if a lobbyist or a politician wanted to make a donation by throwing money through the transom, there was nothing illegal about it. In reality, Long, of course, frequently did receive direct "contributions" in his hands, or in other ways. One close associate vividly remembers the governor of Louisiana, stripped down to his "union suit," lying on a couch in one of Seymour Weiss's suites in the Roosevelt. For several hours, politicians, gamblers, pimps, and lobbyists entered the room and dropped wads of twenties, fifties, and hundreds on Long until he was covered with the cash. No one said a word until Earl finally remarked, "I'll bet that's the most expensive suit of clothes you ever saw."[11]

The 1948 regular session of the state legislature provided numerous examples of the political techniques that made Earl Long such a legendary figure. With an uncanny knack for knowing precisely the right chords to strike, Long had a master's touch in dealing with politicians. Some legislators, he knew, could be bought, and for those, he doled out lavish sums of cash. One of the often repeated Earl Long stories concerned a reporter's asking Earl if he bought legislators the way Huey did. Earl replied, "No, I rent 'em. It's cheaper that way." Earl had little respect for those who sold their votes for money, and the finest compliment he gave a legislator was "He never asked me for a dime." In another instance, Earl asked a senator if he would like to have his wife employed as a legislative clerk or in some other state job, but the senator declined. A surprised look came over Earl's face, and he told the senator that many legislators had wives, children, and other relatives on the state payroll. The senator replied that he just did not operate that way, and for the rest of the session, Earl did not pressure him or attempt to influence his voting. Earl Long summed up the secret of his legislative successes: "Don't write anything you can phone. Don't phone anything you can talk face to face. Don't talk anything you can smile. Don't smile anything you can wink. Don't wink anything you can nod." Almost daily, Governor Long could be found on the house or senate floor, or in a committee hearing chatting, smiling, winking, and nodding. On the opening day of the session, Long actually sat at Senator Willie Rainach's desk applauding as each of his appointees received unanimous senate confirmation. Keeping careful track of the status of legislation, he waited until he made certain of a bill's passage before he allowed it to come up for a roll call vote. Once, a light on the toteboard unexpectedly changed from "yea" to "nay," and a reporter told the governor, "Looks like you lost a vote there." Earl casually replied, "Saves money," and continued strolling down the aisle. In her study of the 1948 session, Lois Nichols observed that Long served "as a one man whip to maintain the organization and discipline necessary to the passage of his bills, a function which otherwise might have been performed by the discipline of a political party."[12]

One of Earl Long's talents was his ability to select young politicians and groom them for careers. In the house in 1948, he chose a young representative from Columbia, John McKeithen, as one of his key floor leaders because he knew instinctively that McKeithen had an innate talent for politicking. (McKeithen would become a two-time governor.) In the senate, he spotted the natural abilities of a first-time senator from Bogalusa,

B. B. "Sixty" Rayburn. Before the session opened, Rayburn met with Earl to ask for favors for his Washington Parish constituents. Appreciating Rayburn's potential as a political ally, Earl did not apply any pressure and simply told Rayburn that he would see what he could do. Rayburn loyally supported Long in the session, and in return, Washington Parish got ninety-eight miles of paved roads, a new charity hospital, and a vo-tech school. For the rest of Earl's life, Sixty Rayburn would remain a close personal friend and a staunch political supporter. Even though he was continually looking for talented newcomers like McKeithen and Rayburn, Earl never allowed anyone to challenge his undisputed role as head of the Long machine. "Earl doesn't believe in grooming successors," Senator Charles Deichman of New Orleans observed. "He always busts up his organization and rebuilds after an election. That way, everybody stays dependent on him, and nobody gets big ideas." As Stan Opotowsky remarked, "The Longs believe in the plantation system of government," with themselves as the planters, and the local leaders the overseers.[13]

No one could devise more ingenious ways of manipulating legislation to maximum political advantage. Earl had the legislature pass a bill creating an Alcoholic Beverage Control (ABC) Board. All other southern states had ABC boards, and in the heavily fundamentalist South, with "dry" counties scattered throughout the region, the boards served as important sources of graft through their legal authority to grant liquor licenses and set liquor prices. But with its large Roman Catholic population and a historical tradition of toleration for drinking, Louisiana had never had an ABC board, and the liquor industry was stunned to see Earl's bill sail through the legislature. The Louisiana ABC Board had the power to set the minimum price on wine, beer, whiskey, and "other intoxicating beverages." With the highest per capita consumption of alcohol in the nation, Louisiana had always had very low liquor prices because of the demand. The Third District assessor in New Orleans and a kingpin of the Old Regulars, Jimmie Comiskey, himself a liquor wholesaler and distributor, commented on the political repercussions of the ABC bill: "The liquor boys got their money and went to the ABC Board, but they told them to go to the governor—everybody went straight to Earl. Earl told me he got the liquor boys to put up a whole season's bets for him at the Fair Grounds. I don't know how much it cost, but I've seen Earl bet $2,000 on a single race." Not coincidentally, the ABC Board took absolutely no action during its brief, four-year existence.[14]

In many other ways, Earl cashed in on the legislative session. Local governments found themselves obligated to him because of a bill appropriating $30,000 in unrestricted funds to every parish in the state, plus an additional $10,000 for the purchase of gravel. "You should have seen the line outside the governor's mansion," one local leader said. "I'll bet every police juror in the state was there, and you should have seen all the politicians who suddenly owned interests in gravel companies. Thirty thousand dollars was a lot of money in 1948, and that money allowed the parishes to get things done without having to raise local taxes on their people. Earl let the local boys rake off a little for graft, but he never let them take too much. When he found a politician getting too greedy, he always cut him off." Yet another measure Earl proposed would have repealed the Louisiana fair trade law. Enacted in 1938, the law prohibited retailers from selling certain merchandise below artificially determined minimum prices. In reality, the so-called fair trade policy incorporated a legal method of price-fixing, costing Louisiana consumers millions of dollars each year. According to Comiskey, it cost the retailers' lobby about $150,000 to get the repeal bill killed in committee.[15]

On October 15, 1948, the New Orleans Field Office of the FBI submitted a "Crime Survey" report to bureau headquarters in Washington. The report flatly stated that "Carlos Marcello had the keys to the front door at Angola since Earl K. Long came to power." Filed twice a year, the FBI "Crime Survey" reports contain detailed documentary evidence of the intimate connection between Earl Long and organized crime in Louisiana. Since the mid-1930s, Long had developed a close relationship with Frank Costello, Dandy Phil Kaistel, and their leader in Louisiana, Carlos Marcello. Long's acceptance of substantial contributions from organized crime for his 1947–48 campaign showed his willingness to have the syndicate's criminal empire in the state. From the time Long took the oath of office in May, 1948, Louisiana witnessed an explosion in wide-open gambling, prostitution, and narcotics trafficking. In Jefferson and St. Bernard parishes, the Old and New Southport clubs, the Beverly Club, the Arabi and Jai Alai clubs, and other establishments increased their operations with the connivance of local law enforcement authorities. When Senator Estes Kefauver's famous committee conducted public hearings in New Orleans and Washington, it reported that under Governor Long, the syndicate functioned openly and illegally with the full cooperation of state and local officials. In testifying before the committee, Jefferson Parish Sheriff Frank "King" Clancy freely admitted allowing the casinos and other gambling establishments to remain open because they provided jobs for parish residents.[16]

According to the FBI, Earl Long received direct payoffs from organized crime. One bureau report stated that "Governor Earl K. Long was the recipient of large-scale graft in Jefferson Parish" from the gambling syndicate, which made annual profits of $18 million. In New Orleans, the bureau reported that the Vieux Carré Gang, a front for the Jefferson syndicate, organized a protection racket in the French Quarter after Long took office because of Long's "close ties" with gamblers and prostitutes. Another FBI investigation revealed that the operators of the Jefferson casinos "take their money directly to Governor Long, and there is no middle man as far as the pay-off is concerned," and the payoffs came in monthly meetings between Long and the casino bosses. In other parts of the state, similar examples of Long's acceptance of graft from syndicate gamblers abounded. In Lake Charles, for example, each gambling house made weekly payments of $50 to $100, with the money divided "among various politicians, including Governor Earl K. Long." In Alexandria, the FBI discovered that a "satchel man" carried graft money to Baton Rouge to make the payoff "directly to Governor Long." In West Baton Rouge Parish, the Club Regent on Highway 190 went so far as to carry out "white slave activities," which Long permitted because the club operators made cash payments to him. Throughout the southern half of the state, slot machines, pinball machines, horse racing handbooks, and whorehouses were rampant since Long had become governor and had such "close ties" to Frank Costello and Carlos Marcello.[17]

From the evidence available, it appears that Earl Long's close association with organized crime figures came from his friendship with Seymour Weiss. Long made frequent trips to New Orleans, where he stayed at the Roosevelt Hotel suite Weiss always held ready for him. Not coincidentally, Costello and Kaistel had suites on the same floor, and Long was often seen in their company. Weiss had a large interest in the Fair Grounds racetrack in New Orleans, which the FBI and other sources connected with organized crime. Weiss also owned the 1-2-3 Club on Baronne Street, which for years dominated the racing handbook and wire service operations in the city. Interestingly, Weiss himself never came under federal investigation because he was a personal friend of Hoover's and may well have been the informant who gave the FBI such strong leads for its exhaustive survey of criminal activities and political corruption during Long's administrations.[18]

The revival of unrestrained spoils politics and the graft and corruption that permeated his administration undermined much of Earl Long's popular support, and his destruction of the municipal independence of the city of New Orleans generated a public rebellion against him. The day after his victory over Sam Jones, Long told a reporter from the New Orleans *Item* that he had no plans for New Orleans and that he had no intention of enacting punitive legislation against the city administration of Mayor Morrison. The next day, he pledged to help everyone in New Orleans, including Morrison, "even though I sure don't love him." In fact, Earl Long had already determined to destroy Morrison politically through a series of maneuvers that would return control of the city to the Old Regulars. There were both political and personal motivations for Long's scheme. The feud between Earl Long and Chep Morrison dated back to the mid-1930s, when Morrison led the anti-Long forces in opposition to Richard Leche. In 1940, Morrison became one of Sam Jones's most active supporters against Long, raising large sums of money for Jones and gathering votes for him, and in the 1940 legislature, he led the fight to have Jones's reform legislation passed. When Morrison defeated Bob Maestri for mayor in 1946, he turned New Orleans into an anti-Long stronghold, seriously weakening the Old Regulars. The New Orleans mayor also represented the "better elements" of society, and his carefully cultivated image of sophistication and respectability contrasted sharply with Long's "country boy" image. Both the local and national press portrayed Morrison with nothing short of adulation, and they depicted Long in the worst possible light. One of Earl's most famous remarks illustrates the differences between the two: "He wears $400 suits. Put one of them $400 suits on Uncle Earl, and it'd look like socks on a rooster." [19]

The day after the second primary, Morrison sent Long a telegram: "I am hopeful that our respective programs may be carried forward for the greater good of Louisiana and New Orleans, and that whenever state and municipal authorities overlap, past political differences may be set aside." Privately, Morrison knew that Long planned punitive action against him. When the legislature convened, what two writers called the "rape of New Orleans" took place: Governor Long's bills and constitutional amendments ridiculed the principles of good government, drastically changed the city's governmental structure, turned the port of New Orleans into a model of spoils politics, and destroyed the political and fiscal authority of the office of the mayor. The anti–New Orleans legislation of 1948 brought out the worst qualities in Earl Long: personal vindictiveness, a disdain for the principles of constitutional democracy, roughhouse politics, and driving ambition to become a second Kingfish. In his desire to destroy Chep Morrison politically, Earl let personal vindictiveness get the better of him. He refused to listen to the counsel of both Russell Long and Bill Dodd, who advised him not to punish New Orleans.[20]

The port of New Orleans, a traditional haven for patronage, fell under gubernatorial attack. In 1940, the Jones administration had reorganized the Dock Board, the port's governing authority. From lists of nominees submitted by New Orleans trade organizations, the governor would appoint board members with staggered terms in office. For eight years, a nonpartisan board of international trade experts had managed the port so capably that New Orleans catapulted from seventh to second place among the nation's seaports. Earl Long had the legislature pass a constitutional amendment giving the governor total control over the port by allowing him to appoint an entirely new Dock Board, whose members did not need expertise in international trade. A legislative act also appropriated $50,000 for an "investigation" of the port by a commission headed by Old Regular Francis Williams. Empowered to recommend to the governor any changes in the port's status, the commission represented nothing more than a thinly disguised attempt by Long to dominate the port.[21]

The politicization of the Dock Board paled in comparison with Long's gross interference in the city government of New Orleans. Sponsored by Old Regulars Senator Frank P. Gipson and Representative William P. Haggerty, House Bill 608 changed the composition of the city government from a mayor and four commissioners, all elected citywide, to an eight-member council comprising the mayor and seven commissioners, with the mayor elected citywide and each commissioner chosen from one of the city's seven assessment districts. Those districts had been gerrymandered—four of the seven represented only 30 percent of the city's population—and the Old Regulars would have a clear majority on the new city commission. The bill went even further. The mayor could make appointments to city offices subject to ratification by a majority of the commission, and if he failed to secure the majority, one of the seven commissioners could propose an alternate appointment. In effect, this provision gave the Old Regulars total appointive authority. The bill also subdivided the city government into eight departments, each headed by a member of the commission. As mayor, Chep Morrison would head only the Department of Public Affairs, an innocuous agency that controlled legal, judicial, and civil service and public relations functions. Such vital city services as police, fire, streets, and public works came under the jurisdiction of the Old Regulars.[22]

Since that bill would take effect after the January, 1950, city elections, Earl pushed other measures to wreck Morrison's political power immediately. One bill revoked the commission's right to transfer a commissioner from one city department to another. In 1948, only one Old Regular, Theo Hotard, served on the commission, and Morrison had shifted him from the patronage-laden Department of Public Property to the Department of Safety. The "Hotard bill" blocked this maneuver, and it stipulated that all unskilled manual laborers hired by the city would not be classified under civil service. Since most of them worked for Hotard's department, the bill gave him greater appointive power than the mayor. A companion bill placed most city jobs under civil service, thus depriving Morrison of a large source of patronage. Yet another bill singled out Morrison by prohibiting mayors of Louisiana cities with populations over 300,000, *i.e.,* New Orleans, from succeeding themselves in office. A final "municipal reorganization" bill turned control of the city police and fire departments to a special eleven-member board dominated by the Old Regulars.[23]

Earl Long not only attacked Morrison's political authority, he also crippled the mayor's fiscal powers. Even though the large tax increases of 1948 doubled state revenues, Long took steps to ensure that Morrison would not receive additional income. The gasoline tax revenue, for example, was divided equally among the state's sixty-four parishes, giving New Orleans only $800,000, though its citizens paid more than $11 million in gasoline taxes. The increase in the tobacco tax was divided among municipalities at the rate of $2 per resident, but the maximum amount each city could receive was $650,000, thereby reducing New Orleans' fair share of the revenue by half. A special legislative session of September, 1948, prohibited all Louisiana cities with more than 300,000 residents from levying a city sales tax of more than 1 percent. Since the city sales tax in 1948 was 2 percent, this bill reduced city revenues by $4.5 million. With his revenues cut nearly in half by Long's actions, Mayor Morrison also found that the governor and the legislature had sharply increased his expenditures. Several bills forced the city government to grant substantial pay raises to many city employees and to make much greater contributions to their retirement funds. As a result of Long's punitive measures, the city of New Orleans faced financial ruin.[24]

In the September, 1948, special legislative session, Earl Long decided that the original bill "restructuring" the city government had not gone far enough, so he pushed through to passage House Bill 434. The bill established a five-member commission council, with the mayor controlling the legal, judicial, police, and recreational functions of city government. Other members had authority over public works, fire protection, assessments, "receipts, expenditures, and accounts of public money," welfare, and public property. Section J of the bill gave the Old Regular–dominated commission council the unrestricted authority to "take over, administer, possess and exercise all executive and legislative powers and duties heretofore had, possessed, and exercised by all other executive, legislative, and administrative offices of the city of New Orleans." In short, House Bill 434 reduced Chep Morrison to political nonexistence and restored to the Old Regulars complete control over the city.[25]

Chep Morrison did not submit meekly to this wholesale attack on his political power. In opposing Long's actions, he enlisted the support of the city's business and civic leaders, and one of his backers, Victor H. Schiro, the president of the Young Men's Business Club, organized a four-hundred-car motorcade to Baton Rouge to lobby against the bills. The New Orleans press unleashed a barrage of editorials praising Morrison and condemning Long. In one editorial, the *Item* went so far as to compare the thirty-six-year-old mayor to William Pitt becoming prime minister of Great Britain at the age of twenty-four, Alexander the Great conquering the world at twenty-two, and Patrick Henry uttering his famous oration at twenty-nine. Earl Long sloughed off the criticisms. When a delegation of New Orleanians tried to meet with him, he refused, saying that he only saw adults and that Morrison was "a boy in a man's job." In a typical gubernatorial harangue, Long had one of his legal assistants, Theo Cangelosi, respond to *Times-Picayune* director Esmond Phelps: "Your little boy blue pretty boy deLesseps (debutante's delight) Morrison says he wants political peace, plus a bigger piece of taxes to spend and entertain Mr. Luce of *Time* magazine at the city's expense so they will write articles telling the nation how great little Cheppie is and how terrible Governor Long is. Oh, give deLesseps more taxes to be a big shot, but don't give Governor Long anything to keep his promises to the people." Long himself lashed out at Morrison, calling him "Dellasoups" and characterizing him as "smoother than a peeled onion." Answering charges that cutting the city sales tax in half would force New Orleans into bankruptcy, Long said that he was merely helping Morrison keep his campaign promises (when he ran for mayor in 1946, Morrison had indeed promised not to increase taxes, but he proceeded to do so anyway).[26]

The national press gave Long's anti-Morrison actions considerable coverage. Ignoring the social legislation Long had enacted, newspapers and magazines portrayed him as a clown and buffoon, a political despot trying to destroy democracy in Louisiana. In 1948, for example, *Time* and *Newsweek* published articles entitled "The Winnfield Frog," "Just Like Huey," "Scandals of 1948," and "Happy Days." Chep Morrison's close friend Henry Luce ordered his staff to ignore journalistic ethics and attack Earl Long. In one story, *Time* crossed the line between legitimate editorial criticism and character assassination, describing Earl as "shifty-eyed" and declaring that "Earl has aped his brother with the beetle-browed assiduousness of a vaudeville baboon learning to roller skate." The article proceeded to portray Earl as "a soft dumpy man with a mushy voice, a flaccid handshake, a venomous temper, and the bearing of a small town pool hall operator." Writing for the *New York Times Magazine,* Cabell Phillips called Long "boisterous, uncouth, and truculent. He has a quick and undiscriminating temper and blasphemes his enemies with vast, genealogical oaths. He has profane contempt for all reporters." Actually, many local reporters liked and admired Earl Long and enjoyed a good working relationship with him. Probably the most perceptive journalistic student of Louisiana politics, Margaret "Maggie" Dixon of the *Morning Advocate,* said that the national press just did not understand Earl and that its stories reflected a northern prejudice against southern politicians, especially the Longs. Dixon contended that despite his periodic outbursts, Earl was a capable administrator who ran the state government quite efficiently. To illustrate Earl's methods, Dixon related the story of a reporter asking Huey about rumors of graft among members of the Highway Commission. "Sure," Huey responded, "but the people have their roads, don't they?" Dixon maintained that Earl operated in the same manner, politicking but doing positive things for the common people. "He was not just a southern demagogue, as Hodding Carter and Ralph McGill and other writers depicted him," Dixon said. "If you look at his campaign promises and then examine his record, you'll find that he kept more promises than any other governor."[27]

Nevertheless, Earl Long's deliberate attack on Mayor Morrison's administration can only be regarded as political reprisal of the most vicious sort. Understandably, Long wanted to reward his friends and punish his enemies, but his gross interference in the municipal affairs of New Orleans exceeded reasonable political behavior. It also provided yet another illustration of Long's sporadic failures to accept political reality. Long interpreted his landslide victory as a popular mandate to revert to the worst features of Longism, but the voters had not cast their ballots with that in mind. Rather, they wanted the social benefits of the Long program without the corruption and despotism so predominant in the 1930s. In a short period of time, Earl Long's power-grab tactics of 1948 would backfire on him and lose for him much popular good will.[28]

One strong indication of the precipitous decline in Governor Long's popularity came in August, 1948, when Russell Long, Huey's son, barely managed to defeat Robert Kennon in a special election for the United States Senate. In May, 1948, Senator John Overton died suddenly, and Earl appointed oil magnate William C. Feazel, one of his wealthy campaign contributors, to fill Overton's term. Long and Feazel reached an understanding that Russell would run as the Long candidate in the August 31 Democratic primary, and that as soon as he reached the age of thirty, the minimum age for U.S. senators, Feazel would resign and Russell Long would serve the remaining two years of Overton's term. Earl selected Russell for the Senate seat because his only experience in politics was as an "executive counsel" to his uncle, and a political novice could be counted on to comply with Earl's wishes.

Aware of the steep decline in Earl Long's popular support and encouraged by the weak candidacy of the inexperienced Russell Long, the anti-Longs decided to make an all-out effort to capture the Senate seat. The faction's leaders, Sam Jones, Chep Morrison, and Hale Boggs, agreed that Robert Kennon would be their best candidate. The Webster Parish judge had run a very strong race in the first gubernatorial primary, and he earned a statewide reputation as a champion of reform. With strong political and financial backing, Kennon promised to give Russell Long a real challenge for the Senate. That same campaign did demonstrate that in Louisiana, political reality has consistently triumphed over factional loyalty. In the August 31 primary, the incumbent U.S. senator, Allen

Ellender, was also running as a Long candidate. Throughout his career, Ellender had been one of the movers and shakers in the Long hierarchy, handpicked by the Kingfish himself and always a close friend and loyal supporter of Earl Long's. Ellender's opponent, Congressman James Domengeaux, was a leading anti-Long, one of Sam Jones's most ardent supporters in 1940 and in 1948. The highly popular Ellender, however, appeared certain to defeat Domengeaux, so most of the anti-Long kingpins, Jones, Morrison, and Boggs, remained conspicuously neutral in that race, thereby ensuring Ellender's victory.[29]

In the campaign, Earl Long took to the stump and emphasized Russell's commitment to his father's ideals. Earl also made his usual contacts with local leaders to roll up a big vote for Russell. Kennon waged a vigorous campaign in which he capitalized on the public's growing disenchantment with Earl. In the primary, Russell Long defeated Robert Kennon, 264,143 votes to 253,668, or a margin of 2 percent of the total. The election had by and large become a popular referendum on Earl Long's performance as governor, and the people had given their verdict. Just six months earlier, Earl had captured 65 percent of the state vote in the second gubernatorial primary, and now his candidate could barely manage to win. Russell Long's narrow margin of victory gave rise to allegations of vote fraud. One unconfirmed story, related by a close associate of Earl Long's, described the scene at Russell Long headquarters in the Roosevelt Hotel on election night. As the returns started coming in, Kennon jumped to an early lead because the large cities, where he won 60 percent of the vote, reported their totals sooner than the Long strongholds in the rural parishes. As the rural returns began to appear, Russell gradually chipped away at Kennon's lead, but after 90 percent of the state vote had been reported, Kennon still held a seemingly insurmountable 3,000-vote lead. Badly depressed, Russell told his uncle that he was ready to concede defeat, but an irate Earl shouted, "Stop crying, you weak-kneed son of a bitch. I told you we were holding up some of the returns from the boys in the country. We'll make up them 3,000 votes." Earl then got on the telephone to his rural leaders, and with the same efficiency as Mayor Richard Daley's machine brought in the late-reporting Cook County returns, the final 10 percent of the state vote went overwhelmingly for Russell Long to give him his victory.[30]

Obviously, no documentary evidence exists to substantiate or to refute the allegation that Earl Long stole the election for his nephew. Kennon did dispute what he called the "phony and baloney" totals from St. Bernard and Plaquemines parishes, which gave Russell 96 percent and 84 percent, respectively. Certainly, Judge Perez performed with his usual efficiency in garnering votes for his candidates, but no hard evidence exists to prove fraud. Ellender swept both parishes with 99 percent of the vote, and the anti-Longs did not dispute the returns. In other areas of the state, the voters followed the historical pattern of the Long candidate winning the rural areas, and the anti-Long the urban ones. However, in the Ellender-Domengeaux race, Ellender, the Long candidate, carried every parish in the state. If there was a pattern to the voting, it was that Earl Long had clearly lost much of his initial popular support.[31]

A curious paradox marked the first six months of Earl Long's first full term as governor of Louisiana. On the one hand, Long provided the people of Louisiana with a host of badly needed improvements in public education, health, welfare, and transportation. On the other hand, his fiscal policies set the pattern for the increasingly heavy reliance of state government on severance tax revenues rather than on more substantial and sound sources of recurring revenue. Long gave the most economically depressed categories of citizens—the poor, the aged, the sick— many benefits that they deserved and needed. At the same time, he resorted to a resurrection of the widespread graft and corruption that had made Louisiana politics notorious. He proved an effective, efficient, and competent administrator of state government, yet he allowed personal vindictiveness to overcome sound political judgment.

8

Dixiecrats and Democrats

The domestic political events of 1948 in Louisiana cannot be considered in a vacuum, for those events were heavily influenced by national issues. When President Harry S. Truman submitted legislation to Congress on civil rights, most of Louisiana's politicians joined a protest movement that culminated in the Dixiecrat revolt. Earl Long, however, remained steadfastly loyal to Truman and to the national Democratic party, and in so doing, he bucked the tide of public opinion and lost the political support of such former Long stalwarts as Leander Perez.

The origins of the Dixiecrat movement deserve careful exploration, for they helped shape the complicated racial and states' rights politics of the 1950s, which had such an impact on Long's career. By the time of the 1944 Democratic National Convention, several prominent southern politicians had organized a movement to oppose the renomination of President Franklin D. Roosevelt, and the Louisiana delegation, led by anti-Long forces, cast their ballots for Senator Harry Byrd of Virginia. Roosevelt, of course, easily won renomination and reelection, but to demonstrate their opposition to his policies, five of Louisiana's Democratic electors resigned rather than cast their ballots for the president. This "mini revolt" of 1944 was not significant in national politics, and most observers considered it a minor expression of anti–New Deal sentiment by a handful of hard-line southern conservatives. In reality, the rump rebellion of 1944 was a dress rehearsal for the Deep South revolution against the national Democratic party four years later.[1]

In Louisiana, Governor Sam Jones led the opposition to the New Deal, which he regarded as a program of federal economic exploitation of the South for the benefit of the North. In particular, Jones viewed federal regulatory policies on natural gas as devastating to Louisiana, for those policies placed strict price controls on gas piped outside the state while allowing much higher prices for gas consumed within it. In 1942, Jones persuaded the legislature to pass a resolution condemning the delivery of Louisiana gas to states that had a steady supply of coal. Jones also publicly attacked Interstate Commerce Commission freight policies that discriminated against southern states. Jones and other anti-Long leaders in Louisiana reflected a historical tradition of conservatism that had characterized much of southern politics since the early antebellum period. Strongly backed by the old Bourbon oligarchy that Huey Long had driven from power, Jones readily sympathized with a coalition of conservative southern Democrats led by Senator Harry Byrd of Virginia and by Senator Walter George of Georgia. The New Deal's enormous expansion of the federal government's authority posed a serious threat to the traditional southern insistence on local control of internal state matters, particularly the race issue, but also the economic situation.[2]

Although Sam Jones led the original Louisiana states' rights movement, Leander Perez became its driving force. While he would gain a national reputation as a leader of Deep South racists, Perez initially supported states' rights because of federal intervention in the energy industry. Originally an ardent supporter of the New Deal, Perez became alarmed when Roosevelt created federal agencies with regulatory control over crude oil, natural gas, and other natural resources. In 1944, Perez joined forces with his erstwhile enemy, Sam Jones, in supporting Harry Byrd at the Democratic convention. In 1946, President Truman publicly advocated federal ownership of the tidelands, a huge oil-rich expanse in the Gulf of Mexico and in innumerable small water outlets between the Louisiana coast and the edge of the outer continental shelf. Under federal law, Louisiana had jurisdiction over the three miles of oil land immediately off its coast, but Truman claimed that the oil derived from that land was a national resource and was therefore under federal control. Perez had more than an ideological commitment to states' rights, he had a heavy personal stake in the outcome of the dispute, since he personally owned vast tracts of the land and earned untold millions from it. When Earl Long became governor in 1948, he appointed Perez as an unpaid special assistant attorney general to prepare Louisiana's claim to the tidelands oil. Apparently, Louisiana did have a strong legal claim because in 1949 the federal government offered a compromise giving Louisiana oil royalties and bonuses within the three-mile offshore limit, plus 37.5 percent of the revenue from oil extracted beyond the limit. It was a generous offer and would have given the state billions of dollars over the next four decades, and Earl Long wanted to accept. Perez, however, insisted that Louisiana fight through the federal courts for 100 percent of all off-shore oil revenue. In agreeing to Perez's argument, Long made a bad mistake, for the tidelands dispute remained in litigation for over a dozen years, and the ultimate settlement was decidedly less favorable to Louisiana than the original 1949 proposal. Perez concerned himself not with promoting the state's best interests, but with keeping the feds out of Plaquemines Parish.[3]

While tidelands oil was not an issue to arouse the general public, the race question was, and on February 2, 1948, President Truman brought the latent states' rights movement into the open. On that date, he submitted to Congress a civil rights program calling for the enactment of an anti-lynching law, the establishment of a Fair Employment Practices Commission (FEPC), and the federal guarantee and enforcement of the right of all citizens to vote. By daring to call to public attention in a presidential election year the most volatile and emotional issue in the South, Truman provoked immediate complaints and denunciations by southern politicians. In Louisiana, Leander Perez responded with a typical racist diatribe, berating those Democrats who continued to back Truman as "political hydrats," mixtures of a socialist "or a Communist or a homo, of whom there have been thousands exposed in Washington lately, which can only produce an illegitimate offspring called a Bastocrat." In more subdued tones, Sam Jones, deLesseps Morrison, and other leading anti-Longs also condemned the president. Governor Earl Long remained silent.[4]

The issue dominated Democratic party politics in Louisiana. On March 6, the State Central Committee met to select delegates to the national convention, and Leander Perez demanded that the state party go on record as officially opposed to Truman's nomination, but Earl Long controlled the committee, and, seeing no useful purpose in such a move, he had Perez's proposal killed. Always loyal to the national party, Earl refused to knuckle under to the increasing pressure from Perez and others, and he had the committee select a delegation that represented all points of view, but that had a majority of loyal Democrats. Perez and his followers gained a handful of slots, but most delegate seats were given to such loyal Trumanites as Allen Ellender, Hale Boggs, George Long, and

Jimmie Comiskey. Earl Long liked Harry Truman and admired the spunky, no-nonsense way he conducted his office. In early May, a week before his inauguration as governor, Earl met with Truman in the White House and told him that Louisiana would faithfully support him at the convention and in the general election. But Long had badly miscalculated the depth and intensity of public opposition to Truman. At the Democratic convention, the Louisiana delegates did not join their colleagues from Mississippi and Alabama and "walk out," but they unanimously cast their votes for Senator Richard Russell of Georgia.[5]

After the Democratic convention, which nominated Truman, had ended, leading politicians from several Deep South states organized a convention of their own. On July 17, 1948, a group of states' rights Democrats, or "Dixiecrats," met in Birmingham, Alabama, and nominated their own ticket, with Governor J. Strom Thurmond of South Carolina for president and Governor Fielding L. Wright of Mississippi for vicepresident. The Dixiecrats made no secret of the reason for their bolting the national party. Their platform solemnly declared that the adoption of Truman's civil rights program would inevitably lead to "forced intermingling with Negroes," a phrase that would gain wide currency in the next decade. The Dixiecrats did not represent the entirety of southern sentiment, and Truman would defeat Thurmond in most southern states, but in Louisiana, the movement spread like wildfire, and Earl Long was caught in the conflagration. Publicly condemning the Dixiecrats as "disloyal" to the national party, Long refused to send delegates to the Birmingham convention and affirmed his support of the national party ticket, unpopular positions that the ever-increasing numbers of his political enemies were quick to exploit.[6]

The rapid growth of the Dixiecrat movement in Louisiana can be attributed to many factors, but race clearly was paramount. Another element was the anti-Longs' exploitation of the 1948 presidential election as a means of destroying Earl Long politically. After the Dixiecrat convention, a group of states' righters worked to have the Thurmond-Wright ticket placed on Louisiana's ballot as the official ticket of the Democratic party. A New Orleans businessman, John U. Barr, one of Sam Jones's leading campaign contributors, organized the Dixiecrat movement in the state. In 1946, Barr had led the drive to have a right-to-work bill passed, and later he would head the Federation for Constitutional Government, an organization of conservatives ostensibly committed to constitutional principles, but covertly working to obstruct public school desegregation. The Dixiecrats in Louisiana also included in their ranks such leading anti-Longs as Sam Jones, Leander Perez, and H. Scott Wilkinson, one of Chep Morrison's top financial backers. Many of the same people who had campaigned for "honest and decent government" in Louisiana now exploited the race issue for political gain against Earl Long. Since Long publicly supported Harry Truman, the Louisiana Dixiecrats directed many of their racist remarks at him rather than Truman. One Dixiecrat circular, derived from a similar Jones campaign circular, charged Governor Long with various sordid acts of political corruption, then continued: "But nothing you have done is quite as low as this. That you should use the power of your office and the tax payers' money to print and distribute Negro newspapers to tell lies about your white opponent, and to foster and urge and demand, on behalf of the Negro, the right to vote."[7]

Like Huey, Earl had rarely employed the race issue in his campaigns. He considered it an artificial issue contrived to disguise the economic neglect of the poor. Because blacks formed the largest segment of poor Louisianians, they received a high proportion of the social, education, and welfare benefits Earl had promoted: old-age pensions, free charity hospital care, welfare prescriptions, etc. Consequently, they rewarded him with their votes. In the 1948 gubernatorial primaries, Earl Long received over 80 percent of the black vote, but this support hardly influenced the outcome of the election. When he became governor in 1948, Earl decided to increase his political strength by registering blacks. During his four-year administration, from 1948 to 1952, black voter registration in Louisiana skyrocketed from 9,200 to 107,844, the highest total in the South. This, of course, left Long vulnerable on the race issue, and many of his enemies did not hesitate to take advantage. It should be noted that the Dixiecrats in Louisiana were led by anti-Longs, but some prominent Longites also joined—for example, Little Eva Talbot.[8]

During the month of August, 1948, Earl Long devoted his time and energy to the very close Senate race between Russell Long and Robert Kennon, and he paid little attention to presidential politics. The Dixiecrats had little difficulty obtaining enough signatures on a petition to have the Thurmond-Wright ticket placed on the ballot as a third party. On September 10, however, the State Central Committee surprised Long by adopting Leander Perez's resolution certifying the Dixiecrat slate as the official Democratic nominees in Louisiana. By this maneuver, Strom Thurmond would be on the ballot as the Democratic candidate for president, and since Truman was also a Democrat, his name would be removed. The Louisiana Democratic party had, in effect, severed its ties with the national party and joined the Dixiecrats. Such men as Leander Perez, Sam Jones, Robert Kennon, John Barr, and Scott Wilkinson had used their political muscle to wipe Harry Truman's name off the ballot, depriving the voters of Louisiana of a free and fair choice in the November election. Even the secessionist fire-eaters of 1860 had not gone as far, placing both the southern Democratic nominee, John Breckinridge, and the northern Democratic nominee, Stephen A. Douglas, on the presidential ballot. In justifying this mockery of the democratic process, the State Central Committee issued an appeal to racist sentiment: "It is the duty of the Democratic party of Louisiana to nominate its presidential electors . . . who will preserve the traditions of the people and their right of self-government, as opposed to candidates . . . pledged to destroy their rights of state government and to force upon them foreign ideologies such as the Russian 'all races law' here called F.E.P.C."[9]

Initially, Earl Long shrugged off the committee's statement: "They did it. I had no part in it." But after reflecting, he decided to take direct action to get President Truman on the ballot. He consulted with J. Howard McGrath, the chairman of the Democratic National Committee, and the organized labor hierarchy in Louisiana, and then he called a special session of the legislature. When the session opened September 21, Long had a bill introduced that would place the Truman-Barkley ticket on the ballot under the "National Democratic Party" label. When the bill got to committee, the Dixiecrats succeeded in drastically altering it. One amendment allowed one hundred voters to sign a petition to place Truman's name on the ballot, but without any variation of the name "Democratic." Another amendment stipulated that the traditional symbol of the Democratic party in Louisiana, the rooster, would be attached to the Dixiecrat slate. The amended bill easily passed the legislature. It is a telling commentary on Louisiana politics in 1948 that Earl Long stood virtually alone among leading politicians in defending the right of Harry Truman to be put on the ballot as the national Democratic party nominee, which he obviously was.[10]

Recognizing the inevitability of a Dixiecrat victory in the presidential election in Louisiana, Earl did not actively campaign for Truman, but he did try to get as high a vote total as possible for him. An analysis shows that Truman received the bulk of the historical Longite vote, though Thurmond easily carried the state, with 204,290 votes to Truman's 136,344, and the Republican candidate, Thomas E. Dewey, capturing 72,657. Truman carried those areas that had traditionally given Longite candidates the most votes—the lower-class and heavily unionized urban areas and the poor white and black areas in the rural parishes. Long's insistence on remaining loyal to President Truman and the national Democratic party took a considerable amount of political courage, since the Dixiecrats had gained such widespread popular support in the state.[11]

The reversal in Earl Long's political fortunes in 1948 led him to a subdued and uncharacteristically moderate role in state politics for the rest of his first full term as governor of Louisiana. On occasion, traces of the old Earl Long would emerge, and he would never forgo his constant yearning for more political power, but on the whole, he did not engage in the free-for-all politicking that marred his first year in office. One reason for the change was his assessment of the political situation in Louisiana, and he spent much of 1949 preparing for two vital elections that would occur in 1950. In one race, Russell Long would run for a full six-year term in the Senate, and in the other, Chep Morrison would run for reelection as mayor. Because the mayoral election would take place in January, 1950, Earl began plotting a strategy to defeat Morrison. In New Orleans, he tried mightily and often to persuade Bob Maestri to run against Morrison. Although Earl Long, Jimmie Comiskey, Captain Billy Bisso, and other Old Regular leaders tried to convince Maestri that he was the only man who stood a chance of winning, Maestri refused their overtures. The former mayor knew that Earl's anti–New Orleans tactics had backfired, greatly enhancing Morrison's popularity in the Crescent City, and that even he had no realistic chance of beating the popular incumbent. Maestri also had had his fill of political office and preferred to spend his time in private business. After a long search, Earl and the Old Regulars chose Charles A. Zatarain, a member of the Louisiana Tax Commission. The selection of a political novice revealed the plight of the Old Regulars in New Orleans. The once mighty political machine had fallen on desperate times, its ranks decimated by defections to Morrison's CCDA, and its political survival threatened by Earl Long's vindictive measures in 1948. Nor did Long help the cause when he publicly hinted at more state money for New Orleans "if harmony prevailed" between the city and the state. With his popularity at an all-time high, deLesseps Morrison swept to an easy first-primary victory.[12]

Morrison's landslide convinced Earl Long to try to salvage whatever political support remained for him in New Orleans, for he still faced Russell Long's Senate reelection bid in August, 1950. Shortly after the mayoral election, Long and Morrison began negotiations. The evidence does not establish which of the two men initiated the discussions, but it does prove that they came to an arrangement mutually beneficial. In exchange for Morrison's promise not to oppose Russell Long's reelection, Long agreed to restore home rule to New Orleans and to return to the city revenues the state had taken away in 1948. In March, 1950, Governor Long called a special session of the legislature to dedicate surplus beer-tax revenues to school lunches and rural roads, and he set back the date of the first senatorial primary to July 25, supposedly to avert a conflict with the spring harvest season, but actually to hold the primary after the regular legislative session, which was scheduled to end in June. When the regular session convened in May, Long's agenda included a much more moderate and decidedly less partisan series of measures. With state revenues burgeoning from the rapid growth of the oil and gas industry, he called for no new taxes, but still found the money to finance increases in spending for roads, bridges, schools, old-age pensions, and health programs. To improve his standing in New Orleans, Earl had bills passed restoring some of the city's lost revenue, giving the mayor control over the police, and granting supervisory regulation over public utilities to the commission council. Long also proposed a $140-million bond issue for highways and for the construction of a badly needed Mississippi River bridge in New Orleans.[13]

By far the most significant of Long's legislative proposals was a bill giving New Orleans home rule. Ever since Huey Long's break with Mayor Walmsley, the city had become a political football, punted around by Longs and anti-Longs alike. Earl's punitive legislation of 1948 clearly pointed to the need for a home rule charter for New Orleans, and for once, Long and Morrison joined together to implement the concept. Morrison wanted a constitutional amendment, and Long wanted a simple legislative act. To resolve the differences, Long appointed a bipartisan panel of two Longites, Bob Maestri and Charles Zatarain, and two anti-Longs, Chep Morrison and Esmond Phelps. The board quickly reached agreement on a legislative act incorporating immediate home rule and a constitutional amendment allowing the city's voters to adopt the home rule charter of their choice. When the panel submitted these recommendations to Governor Long, he pushed the bill and the amendment through the legislature. The amendment, approved by the state's voters in November, 1950, made permanent the right of the people of New Orleans to determine their own form of city government, thus effectively preventing future gubernatorial intervention in the city's municipal affairs.[14]

The anti-Long New Orleans *Item* acknowledged that in salvaging the home rule bill, Earl Long "showed definite statesmanship." Indeed, Long's actions did display the mark of the statesman, finally permitting the city of New Orleans to manage its own affairs after a quarter century of blatant state intervention. Home rule, moreover, meant that New Orleans would inevitably fall under the control of Long's archenemy, Chep Morrison. Governor Long, however, did not act solely out of an altruistic commitment to municipal reform; he did cut a deal with Mayor Morrison. Earl wanted desperately to ensure Russell Long's victory in the senatorial primary on July 25, and he wanted a big win in New Orleans. To get that vote, he needed Morrison's help. On July 28, Earl was admitted to Southern Baptist Hospital in New Orleans to have all his remaining teeth extracted, supposedly to cure the arthritis that plagued him. Before the oral surgery, he held a press conference in his room. Clad in a hospital gown, Long told reporters that his emissaries, Feazel and Sehrt, had met with Morrison five times to work out an arrangement whereby Morrison would not actively oppose Russell's reelection in return for legislation favorable to the city. Both Feazel and Sehrt corroborated the story. Morrison admitted that the meetings had taken place, but he denied that any arrangement had been made. The *Item* backed the mayor's version, arguing that since Morrison publicly endorsed Malcolm Lafargue, Russell's opponent, he could hardly have accepted the deal.[15]

The evidence clearly shows that there was indeed a deal. According to Clem Sehrt, Earl Long and Chep Morrison met at the mayor's Coliseum Street home in early May, 1950. Morrison told Long that to appease his anti-Long supporters in the city, he would publicly endorse Lafargue, but he would privately pass the word to his CCDA ward leaders to support Russell. The story seems plausible. While Morrison did speak publicly for Lafargue, he made little effort to get him elected. His support for Lafargue appears as lip service to satisfy his doctrinaire backers who hated Earl Long. But as a realist, Morrison knew that Russell Long would easily win the election, and that it was to his advantage to make a deal with Earl. Such accommodation between ostensible enemies is not uncommon in Louisiana political history. For his part, Earl Long would hardly have bestowed such benefits on New Orleans in 1950 had the two not made a deal. The most persuasive evidence is the actual election results in New Orleans. Russell carried thirteen of the city's seventeen wards, and rolled up a total city vote of 73,669 to Lafargue's 51,776, or a margin of 60 percent to 40 percent. Obviously, Morrison had not made an all-out effort for Lafargue.[16]

In the statewide senatorial primary, Russell Long defeated Malcolm Lafargue, the U.S. attorney for the Western District of Louisiana, 359,230 votes to 156,918, or 70 percent to 30 percent. In the campaign, Lafargue had tried to capitalize on public opposition to Truman administration policies by assailing Russell's liberal voting record and by denouncing "creeping socialism." Russell, who had a bad stutter, did not campaign much. Instead, Earl took to the stump for his nephew, praising him as "an improvement on his uncle and his father." The election proved to be no contest. Russell carried sixty-three parishes, losing only Plaquemines, where Leander Perez, still furious with Earl for supporting President Truman, gave Lafargue 93 percent of the vote.[17]

To better his standing with the public, Earl Long abruptly reversed himself on civil service. In the 1950 legislative session, he proposed a constitutional amendment for a genuine and more comprehensive merit system than that enacted under Sam Jones in 1940. At a press conference, reporters, skeptical about Earl's sudden reversal, questioned him about the extent of his sincerity. Earl responded that he had the Jones civil service program repealed because it was a sham and did not contain stringent enough prohibitions on partisan political activity by classified employees. Earl's amendment did incorporate a Hatch Act provision against political campaigning by covered state employees, and it did include all the features essential to a legitimate civil service system. Allan Sindler wrote that for Earl, "it was no small concession . . . to endorse what he had repealed a scant two years before." In reality, the new "reformist" Earl Long looked suspiciously like the old Earl. His dramatic change consisted once again of paying lip service to the principle of reform. At no time did he really try to persuade the legislature to pass the civil service amendment. When it came up for a house vote, it lost 47 to 46, or far short of the two-thirds necessary for approval.[18]

Another gesture Long made in the direction of good government came when he endorsed a new state constitution. No one quarreled about the need for one. The current state charter, adopted in 1921, was riddled with inequities, concessions to special interests, and utter absurdities. Amended over three hundred times by 1950, the Louisiana state constitution had become the worst in the nation. Such simple acts as raising a judge's salary or authorizing a Caddo Parish mosquito control commission required a constitutional amendment. In 1946, the legislature had instructed the Louisiana Law Institute, a nonpartisan organization of law school and political science faculty and students, to draft a model constitution. In a massive four-volume study, the institute prepared a project that contained provisions for badly needed improvements in state government.[19]

In both the regular and the special sessions of the legislature in 1950, bills were passed calling for a constitutional convention, with about two-thirds of the delegates chosen by popular vote. The remaining third of the delegates would be appointed by the governor, the chief justice of the state supreme court, and the executive committee of the state Democratic party. In effect, Earl Long controlled at least one-third of the delegates, since he dominated the court and the party executive committee. And since Earl had firm control of about 40 percent of the popular vote, he would get at least another third of the delegates. The bills stipulated that there would be no popular referendum on the new constitution; it would automatically become the new state charter in 1952. Earl Long justified denying citizens the right to approve or reject the new document, asserting that since "the lawyers themselves don't know what a constitution means," the common people, who display "much ignorance," would not know how to cast an intelligent vote. Longite representative Marion Vallie of Jefferson Davis Parish put the matter more bluntly: "My people down in Bayou Chene don't know the difference between a constitution and a free pass to a football game."[20]

Not surprisingly, Earl's call for a new state constitution ignited a firestorm of opposition. With considerable justification, his political enemies suspected that he intended to manipulate the convention to his advantage. This suspicion turned into certainty when the special legislative session in August actually made provision for extending Earl's term as governor until 1954, giving him an extra two years in office. Long protested, claiming his innocence and stating that his only concern was a better form of government for Louisiana. "No state has ever approached a constitutional convention with greater preparatory work," he told the legislature, but his enemies correctly assumed that his preparations would result in a rigged convention. Led by Chep Morrison, the anti-Longs mounted an extensive campaign against the convention, and the public pressure they stirred up forced Earl to abandon the idea. In September, he called a one-day special session, which repealed the call for the convention.[21]

In early 1951, Earl Long turned his attention to the next gubernatorial primary, scheduled for January 15, 1952. Unable to succeed himself as governor, he seriously considered running for lieutenant governor on a ticket with some figurehead, and in March he announced his candidacy. The response was numerous cries of protest that Earl was trying to establish a personal dynasty in Baton Rouge, and he finally dropped the idea. Once again, he failed to realize that people would not tolerate a return to the uninhibited politics of the 1930s. When the public did not respond favorably to a special legislative session in June, 1951, which doled out more money for highways and state institutions, he felt disappointed. Finally realizing that the voters would not in fact accept him as a candidate in 1952, he began looking for someone to head his ticket. Most speculation centered on Lieutenant Governor Bill Dodd, who began publicly stating that he would be the Longite candidate for governor. As a loyal Earl Long man, Dodd believed that he deserved the opportunity to run for governor with Earl's blessing, but at a meeting in the Governor's Mansion, Earl informed Dodd that he would not endorse him. In a public statement, Earl said that in the summer of 1948, while he underwent treatment for his arthritis in Hot Springs, Arkansas, Dodd, who served as acting governor then, fired James Reilly, the director of administration, because Reilly had refused to comply with Dodd's wishes on a state purchasing contract. Long also claimed that while he recuperated from a heart attack in February, 1950, Dodd had tried to take over the state government in a "coup d'etat." As usual, Earl's public remarks concealed his real intentions, for he believed Dodd too capable a person and politician to entrust with the governorship. A former schoolteacher, Dodd had served in the Judge Advocate General's office during World War II and in the state legislature before becoming lieutenant governor. Intelligent, articulate, and able, Bill Dodd was precisely the kind of person Earl Long did not want running the state. He thought losing an election preferable to turning over control of state politics to Dodd, who would inevitably threaten his own domination of the Long machine itself.[22]

After considering several individuals to run as his candidate for governor, Earl finally settled on District Judge Carlos G. Spaht of Baton Rouge. A former mayor of the city and a former head of the LSU Alumni Association, Spaht was virtually unknown outside Baton Rouge and could hardly have been thought a serious candidate in his own right. Throughout the campaign, Spaht's opponents referred to him as "Earl's man." When a friend asked why he picked the obscure Spaht in 1952, Earl replied, "Why not? Hell, Dick Leche was a judge, wasn't he? If Dick could get elected, so can Spaht." The similarity between Earl's selection of Carlos Spaht in 1951 and Huey's selection of O. K. Allen in 1936 was obvious. Not about to allow men of real ability such as Bill Dodd to take over the state, Earl chose Spaht precisely because of his obscurity. Spaht had no real political or personal following and could not contest Earl for leadership of the machine. Superficially, Earl's selection of Spaht was yet another example of his sporadic loss of political acumen, but from a deeper perspective, it proves again his mastery of Louisiana politics. Earl Long picked Spaht because he knew that Spaht would lose. His instinct told him that 1952 would be the year of the anti-Longs, and he correctly predicted to a friend that Robert Kennon would win the governorship and institute a series of good government measures. After four dull, listless years of reform, the voters would once again be ready for a return to Longism, and Earl would triumph spectacularly in the 1956 governor's race. The old trouper also considered his political machine, which, he believed, benefited more from a good, sound defeat than from a series of victories. "When Huey was around," he told a friend, "the boys stayed in power too long, and they got too greedy. Look what happened when Dick was governor. Those sonofabitches stole the state blind. Four years in office is long enough for anybody. You let 'em lose an election, and when the next election comes around, they'll be lean and hungry." Indeed, Earl had a habit of breaking up his machine after elections, purging all those politicians who had seemed too greedy and replacing them with younger, less experienced people. That way, he always stayed on top and did not have to face overly ambitious rivals attempting to undermine his absolute control of the organization. The strategy worked to perfection. After a smashing defeat in 1952, Earl and his machine would triumph four years later.[23]

The gubernatorial election of 1952 attracted a record number of nine candidates, several of whom were not serious. Cliff Liles, the legislature's sergeant at arms, advocated the legalization of all forms of gambling—with the $400 million in annual revenues, the state could repeal most other taxes. Kermit Parker, a New Orleans pharmacist, became the first black candidate for state office since Reconstruction. Dudley LeBlanc also ran, even though Federal Trade Commission injunctions against his advertising of Hadacol and IRS investigations of his tax liability hurt his chances. LeBlanc tried to drop out of the race, but decided to remain in it after Bill Dodd refused to run as his lieutenant governor—the offer having been based on Dodd's raising a quarter of a million dollars. Lucille May Grace became the first woman ever to run for governor. Although she and her husband, Fred Dent, were powers in the Long machine, she had broken with Earl when he did not support the Dixiecrats in 1948.[24]

The main candidates in the race included Bill Dodd, Hale Boggs, James McLemore, and Robert Kennon. Claiming to be the "true" Long candidate, Dodd called for heavy state spending on social programs. Lacking organized machine support and unable to raise money, Dodd found himself eclipsed by the other leading contenders, so he tried the unique tactic of campaigning on television. One of his commercials showed him sitting on a sofa, explaining his platform to the voters. When Dudley LeBlanc saw the spot, he told Dodd that "you can't sell an audience while sitting on your ass on a sofa" and advised him to stand up, shake his fists, and display emotion. Many people considered Congressman T. Hale Boggs the favorite. Boggs had gathered endorsements from a variety of politicians in both the Long and the anti-Long camps—Chep Morrison, Sam Jones, William Feazel, Jimmy Morrison, and Russell Long—yet another example, in which Louisiana history abounds, of politically strange bedfellows joining together. Only a year before, the anti-Longs had bitterly castigated Russell Long for being a tool of his Uncle Earl, but now many praised him for his support of Boggs. Although Boggs had political endorsements and did not lack for campaign funds, his being a New Orleans resident and a Roman Catholic proved fatal handicaps. James McLemore, an Alexandria cattle baron, was not considered a major candidate at the beginning of the race, but his caustic attacks on Earl Long and Harry Truman gained him wide support. Denouncing Truman's "socialistic tendencies" and berating Long for being a "nigger lover," McLemore exploited the growing public concern over the race issue. Although Hale Boggs cut into his strength among the anti-Longs, Robert Kennon became reformism's candidate. As a judge from north Louisiana, Kennon had the advantage of an untarnished record, and his platform, which advocated the reinstatement of civil service, reform of the state penitentiary system, and tax reductions, appealed to the good government crowd.[25]

The multiplicity of candidates guaranteed a second-primary runoff, and since Earl's candidate Carlos Spaht was certain to be in the runoff, the main competition was for places in the second primary. Leander Perez detested Hale Boggs for his pro-Truman voting record, and with Boggs one of the favorites to make the runoff, Perez engaged in character assassination to defeat him. The judge persuaded Lucille May Grace to file a formal complaint with the State Central Committee of the Democratic party challenging Boggs's candidacy on the grounds that as a congressman, he was ineligible to run for state office. Grace also charged that while a student at Tulane University, Boggs had belonged to the American Student Union, a "communist front organization," thus violating a state Democratic party rule prohibiting members of the Communist party from running for state office. The charges, of course, were totally without foundation. In the six previous gubernatorial elections, members of Congress had run for governor, and in 1948, Grace herself had run on the ticket of Congressman Jimmy Morrison. The allegation of Boggs's "pro-communist" sympathies was equally ridiculous and represented nothing more than smear tactics by Grace and her mentor, Perez. In late October, 1951, Governor Earl Long called a special meeting of the State Central Committee to hear the case, and for once, he displayed true statesmanship. Wearing a necktie emblazoned with a Confederate flag, Earl made an impassioned two-hour plea on Boggs's behalf. Pausing periodically to take a swig from a hip flask, he launched a disjointed but scathing attack on Leander Perez, and he told the committee that in the interests of fairness, Boggs should be permitted to remain in the race. After a shouting match between Long and Perez, the committee ruled that since the charges had been improperly filed, Boggs's name would stay on the ballot. The dismissal of the charges on technical grounds has led some writers to argue that since Boggs did not have the opportunity to clear his name publicly, Perez had succeeded in associating the congressman with communism. In fact, the committee's action had no significant effect on public opinion. Even had the charges not been filed at all, Perez could still have accused Boggs of Communist sympathies, and in any event, the Plaquemines boss campaigned all over the state, accusing Earl Long, Hale Boggs, and Harry Truman of participating in a sinister conspiracy to allow the Communists and integrationists to take over Louisiana. Whether the smear hurt Boggs cannot be ascertained. From a careful analysis of the election returns, it appears that Boggs's Roman Catholic religion proved the main factor in his failure to win large numbers of votes in north Louisiana. Earl Long recognized the significance of the religious issue, and in one heavily Protestant section, he proclaimed: "They say Hale Boggs is a Communist. He ain't no Communist because he's a Catholic!"[26]

As the campaign progressed, the political machinations heated up. When McLemore began to win support because he used the race issue, Perez suddenly backed him. Perez had originally endorsed Grace and had promised her plenty of money and machine support. There are conflicting versions of McLemore's candidacy. One holds that Perez wanted to test the political climate for the effectiveness of the race issue. In this version, McLemore's strong showing in the first primary encouraged Perez and the expanding group of segregationist politicians to use that issue to capture control of the state. Not considered, however, is Earl Long's spectacular first-primary victory in the 1956 governor's race, when he defeated McLemore and other candidates without engaging in racist appeals. A more plausible version holds that McLemore was actually a stalking horse for Earl Long, who paid "Mac" essentially to take right-wing votes away from Kennon. Long and McLemore were close friends and business associates. The New Orleans *Item* accused Long of putting up $50,000 in cash and of signing a note for $287,500 to purchase McLemore's cattle auction barn in Alexandria, using a mutual friend as an intermediary. McLemore did admit selling the facility to a Robert "Brother" Blackman, who acknowledged that Earl Long did give him the money and the note to make the purchase. Russell Long added to the controversy by charging that his uncle paid McLemore to enter the race. Clem Sehrt corroborated Russell's story, claiming that Long paid McLemore $100,000 to file his candidacy and capture the anti-Truman vote. Obviously, there is no record of this transaction, though the story does accord with Long's history of manipulating the political process to his advantage.[27]

In the first primary, Carlos Spaht, as expected, led the pack, with 22.8 percent of the vote. Robert Kennon came in second, with 21.5 percent; McLemore, Boggs, and Dodd trailed. Although Earl did actively campaign for Spaht in the second primary, that election was no contest. All the defeated first-primary candidates jumped on the Kennon bandwagon, and the Minden judge won an easy runoff victory, capturing 482,302 votes, or 61.4 percent, to Spaht's 302,743, or 38.6 percent. Anti-Long candidates also won decisive majorities in both houses of the legislature, and they took a majority of local and parish offices. The election appeared once again to spell Earl Long's political demise, but Earl had already started making preparations for the next race. Years later, he reminisced about the Kennon-Spaht campaign: "I told Spaht the way to win was for me to run for lieutenant governor with him, but he didn't want it that way. . . . I did everything I could for Judge Spaht. . . . Fact is, I spent my own money . . . and I spent money for Spaht that I should have kept for Earl."[28]

9

"Huey Never Done That!"

The smashing victory that Robert Kennon and the anti-Longs scored over Carlos Spaht and the Longs in the 1952 state elections once again prompted many observers to proclaim the end of Earl Long's political career, but Long correctly perceived that his eclipse would prove only temporary. In the 1955–56 gubernatorial primary, he had made the preparations necessary to stage yet another spectacular comeback, and he won a sensational first-primary victory in the election. In its first three years, Earl Long's second full term as governor continued to illustrate both the social programs and the political methods that made him the dominant figure in Louisiana politics.

When Robert Kennon took the oath of office as governor of Louisiana in 1952, he promised to fulfill his campaign pledge of a "civics book approach" to state government, and in a style reminiscent of Sam Jones in 1940, he persuaded the legislature to enact a series of reform measures. State civil service was reinstated and given constitutional protection by voter approval of a civil service amendment. The state Budget Office was reorganized, and the state auditor was given greater control over expenditures. The penitentiary system was overhauled, and for the first time, the main penal facility at Angola was placed under professional management. Boards governing state colleges and universities, mental institutions, highways, wildlife and fisheries, and welfare were reconstituted and made more independent of gubernatorial control. The first "sunshine," or open meeting, law was passed, and voting machines were mandated for all precincts in the state. In 1954, the legislature passed a right-to-work bill prohibiting companies from hiring only members of labor unions, and the voters approved a constitutional amendment requiring two-thirds legislative approval of all tax increases. Kennon also reduced the

The pea patch farm, 1960
Authors' collection

Long (left) and "Sixty" Rayburn (right) feeding hogs at the pea patch farm,
1956.
Earl K. Long Papers, Louisiana and Lower Mississippi Valley Collections,
Louisiana State University Libraries

Long (wearing white hat, holding basket) and friends at the pea patch farm, 1956.

Long on tractor at the pea patch farm, 1956
Earl K. Long Papers, Louisiana and Lower Mississippi Valley Collections,
Louisiana State University Libraries

Governor Long during his famous tirade before the legislature, May, 1959
State Library of Louisiana

Governor Long during his famous tirade before the legislature, May, 1959
State Library of Louisiana

Governor Long in the basement of the East Baton Rouge Parish Courthouse, just prior to his transfer to Mandeville, 1959.
State Library of Louisiana

Governor Long leaving the Covington Junior High School gymnasium after securing his legal release from Mandeville, June, 1959.
Shreveport Times

Earl K. Long (left) and James A. Noe (right) announcing their ticket in the 1959 state elections.
Shreveport Times

Long at Ville Platte, July 4, 1959
Glen Ducote for Shreveport Times

Long with a new pair of cowboy boots, Fort Worth, July, 1959
Shreveport Times

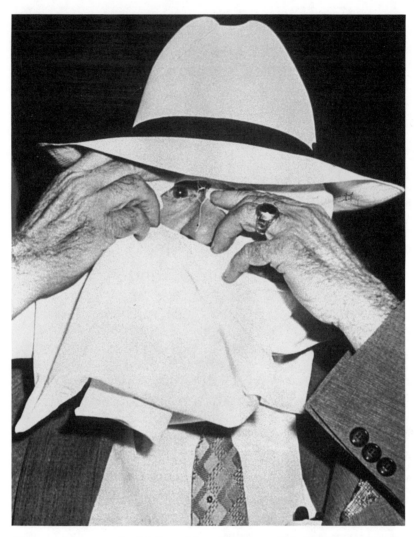

Governor Long covering his face with a pillowcase to hide from the press at the Forth Worth airport, July, 1959.
UPI

Governor Long campaigning in New Orleans' French Quarter, August, 1959
Authors' collection

Typical Earl K. Long rally, Haynesville, August, 1959
Langston McEachern for Shreveport Times

YOU KNOW ME

Anti-Long propaganda, 1959
State Library of Louisiana

Governor Long stumping for lieutenant governor, West Monroe, November, 1959.
Courtesy of C. J. "Bobbie" Dugas

gasoline tax by two cents a gallon, and he raised the number of exemptions to the state income tax, these measures helping to offset the continuing rapid increase in state revenues from oil and gas severance taxes. Finally, to emphasize his commitment to clean government, Kennon allowed Superintendent of State Police Francis X. Grevemberg to launch a massive crackdown on the wide-open gambling that had flourished in south Louisiana during Earl Long's administration. By the time Kennon left office, most of the casinos and pinball and slot machine parlors had been forced to close.[1]

Much like Sam Jones, Kennon blended reformist, anti-Long sentiments with an equally intense devotion to states' rights and racial segregation. In 1948, Kennon had backed the Dixiecrats, and, as governor, he openly opposed the policies and candidates of the national Democratic party. In January, 1952, the party's State Central Committee selected Earl Long and Mary Evelyn Dickerson as Louisiana's representatives to the Democratic National Committee, but as soon as Kennon gained control of the state government, he replaced them with two of his own people. At the Democratic National Convention of 1952, the Kennon-led Louisiana delegation voted as a unit for Senator Richard Russell of Georgia for president, and it refused to support the party platform, which had a civil rights plank that Kennon characterized as "repugnant to right-thinking Democrats in Louisiana." In the 1952 presidential election, Governor Kennon broke with the state's historical policy of backing the Democratic candidate by openly supporting the Republican candidate, Dwight Eisenhower. That presidential election brought the Long versus anti-Long struggle into sharp focus. Virtually all the leading anti-Long "reform" politicians in the state—Robert Kennon, Sam Jones, Leander Perez, Chep Morrison—either openly or covertly threw their backing to Eisenhower; Earl Long and his followers backed the Democratic candidate, Adlai Stevenson. In a close election, Stevenson carried Louisiana by winning the historic Long vote: blacks, organized labor, and those in poor rural areas.[2]

Almost from the time Kennon assumed office, Earl Long began to plan for the 1955–56 governor's race. Ambitious as always, Earl knew that the anti-Long sweep in 1952 marked yet another seesaw in recent Louisiana politics, and that 1956 would provide him the opportunity for victory. And he wanted to ensure that this win would be his greatest, something that not even Huey had secured, a first-primary victory for governor. So the cagey old politico started making the essential deals. He began by persuading such potentially strong rivals as Sam Jones and Jimmie Davis not to make the race. At the same time, he employed intermediaries to convince several weak candidates to enter the race. For example, Earl had many of his rural supporters write letters and send telegrams to Chep Morrison encouraging him to run. One local leader delighted in recalling that "Earl really got a kick out of that scheme. He really made Morrison believe that he had a lot of support in the rural parishes." Earl also sent two men with $5,000 each to get Chep into the race. As usual, Earl recruited politicians unhappy with Kennon's reform measures, which reduced their patronage considerably. For example, many sheriffs in south Louisiana had used the kickbacks from gamblers as important sources of revenue. "We were hungry," one sheriff said. "Kennon and Grevemberg cut off our money, and Earl promised to give it back to us." One of the legendary sheriffs in recent times, C. J. "Cat" Doucet of St. Landry Parish, who received his nickname from the prostitution that flourished under his benevolence, stated frankly that "Earl would let me open up the cathouses again, and he promised to let me get my fair share of the take from the bookies."[3]

Earl Long's platform for the 1955–56 race included the typical pledges of large increases in state spending on a variety of health, education, and welfare programs. His ticket included Lether E. Frazar for Lieutenant Governor; Jack P. F. Gremillion for Attorney General; Bill Dodd for State Auditor; Shelby M. Jackson for Superintendent of Education; Lucille May Grace for Register of the State Land Office; and Dave L. Pearce for Commissioner of Agriculture. Earl's main concern in selecting a ticket was representation from all regions of the state, and he did not pay much attention to the individuals on the ticket, except, of course, to ensure that they would pose no threat to his absolute control of the machine. Earl's close friend and political supporter Sixty Rayburn related the story of how Jack Gremillion came to appear on the ticket. Earl had originally intended that his friend Camille Gravel, an Alexandria attorney who had worked with him in getting out the black vote, run for attorney general, but at the last minute, Gravel decided not to file for the office. On the day before the deadline for filing, Earl called a friend in Baton Rouge and told him to pick someone to file for attorney general on his ticket. The friend selected Gremillion, and the next morning, Earl, who had never met Gremillion, invited him to the pea patch farm in

Winnfield. After talking with Gremillion for a few minutes, Earl went into the house to speak privately with Sixty Rayburn. "Lord God, where do you reckon they found him?" Earl asked, and Rayburn said, "Governor, I don't know." Earl said, "Well, we're going to have to get him some tomwalkers [stilts] because nobody'll ever see him in a crowd," a reference to Gremillion's being barely five feet tall.[4]

Only four candidates challenged Earl Long in the 1955–56 governor's race, and of them, only deLesseps Morrison could be considered a serious foe. Despite Earl's efforts to convince him that he could win, Morrison in all probability figured that this race would give him the statewide publicity he needed to make a successful run four years later. Relishing the lavish, laudatory coverage of his anti-gambling crusade, Grevemberg told himself that the voters would cast their ballots for a man of proven integrity. Grevemberg, however, was too strongly doctrinaire in his views, and he had alienated numerous politicians with his crackdown on gambling. A third candidate, Fred A. Preaus, was highway director under Kennon and had the governor's backing, but he failed to generate any mass support. Finally, James McLemore of Alexandria again ran as a segregationist candidate.[5]

With a weak field opposing him and with backing from most of the state's political powers, Earl Long felt assured of victory, and he took to the stump with enthusiasm, for of all the elements of politics, the one he enjoyed the most was campaigning. Typically, he traveled throughout the state, appearing in virtually every town. And he invariably attracted large crowds, drawn by the promised entertainment and giveaways, as well as the unique Long stump harangues. One person recalled Long at a rally in Marksville, tossing loaves of bread and other foodstuffs to the audience and thoroughly entertaining people with his shenanigans. When native son Edwin Edwards opened his 1983 campaign in Marksville, one old-timer recalled that he drew a larger crowd than any other candidate he could remember, except for Uncle Earl. After arriving over an hour late, Earl sat on the platform while other members of his ticket gave short speeches, but he always remained the center of attention. Frequently taking ships from a glass of soda or grape juice, swatting mosquitoes, waving his handkerchief over his head, he held the crowd's interest. After he finished talking, Earl would throw money and peppermint sticks to the children, then sit on the back of a pickup truck to shake hands with the townspeople. Earl's speeches highlighted his campaign, and nothing delighted his audiences more than to hear him launch one of his vaunted personal attacks against his opponents. Even though Chep Morrison went so far as to campaign on water skis, in an attempt to shed his image as a sophisticated urbanite, Earl simply demolished him on the stump: "I'd rather beat Morrison than eat any blackberry or huckleberry pie my momma ever made. Oh, how I'm praying for that old stump-wormer to get in there. I want him to roll up them cuffs, and get out that little old tuppy [toupee] and pull down them shades, and make himself up." Fred Preaus fell victim to one of Earl's classic put-downs. In one of the numerous versions of the story, Earl was campaigning in West Monroe and told the audience about Preaus, an automobile dealer from Farmerville: "Now, that Fred Preaus, he's a good, God-fearing, honest man. If I wanted to buy an automobile, I'd go right to Fred's dealership and buy it from him, 'cuz I know I'd get a good, honest deal from him. But if I wanted to buy *two* cars, I'd have to go somewhere else, 'cuz that's too big a deal for Fred to handle!" Nor did Grevemberg escape his share of Long ridicule: "Now, if you want to vote for a pretty man, you vote for Mr. Grevemberg. He's got nice wavy hair, and he's a fine husky man. He looks better without makeup than Dellasoups 'Storytelling' Morrison does with it."[6]

Earl's only real threat came from Chep Morrison, but the New Orleans mayor quickly discovered that his alleged popularity outside the city did not exist. Morrison's correspondence contains many letters to politicians seeking their support, but Earl had outmaneuvered him by lining up backers a year in advance. In desperation, Morrison found himself making lavish promises just to get the endorsement of minor officials. Dudley LeBlanc, for example, would get to select the new highway commissioner and the state purchasing agent, and would have a veto over all gubernatorial appointments in two congressional districts. And LeBlanc's influence was limited to a small area of south Louisiana. LeBlanc summarized one of Morrison's greatest weaknesses, one that he would fail to overcome in three gubernatorial campaigns: "You don't know anything about country politics."[7]

Earl Long, of course, knew his country politics inside and out, and he used this knowledge with his customary skill. Encountering no difficulty raising money—he received over a quarter of a million dollars from the Carlos Marcello organization alone—he spent generously to ensure a heavy voter turnout. As election day approached and an Earl Long first-primary victory appeared possible, he was besieged by politicians eager to jump on his bandwagon. Earl's cousin, David Bell, who served as the bagman for the Long campaign, remembered that "Earl sent me all over the state collecting money. He charged sheriffs $25,000 apiece, legislative candidates $50,000, assessors $30,000, and minor candidates $5,000. Big contributors Earl handled personally." Once again, those "big contributors" included Frank Costello and Carlos Marcello. According to the FBI, Costello donated $250,000 to Earl's 1956 campaign, an amount matched by Marcello. "Part of this payment," an FBI report stated, "was for the pardoning of narcotics peddlers in confinement at Louisiana State Penitentiary at Angola who have worked for Marcello." Other large contributors to the Long campaign were oilman Louis J. Roussel, a group of wealthy people interested in establishing a new racetrack in Jefferson Parish, and organized labor. Although no accurate figures exist, it appears reasonable to estimate that Long raised well over a million dollars for his race.[8]

January 17, 1956, was one of the happiest days of Earl Long's life, for he scored a smashing triumph in the governor's election. With 51.5 percent of the total vote, Long won in the first primary, giving him the governorship without a runoff. And so all Long candidates for statewide office were automatically elected, whether or not they had majorities in the first primary. In addition, over 80 percent of the Long candidates for the legislature and for local and parish office won election. It was a great victory, with Earl taking especial delight in outperforming the great Kingfish himself by winning the first primary. "Huey never done that!" he told anyone who would listen. Earl also relished the thrashing he had administered to his political enemy, Chep Morrison. Along with a large contingent of friends and political supporters, Earl celebrated in his suite at the Roosevelt Hotel. There were copious quantities of food and drink, as well as recordings of Chep Morrison's desperate phone calls to his ward leaders around the state. Some of Long's supporters hired private detectives to place a wiretap on Morrison's home telephone, and Earl gleefully listened to all the conversations on election night. Because the wiretap involved a violation of federal law, the FBI conducted an exhaustive investigation, but failed to uncover any evidence implicating Earl.[9]

Earl Long carried sixty-two of the sixty-four parishes, losing only Orleans and Plaquemines, where Leander Perez threw his support to Fred Preaus. Long swept the rural areas of the state, and he rolled up an impressive vote in the urban areas because of his very strong support from organized labor and blacks. The most surprising vote came in New Orleans, where Morrison had counted on a huge lead to offset Long's heavy country vote. Long amazed everyone but himself by losing the city to Morrison by only two thousand votes. Long won the poorer wards and nearly two-thirds of the black vote. One black leader explained why: "We got a friend in Mr. Long and we have a friend in Mr. Morrison. If we vote to beat Mr. Long and put Mr. Morrison as governor, that leaves us just one friend. We're [*sic*] Mr. Morrison to stay as mayor, and want our other friend to stay as governor. That way we will have two friends." During his campaign, Earl had told New Orleans blacks that they ought to vote for Chep for mayor and vote for him for governor "so they would have both of us around." [10]

Once again, Earl K. Long was Governor of Louisiana. His May 12, 1956, inauguration was considerably more subdued than the 1948 extravaganza because the Kennon administration had enacted a law limiting inauguration expenses to $5,000. When the legislature convened later in May, Earl followed tradition by requesting tax increases to fund his program of substantial boosts in spending for health, education, welfare, and highways. He asked for increases in the taxes on racetrack betting, sulfur, natural gas, and timber, but unlike 1948, when he encountered only pro forma opposition, Earl discovered that the 1956 legislature had a more conservative fiscal approach. One of Kennon's constitutional amendments approved by the voters required a two-thirds legislative majority for all future tax increases. This meant that since there were one hundred members of the house, Earl would have to get sixty-seven votes to pass a tax increase. Under intense pressure from lobbyists representing the industries subject to Long's proposed taxes, house members displayed a rare rebellious nature. Even though Earl personally worked the house floor, subjecting the representatives to his ordinarily effective methods of persuasion, he fell one vote short. A solid coalition of anti-Longs and some Longites formed the famous "34 Club," which refused to budge from its adamant opposition to the tax increases. [11]

One reason Earl failed was that he had already used up many of his political favors in getting the Louisiana right-to-work law repealed. Enacted in 1954 under the conservative Kennon administration, the law prohibited employers from requiring their employees to join labor unions as a condition of employment. In most states, if a majority of a company's employees voted to organize a union, all the employees had to join, since they would benefit from collective bargaining. But in the South, right-to-work laws effectively prevented this practice, and the pro-business Kennon administration used its right-to-work law as a means of weakening organized labor in Louisiana. During the 1955–56 campaign, Earl Long had courted the union vote and received over 80 percent of it in the election. In return, he made the repeal of right-to-work the priority item on his legislative agenda. Business interests lobbied assiduously against repeal, offering one senator $25,000 for his vote. Typically, the politico reported the offer to Earl, who would, he said, have to top it to get his vote. Earl matched the donation and appointed the senator's brother to a $7,500-a-year seat on a meaningless state commission. Through such tactics, Long won the repeal of the right-to-work law. Repeal proved a boom for organized labor. With union membership rapidly increasing, Louisiana became the most heavily unionized state in the South.[12]

During the first three years of his second full term as governor, Earl Long expanded his program of providing large increases in social benefits to the people of Louisiana. Even though Long had failed to enact the tax increases he sought, state revenues rose because of the continuing growth in oil and gas production. Between 1956 and 1960, state spending went from $471 million to $566 million, ranking Louisiana eleventh in the nation and first in the South in per capita expenditures. A large proportion of the money funded increases in social spending, with Louisiana ranking first in the South in per capita expenditures for education, highways, health, and welfare. Old-age pensioners saw their monthly checks rise from $54.01 per person in 1956 to $71.06 in 1960, and schoolteachers enjoyed a $1,000, or 28 percent, pay raise. Despite his reputation as a free spender, Earl Long did exhibit a sense of frugality. He vetoed a large number of appropriations bills because the state did not have the money, and he refused to obligate future generations of Louisianians through issuing state bonds. Each year during Long's second term, the state had a balanced budget, not only on paper, but in fact. It was a period of general prosperity, with industry and employment rapidly expanding in Louisiana, and he took advantage of that economic boom to fund his programs without raising taxes. Because the existing tax structure proved more than adequate for his needs, Earl made no effort to provide the state a solid, stable source of revenue for the future. Indeed, he recognized the political benefits from pursuing the opposite fiscal policies. For example, he encouraged parish assessors to assess property at unrealistically low levels, thus exempting the vast majority of property owners from paying any taxes at all to the state. While politically popular, this policy would perpetuate a notion still held in Louisiana that homes, businesses, farms, and real estate should remain tax exempt. Because state revenues from severance taxes, mineral leases, and royalties from the energy industry were increasing at such a rapid pace, Long also kept direct taxes, such as those on sales, income, gasoline, and tobacco, at very low levels, also encouraging a strong popular aversion to tax increases of any kind.[13]

Even though he lost his fight for the tax increases, Earl handled the legislature with his usual mastery, obtaining legislative approval of 92 percent of all the bills he proposed, compared with 62 percent approval during Huey's governorship. "Earl knew everything that was going on about the legislature," House Speaker Robert Angelle remarked, "and he kept it all in his head. Even before a bill got out of committee, he could tell you the exact vote it would get." Other veteran politicos made similar comments, that no one possessed a more profound knowledge about the inner workings of the capitol than Earl Long, and all agreed that the methods he employed to get things accomplished were ingenious and effective.[14]

Among those methods, the "divide and conquer" tactic prevented potential political rivals from emerging within his organization. Every now and then, a Longite politician would try to wrest control of the machine from Earl, and Earl would quickly cut him down to size. One example involved the famous feud between Earl and Secretary of State Wade O. Martin, Jr. Martin's father, Wade Sr., a long-time member of the Public Service Commission, had been a loyal Longite since the late 1920s, but when he ran for reelection in 1952, Earl put two candidates against him, and the frail Martin had to withdraw because he did not have the stamina for a rigorous campaign. Furious with Earl for this betrayal of his father and ambitious in his own right, Wade Jr. began to assert his independence of Earl and hinted that he might run for governor in 1959. When Martin took office in 1956, the secretary of state controlled the state insurance business, regulated voting machines, certified voting commissioners, and promulgated official election results, so Martin had a secure power base from which to challenge Earl's authority. Aware of Martin's ambition, Earl decided to teach him a lesson in power. He had bills introduced depriving the secretary of state of control over the lucrative insurance business and of authority over the voting machines. Stripped of these functions, Martin would be reduced to certifying election returns, swearing in public officials, administering the state archives, and other politically insignificant duties. Enraged by Earl's actions, Martin fought desperately to get the bills killed. At a committee hearing, Martin and Long shouted insults at each other, nearly came to blows when they wrestled over a microphone, and both had to be restrained. Martin threatened, cajoled, and pleaded with legislators, but to no avail. Knowing that Earl dispensed the patronage on which they nourished, the legislators passed both bills by overwhelming margins.[15]

During his second term, Earl Long and Leander Perez waged an almost continual battle. Since their split over the Dixiecrat issue in 1948, Long and Perez detested each other, and during the gubernatorial campaign, Perez saw Long on Canal Street in New Orleans and asked how he could help him win election. Earl replied, "Come out against me as soon as possible," and walked away. The undisputed boss of Plaquemines Parish, Perez had made repeated attempts to extend his domain into neighboring St. Bernard, but he met resistance from Sheriffs L. A. Meraux and Celestine "Dutch" Rowley, both Earl Long stalwarts, who naturally did not want Pererz muscling in on their territory. When Dr. Nicholas Trist became sheriff in St. Bernard in 1952, he and Perez entered into a secret arrangement whereby they would divide the parish patronage without Earl Long's knowledge. Crafty and well-informed as ever, Earl found out about the agreement, and he decided to teach Perez a lesson by stripping him of political control of his bailiwick. Several levee districts in Plaquemines had legal authority over the parish's numerous waterways. Appointed by the Perrez-dominated police jury, the levee board members allowed him to amass a huge personal fortune from the mineral-rich land beneath the swamps and marshes and to use the levee districts as a patronage empire. In 1956, Perez tried to expand that empire, and his legislative puppet, Representative E. W. Gravolet, Jr., introduced a bill giving those levee districts legal control of submerged lands in the Gulf of Mexico. By the time Gravolet's bill passed a house committee, Earl's people had changed it completely, sending to the house floor eleven bills that effectively demolished Leander Perez's political power. One bill gave the governor the authority to appoint twelve new members of the Plaquemines Police Jury, giving him a controlling vote on all matters pertaining to parish government. Two other bills allowed Earl to appoint the members of the levee districts and to change boundaries and jurisdictions. An enraged Perez vowed to "fight to hell and back" against that "son of a bitch," but Long prevailed, and all eleven bills passed. When

Earl's people assumed their seats on the police jury, they took further measures to undermine Perez's authority. In both Plaquemines and St. Bernard, Long partisans removed Perez's people from parish payrolls, totally eliminated the salaries of many Perez appointees, and, in a personal affront, reduced the salary of Perez's son, who served as second assistant district attorney, from $200 a month to $62.50.[16]

Earl Long's record of success in the legislature rested primarily on his adroit use of patronage and money. On rare occasions, his opponents managed to defeat his measures. When the tax increases came up for a vote, Long discovered that well-heeled lobbyists had spent generously against them. One legislator recalled that "you can take $100,000 and block any measure in the legislature. The sulfur company has spent enough money to kill the tax to pay for it the first year. I've seen enough money flashed in the last few days to buy half the Heidelberg Hotel." The defeat of the tax increases, however, proved an unusual exception to the general rule that what Governor Earl Long wanted, the legislature gave him. One method involved a state law allowing the governor to fill vacancies in local offices. In his 1956–60 term, Long appointed 71 school board members, 49 police jurors, 117 justices of the peace, 119 constables, 16 coroners, and he filled 325 other positions in parish government. He also appointed a total of 803 members of levee boards, water and drainage districts, and other regional boards and commissions. In state government, he added over 4,000 people to the civil service lists and hired thousands more unclassified employees. And he named the members of 217 state boards and agencies and hired 1,329 people in the executive branch. Some of these appointments, like the members of the LSU Board of Supervisors, entailed real responsibilities while others, like the members of the ABC Board, the Art Commission, and the Old State Capitol Memorial Commission, existed solely for patronage. Some were extremely lucrative. In 1960, the attorney for the inheritance tax collector in New Orleans, a position Earl himself had held, earned $138,292 in fees. Earl, of course, hired relatives, friends, and supporters of important politicians to fill the positions. One of his most ingenious patronage devices was the "inspector." He appointed hundreds of "marsh inspectors," "swamp inspectors," "ditch inspectors," "pothole inspectors," "mosquito inspectors," and "coal mine inspectors." In 1958, the Lafourche Parish Levee Board, whose nine members Earl appointed at annual incomes of over $10,000 apiece, paid $65,000 for "inspections."[17]

Like George Washington Plunkitt, Earl Long drew the distinction between "honest graft" and "dishonest graft," the latter entailing bribes and kickbacks, the former incorporating the universal practice of rewarding friends with government business. With a magician's touch, he seemed to know precisely the right people to whom to award lucrative state contracts. The state insurance business, for example, ran into the hundreds of thousands of dollars. One legislator, whose insurance agency in New Orleans got the contracts for state vehicles and office buildings in the city, recalled that Earl "never threatened me, but there was always the implied threat that if I didn't cooperate, someone else would get the business." Similarly, Earl awarded contracts for the construction of buildings, the paving of roads, and innumerable other projects to political supporters. He also had at his disposal such functions as the purchasing of state supplies and equipment, the chartering of new state banks (free from the much more stringent federal regulations), the investment of idle state funds, the issuance of building and health permits, the advertising of state business, the leasing of state mineral lands, and a variety of other operations.[18]

With a deserved reputation as an expert in wheeling and dealing, Earl Long proved a surprisingly efficient administrator of state government. State officials such as the superintendent of education, the state auditor, the commissioner of agriculture, and others learned quickly that Earl ran their offices. "If you wanted something done," a former Highway Department official said, "you went straight to Earl, no matter how small and trivial it might be. He knew every pothole in every road in the state." Contemporaries still marvel at his ability to maintain a constant watch over the expenditure of virtually every cent of the state budget and at his encyclopedic knowledge of the intricacies of state government. Typically, he had a disdain for bureaucratic red tape, and when a problem arose, he handled it personally. Senator Sammy Downs remembered one occasion when an elderly constituent lost her old-age pension check: "I called Earl, and she got a new check in the mail the next day. Today, she would have to fill out two hundred forms and wait three months." Representative W. L. "Buddy" Napper of Lincoln Parish, who voted against the tax increases, remembered how he could still get favors just by picking up the phone and calling "Ole Earl." Long would often conduct unannounced, spur-of-the-moment tours of the state to check on projects and to see what work needed to be done. He also spent countless hours on the telephone, calling people all over the state to keep current with local matters. An example of Earl's attention to details came when Dr. Edwin A. Davis, a renowned LSU historian, asked Earl for money for a state archives. Without even referring to the budget, Earl instantly agreed that the state would provide the funds.[19]

Earl often combined political control with clever ways of accomplishing his goal of providing assistance to needy people. One unique device he invented was for the many young people from poor families who could not afford to go to college, even with the extremely low tuition rates then prevailing. Earl thought of the legislative scholarship. Each member of the legislature received a number of vouchers worth $25, $50, and $100 to give to the sons and daughters of constituents. These vouchers could be used at state colleges and universities for the payment of tuition, room and board, books, etc. To get a "scholarship," a person simply went to his legislator and collected the voucher on the spot. "It saved a hell of a lot of paperwork," remarked Representative George Tessier, "and it helped a lot of poor kids go to college. The $25 or $50 made the difference between being able to afford books and lunch for them."[20]

Although Earl Long insisted that he always adhered to the law in his political dealings, the evidence demonstrates otherwise. During his second full term as governor, Long again cooperated with organized crime in gambling and vice operations, and he engaged in numerous acts of political corruption. As soon as he became governor in 1956, Long approved the reopening of gambling casinos in Jefferson Parish, and slot machines, bingo, and keno parlors were flourishing in New Orleans. An FBI investigation revealed that Long received regular payoffs from gamblers throughout southern Louisiana. In Calcasieu Parish, for example, an FBI report noted, gamblers were paying $50 to $100 apiece to politicians, "with Governor Long receiving his share." In St. Landry Parish, Long's ally Sheriff Cat Doucet reopened the large number of cathouses between Krotz Springs and Opelousas, "with Long receiving payoffs." Unlike Robert Kennon, who ordered the State Police to rigorously enforce antigambling laws, Earl Long instructed them to "patrol the highways," leaving that enforcement to parish authorities. Since many of the local officials had a vested interest in maintaining gambling, enforcement remained lax. Jefferson Parish Sheriff William S. Coci quickly gained a reputation as a pawn of Carlos Marcello and a close ally of Governor Long.[21]

Despite his cooperation with organized crime, Long discovered that he could not reinstate the wide-open gambling that existed during his 1948–52 administration. The Kennon-Grevemberg crackdown on gambling had received widespread public support, and Long came under increasing pressure to enforce the laws against vice. Numerous citizens' groups and religious organizations joined together to force Long to do so. Leading newspapers attacked Long for his policies and demanded that he put the gamblers out of business. Long meekly responded that it was difficult to put an end to gambling because so many people engaged in the practice, but he reluctantly agreed to try to enforce the laws. By 1958, much of the gambling and vice had gone underground, and the casinos were beginning to lose money because of the rapid rise of legalized gambling in Las Vegas. Nevertheless, Long continued to cooperate with the illegal gambling industry in Louisiana, and for the rest of his governorship, the FBI would find instances of that connection. In one report, the bureau discovered that a "satchel man [carries] gambling graft" from the Marcello organization in Jefferson Parish to Baton Rouge and "delivers the graft money directly to Governor Long." In other investigative reports, the FBI also detailed Earl's personal addiction to betting on horse races with bookies all over the country, especially several notorious bookies in West Baton Rouge Parish, where Long regularly placed bets of $1,000 to $2,000 on horse races.[22]

The "Crime Survey" reports also contain elaborate documentation of innumerable acts of political corruption during Long's 1956–60 administration. One report stated that the Kenner Corporation, in which Long owned stock, paid Long $50,000 and three members of the Louisiana Racing Commission $15,000 each to reject a routine request by the Magnolia Racetrack in Kenner for a license to hold a racing season in 1956. Deprived of its revenue, the track would be forced into bankruptcy, and the Kenner Corporation would be able to buy it cheap. The following year, the track would reopen as the much larger and more profitable Jefferson Downs. From the available evidence, it is not possible to ascertain the accuracy of this report. The Kenner Corporation did purchase the Magnolia Racetrack and reopen it as Jefferson Downs, but the corporation's records do not reveal Earl Long as a stockholder, though Long may have used a dummy stockholder. The same FBI report also alleged that new-car dealers in New Orleans paid Long $10,000 to get a bill passed prohibiting used-car dealers from selling automobiles less than two years old. No such bill passed the legislature during Earl's term. That, of course, does not preclude the possibility of the bribe.[23]

The FBI accumulated evidence of Long's receiving payoffs from several sources within organized labor. It reported that the state AFL-CIO paid the governor $100,000 for his success in getting the right-to-work law repealed. In another report, the bureau accused the Bar Pilots Association and "several steamship companies" of paying the governor $100,000 to veto a bill allowing any qualified person to join the union. In yet another investigative report, the FBI stated that James R. "Jimmy" Hoffa, the notorious head of the Teamsters Union, gave Earl Long $250,000 to $300,000 "for his assistance in a labor strike at the ESSO Refinery in Baton Rouge." The report claimed that Earl buried the money beneath the support pillars of his house at the pea patch farm in Winnfield. These assertions cannot be substantiated through independent sources, but each does have partial verification. Although the $100,000 mentioned by the FBI appears far too high, several legislators have confirmed that organized labor spent large sums of money, channeled through Governor Long, to get right-to-work repealed. The report of the Bar Pilots Association bribe is partly confirmed by a story in the *Morning Advocate,* which stated that "federal agents were looking into . . . the veto of a Mississippi River Bar Pilots bill passed in 1956." Columnist Drew Pearson reported that Long had accepted a $5,000 bribe from a New Orleans steamship agent and lobbyist, Earl S. Billings, for vetoing a bill that would have increased the fees pilots could charge the shipping companies. Pearson's allegation was confirmed by Louis J. Roussel, who said that he had acted as the courier for the money. The most sensational of the FBI's accusations, that Jimmy Hoffa paid Earl Long a bribe of $250,000 to $300,000, hardly seems credible. Yet, it is known that the head of the Louisiana Teamsters, Edward Grady Partin, was a Hoffa intimate and a strong ally of Earl Long's. Interestingly, the strangest part of the FBI report, that Earl buried the money at his farm, may well be true. In 1962, two years after Long's death, the farm was destroyed in a fire, the cause of which has never been officially determined. In interviews, two close friends of Earl's, Clem Huffman, the manager of the pea patch farm, and Ernest S. Clements, a former Public Service commissioner, said that the fire was deliberately set by a disgruntled Long supporter whom Earl had failed to appoint to a promised position. When that person heard that Earl had "hundreds of thousands of dollars" buried at the farm, he torched the place, but he did not find any money.[24]

Among numerous other instances of Long's receiving payoffs, the FBI reported that Earl told a "racehorse tout" to pay him $5,000 before he would allow the legislature to issue a license to a finance company, that Long was paid $15,000 from "loan sharks and stock brokers," and that the governor charged $3,000 to pardon or to commute the sentence of an inmate at Angola. Shocked by the seemingly endless list, Hoover wrote to his main associate, Clyde W. Tolson, "Shouldn't we call to attn. of IRS some of the Louisiana deals of Governor Long?" Hoover did, in fact, notify the IRS of the information he had obtained, and the IRS conducted a lengthy probe into Long's finances. After Long's death, his estate settled with the IRS for $34,391.37 in back taxes and penalties for the period from 1956 to 1960. Hoover also wrote Attorney General William P. Rogers requesting that the Justice Department consider prosecuting Long for violating federal law, but the department concluded that Earl had not done so. So indignant did Hoover become about Long's shenanigans that when the governor asked him to speak at a Louisiana Health Council meeting in 1958, Hoover not only declined the invitation, he instructed the FBI not to let any future communications from Long reach his desk. At the bottom of Hoover's response to Long, the FBI file copy contains the interesting comments: "Gambling and vice rampant in Louisiana. Files also reflect that Governor Long is possibly mentally unbalanced and has been influenced in legislative matters by monetary payments . . . there are large-scale payoffs from racing officials and insurance kickbacks involving Governor Long." [25]

For the first three years of his second full term as governor, Earl Long remained in the public spotlight, but he did not attract undue attention. For the most part, his administration was dramatically less controversial than the previous one. In 1959, however, Long would more than compensate for his unusual reticence by engaging in a series of actions that would focus national attention on him. Those actions stemmed both from erratic personal behavior and from his stance on the increasingly volatile race issue.

10

The Politics of Race

Throughout his political career, especially in the late 1950s, Earl Long had become embroiled in the race issue. Long's programs of heavy state spending for health, education, and welfare provided many benefits for Louisiana's black citizens, and he recognized that they formed a potentially powerful voting bloc to add to the hardcore Long vote among poor whites and members of labor unions. In his 1948–52 administration, Long therefore substantially increased the size of the black vote in Louisiana by registering over 100,000 formerly disfranchised citizens, and they rewarded him by casting their ballots for him on election day. In his 1956–60 administration, however, Long found that his political opponents used his support for black voting rights and for other benefits to blacks as effective campaign tactics against him. Long fought back, refusing to give in to his opposition, even while the growing intensity of the race issue in the late 1950s threatened to destroy him politically.

Earl Long grew up in a state where both by law and by custom, blacks were victimized by a rigid caste system of racial segregation and discrimination. Public facilities, schools, churches, and cemeteries were segregated, and blacks were denied the right to vote, to hold public office, to serve on juries. In short, they possessed none of the privileges of American citizenship. Blacks were also denied the opportunity for economic and social independence, with the great majority destined to spend their lives in poverty and privation. Since blacks had no political power, white politicians campaigning for office customarily voiced their support for the continuation of these practices. Not even the great Huey, who generally eschewed race-baiting in his campaigns, dared to challenge the entrenched system of white hegemony.[1]

Earl Long shared the view universally held by white Louisianians that racial segregation afforded the only practicable means of maintaining a biracial social and political system. On numerous occasions throughout his career, Long spoke of his strong support for segregation, his belief in the superiority of the white race, and his opposition to civil rights for blacks. As a politician, Long did not hesitate to use whatever techniques he deemed necessary to win, and the exploitation of the race issue was one of them. In the 1948 gubernatorial campaign, Earl advised his Old Regular backers in New Orleans to spread racist propaganda against his opponent, Sam Jones, and against Jones's leading supporter in the city, Mayor deLesseps Morrison. One Long–Old Regular campaign broadside, widely distributed in lower-class white areas, appealed outright to racist sentiment: "WARNING TO THE WHITE PEOPLE OF NEW ORLEANS! Morrison betrays the white race! Mayor of New Orleans gives Negroes Equal Political and Social Rights! It is even reported that King Zulu [the monarch of the all-black Mardi Gras parade] will take Rex's place at the next Mardi Gras!" In that same race, Long's people spread doctored photographs of Morrison swimming in a public pool with blacks. In the 1951–52 gubernatorial campaign, Long used the race issue against Bill Dodd. In a circular letter mailed to hundreds of thousands of white voters, Earl called his lieutenant governor "a friend of the colored" and warned that if elected, Dodd would give blacks equal rights with whites. In the 1955–56 governor's race, Long again denounced Morrison for his racial moderation. One Earl Long circular advised white voters, "If you want your children to Attend School With Blacks, vote for Morrison." In that campaign, Earl publicly proclaimed his "one thousand percent support for segregation."[2]

When he became governor again in 1956, Earl Long responded to the growing white voter opposition to *Brown* v. *Board of Education of Topeka* (1954), in which the Supreme Court ruled unconstitutional state laws mandating racial segregation in public schools. That decision touched off a storm of defiance throughout the South, with white politicians trying to outdo one another in their public support for segregation. In both the 1956 and 1958 sessions of the legislature, Governor Long supported and signed into law several bills designed to expand racial discrimination. One law segregated all athletic and recreational facilities in Louisiana. Another required letters of "good moral character" for all high school graduates applying for admission to white colleges and universities, an obvious attempt to exclude black students from those institutions. Another measure suspended the compulsory school attendance law, thereby permitting white students to withdraw from any schools integrated under federal court order. A final segregationist act passed under Long "interposed" Louisiana's authority between the federal courts and the state's public schools. A favorite device of the advocates of states' rights, the doctrine of interposition was designed to give the governor the legal authority to block the integration of the public schools.[3]

Both privately and publicly, Earl frequently indulged in vicious racist remarks, and he ridiculed and disparaged blacks. Campaigning before black audiences, he often proclaimed, as he held up a smoked ham, "I want the biggest, blackest, ugliest nigger in the crowd to come up here and get this ham." At a press conference, he told a group of reporters, "Why, the colored have made the greatest progress of any race in history. A hundred years ago, they was eatin' each other." After stump appearances, when people came to greet him and shake his hand, Earl always kept his pockets stuffed with peppermint sticks. When a black person reached out for a handshake, Long would put a peppermint stick in his hand, "so I don't have to shake hands with them." In the Governor's Mansion, he often entertained white guests by having black servants dance "jigs" and perform "Stepin' Fetchit" routines, which stereotyped blacks as lazy, shiftless, and ignorant.[4]

Earl Long, then, could hardly be called a flaming liberal on the race question. Like virtually all whites, he supported racial segregation and maintained a firm belief in the superiority of the white race. Yet he gradually developed into one of the South's leading white defenders of the right of black citizens to receive certain benefits from state government and to have their political rights as voters protected by the state. Near the end of his career, Earl Long became the only significant southern political figure to champion the right of blacks to vote, and he defied the prevailing and growing racist element in Louisiana politics to publicly defend that right. Long's reasons for doing so were rooted both in his general political philosophy and in his assessment of the political situation in Louisiana.

Throughout his political career, Earl Long consistently advocated and implemented substantial increases in state spending on a variety of programs in health, education, and welfare aimed at providing the poor people of Louisiana with state assistance. Realizing that blacks formed the poorest, least educated, and most deprived class of people in the state, Long ensured that they would receive the benefits he promoted. From his boyhood experiences in Winn Parish and through his constant travels around the state, Earl witnessed firsthand the poverty, illiteracy, and deprivation that affected blacks and poor whites alike, and in his determination to help these people, he made no distinction between the races. "A poor man is a poor man," he told a friend, "it makes no difference what color he is." Since blacks were at the bottom of the economic scale, he realized that they would receive a disproportionate share of the benefits he enacted. The $50 monthly old-age pension program, for example, provided enormous assistance to elderly blacks, for it was the only source of income for many of them. Another Long program that blacks availed themselves of was welfare prescriptions, whereby poor people could obtain prescription drugs at no cost. Combined with his greatly expanded charity hospital system and a statewide network of free health clinics, Earl provided tens of thousands of blacks with free health care for the first time in their lives. Other social programs funded and administered by the state were aid to families with dependent children, aid to the needy blind, vocational training, and adult illiteracy programs. Of the total increase in state spending during Long's 1948–52 administration, during which period the state budget nearly tripled, over half went to Louisiana's blacks, who were slightly less than a third of the population.[5]

Earl sincerely believed that blacks deserved these benefits—and he also perceived the political advantages in this policy. Unlike most of his contemporary southern political leaders, Earl Long actively promoted the right of blacks to vote. Disfranchised since the late nineteenth century, Louisiana's blacks remained cut off from political power until Earl Long became governor in 1948. Not even Huey, who had abolished Louisiana's poll tax to win the votes of poor whites, dared register blacks. Only 22,572 blacks were registered to vote. Earl realized that blacks were the largest single potential voting bloc in the state, and a carefully nurtured program of registering them would increase the Long vote in elections. When combined with the historically hardcore Long support in the rural parishes and among labor unions, blacks would give the Long machine over 40 percent of the state vote at the outset of an election. Therefore, as soon as he became governor in 1948, Earl passed the word to parish registrars: sign up black voters. Until that time, the literacy test was used to prevent blacks from registering. To register to vote, a person had to read and interpret, to the satisfaction of the parish registrar of voters, a section of the United States Constitution, and not surprisingly, registrars disqualified those few blacks who even tried to take the test. If applied impartially, the literacy test would also have disqualified the many white applicants who were either illiterate or poorly educated. Of Louisiana's 885,439 registered white voters in 1948, there were 55,103 who were totally illiterate and marked their ballots with an X, but of the 22,572 registered blacks, only 275 were illiterate. With the literacy test and a historic southern tradition of intimidation, Louisiana systematically deprived blacks of the right to vote.[6]

This situation changed dramatically in 1948, when Earl Long became governor. Long's program of black voter registration during his 1948–52 administration has received scant attention from scholars. For example, the most comprehensive study of black voting rights in the postwar South ignores Earl Long—even though by the end of his first full administration, Louisiana had the largest number and the highest percentage of registered black voters in the South. Long's motivation was, of course, to sign up new Long voters, but the result was impressive. During the first two years of that administration, between 1948 and 1950, the number of white voters in Louisiana actually declined, from 885,439 to 756,356, while the number of registered blacks skyrocketed, from 22,572 to 61,675. By the end of his term, in 1952, Louisiana had 107,844 registered black voters, an increase of 85,272 since he took office. In 1948, blacks were only 2.4 percent of Louisiana's registered voters; by 1952, that figure had risen to 12.6 percent; and by the end of Long's second full term as governor, the figure was 15.6 percent. That Long brought about such a dramatic increase in the black electorate mainly to win votes for himself should not detract from this considerable achievement, coming as it did without any pressure from the federal government and over a decade before the Voting Rights Act of 1965.[7]

Perhaps the most substantial gains blacks made under Long's governorships were in education. During his eight years as governor, Louisiana witnessed the construction of fourteen new trade schools for blacks and over a hundred new public schools, the hiring of over two thousand new black schoolteachers, paid on an equal salary scale with white teachers, a 50 percent reduction in black illiteracy, and a tenfold increase in spending for black colleges. Dr. Ralph Waldo Emerson Jones, the longtime president of Grambling State University (then College), called Earl Long "the best friend Negro school children in Louisiana ever had. Sure, we had segregation then, but Governor Long did more for black school teachers and black students than any other governor." Characteristically, Earl employed unique methods to effect these educational gains for blacks. In 1948, he visited the Grambling campus, and Dr. Jones took him on a tour, pointing out all the areas that needed improvement. Afterwards, Jones and Long had an hour's private talk. Earl later told his nephew, "You know what? That black son of a bitch conned me out of a million dollars! *But he needed every penny of it!*" On another occasion, Earl visited the site of a north Louisiana state hospital that had recently been closed; he was to decide what to do with the furnishings, the buildings, and a prize herd of Jersey cows. When he arrived, Earl spotted Dr. Jones waiting for him. "Well, well," he exclaimed, "if it ain't Ralph Waldo Emerson himself. What do you want, Ralph?" Jones protested that he was just there to greet Long, but Earl retorted, "Hell, Ralph, I know you better than that. What do you want?" After praising Long for all the good things he did for Grambling, Jones said that "there is one more thing Grambling students need—it's milk for their breakfast cereal." Knowing that he had been hoodwinked, Earl said, "Take the damned Jersey cows, Ralph. They're yours."[8]

After the Supreme Court's school desegregation decision of 1954, the race issue intensified in Louisiana, as it did elsewhere in the South. As federal courts began to order the integration of public school districts in southern states, and as Dr. Martin Luther King's civil rights movement began to attract national attention, politicians all over the South used racist appeals to win election and to retain public support. Even Earl Long publicly endorsed racial segregation, and in 1956 and 1958, he signed several segregationist bills into law. Privately, however, he recognized and accepted the inevitability of integration. After President Eisenhower federalized the Arkansas National Guard in 1957 and used it to enforce a federal court decree at Little Rock's Central High School, Earl told a friend, "Well, that's it. The feds are behind the niggers. I'll be damned if I'll make a fool of myself like Faubus." Long believed, unlike Faubus, that resistance to federal authority was futile, an issue settled by the Civil War, and he had already taken several small steps to help Louisiana make the transition to the new age of racial equality. During his first full administration and in his second, Governor Earl Long quietly ordered the racial integration of several state colleges and universities, and some few black students were admitted to institutions in Baton Rouge, Lafayette, Hammond, and Thibodaux. The handful of blacks represented nothing more than token integration, and Earl doubtless would have preferred to let matters rest at that. But in 1958, he moved into a much more open position of support for racial equality.[9]

In late 1957, a federal court in New Orleans directed the New Orleans Public Service company to remove the racial barriers on its busses and streetcars by early 1958. In a rare display of cooperation, both Governor Long and Mayor Morrison urged compliance with the court order. The two men agreed that New Orleans should avoid the adverse publicity generated by the Montgomery, Alabama, crisis in 1955 and 1956. There, King led the city's blacks in an economic boycott of the downtown business area until the city authorities relented and desegregated the busses. In New Orleans, such a boycott would have devastated the local economy, as well as its national image, so Long and Morrison agreed to enforce the federal court order. Segregationist politicians in the legislature, however, tried to circumvent it. Plaquemines representative Gravolet sponsored a bill allowing a person in a seat on a bus or streetcar to decide who could sit next to him. Gravolet's bill passed the legislature, but Governor Long vetoed it as a ridiculous attempt to retain segregation in public transportation. Ironically, one of Long's enemies, Dr. Emmet L. Irwin, the head of the racist White Citizens Council of Greater New Orleans, praised the governor because the bill would have placed "respectable white ladies" in the intolerable position of having to ask the permission of Negroes to be seated. Long's veto ensured that New Orleans' busses and streetcars would be desegregated, and they were in 1958 without serious incident.[10]

During his campaign for governor in 1956, Earl Long promised to establish a branch of LSU in New Orleans. City residents favored the plan, which would enable many poor New Orleanians, who could not afford the cost of room and board at the Baton Rouge campus, to go to college. For many years, the powerful LSU lobby had blocked legislation that would establish the school because enrollment at the Baton Rouge campus would drop. In 1956, Earl kept his campaign promise by pushing through to enactment a bill creating Louisiana State University in New Orleans, with funds appropriated for the construction of buildings, the hiring of a faculty and staff, and other necessary costs of operation. As the site for the new campus, Earl selected an abandoned United States Navy base located on a choice piece of land adjoining Lake Pontchartrain, directly across Lakeshore Drive from the Pontchartrain Beach amusement park. The Orleans Levee Board had legal jurisdiction over the land, and Earl ordered the board to lease the land to the state for a nominal fee, but the Levee Board president, Louis J. Roussel, refused. Although Roussel had for years been a financial contributor to the Long machine, he and Earl had a falling out during a lobbying dispute in the 1956 legislative session. Roussel intended using his control over the Levee Board to thwart Earl's LSU-NO proposal, but he miscalculated. In characteristic fashion, Long fired Roussel and replaced him with businessman Claude W. Duke, and he got rid of the Roussel people on the board and replaced them too. The new board quickly complied with the governor's wishes, signing a ninety-nine-year lease, allowing the state to use the lakefront site for a total rental of one dollar. In June, 1958, the legislature appropriated $8.1 million for LSU-NO, and with remarkable speed, the new university opened its doors in September of that year.[11]

While LSU-NO clearly benefited the people of New Orleans, it also became part of the race issue. The federal courts obviously would not permit the state to establish a new, racially segregated university, so LSU-NO was officially open to all students regardless of race. To minimize the potential for racial unrest, Earl also had the legislature establish a branch of Southern University in New Orleans (SU-NO), less than a mile from the LSU-NO site. Earl intended that black students attend SU-NO and whites attend LSU-NO, thus maintaining segregation in practice, even though both institutions were integrated by law. No whites attended SU-NO, but more than two hundred black students joined over one thousand whites in registering for classes at LSU-NO. Thus, without meaning to, Earl Long had established the first public, state-supported university in the Deep South that admitted all students without regard to race. Other southern universities, including several in Louisiana, had integrated before LSU-NO, but they had done so only on a token basis. At LSU-NO, the two hundred black freshmen made that institution a fully integrated one. Earl Long doubtless would have preferred to open LSU-NO as a segregated university, but he accepted the fact that he was bound by federal court regulations, and he wanted to open the university because of the demonstrated need for it. Determined to make LSU-NO a quality institution, he provided it with a top-rank administration and faculty.[12]

As with his aggressive promotion of black voting rights, Earl Long has received virtually no recognition for his crucial role in enforcing the peaceful opening of a fully desegregated university. Civil rights scholars have discussed the violence that accompanied the admission of a single black, James Meredith, to the University of Mississippi in 1962, and they have praised such southern political leaders as Mayor William Hartsfield of Atlanta, who presided over the peaceful, token desegregation of some public schools in 1960. Several accounts treat the violence that marred the admission of only three black pupils to two previously all-white public schools in New Orleans in November, 1960. At that time, both Mayor deLesseps Morrison and Governor Jimmie Davis tried desperately to prevent integration, and they encouraged white parents to withdraw their children rather than let them attend school with blacks. At LSU-NO, the potential for serious racial violence clearly existed, with two hundred black students trying to register for classes and the White Citizens Council and other racist organizations publicly trying to disrupt the orderly beginning of school. Governor Earl Long, however, quickly put an end to any thoughts of violence. He graced the university's opening with his presence, and he spoke extemporaneously about the educational benefits it would bring to the city. Like Mayor Hartsfield, Governor Long placed educational necessity above personal racial views, and Long made it clear that he would use the power of the state to enforce the peaceful functioning of LSU-NO. To illustrate his message, he brought a contingent of state troopers with him to the campus, and their presence discouraged those who had intended to obstruct the registration process. Because of Long's actions, the first fully integrated public university in the Deep South held its first year of classes without a single incident of racial violence, and in ensuing years, LSU-NO continued to maintain its academic integrity and an integrated student body.[13]

Long's support for black voting rights, his providing black citizens with state benefits, and his enforcement of the nonviolent integration of busses and streetcars and LSU-NO gave his political opponents plenty of ammunition, and as the gubernatorial election campaign of 1959 approached, the anti-Longs decided to use the race issue to destroy Earl Long. By 1959, the segregationist faction in Louisiana politics had gained considerable strength. Such politicians as Leander Perez and State Senator Willie Rainach, who represented Claiborne and Bienville parishes, preyed on white prejudice. Rainach had been a prominent anti-Long legislator since his election to the house in 1940, and he became known as one of the most conservative members of the legislature. In 1954, Rainach had led the successful attempt to enact a right-to-work law, but it was as chairman of the Joint Legislative Committee on Segregation that he won public recognition. After the Supreme Court's *Brown* decision, the Kennon administration had the legislature establish the committee to preserve racial segregation in Louisiana. As chairman of the committee, Rainach held hearings and made speeches supporting segregation and denouncing the federal courts. After Earl Long became governor in 1956, Long reduced the committee's funding, so Rainach joined Leander Perez in using the White Citizens Councils as the chief organs of segregationist propaganda in the state. In 1958, Rainach served as national chairman of the Citizens Council of America. Also joining the segregationists were Representative Wellborn Jack of Shreveport, Mayor Jack Christian of Baton Rouge, and Mayor W. L. Howard of Monroe. These men were all prominent political opponents of Earl Long, and Long used his political muscle to hamper their efforts to stir up the race issue in Louisiana.[14]

By late 1958, this original group saw their cause become considerably more vital when many of the traditional anti-Long powers actively joined them. Such men as Sam Jones, Robert Kennon, Jimmie Davis, and de-Lesseps Morrison harbored ambitions for another run for governor in 1959, and they intended to exploit the race issue to win against the Long candidate. Their design took on an added measure of urgency when they heard rumors that Earl Long intended to resign as governor in 1959 so he could legally run for reelection. To block Long's plan, these anti-Long leaders decided that the governor's vulnerability on the race question, *i.e.,* his moderation, formed his greatest liability and that a united front (anti-Long and segregationist factions using race as their main campaign issue) would result in a Long defeat. Of all the anti-Longs, none proved as ambitious for statewide office as Chep Morrison, and his political maneuverings in the 1958–59 campaign provide an instructive commentary on the manner in which Louisiana politics at that time became consumed in the race issue.[15]

Elected to his fourth term as mayor in 1958, Chep Morrison had earned a reputation as a racial moderate. Cultivating the support of New Orleans' growing black community, Morrison had included blacks in many of his civic projects—new playgrounds, swimming pools, and gymnasiums, for example. The police and fire departments began hiring blacks, and other city departments increased the number of black employees. In return for these favors, blacks rewarded Morrison with their votes in all his mayoral campaigns. Within the city, this policy of racial moderation benefited Morrison politically, but outside New Orleans, it hurt him. When Morrison ran for governor in 1955–56, Earl Long branded him an integrationist, and in the rural areas of the state, Morrison was considered "soft" on race, a fatal political handicap. Morrison realized that to become governor in the 1959 election he would have to win over the segregationists. The mayor began adopting a much harder position on race, and he began actively courting the support of racist politicians. To demonstrate his commitment to the segregationist cause, Morrison publicly opposed many of Earl Long's legislative proposals, even those that benefited the city of New Orleans. A case in point was Long's program for establishing LSU-NO. Even though a New Orleans branch of LSU had for years been considered essential, Morrison strenuously fought against the proposal, and he instructed the CCDA delegation in the legislature to vote against the bill, and he used his influence with the city's press and business community to organize active opposition to LSU-NO. After Earl Long died, Dr. Homer Hitt, LSU-NO's first chancellor, praised his support of the university "despite the opposition of the New Orleans press, the Chamber of Commerce, and City Hall." Besides attacking LSU-NO, Morrison also tried to obstruct the integration of city recreation facilities, and he publicly denounced a federal court order mandating public school desegregation in New Orleans.[16]

Chep Morrison's political papers contain a large volume of manuscripts covering his efforts to gain the backing of the racist politicians in the 1959 governor's race. By the early spring of 1959, rumors flourished about Earl Long's plot to resign his office so he could run for governor in 1959. Long was sixty-three years old, and his health had deteriorated. The old trouper knew that he might not have another four years, so he decided to attempt a unique evasion of the constitutional prohibition against a governor's succeeding himself. By resigning as governor in 1959, Long would become eligible to run again, since under the state constitution, Lieutenant Governor Lether Frazar would take over as governor as soon as Long resigned. If Long won the election, he would be sworn in as governor in 1960 and, technically, would succeed Frazar.[17]

Apprehensive about Long's scheme, Morrison decided to join with the segregationists to defeat Long in the election. In the spring of 1959, he called a series of meetings around the state, with the purpose of "ultimately building a ticket." The first one was held at the Bellemont Hotel in Baton Rouge on April 7. Morrison met with Secretary of State Wade O. Martin, Jr., a staunch anti-Long, and with Representative John Garrett of Claiborne Parish, a prominent segregationist and a protégé of Willie Rainach's. They decided that future meetings should be held in April and May to form a united segregationist front against Earl Long before the legislative session convened in May. Two weeks later, on April 21, the second meeting took place at the Bentley Hotel in Alexandria, shortly after Earl publicly announced that he would indeed run for governor again. The participants included Morrison, Leander Perez, Jack Christian, Jack Howard, and Sheriffs Nicholas Trist of St. Bernard and Chester Wooten of Plaquemines. Agreeing strongly that attacking Long for his racial moderation afforded the best chance of defeating him, they discussed potential candidates for their slate. Morrison offered himself for governor, but Jack Howard argued that as a Catholic from New Orleans, Morrison could not carry north Louisiana, and he proposed Willie Rainach for governor and Morrison for lieutenant governor. The "Better Government Group," as Morrison called the participants, next met at the Bellemont Hotel on May 12, the day after the legislature convened. Morrison, Perez, Gravolet, Garrett, and others plotted to exploit the legislative session to draw public attention to Earl Long's vulnerability on the race issue. They unanimously agreed to support Rainach's purge of black voters to deprive Long of one of his largest voting blocs, thus forcing him to take a public stance on black voting rights.[18]

Earl Long had successfully defused the race issue in Louisiana, but his political opponents would bring it into the open in the gubernatorial campaign of 1959. Morrison, who for nearly two decades had denounced Long for his abuse of power and for his corrupt methods, now plunged into the depths of racial hatred to further his political prospects. In a revealing letter to Leander Perez, written on May 17, 1959, Morrison provided an insight into his campaign strategy: "I am making substantial and rather definite plans to make the race for governor. I would appreciate your support in getting Rainach, Trist, and Howard to back me. With a united front, I am sure that we can defeat Earl Long and *return good government to Louisiana*." Morrison thus linked support from the leading racist elements in Louisiana politics to the cause of "good government," the traditional slogan of the anti-Longs. It should be noted that despite his strenuous efforts to win the backing of the segregationists, Morrison ultimately failed. Leander Perez and others decided that the New Orleans mayor was too ambitious and headstrong, and they threw their first-primary backing to Willie Rainach. In the runoff, they rejected Morrison and supported the much more docile Jimmie Davis, who won the election.[19]

This concerted attack against Earl Long by anti-Long and segregationist politicians paled in comparison to Rainach's full-fledged effort to employ the race issue against Long in the legislative session of 1959. That session, which convened on May 11, became the most tumultuous since the impeachment session thirty years earlier: it featured Governor Earl Long's public outbursts against Rainach and other political opponents. And Earl's actions persuaded his family to have him committed to mental institutions in Texas and Louisiana. Those outbursts came when Rainach attempted to deprive black voters in Louisiana of the franchise. Willie Rainach had found what he considered the ideal vehicle that he could ride to victory in the governor's election. By 1959, Louisiana had over 150,000 registered black voters, the largest number in the South, the vast majority of whom were Earl Long supporters. By disfranchising these people, Rainach believed that he would drastically reduce Long's power and that he would place Long in the politically untenable position of having to defend black voting rights at a time when white sentiment was clearly leaning toward segregation. Taking advantage of his chairmanship of the Joint Legislative Committee on Segregation, Rainach had begun challenging the credentials of registered blacks in certain parishes. In 1958, for example, Rainach had actually tried to disfranchise Earl's black cook by personally challenging the legality of her registration at the Winn Parish courthouse. Earl himself called the parish registrar and ordered her not to remove any blacks from the rolls. When Rainach backed down, Earl mistakenly thought that the matter had ended. In fact, Rainach's campaign had just begun.[20]

New documentary evidence from declassified FBI files reveals that Rainach and the racist elements in Louisiana politics in 1959 intended nothing less than removing all blacks from the voter registration rolls across the state. An FBI memorandum of August 3, 1959, states that the "Civil Rights Commission has obtained secret minutes of the Louisiana White Citizens Council revealing plans to bar all Negroes from voting in

Louisiana. This is one factor behind the political battle over Governor Earl K. Long because Long has championed the right of Negroes to vote." Under state law, any two registered voters could challenge another person's legal qualifications to vote, and if an investigation turned up inaccuracies in his registration application, he would be removed from the rolls. A literal application of the law would mean that voters who had made even minor errors in spelling on their applications could be struck from the rolls. Since large numbers of white and black voters in Louisiana were either illiterate or had only a rudimentary education, many thousands of them had indeed made minor mistakes filling out the forms. Applied impartially, the law would have disfranchised hundreds of thousands of white voters, as well as blacks, but Rainach, of course, intended to purge only blacks. Between 1956 and 1959, with the connivance of friendly registrars, Rainach had succeeded in purging the names of 15,326 blacks. In Washington Parish, the number of registered blacks fell from 1,783 in 1956 to 241 in 1959; in East Feliciana Parish, it dropped from 1,349 to 70. As the legislative session opened in May, Rainach announced that the process would take place throughout the state.[21]

This purge placed Earl Long in an impossible political situation. If he allowed it to continue, he would lose tens of thousands of loyal supporters, but if he tried to stop it, he would leave himself wide open to attacks by the racists. Although he appreciated the considerable risks involved, Long did not hesitate to choose the latter. It is to his lasting credit that he opted, squarely and decisively, to defend the right of his black constituents to vote. To block the Rainach purge, Earl had several bills introduced in the legislature that prohibited the challenging of any voter whose name had been on the rolls for more than one year and that prohibited the removal of anyone who had made insignificant errors in registration. Long badly miscalculated the volatility of the race issue, especially in an election year, and in a rare legislative defeat, the senate rejected his bills by a vote of 19 to 13. One Longite senator remarked, "We just couldn't be seen as soft on the nigger question." Undeterred by the reversal, Earl had his house floor leaders tack the bills as amendments on another measure dealing with assistant voter registrars. The amended bills were scheduled for a public hearing before the "B" section of the House Judiciary Committee on May 26, and when the names of both Willie Rainach and Earl Long were listed among those testifying, spectators jammed the gallery. Heavily pro-Rainach, the audience cheered when the senator from Summerfield launched a racist diatribe, the content of which would set the tone for much of the political campaign of 1959: "Our registration laws are based not on education, but on intelligence, something that is bred into people for thousands of years. It's been bred into the white people of this world."[22]

Earl Long and his supporters shot back at Rainach. At considerable personal political risk, a pro-Long committee member, Representative Ben Holt of Alexandria, informed Rainach that "you've got to let them vote. A colored man is still a man—a human being with a soul like you and I have. You can't kick him around like a farm animal!" When Governor Earl Long appeared before the committee, one of the most dramatic incidents in the history of the Louisiana legislature occurred. Anticipating the usual dose of Long humor, the committee and the gallery were shocked when Long suddenly began cursing and shouting. Pacing back and forth, taking swigs from a Coke bottle filled with heavily spiked grape juice, Earl screamed at the committee members and erupted into a torrent of graphic obscenity, a tirade that embarrassed many of the spectators, whose numbers included some nuns and grammar-school children. State Board member Joe Waggonner of Plain Dealing apologized for Long's behavior and told him: "I've heard it said you were sick, but since I've been here this morning, I've been able to diagnose you as sick. If I've ever seen a man in my life with constipation of the brain and diarrhea of the mouth, you're that man." Brushing aside Waggonner's chastisement, Long continued his irrational behavior, denouncing Rainach for his racist remarks and adding, "That goes for people that sleep with them at night and kick them in the street in the daytime." To one committee member, he yelled, "I can interrupt that bastard any time I want!" and he claimed that it was better to say "damn" than to "sleep with a nigger woman at night!" Finally finishing his incredible performance, Long stalked out, and the committee formally voted to reject his bills.[23]

The following night, Earl Long appeared before a joint session of the entire legislature to apologize for his behavior and for his vulgarity at the committee hearing. Instead, he repeated the amazing performance in even more remarkable fashion and was soon whisked off to a mental asylum. The sensational publicity surrounding Long's breakdown has obscured the immediate events that touched off this most spectacular episode in his life, and in a broader sense, it has also obscured Long's role in the racial turmoil in the South in the late 1950s. A summary of that role is appropriate, for it covers a significant chapter in the recent history of Louisiana.

T. Harry Williams wrote that in his defense of black voting rights, Earl Long "said some brave things that needed to be said and in so doing he opened up a new vista in Louisiana and southern politics—he showed that the segregation issue could be and should be frankly discussed." Virtually every southern political leader, including such "statesmen" as Lyndon Johnson, Sam Rayburn, and J. William Fulbright, was trying to out-perform his rivals in proclaiming his defense of racial segregation and of the superiority of the white race. Earl Long, however, publicly chal-lenged one of the foundations of white political hegemony in the South, that southern blacks could not vote. Long courageously stood up to and defied the racists; championing the right of blacks to vote would, he knew, cost him substantial numbers of white votes. In short, Earl Long placed human rights above political expediency. What can one say about Long's opponents, men like Chep Morrison and Jimmie Davis, and about their editorial backers, the *Times-Picayune* and the *Morning Advo-cate,* who had so often promoted the cause of "reform" and "good gov-ernment"? These politicians and these newspapers supported Rainach's purge and denounced Long. The jockeying for position in the upcoming governor's race, in which "nigger baiting" would become a prominent theme, would produce a strange alliance between the advocates of decent and honest government and the racial bigots.[24]

It should be emphasized that Earl Long could in no sense be consid-ered a supporter of civil rights for black citizens. He was a segregationist himself, and at no time did he favor such changes as the desegregation of public facilities and equal employment opportunity. And it needs to be repeated that his defense of black voting rights stemmed from the fact that blacks voted for him; he wanted blacks to remain registered because he needed their votes. Yet Long also saw that the era of racial segregation was coming to an end, that the federal government's enforcing Court-ordered desegregation inevitably meant the demise of the Jim Crow sys-tem. Rather than stir up popular prejudices and passions and engage in futile gestures to resist the era of civil rights, Long believed that it was in Louisiana's best interest to accommodate itself to that era. In a famous remark to Leander Perez, Earl summarized his eminently practical attitude toward the civil rights question: "Whatchya gonna do now, Leander? The feds have got the atom bomb." So he peacefully opened the integrated

LSU-NO, preserved the right of blacks to vote, and generally blocked all attempts by the racists to obstruct desegregation. Interestingly, even though his bills were defeated in the legislature, Long used his political muscle to stop Rainach in his tracks, and the purge of black voters came to an abrupt end. Within the context of the time in which he lived, Earl Long can justifiably be called the first prominent southern politician to confront head-on what one historian called the "central problem of southern history," the race issue.[25]

11

"Just Plain Crazy"

On June 15, 1959, *Time* magazine solemnly reported that "the fact was clear: Earl Long had just gone plain crazy." The local press concurred in *Time*'s diagnosis. The Shreveport *Journal* entitled an editorial "Earl Long—Louisiana's Disgrace" and indignantly declared that "there are no words strong enough to indict Governor Earl K. Long for the shame and humiliation he has brought upon Louisiana and the entire South." The Baton Rouge *Morning Advocate* agreed, predicting that "for Long to continue in office can bring chaos from which the state may take years to recover." In countless articles and editorials, newspapers and magazines in Louisiana and across the nation voiced similar sentiments, depicting Governor Long as mentally unstable and clearly unfit to retain his office. Almost without exception, their conclusion was that the people of Louisiana had finally gotten what they deserved for electing Longs to political office.[1]

The occasion for the adverse publicity was Earl Long's famous "mental collapse" in May, 1959. During an address before a joint legislative session, Long had spoken incoherently and irrationally, personally denouncing his political opponents and launching into outbursts of obscenities. After speaking extemporaneously for an hour and a half, Long could not continue and had to be escorted from the podium. Taken to the Governor's Mansion, he was confined to an upstairs bedroom, with two burly hospital attendants as guards. After consulting with family members and with physicians, Long's estranged wife, Blanche, sister Lucille, and his nephew, Russell, decided to have him committed to a mental institution. The following morning, Long was flown in a Louisiana National Guard airplane to Galveston, Texas, where he was admitted to the Titus Harris Psychiatric Clinic of John Sealy Hospital, a respected facility that had agreed to admit him. After spending over two weeks at the Galveston facility, Earl secured his release by filing a habeas corpus lawsuit against Blanche and by promising to undergo treatment at the Ochsner Foundation Hospital near New Orleans. The governor did indeed go to Ochsner's, but he stayed only a few hours and departed for Baton Rouge. Upon learning of his action, Blanche notified the East Baton Rouge Parish coroner to draw up the legal papers necessary to have her husband committed to a state mental institution. When Earl reached the East Baton Rouge Parish line, he was met by sheriff's deputies, who transported him to the parish courthouse. After a perfunctory psychiatric examination, he was forcibly and involuntarily taken to Mandeville in St. Tammany Parish, where he was committed to the Southeast Louisiana Hospital. Earl remained in Mandeville for nine days, during which time he had his attorney, Joe Arthur Sims, file a separation suit against Blanche, thereby legally preventing her from recommitting him. Earl then fired the head of the state Hospital Board, Jesse H. Bankston, and replaced him with a friend, Charles Rosenblum. Rosenblum persuaded the board to fire the acting superintendent at Mandeville, Dr. Charles H. Belcher, and hire Dr. Jess H. McClendon. A close friend of Earl's, Dr. McClendon immediately ordered him released from Mandeville. In a highly publicized court hearing in nearby Covington, Judge Robert Jones ruled that Governor Long could no longer be legally confined in the institution and was therefore a free man. After resting for a few days in Covington, Earl opened his campaign for governor on July 4, but he appeared weak and tired, so he went to his pea patch farm in Winnfield for a week's rest. Then he embarked on an eighteen-day tour of several western states and Mexico.[2]

The events of May 26 through July 29, 1959, served to underscore the general perception of Earl Long as a crazy old man unfit to continue as governor and as a definite candidate for the insane asylum. Certainly, many of Long's actions during that two-month period seemed to justify the verdict. On two consecutive days, he made public appearances in the legislature, where he screamed, shouted, cursed, and behaved in a decidedly irrational manner. At the Governor's Mansion, he flew into a violent rage, breaking furniture and windows and shouting "Murder!" from his bedroom window. At Mandeville, he became violent and threatened administrators and staff. On his western tour, he bet thousands of dollars on horse races, openly visited notorious night spots, covered his head with a pillowcase, cursed newspaper reporters, and engaged in other out-landish acts. Not surprisingly, the press devoted considerable attention to these most atypical actions by the governor of a state, and Earl Long be-came the object of derision and ridicule. The titles of some of the na-tional magazine articles written about him suggest the thrust of their content: "Louisiana Melee," "Strange Behaviors," "His Worst Enemy," "A Portrait of Earl Long at the Peak of His Crack-Up," "Still More Trouble for Ol' Earl Long," "Louisiana Ruckus," "State in a Stew."[3]

Over a quarter century later, the events surrounding Earl Long's "men-tal breakdown" and confinement at the institutions remain the subject of speculation, sensationalism, and confusion. No objective scholarly ac-count of these two remarkable months in Long's life has been written, and the journalistic studies suffer from a lack of objectivity and from their authors' tendency to focus on the colorful and the spectacular. For the first time, a serious, accurate account based on the most reliable evidence is presented here. To understand the events of May, June, and July of 1959, it is necessary to investigate Long's personal life prior to those events, for that way of life proved responsible for his collapse.

From the time they were married in 1932 until 1958, Earl and Blanche Long had, by all accounts, a happy marriage. Although they had no chil-dren, a personal disappointment to Earl, their relationship was a close one. Blanche Long had been a steadying influence on her husband. After they were married, Blanche managed to restrain Earl from indulging in alcohol, and she took care of the family finances. She also provided sound political advice, helping Earl avoid some of the mistakes that plagued his early career. On the campaign trail and in the corridors of the legislature, Blanche turned into one of Earl's most capable political assistants, and as the governor's wife, she presided over official dinners and social functions with grace and style. When Earl suffered a major heart attack in 1950, Blanche nursed him back to good health, and she persuaded him to give up cigarettes. At her urging, he was baptized in the Baptist faith, and for several years, Earl and Blanche regularly attended First Baptist Church in Baton Rouge.[4]

During Earl's second full term as governor, this close marital relation-ship steadily deteriorated until he and Blanche stopped living together. A lady of genteel upbringing, Blanche had never grown accustomed to Earl's habitual earthiness and crudeness. She loved fine clothes, food, and furnishings; he retained his passion for the simple life. On his numerous visits to the pea patch farm, which grew more frequent in the late 1950s, Earl constantly appalled Blanche by donning coveralls and heading into the fields to hoe cotton or plant corn. She was shocked at the sight of her husband, the Governor of Louisiana, caked with blood and drenched with sweat after slaughtering some of his hogs. According to Clem Huffman, who managed the farm, Blanche often visited there with Earl, but she did not disguise her dismay at seeing him behave like a "common country farmer." Try as she might, Blanche could not break Earl of some of his crude habits, such as spitting on the carpet and lounging around in various stages of undress.[5]

In 1959, Earl explained the situation between Blanche and him to Blaze Starr: "Honey, I'm married . . . but my marriage has been very miserable. My wife, Miz Blanche, is one of those high-society women. She's all the time telling me what I should do and what I shouldn't do. And it is just getting on my nerves. . . . We haven't slept together in over two years." This, of course, was Earl's highly colored version. In fact, Blanche made strenuous efforts to keep the marriage from collapsing, but Earl resisted her. During 1958, his health declined—he lost weight and began to eat irregularly. Going for days without sleep, he seemed to be stretching himself beyond the limits of physical endurance, and he refused to listen to Blanche's advice to slow down. Instead, Earl drove himself even harder, and toward the end of the year, he began drinking heavily, and he started smoking again. The final break came when Blanche's dream house was completed. For years, she had wanted to live in a large, comfortable home, and in 1957, Earl finally allowed her to plan it. Blanche threw herself into the project with enthusiasm, personally supervising almost every phase of the construction and spending many hours selecting carpeting, wallpaper, and furnishings. The house, completed in late 1958, was located on Baton Rouge's "millionaires' row," fronting on the lake near the capitol. The $150,000 home had 4,433 square feet of living space and featured elaborate decorations and exquisite furniture. After it was finished, Earl took one look and said, "It's too big," and returned to the Governor's Mansion. Blanche moved into the new house in February, 1959.[6]

With Blanche gone, Earl seemed to lose all semblance of self-control, and during the first five months of 1959, his pace was hectic and his way of life wild. One close friend remarked that during this time, "Earl was trying to act like an eighteen-year-old boy who had just left the family farm and had discovered New Orleans for the first time." A relative said that

"Earl behaved like a kid brought up by strict Baptist parents who had never seen a cigarette, a bottle of whiskey, or a loose woman in his life." Almost every night, Earl would order a state trooper to drive him at breakneck speed to the French Quarter in New Orleans, where he frequented almost all the night spots. Typically, Earl would enter a nightclub, sit at a table near the stage, and drink heavily while he enjoyed the floor shows, staying until the last performance was over, at two or three o'clock in the morning. Then he would return to Baton Rouge, catch a couple of hours' sleep, and awaken at six o'clock. Skipping breakfast, he began drinking as he scoured the racing spreadsheets and placed his bets on the horses. This pace naturally exhausted the sixty-three-year-old Long, and to keep going, he started consuming huge quantities of Dexedrine.[7]

Bourbon Street regulars grew accustomed to seeing the governor's black Cadillac limousine or a state police car parked outside one of the French Quarter's fleshpots. Phil Johnson, then a television reporter, remembered one occasion when Earl's car was parked on Bourbon Street. He and several other reporters heard grunts and groans coming from inside a "house." After an especially loud shriek by a female, Earl's state police chauffeur knocked on the door and inquired whether he was all right. Red with rage, a disheveled Long opened the door and bellowed, "You stupid ass! I told you to come to get me if *I* screamed, not if *she* screamed!" One night Earl was making his usual rounds of the French Quarter, and he entered the Sho-Bar, which featured the striptease artist Blaze Starr. Earl watched her perform and immediately fell in love. "He was mad for her," the club's owner said. "He came back nearly every night for two weeks." Earl and Blaze soon started dating, and she visited him at the Governor's Mansion, the pea patch farm, and his Roosevelt Hotel suite. Naturally, the story of the sixty-three-year-old state governor openly consorting with a twenty-three-year-old stripper made good newspaper copy, and the New Orleans and Baton Rouge press began publicizing Earl's escapades with the young woman. With justification, Earl raged at the newspapers for sensationalizing his private foibles while carefully avoiding those of such favorites of the urban press as Chep Morrison. The governor, however, had himself primarily to blame. As a public official, he should have realized that the press would publicize his exploits, especially since he made no attempt to keep them private. An example came at the Kentucky Derby of 1959. Governor Earl Long showed up at Louisville's Churchill Downs with much fanfare and drew attention to himself by betting thousands of dollars on the races and by sitting in his box with attractive young women on each knee. Shortly before his outbursts, Earl flew to Atlanta in a National Guard airplane and returned to Baton Rouge with a cargo of "entertainers," a bevy of strippers he had procured in the Georgia capital to amuse his guests at a wild party he threw in the Governor's Mansion.[8]

The excessive drinking and smoking, the ingestion of inordinate quantities of Dexedrine, and the frantic pace all took their toll on Governor Long, and by the time the legislature convened on May 11, 1959, friends and political associates were shocked by his appearance. Earl seemed to age ten years in less than six months, and he behaved oddly and talked incoherently at times. To those who knew Earl, it came as no surprise that he had acted in such a shocking manner before the House Judiciary "B" Committee. After his performance at the committee hearing, Earl realized that he had made a serious mistake, not only by offending the public, but also by alienating key legislators whose support he needed for getting bills passed and for the upcoming governor's race. The evening of May 25 saw Earl and close political advisors gathered at the Mansion discussing his best means of making amends, and they decided that a public address to a joint session of the legislature, in which Earl would read a carefully prepared apologetic speech, would minimize the political damage. So, the following evening, May 26, the house and senate assembled in the house chamber to hear the governor apologize. Because of all the adverse publicity he had received, large numbers of newspaper reporters and television cameras were ready to record his message. If Earl had listened to the advice of his friends and had read the address exactly as typed, he could have gained widespread popular admiration for his statesmanlike manner.[9]

"The minute he started to talk," Gaston Ducote, Earl's intimate associate, recalled, "I knew we were in trouble." The reason for Ducote's concern was that Earl started speaking extemporaneously and quickly forgot about the printed speech, which he had set aside on the lectern. "Once Earl got started talking," his cousin David Bell, said, "you never knew what he would say because he would say anything that popped into his head." On the night of May 26, 1959, Earl K. Long, still feeling the effects of the alcohol and drugs he had consumed shortly before he went to the capitol, erupted: his outburst lasted an hour and a half and would gain national attention. Ranting and raving, Earl shouted and screamed at individual legislators; his rambling, incoherent words could hardly be termed a speech. Pounding his fist on the lectern, pointing his finger at legislators, he lashed out at those who opposed him politically. When it seemed that he could no longer stand the physical strain, he suddenly grew subdued and reflective, reminiscing about his boyhood days in Winnfield. Then, spying a hostile politician, he would become excessively loud and belligerent. On several occasions, friends tried to restrain him, but he brushed them off and continued his tirade. Ordinarily, in public, Earl would not curse, but on this night, he did. Spotting Representative Frank Fulco of Shreveport, one of his opponents, Earl called him a "damn Dago." When he saw Willie Rainach, he told the story of Rainach's uncle who was killed by an outraged black man who caught him in bed with his wife. Rainach, the members of his Joint Legislative Committee on Segregation, and William Shaw, the committee's counsel, came in for especially vivid attacks. On occasion, Earl regained his composure and spoke calmly and eloquently about the race issue, and he displayed flashes of his legendary sense of humor. In one of the classic remarks he made, Earl told the legislature that "after all this is over," Rainach will "probably go up there to Summerfield, get up on his front porch, take off his shoes, wash his feet, look at the moon, and get close to God." Then, after a lengthy pause, Earl stared at Rainach and, pointing at him, shouted, "And when you do, you got to recognize that niggers is human beings!" After an hour and a half of nonstop harangue, Earl visibly weakened, and the legislature's sergeant at arms finally managed to persuade him to stop. House Speaker Robert Angelle, Earl's aide, Gaston Ducote, and reporter Maggie Dixon of the *Morning Advocate* helped him to walk out of the chamber.[10]

Earl was rushed to the Governor's Mansion, where he was locked in a second-floor bedroom. Concerned about Earl's mental and physical health, several Long family members, along with trusted political advisors, were at the Mansion to decide on a course of action. Present at the extraordinary gathering were Blanche Long; Russell Long; Lucille Long Hunt, Earl's sister; Dr. Arthur Long, Earl's cousin; John Hunt, Lucille's son; Victor Bussie, the Louisiana labor leader; and Gaston Ducote. They all agreed that Earl needed immediate psychiatric attention, a decision reinforced by Earl's behavior after being locked in the bedroom. He grew violent and irrational, ripping the front of his bed from the frame, throwing a bottle of milk of magnesia and an ashtray through a window, then standing at the broken pane and shouting "Murder!" Two hospital attendants who were acting as guards rushed into the room and restrained him until family members talked to him and he calmed down. At a family conference, Dr. Arthur Long said that Earl suffered from manic depressive psychosis, with a tendency to violence, and that they should commit him to an asylum. At first, the family wanted to commit him to the Southeast Louisiana Hospital in Mandeville, but under Louisiana law, he would still remain governor. So, after lawyers told them that committing him to an out-of-state asylum would not leave them liable to kidnapping charges, the family decided on a psychiatric clinic in Galveston, Texas.[11]

The following morning, May 27, Lucille told Earl that he was going to be taken to a hospital in New Orleans for treatment, but Earl protested. So Dr. Long injected him with two doses of sedatives, but the medication had no effect. Earl screamed that he would not allow them to take him to a hospital. Unable to persuade Earl to come quietly, the family had him strapped to a hospital stretcher and brought downstairs to a state police station wagon. Then Earl was driven to the airport, where he was placed in a National Guard airplane and flown to Galveston. In the meantime, Russell Long addressed the legislature and informed the lawmakers that Earl had had a breakdown and needed an extended period of rest. With Earl in Texas, Lieutenant Governor Lether Frazar became acting governor, a situation that Russell said might last "for a considerable period of time."[12]

On the morning of May 30, 1959, Governor Earl K. Long of Louisiana was formally admitted to the Titus Harris Psychiatric Clinic of John Sealy Hospital in Galveston. At the entrance to the clinic, Long informed Dr. Titus Harris, the facility's director, that he was there against his will, and he insisted that he did not require treatment. Long was not the first governor to be treated at Sealy, but unlike the others, whose confinements remained closely guarded secrets, Long's stay was inordinately publicized. A circus atmosphere became part of an already sensational case. In general, Earl was a cooperative patient and allowed the hospital staff to administer a battery of psychiatric and physical examinations, but, understandably, he wanted to be released, and he threatened his wife and his nephew with lawsuits, charging that they had kidnapped him across state lines against his will. Because kidnapping was a federal offense,

Russell Long called the FBI to try to ensure that the bureau would not attempt to conduct a criminal investigation. Satisfied through his political connections in Washington that the Justice Department would not prosecute them, Russell called Blanche and told her to sign the necessary legal papers for an extended commitment. Blanche did so, and Earl remained at Sealy for a total of seventeen days. Biding his time, Earl visited and chatted with other patients, and he received visitors, who smuggled in cigarettes and whiskey to him. He calmed down considerably after Lucille arrived and cooked him a meal of fried catfish, mustard greens, cornbread, and huckleberry pie.[13]

In signing the papers for a formal confinement, Blanche had requested a sanity hearing to determine whether or not Earl was capable of making rational judgments. Earl countered with a formal petition for a habeas corpus hearing to determine whether he was being held against his will, and he signed the document "Earl K. Long, governor in exile, by force and kidnapping." The habeas corpus petition had legal priority over the sanity petition, and a formal hearing was scheduled for June 17. On that date, Major General Raymond A. Hufft, the adjutant general of the Louisiana National Guard, testified that Long had indeed been forcibly and involuntarily taken to Galveston. Judge L. D. Goddard announced that he would render his decision in one week. Earl had a solid legal case, for he had clearly been transported across the state line against his will, and Blanche began having second thoughts. If Judge Goddard ruled in Earl's favor, as appeared likely, Earl would have to be set free immediately, and the sanity hearing could not be held. Earl would then return to Louisiana as governor, and, as one politician remarked, "all hell would break loose." Of greater concern to Blanche was Earl's repeated threat to sue her and Russell for kidnapping. To avert this possibility, Blanche had intermediaries arrange a deal with Earl. In return for his agreement to receive proper medical attention in Louisiana, she would withdraw the sanity petition. Always careful, Blanche also had Earl sign a statement releasing from legal liability all persons responsible for his abduction and confinement. The withdrawal of the sanity petition meant that Earl could no longer be legally confined in Galveston, and on June 17, a National Guard plane flew him to New Orleans. A police car took Earl from the airport directly to the Ochsner Foundation Hospital in Jefferson Parish for medical consultation. Earl had promised Blanche that he would undergo treatment there, but once he arrived, it became apparent that he had no intention of keeping the promise. For over three hours, Ochsner physicians pleaded with the governor, but Earl claimed that he could obtain the rest he needed in Baton Rouge and at his pea patch farm. Blanche begged Ochsner officials to confine Long there, but the hospital's attorney informed her that the institution had no legal grounds for detaining him, and Earl left Ochsner's in the late afternoon.[14]

Upon learning of her husband's decision, Blanche Long telephoned Dr. Chester Williams, the coroner of East Baton Rouge Parish, and told him to prepare the legal papers required to have Earl committed to a state mental institution. Then she drove to Baton Rouge, arriving there before he did, so she could ensure that all preparations necessary for his second confinement had been made. Dr. Williams had done as Blanche requested, and he took the precaution of going to a prominent anti-Long judge, Fred S. LeBlanc, to get court approval for the committal papers. Then Williams called Dr. Sparkman Wyatt, a Baton Rouge psychiatrist, to meet him at the East Baton Rouge courthouse for a lunacy hearing. Williams also directed that sheriff's deputies stop the governor's car at the parish line and take him directly to the courthouse basement. After leaving Ochsner's, Earl got into a state police car and headed for Baton Rouge. When the vehicle reached East Baton Rouge Parish, sheriff's deputies stopped it and drove the car into the city. Thinking that he was being treated to a cordial homecoming by local officials, Earl relaxed, but when he realized that he was going not to the Governor's Mansion but to the courthouse, he loosed a torrent of obscenities. As the car entered the basement parking garage of the courthouse, Earl refused to leave the vehicle.[15]

At about 6:30 P.M., on June 18, 1959, there occurred in the parking garage of the East Baton Rouge Parish courthouse what surely must rank as one of the most extraordinary lunacy hearings ever. Serving as a court-appointed lunacy commission, Doctors Chester Williams and Sparkman Wyatt climbed into the back seat of the state police car and conducted a forty-five-minute examination of Governor Earl K. Long. Throughout the interview, Long screamed and cursed, leading Wyatt to diagnose his condition as "paranoid schizophrenia with cycles of manic-depressive activity." The two physicians then recommended Long's commitment to a mental asylum, and Judge LeBlanc signed the formal court order for the committal. Against his will, Earl was driven to the Southeast Louisiana Hospital in Mandeville, a small town bordering Lake Pontchartrain. By the time he arrived, Governor Long was in an absolute fury. Upon entering the hospital, he was greeted by Dr. Charles H. Belcher, the facility's acting superintendent, who said, "How do you do, governor? I'm Dr. Belcher." Instantly, Earl blurted his reply, "The hell you are! You *were* Dr. Belcher!" Stripped naked and locked in solitary confinement, Long cursed the hospital staff and threatened to fire all of them. Later, he said of his confinement, "When I got there, I wasn't wearing enough clothes to cover a red bug, and when I left, I was enjoying the same wardrobe." He also complained about being "stuck with hypodermics and harpoons."[16]

The pandemonium at Mandeville generated repercussions in Baton Rouge, for no one seemed to know the exact status of the executive branch of the Louisiana state government. The state constitution stipulated that the lieutenant governor would become the state's chief executive if the governor were "incapacitated," but Lieutenant Governor Lether Frazar adamantly refused to betray his close friend, Earl Long. With an eye to the upcoming state elections, Attorney General Jack P. F. Gremillion ruled that Earl's confinement at Mandeville rendered him officially unable to carry out the duties of his office, but Secretary of State Martin refused to sign the papers authorizing Lieutenant Governor Frazar to serve as acting governor. Martin's motive was political revenge for Earl Long's having practically destroyed the powers of his office in 1956. By refusing to allow Frazar to take over as governor, Martin hoped that the courts and the Mandeville authorities would be forced to have Long declared legally insane, thus ending his political career, but the scheme backfired. Martin thought that after Long was declared legally insane, a special legislative session would convene to impeach Long and remove him from office. Frazar, however, remained loyal to his friend and told Martin that even if he were officially recognized as acting governor, he would not under any circumstances call a special session to impeach Long. Thus, Martin, by refusing to sign the state papers making Frazar acting governor, effectively allowed Earl Long to remain governor throughout his stay in Mandeville.[17]

Physically exhausted and emotionally drained, Earl Long nevertheless retained enough of his mental faculties to concoct an ingenious plan whereby he would secure his release. Distrusting his regular attorney, Theo Cangelosi, Earl called a close friend, Joe Arthur Sims, a lawyer from Hammond, and told him to come to Mandeville right away. Several hours later, Sims appeared in Long's room and discovered him stark naked, yelling, "JOE SIMS, WHERE THE HELL YOU BEEN?" Earl instructed Sims to file a suit of legal separation against Blanche, thus nullifying her legal authority as his spouse to have him recommitted. Then Earl told Sims to file a formal petition for a habeas corpus hearing, which Sims did, and the hearing was scheduled for June 26 in the St. Tammany Parish seat of Covington. Finally, Earl told Sims to convene a meeting of the state Hospital Board, which had formal political jurisdiction over the Mandeville institution.[18]

On the morning of June 26, 1959, the quiet little community of Covington, Louisiana, found itself the center of national attention. Because the parish courthouse was being renovated, the habeas corpus hearing would be held in the Covington Junior High School gymnasium. Over a thousand reporters and spectators packed the gym, and the school PTA took advantage of the occasion to sell soft drinks to the crowd. Most people thought that the court would conduct a sanity hearing and that Judge Robert D. Jones of the Twenty-second Judicial District would rule on that issue. In fact, however, the only purpose was to determine whether or not the governor was being confined against his will. The anticipated fireworks did not take place, for Earl Long had pulled another trick out of his political hat. While in Mandeville, he had placed strategic phone calls to allies around the state, informing them of a clever plot by which he could win his discharge. Earl had secretly planned with his loyal supporters on the state Hospital Board to get rid of the director, Jesse H. Bankston, who had refused to help Earl secure his release. At 9:00 on the morning of June 26, the Hospital Board met and voted to support Earl in his plan to fire Bankston. Then the board elected as its new director one of its members, Charles Rosenblum, a Hammond merchant and a close friend of Earl's. As soon as he was sworn in, Rosenblum requested that the board fire the acting superintendent at Mandeville, Dr. Charles Belcher, and the board complied. To replace Belcher, the board appointed Dr. Jess McClendon of Amite, another close friend and loyal political ally of Earl Long's.[19]

At 10:00 A.M. the habeas corpus hearing convened in the junior high school gym, and ten minutes later, it was over. Joe Arthur Sims read the official letters from the state Hospital Board announcing the appointments of Rosenblum and McClendon. Sims then read a statement from McClendon certifying Earl Long as completely rational and declaring that he would be immediately released from the institution. The only other person to testify at the hearing was Attorney General Jack Gremillion, whom Earl had threatened with political reprisal if he did not reverse his previous stand. Apprehensive about his future, Gremillion did exhibit a change and testified that Louisiana joined attorney Sims in a motion to dismiss. Since neither Blanche Long nor any other person who had originally supported Earl's confinement showed up to testify, Judge Jones dismissed the entire case. Because of McClendon's statement, the judge said, Earl was not a patient any longer, so no habeas corpus hearing could legally be conducted. In effect, Earl Long had gained his freedom. As soon as the judge concluded his remarks, a tumultuous cheer went up from the throng, and a crowd of well-wishers rushed to Earl's table to offer their congratulations. Earl sat at the table shaking hands and chatting with the people. Always ready to seize an opportunity to raise money, he had ordered one of his assistants to place a cap upside down on the table, and the sympathetic crowd quickly filled it to overflowing with more than $2,500 in donations. Around noon, Earl went to the Pine Manor Motel in Covington, where he announced the firing of John Nick Brown, the superintendent of the State Police. Earl Long had survived another personal and political crisis.[20]

Even today, many people in Louisiana are quick to formulate opinions about the condition of Earl Long's mind. As A. J. Liebling pointed out, those opinions can usually be summarized as "crazy" or "not crazy," like "pregnant" or "not pregnant," a condition admitting of no variations. A recent television documentary about Long contributed to the sensationalism and misleading information by portraying Long as mentally unbalanced, showing brief excerpts from some of his most outrageous remarks, and erroneously referring to the court session in Covington as a sanity hearing. Both the electronic and the print media devoted an extraordinary amount of coverage to the events of May and June, 1959, and their coverage concentrated on the sensational. Earl Long was almost invariably depicted as a man who had disgraced the people of Louisiana through his actions and whose irrational behavior completely justified his committals to mental institutions. Journalists made little effort to ascertain the complex facts of the case. Instead, they generally agreed with Time's conclusion that Earl Long was "just plain crazy."[21]

Unfortunately, because of laws protecting the privacy of patients and their families, Long's official medical records at both the Titus Harris clinic and at the Southeast Louisiana Hospital remain unavailable for research. It is, however, possible to present an objective and balanced summary of the available evidence, which was obtained from a variety of sources. One category includes the oral and written statements by physicians who examined Earl Long during the controversial period. Dr. Arthur Long, who saw Earl briefly at the Mansion after his outburst, diagnosed his condition as manic depressive psychosis with a tendency to violence. Dr. Titus Harris, the head of the Galveston clinic, wrote to a researcher that Earl had suffered "a series of light strokes which could have brought about a change in personality accounting for the symptoms he had." Harris believed that the strokes damaged those portions of the brain that control the emotions and inhibitions, but not those that control the intellect. In another public report, the "lunacy commission" of Williams and Wyatt described Earl's condition as "paranoid schizophrenia with cycles of manic-depressive activity." State Senator Ralph King, a physician who had treated Earl for a heart attack in 1950, told the press that "there is nothing wrong with Governor Long's mentality. I placed about 20 or 25 long-distance calls for him at Vidalia, and he gave me all the phone numbers from memory." McClendon was quoted at the Covington court hearing as proclaiming Long completely rational. The three psychiatrists who visited Long in his motel room the night of the hearing, Doctors Robert Heath and Victor Leif of the Tulane medical school and Doctor Charles Watkins of the LSU medical school, told reporters that Earl had had "a nervous breakdown as the result of a stroke, a small stroke, or a series of strokes." They added that he was "better mentally than physically," and that "at the present [June 26, 1959] the governor is rational, with no intellectual impairment."[22]

Although these public comments should be given serious consideration, coming as they did from physicians, they do not provide sufficient information or list the necessary clinical criteria for a definitive diagnosis. In the absence of the actual medical records from Galveston and Mandeville, it is possible to analyze the known evidence about Earl Long's life and to arrive at a tentative assessment of the mental condition that precipitated the remarkable events of May and June, 1959. This assessment is based on a careful review of the relevant psychiatric literature and on consultation with experts in the field.[23]

In all probability, Earl Long suffered from bipolar disorder. Formerly called manic depressive psychosis, bipolar disorder is a mental illness characterized by extreme fluctuations in mood, ranging from an elevated "high" to a severe depression. The typical manic patient will exhibit periods of being hyperactive, excessively talkative, and fanciful. Often, the manic harbors an inflated sense of self-esteem that becomes grandiose.

He also displays a greatly decreased need for sleep, finds himself distracted by trivial matters, and engages in activities that have a very high potential for risk. During these "highs," the manic frequently is unusually creative. During the periods of severe depression, the manic often considers suicide. Trained clinicians have little difficulty recognizing full-blown cases of bipolar disorder.[24]

To explain bipolar disorder, we must provide certain specific examples of how individuals with the psychosis behave. Although individual human beings vary widely in their behavior patterns, manics do exhibit some common tendencies. The first, hyperactivity, involves an extraordinary degree of physical and mental energy. Manics can go for days with little or no sleep, and instead of becoming exhausted, they seem to perform their work with unusual efficiency. A manic housewife may go to sleep at midnight, awaken at 2:00 A.M., and complete all her daily household chores by 4:00 A.M. A manic salesman may exceed his monthly quota in just two days of incessant work. A second characteristic of manics is pressured speech, in which the manic's thoughts flow so rapidly that his speech cannot keep up. The impression is that he is speaking incoherently and irrationally. The manic often talks on the telephone for hours, day and night. Frequently, the manic's mind has recurring ideas he feels compelled to express in words. A third common trait is reckless behavior that entails a high degree of personal risk. Manics, for example, often consume large quantities of alcoholic beverages, sometimes adding amphetamines, barbiturates, and other drugs. They also have a tendency to spend huge sums of money—compulsive gambling is common. Manics also have been known to engage in such potentially destructive behavior as reckless driving and sexual promiscuity. Almost invariably, manics resist attempts to provide them with the proper psychiatric treatment, and they believe that there is nothing wrong with them.[25]

In light of these general characteristics, it is quite evident that Earl Long suffered bipolar disorder throughout his adult life. Hyperactivity was certainly an Earl Long trademark. In numerous interviews, friends and political associates remarked on his seemingly inexhaustible reserves of energy. During Huey's crisis in 1929, a legislator could not restrain his amazement that "Earl never slept during the impeachment." While on the campaign trail and during legislative sessions, Earl always appeared constantly vigilant and alert to every opportunity. When questioned about the secret of his political successes, Earl himself told a reporter that "while the rest of 'em are sleeping, I'm politicking." Earl also had a chronic case of telephonitis, and his political aides, newspaper reporters, and acquaintances resigned themselves to being awakened at two or three o'clock in the morning by a phone call from Governor Long. During his eighteen-day swing through several western states and Mexico immediately following his release from Mandeville, Earl astonished observers with his boundless energy, physically exhausting members of his entourage who were less than half his age. In his final campaign, when he won election to Congress, Earl's whirlwind campaign carried him through every city, town, and hamlet in the sprawling Eighth Congressional District. In the six-month period prior to his outburst before the legislature, Earl caroused in the French Quarter until the wee hours almost every night.[26]

In his tirades before the legislature in late May of 1959, Long displayed another characteristic, pressured, rapid speech. Because his mind operates much faster than he can voice his ideas, the manic appears incoherent, and that is precisely what occurred when Earl spoke before the Judiciary "B" Committee and before the joint legislative session. Almost certainly, Earl's mind was consumed with a rush of ideas that compelled him to speak more and more rapidly, trying to express them all. Thus, in speaking about the race issue, he spotted Willie Rainach, and his mind flashed negative impressions. Then he would suddenly jump to another topic, then another. This compulsive desire to talk is typical of manics. In his campaigns, Earl became widely known for his one- and two-hour stump harangues that followed no logical pattern and switched abruptly from one subject to another. In normal conversations with friends, Earl talked more than anyone else and was the center of attention. At times, he would talk nonstop for hours.[27]

As we have seen, Earl Long loved to spend money, and he became legendary for his habit of stopping at small country stores and urban supermarkets to try to bargain for good deals on almost everything. As Dr. Ronald R. Fieve, a prominent psychiatrist, wrote in his well-known study of bipolar disorder: "The lifestyle of the manic-depressive who is in a high tends to be a glorious scattering of money. He looks for new and interesting ways to spend it. He goes on buying sprees for the sheer joy of spending." On one excursion to Schwegmann's supermarket in New Orleans, Earl purchased one hundred pounds of potatoes, three hundred dollars' worth of alarm clocks, eighty-seven dozen goldfish, and two cases of Mogen David wine. In his countless excursions around Louisiana, Earl bought ropes, goats, chickens, hogs, corn, seed, hoes, hats, shoes, earthworms, and a variety of other items that he had no use for, and he almost invariably gave them away.[28]

Closely related to excessive spending is the tendency to gamble compulsively. From the time Dudley LeBlanc introduced Earl to pari-mutuel betting around 1927 until he died, Earl played the horses with reckless abandon. Upon awakening in the morning, the first thing he did was to open the racing spreadsheets, make his selections, then call in his bets to bookies around the country. In his travels, Earl selected places where racetracks were located. In 1956, when he led the Louisiana delegation to the Democratic National Convention in Chicago, Earl spent nearly all his time at Arlington Race Track. During racing season, he had a special reserved box at the Fair Grounds, and he frequently visited Churchill Downs in Louisville. Like most compulsive gamblers, Earl derived his greatest pleasure not from monetary considerations, but from the challenge of devising a perfect system that would beat the odds. He rarely paid attention to the actual amounts of money he won or lost, but he found a lot of excitement in his "systems" for playing the horses and in placing his bets with the bookies.[29]

Many manics are highly successful businessmen and women who find release for their emotional "highs" in such tension-laden professions as stock broker and financial investor. The constant wheeling and dealing, the strategies for investing in certain stocks, the physically and mentally exhausting routine of high finance, all have great appeal for manics. In Earl Long's case, Louisiana politics substituted for financial transactions—no one relished political wheeling and dealing more than he did. Manics love power, being in control of situations, and Earl became a master of even the most minute aspects of the complexities of state politics. Even when he was assured of winning a legislative battle, he would still engage in back-room deals. The world of politics held a magnetic attraction for Earl Long, and with his enormous physical energy, his relentless drive to achieve perfection in the political arena, and his continual efforts to improve his mastery of state politics, he had real advantages over the opposition. Louisiana politicians have related many tales of Earl's enormous satisfaction in winning a political struggle through his ability to touch the right people in just the right manner. One legislator recalled: "When Earl would start to strike a bargain with a politician, his eyes would light up, they would seem to sparkle." To many, this display of enthusiasm is perhaps excessive. Manics, however, typically devote large amounts of time to their work, which is for them a source of pleasure.[30]

Earl Long, then, manifested many of the classic clinical symptoms of bipolar disorder well before his "mental collapse" of 1959, and in the first half of that year, his behavior demonstrated that he had fallen into the most severe stage of the disorder. His resumption of cigarette smoking, his excessive indulgence in alcoholic beverages and amphetamines, his carousing in the French Quarter, his public appearance at the Kentucky Derby with two call girls, his constant hyperactivity, all these were clear signals that he was rapidly approaching the dangerous stages of bipolar disorder, when patients must receive immediate medical and psychiatric attention because they are a real, violent menace to themselves and to others. The climax came during Governor Long's appearances before the legislature, when his actions met precisely the criteria by which Dr. Fieve rates the "medical emergency" stage of bipolar disorder. The patient then exhibits the following symptoms: "wildly manic and psychotic; can't stop talking; incoherent, overactive, belligerent, or elated. Not sleeping at all. At times delusional; hallucinating. May be either violent or paranoid."[31]

By the time Earl finished his outburst before the joint session of the legislature, he had become rambling and incoherent, unable to walk without support. After being led to the Governor's Mansion, he grew increasingly belligerent and violent. In a declassified FBI memorandum, assistant director Albert Rosen reported to Hoover on a conversation he had with Russell Long: "Senator Long stated that Governor Long had the idea that he was a Napoleon or a Julius Caesar." Delusions of grandeur are yet another classic symptom of bipolar disorder. The family's decision to have Earl committed to the Galveston clinic probably saved his life: by the morning after his confinement in the Governor's Mansion, he was violently resisting efforts to move him, vehemently insisting that nothing was wrong with him, feeling no effects from two injections of morphine. Earl Long had clearly lost control of his physical and mental processes.[32]

Long's release from the clinic at Sealy Hospital came about not because the medical staff recommended it, but rather because he sought his right of habeas corpus. His behavior in the East Baton Rouge Parish courthouse parking garage, when he was examined by Doctors Williams and Wyatt, showed that he definitely remained psychotic. The confinement at Mandeville had a calming effect on Long, enabling him to regain control over himself, and above all, it gave him the desperately needed period of rest that his sixty-three-year-old body required. Even after that, however, Earl continued to manifest symptoms of bipolar disorder. When he ran for Congress in 1960, he ignored the advice of his physicians, who warned him that because of the weakened condition of his heart, another grueling campaign would kill him. This self-destructive driving ambition also fits the pattern of bipolar disorder.[33]

Although the exact treatment Earl Long received remains unknown, he certainly did not get carefully monitored doses of lithium, which is now the medically approved treatment. In 1959, not only were approximately 50 percent of all cases of bipolar disorder misdiagnosed as paranoid schizophrenia and other psychoses, but the remarkably effective lithium treatment was virtually unknown or resisted. In any event, once he secured his release from Mandeville, Earl successfully blocked all attempts by family members and friends to get him voluntarily to obtain professional assistance. Instead, he lived the remaining thirteen months of his life still afflicted with bipolar disorder, and it again grew progressively worse. Aggravating this problem was Long's rapidly progressing case of arteriosclerosis. In the last two years of his life, he often needed oxygen and had to take daily medication.[34]

Although it is impossible to give a definitive psychiatric analysis of Earl Long, the strong correlation between his well-known mannerisms and behavior and the clinical criteria for bipolar disorder allows an explanation for the innumerable eccentricities that characterized him. The probability that Earl had bipolar disorder enables us to explain those eccentricities as the demeanor not of a "crude" or "crazy" man but of someone afflicted with a mental disorder that required regular treatment. In the absence of appropriate medication, the disorder grew worse over the years, ultimately climaxing in the traumatic events of May and June, 1959. Typical of manics, Earl never realized the nature of the disorder and indeed insisted that he had no need for treatment. The nearly one month of confinement at Galveston and Mandeville gave him the rest he desperately required, and allowed the disorder to mitigate. He was not cured, however, and shortly after his release from Mandeville, Earl Long would embark on a raucous, eighteen-day "vacation" swing through several western states and Mexico, an excursion that would add more material to the Earl Long saga.

12

On Vacation

Louisiana's seriously ill governor was told by several physicians that if he did not go away somewhere for a rest, he might die at any time. After his release from Mandeville, Earl spent several days in his Covington motel room, then he retired for nearly a week to his pea patch farm in Winnfield to get a respite from the constant publicity. But he discovered that he could not run away from controversy. In early July, 1959, Cora Schley, one of Long's public relations advisors, announced that she had told federal agents investigating Earl's finances that she held $7,000 in campaign funds for him in a safe-deposit box at an Alexandria bank. Earl denied the story but, for reasons never publicly disclosed, tried to prevent Cora Schley and her husband from adopting a child. When the Schleys' lawyer, Camille Gravel, accused Long of deliberately blocking the adoption, Earl replied that Gravel, a former political ally, was a "very pompous man" and that Gravel and Cora Schley had "heads as hard as bricks." After sending a state trooper to Alexandria to collect the campaign money, Long suddenly dropped his opposition. Governor Long also came under attack for allegedly accepting a $5,000 bribe from Earl S. Billings, a New Orleans steamship lobbyist, for vetoing a river pilots' bill. Louis J. Roussel, whom Earl had fired as head of the Orleans Levee Board, publicly confirmed the charges.[1]

Despite the continuing adverse publicity, Earl Long refused to remain outside the political arena, and on July 4, he opened his campaign for governor with a stump speech in Ville Platte, and he spoke in several other towns around the state. As usual, all announced candidates for governor—including State Comptroller Bill Dodd, former governor Jimmie Davis, Mayor deLesseps Morrison, and State Senator Willie Rainach—and for other offices appeared together, with each speaking in turn. Curious to see Earl Long make his first public appearance since his commitments, a large crowd gathered in Ville Platte. Although he had not yet recovered from his ordeal of the past month and a half, Earl showed flashes of his unique campaign style. He called Bill Dodd a "genuine faker," and his other opponents "cowards and liars." He accused Dodd and Morrison of being pawns of Carlos Marcello, labeled Jimmie Davis "the biggest jelly bean that ever lived," and promised to "reduce" Willie Rainach "to a good, kind, ordinary, indulgent citizen." The caravan moved to Cameron in southwestern Louisiana, where Earl handed out one-dollar bills to children, and the candidates finished their first day of campaigning at Lake Providence in north Louisiana, where the Miss Louisiana pageant was being held. There Earl told the sizable gatherings, "I just wanted you to judge for yourself what a nutty man looks like."[2]

Astute observers noticed that Earl Long was clearly but a shadow of his old self. During the July 4 stump tour, he was visibly weak and tired, and he restricted his ordinarily lengthy stump harangues to only a few minutes. As soon as the speaking at Lake Providence had ended, he returned to the pea patch farm, and at a meeting of his campaign staff the following morning, he suddenly fell asleep. The next day, Earl went to the Governor's Mansion, but was too exhausted to take care of any official duties. After being fitted with a new set of false teeth (the old ones no longer fit because of all the weight he had lost), he returned to Winnfield on July 7 and rested there for three more days. During that time, he decided to take a vacation trip to the West, to regain his strength for the grueling campaign that lay ahead. On July 11, Long boarded a plane in Shreveport and headed for Fort Worth, Texas, the first leg of a whirlwind, eighteen-day swing that would add considerable material to the growing legend of Earl Long.[3]

Earl had made a number of previous trips to the West, and they had always rejuvenated him. This time, he simply wanted to do the things he enjoyed the most: visiting friends, eating and drinking what he wanted, going to the racetrack, and just enjoying the scenery. Long's doctors had warned against the trip, telling him that he could not stand the rigors of a long journey, but he ignored their advice. He mainly wanted to get away from Louisiana, from politics for a while, and especially from the hordes of reporters that constantly hounded him. But he soon discovered that the press would not leave him alone. He made good copy, and newspapers from around the country and even from some European countries had sent reporters to cover his every move. Throughout his trip, Earl was badgered by prying reporters, and he actually discovered one trying to crawl through a transom in his hotel room in El Paso.[4]

Early in the morning on Saturday, July 11, 1959, Governor Earl K. Long watched some of the workers at the pea patch farm brand cattle, and he paid a visit to his hog pen. Then, accompanied by several friends, including Senator B. B. "Sixty" Rayburn, Representatives Jesse McLean and J. M. "Pete" Menefree, and escorted by a couple of state troopers, Earl got into an automobile for the drive to Shreveport. En route, he stopped in Ruston to borrow $4,000 from his sister Lucille. Earl's commercial flight stopped briefly in Dallas, and during the interval, pandemonium broke out on the plane. A horde of reporters rushed aboard, but Earl refused to see them. When they persisted, he pulled a pillowcase over his head, then put his hat on. After Earl's plane finally took off for the short flight to Fort Worth, the reporters got into their automobiles and sped recklessly to get to the airport before Long deplaned. Aware that the reporters would be waiting for him, Earl refused to take the pillowcase off, so Sixty Rayburn cut some breathing holes in it. Naturally, the press had a field day when Earl left the plane. On Sunday, newspapers all over the country published photographs of the Governor of Louisiana, just released from two mental institutions, walking across the tarmac and looking like a child dressed for trick-or-treating.[5]

After cursing and fuming at the reporters, Earl arrived in the waiting room, where he removed the pillowcase. Eventually, Earl was driven to the Hotel Texas, where he had reserved a suite on the twelfth floor. He had Sixty Rayburn telephone the governor of Texas, who was unavailable. Rayburn then called Waggoner Carr, the speaker of the house, to ask if Long could address the Texas legislature, but Carr was noncommittal. Earl spent the night in the hotel—four or five newsmen slept in the hall. On Sunday, July 12, Earl stayed in his room, and he placed several phone calls to Louisiana officials. He also called Dr. Titus Harris in Galveston and talked about his constant harassment by the press. He issued a public statement: "I'm still a sick man and I need a rest. Reporters and photographers have been chasing me like a wild animal and they could drive me insane." Indeed, Earl discovered that he could not go anywhere without reporters and cameramen. When he entered a hotel elevator to go up to his room, he found a reporter waiting there for him. He whispered something to State Police Lieutenant Russell Willie, who punched the newsman in the jaw, knocking him unconscious. Later, Willie apologized for his behavior, but the press never left Earl alone during his vacation trip. The reporters were simply doing their job. An Earl Long story made a certain Page One headline, and they were determined that he would go nowhere without their knowledge.[6]

On Sunday night, Earl took an unscheduled tour of the city, stopping at the railroad terminal, where he chatted briefly with several Louisianians, and visiting a cattle ranch. The following morning, Monday, July 13, a clean-shaven Governor Long, clad in cowboy boots and ten-gallon hat, held a roving press conference in the hotel lobby. After apologizing for his actions of the previous two days, he answered questions in his usual eccentric manner. Asked about oilmen, he said that some were good citizens, but others "wouldn't pay a dime to see Christ rescued from the cross." He also said that he intended to revise drastically Louisiana's laws about confining people to mental institutions. "Before a man can be put into an asylum," he said, "they will have to have ten close friends and three doctors who live in the neighborhood to approve." He also ventured his opinion of psychiatrists: "The longer a man is a psychiatrist, the crazier he gets." At a more formal press conference later in the day, Earl alluded to the racial context of his famous outburst before the legislature: "When I addressed the legislature, I stepped on the toes of some sleeping cats." And in one remarkable statement, he criticized the Confederacy, branding the Civil War a "useless war, one that shouldn't have been fought," and he even went so far as to praise Abraham Lincoln as "a great man, Republican or no Republican," concluding that "Lincoln was right."[7]

During the day, Earl called his aide, Dupree Litton, and told him to bring Lieutenant Governor Lether Frazar and Representative Spencer Myrick, plus $10,000 in cash, to Fort Worth. They complied immediately. Later, Earl and Sixty Rayburn went on a shopping spree. At a western store, he bought twenty pairs of boots, which he kept, and assorted other items, which he sent back to Louisiana to be distributed to "old people of Earl's choosing," as one account stated. Long also visited a Fort Worth restaurant, where he showed the chef how to dice vienna sausage into cream of chicken soup. A Baton Rouge reporter dubbed the concoction "Earl Long Soup," a label the chef advertised to attract customers. Earl had intended to fly to El Paso on Tuesday, but he stayed in Fort Worth one more day because he accepted an invitation to address the Jaycees. On Wednesday afternoon, July 15, Earl Long gave a masterly performance before a sellout crowd. Artfully blending his unique humor with serious remarks about important issues, the Louisiana governor left everyone convinced that he had completely recovered from his "breakdown" a few weeks earlier. Indeed, the vacation actually seemed to invigorate the sixty-three-year-old Long. After four days in Fort Worth, Earl looked better and felt better than he had in six months.[8]

After posing for photographers, Governor Long's entourage began the long trek from Fort Worth to El Paso. Because of unstable weather, he had to cancel his plans to fly and instead made the trip in a caravan of automobiles. Long had told reporters that he would stop overnight in Snyder, but when they reached the small town, all they found was one of Earl's station wagons. Earl had actually driven to Webb Air Force Base in Big Spring, where he spent a restful night in the officers' quarters. The following day, Thursday, July 17, the Long caravan drove at high speeds across Texas, making several stops along the way. At a small store in Pecos, he bought twenty crates of cantaloupes, sending eighteen of them c.o.d. to friends in Louisiana. At 5:30 P.M., Earl's party arrived at the Hilton Hotel in El Paso, and the waiting reporters were treated to the sight of the governor's black Cadillac sedan with two crates of cantaloupes perched on its roof. Earl invited the press to his seventh-floor suite for another news conference. When a reporter asked about his desegregation of Charity Hospital in New Orleans, Earl replied that 70 percent of the facility's patients were black. One newsman asked him if he planned to get a quickie divorce from Blanche in Juarez, just across the border from El Paso, and Earl said, "Say, I hadn't thought of it, but that's not a bad idea!" His personal physician, Dr. M. O. Miller, told the press that if the governor continued to improve as rapidly as he had in the past week, he would be ready to start campaigning in ten days.[9]

Earl had told the reporters that he would go to Juarez later that night, and he was true to his word. Once he crossed the border, there began a series of events that would capture headlines all over the nation. Long went to the Charmont Café as the dinner guest of his good friend William Stevens, who owned a ranch near El Paso. As the governor sat at the table to sample the feast Stevens had ordered for him, reporters, photographers, and curiosity seekers surrounded him. Earl suddenly flew into a violent rage, yelling "Out!" When they did not clear away fast enough, he shouted, "I'm going to shoot the bastards!" Witnesses said that Long had a knife in his coat pocket and that his aides had to restrain him from using it. Unable to enjoy his meal in peace, Earl stalked out of the café. Later, Earl said that he and his party drove around Juarez and stopped to drink "some of that cheap champagne," but in reality, he headed for a well-known night spot, Irma's Whorehouse. Bribed by Long aides, the Juarez cops chased the reporters back across the border, leaving Earl to savor the pleasures of Irma's without harassment. After an all-night carousal, Earl finally returned to his hotel in El Paso at six o'clock in the morning. Most of his entourage had been worn out by the long drive to El Paso and by the revels in Juarez, and they had returned to the Hilton for a rest, but Earl stayed up all night, still fresh and vigorous. Enraged because his party had deserted him, Earl marched down the seventh-floor corridor banging on doors and shouting "Wake Up!" State Police Captain Douglas L. Durrett tried to calm Earl down, but he gave up. "They say he's sick," Durrett said, "but right now, he could lick any fifty men in Texas." Someone else in the hall marveled at Earl's energy, shook his head, and said, "That Earl Long is worth fifty men." [10]

After only four hours' sleep, Governor Earl Long awoke on Friday morning with a hangover, but he managed to consume a breakfast of ham and eggs and "about a barrelful of coffee." Most of his party, completely exhausted though considerably younger than he, departed for Baton Rouge. Earl spent most of the day in his hotel room, where he made numerous long-distance telephone calls. With his permission, two Baton Rouge newsmen, Brooks Read and Bud Hebert, recorded his phone calls to them; these were later incorporated into a record album entitled *The Last of the Red Hot Poppas*. Long made only one public appearance during the day, vividly described by the El Paso *Times*: "Gov. Earl K. Long of Louisiana behaving like an old grey bear hemmed in by hounds, stuck his head out of his seventh floor lair in the Hilton Hotel only once during the daylight hours Friday—to snarl at newsmen. He was clad in his drawers and a white shirt." On Friday night, Earl made a deal with reporters: he would hold a wide-open press conference if they would not dog his trail. So, once more free from prying newsmen, he took off for Juarez, ending his spree at Irma's. This time, however, he did nothing more than cuddle a couple of the girls who sat on his lap. When the local police started to move in on Earl's table, Bryce Miller, a Baton Rouge newsman, threw a twenty-dollar bill on the table, and the party made a hasty departure. [11]

The next morning, Saturday, July 18, Earl awakened early, as usual, and spent several hours on the phone. He placed one call to his farm in Winnfield to check on his chickens, cows, and hogs. Shortly after noon, Earl left the Hilton Hotel, and he spent a half hour in a fruitless attempt to shake off the press. Dashing through the hotel kitchen, he caught a waiting taxi and went to the airport. Shielding his face with his hat, he boarded a chartered plane, which took off immediately. Much to Earl's chagrin, the press had chartered five planes, and they followed his to the next destination on the excursion, Ruidoso, New Mexico. At Ruidoso, Earl went straight to the racetrack, where he was escorted to the manager's private quarters so he could recover from the air sickness he had suffered on the flight. While he rested, Earl swapped dirty jokes with his friends and played the horses according to the posted odds. Without a racing form, he relied on his hunches and lost about $300 per race. When Earl walked into the public clubhouse, he spotted a table marked "Welcome Gov. Long," but he refused to sit there. In the grandstand with his friend Pete Menefree, Earl bet on the long shots and lost heavily, but he soon began playing the favorites and recouped some of his losses. When Earl got up and moved to another part of the grandstand, the sheriff politely asked him to return to his seat. Earl went into another of his violent rages, with the usual graphic language and gestures, and he was led to the jockey club. Altogether, Earl had wagered between $12,000 and $15,000 on the horses, and he claimed that he came out "a couple of hundred dollars ahead." [12]

Still feeling the aftereffects of air sickness, Earl accepted the track's offer to drive him back to El Paso. During the two-hundred-mile journey, he made several stops. One was at a country store in Tularosa, New Mexico, where Earl sat on a portable bread rack and ate a meal of vienna sausage, cheese, crackers, sardines, and milk. He thoroughly enjoyed the food and did not seem to mind the crowd of reporters and onlookers who had gathered to watch him eat. He arrived at the Hilton Hotel in El Paso about ten o'clock that night and, for once, settled down and stayed there. On Sunday morning, Governor Long and his party attended services at the First Baptist Church of El Paso, where Earl, who claimed that he was a "back seat Baptist," sat in the rear of the church. Throughout the service, he whispered and coughed, much to the annoyance of the congregation. Afterwards, Earl signed autographs for children, and he told the minister, the Reverend W. Herschel Ford, "That's good preaching. It was only thirty-five minutes long. In the country, they used to preach for an hour and a half. That's too long for an old man to sleep." Waiting for him outside the church was Mrs. A. D. Long, the mother of Dr. Arthur Long, who had originally recommended his commitment. Growing loud and animated, Earl told her, "I love you, but I'm going to sue the whole bunch for every dime they've got, and I'm going to give it all to the church."[13]

After spending the rest of Sunday in El Paso, Earl and his party departed for Denver, Colorado, early in the morning on Monday, July 20. Followed by reporters, his caravan drove at the usual torrid pace northward to their original destination, Albuquerque. Earl had read in the city's newspaper that the sheriff had stated that Governor Long and his people would have to surrender their guns. So when they reached Albuquerque, Earl ordered his driver to head for Santa Fe. On the expressway to Santa Fe, a suitcase from on top of Earl's car flew off and struck a car in which two reporters were riding, causing them to swerve into a ditch. No one was hurt, and the car was not damaged. As state troopers collected his clothing that had been strewn along the highway, Earl laughed. "This is one way to stop them God Damn newsmen from following us." The remark broke everyone up, and from then on, Long and the press enjoyed a real rapport. Exhausted by their journey, the party arrived in Santa Fe well after dark, and Earl's aides found rooms at the Town House Motel. Earl quickly fell asleep, and Pete Menefree became alarmed when he saw that Earl appeared comatose. Menefree could not rouse him and called a doctor. The physician, Dr. Richard Landmann, arrived and started to examine Earl, who suddenly woke up and started to curse. A nurse said, "He must be feeling better; he just God-damned me." Dr. Landmann briefly examined Earl and said that perhaps Santa Fe's altitude, 7,000 feet above sea level, contributed to the spell, but he could not make a firm diagnosis. Regardless of what had stricken him, Earl fell back into a normal sleep and awakened the next morning ready to go. Displaying no signs of the nighttime problem, Earl had breakfast with Governor John Burroughs, then resumed his voyage to Denver.[14]

During the trip, Earl stopped in Taos, New Mexico, where he haggled awhile with the proprietor of an army-navy surplus store. As usual, he attracted a crowd of spectators, and the Taos police had to be called to restrain the throng. One elderly lady said that she wanted to get near enough to "hear him cuss." Earl eventually bought $160 worth of sundry items, which he had shipped to the pea patch farm. Upon taking to the road again, Earl seemed to settle down, and he enjoyed the beautiful scenery of the Rocky Mountains. The caravan did not reach Denver until late evening; in front of the Brown Palace Hotel, another horde of reporters waited, eagerly anticipating more misdeeds and foul language from the tempestuous Louisiana governor. This time, they were sorely disappointed, for Earl Long spoke to them calmly and quietly, promising to hold a press conference the next morning. That morning, after he called former president Harry Truman and made an appointment to see him in Independence, Missouri, Earl Long faced a room full of reporters. Long handled their questions easily. He told them that he felt better than he had since his abduction to Galveston, and that he wanted to talk with Truman about the 1960 presidential election. He also said that his political opponents in Louisiana had "the chance of a snowball in hell" of impeaching him, and that he and Blanche would never reconcile. He also said that he would go to Kansas City, Missouri, and Hot Springs, Arkansas.[15]

The two days Earl Long had in Denver, Wednesday and Thursday, July 22 and 23, 1959, were perhaps the most pleasurable of his entire vacation, for he spent them at Centennial Race Track. On Wednesday, he appeared unkempt and unshaven. Accompanying him were Gene Henley, manager of the Ruidoso track, and Fred Piper, regional director of the AFL-CIO and an old friend of Earl's. Earl enjoyed his day at the track, but he lost about $3,000. Lieutenant Bill Wisner of the State Police bet money on the wrong horse for him, and Earl raged at him. Later, he made a pass at two women sitting in front of him, and when they told him they were married, Earl said, "I'm divorced [*sic*] and I'm on the loose." On Wednesday night, Earl was supposed to go to a nightclub to watch stripper Tempest Storm, but he was exhausted, and he went to sleep at eight o'clock. The next morning, Governor Stephen McNichols paid a courtesy call, and then Earl went to the hotel barbershop for a shave and a haircut. He went straight to still another press conference. He reiterated his intention to run for governor again, and he told reporters that he had gained nine pounds on his trip and that his health was improving. When a reporter told him that his former lawyer Theo Cangelosi, who had refused to assist him during his confinements, had resigned as attorney for the Greater Baton Rouge Port Commission, Earl sarcastically replied, "I guess that port is about to collapse without that windjammer." Concerning his having been committed, he said, "Mandeville was by far the worse. They wouldn't let you get a postcard in there. A dungeon in hell was no worse than Mandeville, and the food is as bare as a cupboard in a poor man's house." After fielding questions for over an hour, a buoyant Long concluded the session.[16]

Being driven around Denver, Long had his chauffeur park in front of a building entrance, and a crowd of about three hundred people cheered as Officer Katherine Gerkin issued the Long party a citation for illegal parking. Earl did not complain, and he sent an aide to traffic court to pay the fine. A little later, Jerry McNeill, a Dallas reporter for the Associated Press, who had been with Earl the entire trip, drove him to a western store, where Earl bought four saddles, two straw hats, two wool shirts, and many other items. Then Earl went to the airport, where he caught a delayed flight to Kansas City. He arrived in the Missouri city early in the morning on Friday, July 24. Even at that hour, between two and three hundred spectators jammed the observation deck to get a glimpse of the controversial Louisiana governor. After a quick wave to the crowd, Earl was whisked away to a hotel.[17]

After a few hours' sleep, Earl motored to the Truman Library in Independence, Missouri, a short distance from the hotel, to keep his appointment with his old friend Harry Truman. After a private forty-five-minute talk with the former president, a smiling Earl Long emerged and gave a guard a $100 bill. On the back steps of the library, he held another marathon news conference. He said he told Truman "a lot of dirty jokes. He didn't tell me any, but he acted like he hadn't heard any of mine." Also, he and Truman agreed that the best ticket for the Democratic party in the 1960 presidential election would be Missouri senator Stuart Symington for president and Massachusetts senator John Kennedy for vice-president. Briefly touching on the race question, Earl denounced both the NAACP and the "grasseating racists," and he said he hoped to stop in Little Rock to give Governor Orville Faubus "some of my philosophy on that Central High School situation." Off the record, he said Faubus had been "dead wrong" to oppose the integration of the school and that President Eisenhower had acted "correctly" when he sent in troops to enforce the federal court desegregation decree. Typically, the press conference covered a variety of subjects. Earl said, accurately, "I'm for the women. I've appointed more women than all other Louisiana governors put together." Asked about an IRS investigation of his finances, he said that he wasn't concerned: "I've seen to it that all records and books they could harass me with have been destroyed." [18]

Later, in his hotel suite, Earl joined an impromptu party that started when several American Legionnaires and their wives, attending a convention in Kansas City, dropped in to meet the governor. Earl invited them to join in a songfest around the piano Truman often played. Early on Sunday morning, July 26, Earl flew from Kansas City to Little Rock. He deplaned unshaven and brandishing a book of poetry. Governor Faubus was out of town, so Earl signed a few autographs at the airport. Then he got into a car owned by Mr. and Mrs. Frank Matthews, a lumberman and his wife from Mansfield, Louisiana, and they drove to Hot Springs. Two hours later, Earl and his party checked into Hot Springs' DeSoto Hotel, where Earl had often stayed when he visited the resort town for its mineral baths and its racetrack. At a press conference in the lobby, he proved calm and even-tempered. When he asked reporters to quote him as saying "son of a gun" instead of "bastard," which he actually said, they gladly obliged. As Earl walked in the lobby, four-year-old Janet Kay Harrison of El Dorado, Arkansas, went to him to shake his hand. Touched by the gesture, Earl asked the child if he could take her home to the pea patch farm with him, but she emphatically refused. When he reached his hotel room, Earl found a number of Louisiana politicians waiting for him; after a brief talk with them, he took a four-hour nap. [19]

Earl arose at seven o'clock Monday morning and, after a breakfast of a cigarette and a cup of coffee, left his seventh-floor suite for the hotel's thermal baths. Clad in a lightweight charcoal robe, with a cigarette dangling from his mouth, the Louisiana governor looked comical on his way to the bathhouse. An hour and a half later, Earl moved to the mezzanine, where he held yet another press conference. At this one, the spectators outnumbered the reporters. Once again, the old stumper treated newsmen to choice samples of his humor. On an attempt by a legislator to have him impeached: "I welcome the opportunity for this little upsquirt to try and impeach me. He'll end up lighter and wiser." On integration: "Why, the colored people have better schools than we do." On southern blacks: "I'll bet that in fifty years colored people would rather be in the South than in the North." On the influence of money on politics: "Money talks." On psychiatrists: "If you heard one of them talk, you'd think he brought the sun up in the morning." On Chep Morrison: "My garters are not quite as snappy as they once were, but I'm oversupplied as far as he is concerned." [20]

During this press conference, an incident occurred that provided plenty of material for more sensational stories about Earl Long. Ann Scott Billings, a divorced woman about thirty-five years old, came up from the lobby and introduced herself to Earl. The governor told the press that she was a "smart looking woman." The two arranged to meet later in the afternoon. Earl showed up clean-shaven and all spiffy, wearing a brown silk Italian suit and two-tone shoes and—true to form—his favorite old battered Panama hat. Mrs. Billings wore a handsome black dress and white gloves. Accompanying her were her aunt and her two children. Lieutenant Bill Wisner drove the party around the Arkansas highways. Reaching speeds of seventy-five miles per hour, Wisner tried to shake the two carloads of reporters, but he failed to do so. Along the way, Earl had Wisner stop at a country store because he wanted to buy some hams, but the store had none, so he settled for a basket of peaches, a dozen bananas, and a few nectarines. Three hours after their departure, the party returned to the hotel. Two hours later, Earl went to a cafeteria not far from the hotel, where he ate supper. In the meantime, more than three hundred people thronged the entrance to the hotel. As Long aides talked to the press, Earl's limousine suddenly roared away from the parking lot, with Mrs. Billings at the wheel. After picking Earl up in front of the cafeteria, she sped off before reporters could get to their cars to follow her. Around midnight, Governor Long and Mrs. Billings returned to the hotel and sat in the parking lot chatting. After Long left, she told reporters that "he's got a brilliant mind, and I don't care what they say. We talked about politics, law, and where Sherry [her daughter] would go to college." [21]

Naturally, the press had a field day with the story of Earl Long's "consorting" with an "attractive divorcee." Actually, there was nothing to indicate that Long and Billings did anything more than take a couple of drives together. Billings told reporters that her date with Governor Long was a "casual encounter," and that she had no plans to meet with him again. Instead, she would return to Memphis to help her ailing mother manage a house they owned there. For his part, Earl Long said that while he thought Ann Billings was a very attractive woman, he had better forget her because the difference in their ages was so great. The highly publicized "tryst" thus lasted less than one day, and Long and Billings never saw each other again.[22]

As Governor Earl Long neared the end of his vacation, and as he drew closer to Louisiana, more of his friends and political allies from the state visited him. These included such people as Joe Arthur Sims, Charles Rosenblum, and Sammy Downs. After spending a quiet Sunday and Monday, July 26 and 27, in Hot Springs, Earl took the last automobile ride of his trip on Tuesday afternoon. An aide took him on a sight-seeing tour along a scenic route through the Ozark Mountains. Near Benton, Arkansas, Earl spotted a gift shop and insisted that they stop. He and the shop owner, R. E. Keathley, Sr., joked and haggled over prices. Finally, Earl bought about $80 worth of assorted goods, including two hams, a side of bacon, and some jugs and corncob pipes. After passing out sides of bacon to the newsmen who followed him, he headed back to Hot Springs, where he arrived at 8:30 P.M.[23]

At 10:04 A.M. on Wednesday, July 29, 1959, a private plane owned by Monroe businessman Monte Carhone touched down at Monroe's Selman Field, ending the eighteen-day vacation of Governor Earl K. Long. To the astonishment of almost everyone, the controversial tour had done wonders for Long's mental and physical condition, and he returned home calmer, heavier, and more energetic than when he had departed. He had defied his doctors, who predicted that such a strenuous trip would surely kill him. Although on occasion Earl lost his temper, in general he behaved normally. Most of the reporters who followed him around publicized his various exploits as those of an eccentric old man clearly not acting in a rational manner. But the reporter who saw more of him on the vacation than did anyone else had a different impression: "Earl Long was eccentric compared to the normal person. He probably did nothing on his vacation trip he had not been doing for years. The difference was that he was closely covered by dozens of newsmen who kept copy on him rolling to their bosses. He still met the press in his BVD's, and he still bought nutty things and gave them away. His antics on this trip were not those of a crazy man." As he stepped off the plane at the Monroe airfield, a refreshed Earl Long looked forward to another fling with his favorite, Louisiana politics.[24]

13

The Last Campaigns

On July 29, 1959, Earl Long returned to the pea patch farm in Winnfield for a brief rest before beginning yet another campaign for governor. Although Louisiana's constitution prohibited a governor from succeeding himself, Earl planned to evade that obstacle by resigning his office just before the election. Since Earl would no longer be governor, he would therefore be eligible to run again. To implement this bizarre scheme and build up popular support, he took to the stump in August. Because of all the recent publicity, larger crowds than usual were in attendance, with many people coming to see "a crazy man." Instead, they witnessed vintage Earl Long, a man still capable of entertaining his audience. "I'm against gambling," he preached and was booed resoundingly. But he added, "For those who can't afford it." He also said that if "Willie Rainach and the NAACP would leave us alone, we'd be all right." When the Young Men's Business Club in New Orleans demanded his removal from office for "irrational, bizarre, and undignified behavior," Earl responded that he had conducted himself "just like good Christian women would want me to." After announcing the calling of a special legislative session on August 10, Earl stated that he had every intention of running for governor in the December, 1959, primary and that he would resign at the beginning of December.[1]

The large, enthusiastic crowds during his stump tour led Earl Long to believe that he would win an unprecedented third term in the governor's office, but Earl had failed to grasp the rapidly changing political situation in Louisiana. What he did not realize was that the adverse publicity about his confinements, his antics during the vacation trip, and his public denunciations of Rainach and the segregationists convinced all but his most faithful supporters that he had no political future. His announced intention to resign so he could succeed himself also alarmed many politicos, for he threatened to establish a personal dynasty. When Earl implemented his plans for the special legislative session, he received his first dose of the new political realities. As soon as the session convened, Representative Ben Holt of Alexandria, a Long ally, moved to adjourn, and the house immediately passed the motion, 71 to 25. Shortly afterward, the senate also voted to adjourn—the count was 26 to 9. A surprised Governor Long rushed to the senate floor, and many legislators were apprehensive that he might repeat the fiasco of May 28, but Earl gave a short, mild speech, declaring that he had no hard feelings and that he would let the people decide his political future.[2]

That future, however, rested in the hands of the State Central Committee, which would rule on whether or not Earl could resign as governor to run for the office in the Democratic primary. Earl had publicly stated that he would not resign before mid-October, but the deadline for qualifying for the race was September 15. When the committee met on September 4, it would have to rule on a motion by N. B. Carstarphen of Shreveport, one of Jimmie Davis' people, that Long would have to resign before September 15. It was a clever maneuver. If the committee passed the motion, Long would have to give up the governorship a full seven months before his term expired, thus depriving him of the vast patronage and monetary resources of the office. Earl surveyed the full 101-member committee, and he discovered that the resolution would pass easily, so he made no effort to block it. At the September 4 meeting in Baton Rouge, Earl astonished the packed gallery by remaining quiet and subdued throughout the proceedings. After some discussion, the committee voted 93 to 1 to allow Earl Long to qualify to run for governor provided he resign before September 15. Long himself voted for the motion.[3]

On the day of the deadline, September 15, Earl Long announced that he would run for lieutenant governor on a ticket headed by his former enemy Jimmie Noe. Earl knew that giving up the governorship so long before the election would prove disastrous, and he talked Noe into being on his ticket. Noe had been inactive in Louisiana politics since 1948, spending most of his time building up his personal fortune in oil and gas and in radio and television programming. Why he agreed to run for governor in 1959 remains a mystery. Bobbie Dugas, who ran for state comptroller on the Noe-Long ticket, wrote that he, Earl Long, and legislator Oscar

Guidry met with Noe in West Monroe. "After two hours of bickering," Dugas wrote, "Noe finally 'gave in' as a candidate for governor with Earl as his running mate." Gaston Ducote, a Long intimate, believes that in 1959, Earl tried to revert to the tactics of the 1930s. Ducote contended that Noe and Long agreed that Noe would resign as governor shortly after his inauguration, thereby propelling Long into the governorship, and Long would allow Noe to appoint the members of the state Mineral Board, which regulated the oil and gas industry. It does not appear likely that such a deal was made. Both Long and Noe knew very well that the public and the press would not stand for such a flagrant violation of the democratic process. In all probability, Earl ran for lieutenant governor because of his compulsive need to campaign. He had run in almost every state election since 1932—the only exception was in 1952—and he just could not sit this one out. So he talked Noe into making the race. He knew that without any organized machine support, they had no chance of winning, but with the multiplicity of candidates, a second primary was certain. Then he and Noe could make deals with the candidates, thus establishing Long's base for the next race.[4]

Earl Long and Jimmie Noe opened their campaign before a large crowd at the Neville High School auditorium. To entertain the audience, they brought in country comedy star Minnie Pearl and, in a unique addition to the Louisiana political scene, the Jewish raconteur from New York Sam Levinson. Although Jimmie Noe headed the ticket, the people came to see and hear Earl Long, and Earl did not disappoint them. In a series of scathing attacks, he lashed out at his opponents. "If the NAACP and that little pin-headed nut Willie Rainach will just leave us alone," he proclaimed, "then sensible people, not cranks, can get along in a reasonable way. That Rainach wants to fight the Civil War all over again." He characterized Jimmie Davis as "a sweet-smelling guitar player who's in North Louisiana Sunday morning singing 'Nearer My God to Thee,' and Sunday night in South Louisiana singing 'Bed Bug Blues.' His pockets are lined with oil money, gambling money, and 'Bed Bug Blues' record money." On another occasion, Earl devastated Davis with a classic one-liner: "Jimmie Davis loves money like a hog loves slop." Earl stumped the state. In Alexandria, he attacked Bill Dodd: "Big Bad Bill has at least six streamlined deadheads on his payroll that couldn't find Bill's office if they had to. But they can find that *Post Office* every month to get their salary check—Ohyeah!" Spotting Camille Gravel in the audience, he said, "On account we got so few crazy people, we can afford to let Camille Gravel run around."[5]

The 1959 campaign showed Earl Long in vintage form. Wearing red suspenders, dressed in a loose-fitting cream-colored Palm Beach suit, Earl would enter a town, usually over an hour late, take his seat on the platform, and immediately gain the audience's undivided attention. While other members of his ticket spoke, he would arrange his chair at an angle, cross and uncross his legs, snap his red galluses, and catch in midair the flies, mosquitoes, and gnats swarming around the lights. At times, he would pick his nose; at others, he would scratch his crotch. Invariably, in the steamy afternoons and evenings, he would douse himself with cold Coca-Cola, to the crowd's obvious delight. "Cool yourself off, Earl," one spectator yelled, and Earl piped back, "I'm a red-hot poppa," then resumed smoking his cigarette. After about thirty minutes, Earl would suddenly snatch the microphone, no matter who was speaking, and erupt into one of his tirades. He attacked anyone and anything—newspaper editors, politicians, oil and gas magnates, New Orleans' fashionable Boston Club, Communists, rich people, psychiatrists, and lawyers all received their share of the vitriol. In between personal denunciations, he would preach to the audience in the manner of a hellfire-and-brimstone evangelist. But he illustrated his lessons with innumerable anecdotes, many of them slightly ribald. Throughout his discourses, people shouted, "Amen!" and "Hallelujah!" and "You tell 'em, Earl." In his inimitable manner, Earl knew just the right rhetorical tones to reach the poor black and white farmers who made up the majority of his audiences. Attacking the editor of the Alexandria *Daily Town Talk,* he said, "I've been accused of saying the fella who owns the paper is a kept man. Maybe he ain't, but I'd like to be kept as good as he is. He married a rich woman. That's about the best way I know to save yourself about ninety-eight years' hard work." Filled with common laborers, the crowd would cheer in appreciation.[6]

The Noe-Long platform of 1959 contained typical Longite promises of something for everyone: more charity hospitals; larger homestead exemptions; $3 automobile license plate fees; more roads and bridges; higher old-age pensions; pay raises for schoolteachers, state police, and civil service employees; support for organized labor; more money for colleges and universities; and "peaceful race relations." This last was an unsubtle slap at Rainach's flagrant appeals to racial bigotry. In the campaign, Earl openly stated, "I want the nigger vote, and I don't make any secret of it. And I get it because the colored people know I've tried to help 'em." Despite his vigorous public campaign, Earl Long knew he would lose. Well before the primary, he predicted that Jimmie Davis and Chep Morrison would come out on top in the first primary, and that Davis would defeat Morrison in the runoff. Further, he estimated the vote count within 1 percent of the actual total. Most of the smart money people had lined up behind Jimmie Davis because Rainach and Morrison were too unreliable. Rainach had stirred up the race issue, and Morrison was overly ambitious. Former governor Davis could be counted on not to rock any of the traditional political boats. In the first primary, just as Earl had predicted, Morrison won and Davis was second, with their running mates in the same positions. Earl Long ran third in the lieutenant governor's race, with 157,452 votes, most of them coming from blacks and poor whites. The old trouper still had a loyal following, and he ran well ahead of Jimmie Noe and the others on their ticket. But his elimination in the first primary, as well as his surprising defeat for the Winn Parish seat on the Democratic State Central Committee, led many prognosticators to conclude that Long's stormy career in Louisiana politics had finally come to an end. Once again, they would be proven wrong.[7]

For the rest of his administration, Long remained a subdued man, avoiding the limelight and staying out of controversy. When his successor, Jimmie Davis, took the oath of office as Louisiana's new governor in May, 1960, it appeared to many that Earl Long would live the rest of his life in quiet retirement. Earl, however, had no such intention. After Davis' inauguration, he moved into a state-owned apartment in the Pentagon Barracks near the capitol. Dividing his time between Baton Rouge and New Orleans, the former governor resumed his hectic frequenting of the Fair Grounds racetrack and the French Quarter night spots. After the Fair Grounds season closed in mid-May, Earl went on a five-day fling to Baltimore, taking the striptease artist Candy Cane with him to Pimlico. On May 24, Earl took a stripper from the "2 P.M. Club" in Baltimore with him to New York City, where, according to the FBI, they spent a "free-wheeling and free-spending night." In mid-June, he became involved in a minor traffic accident on Gentilly Boulevard in New Orleans. When the New Orleans Police Department investigated, Earl used obscene language and resisted arrest for reckless driving and for not having a proper license. The FBI said that the city police had "had enough of

Long" because he had twice before been involved in traffic accidents while he was drunk.[8]

Despite these personal excesses, Earl once again felt the tug of politics, and after he recovered from prostate surgery at New Orleans' Baptist Hospital, he formally filed his candidacy for the Eighth Congressional District seat in the United States House of Representatives. "I know it's gonna kill me, but I just gotta do it," Earl confided to a friend about his race for Congress. "My doctors tell me my heart's too weak; it can't stand another campaign; but I have to make the race." Earl seemed to have a premonition of death. In his farewell address to the people of Louisiana, televised statewide on May 3, 1960, he waxed philosophical: "I know that I must go to a far and distant land and that I will have the satisfaction of carrying my deeds with me for judgment in the next world." That is why he decided to make a final effort to win an election. As he once told a friend, "I am going to stay in politics until I am taken from this earth." Fully aware that a grueling campaign would undoubtedly kill him, he nevertheless decided to challenge incumbent congressman Harold McSween. He would die doing what he loved best: politicking.[9]

The largest congressional district in Louisiana, the Eighth covered much of the central and northwestern region of the state. Other than Alexandria, the district contained no large cities, and it had only two fairly large towns, Marksville and Natchitoches. In the rest of the sprawling district were small towns such as Winnfield and Bunkie and many hamlets like Florien, Lecompte, Glenmora, Simmesport, Boyce, and Bordelonville. Innumerable isolated farmhouses were scattered throughout the region. Candidates for elective office had to cover thousands of miles in remote rural areas, a schedule that would have taxed the energies of a much younger man than the sixty-four-year-old Earl Long. But Earl looked forward to making the race, and he plunged into it with enthusiasm and energy. Ignoring the incessant demands by his friends and physicians to slow down, Earl drove himself harder and harder, almost as if he knew that this would be his last campaign and he wanted to go out a winner.[10]

The Eighth Congressional District campaign of June, July, and August, 1960, was one of the most exciting in Louisiana political history, made so by the presence of Earl Long. He faced two opponents—the incumbent, Harold McSween, who had garnered nearly all the organized machine backing and was the heavy favorite; and State Representative

Ben Holt of Alexandria, a former Long ally. With the rapidly growing influence of television on electioneering, this would probably be the last campaign in which the candidates devoted nearly all their time and money to appearing personally in every town in the district. As the campaign opened on June 3, the contenders had promised to avoid mud-slinging, but with Uncle Earl in the race, everyone hoped for a round of name-calling and invective. They soon got their wish. Earl told a reporter that McSween was "the only guy I ever saw that can talk out of both sides of his mouth, whistle, and smoke a cigarette at the same time." Generally, though, in the initial stages of the campaign, the candidates emphasized their platforms. McSween stressed his efforts in Congress: trying to balance the federal budget, fighting to reactivate Fort Polk as an army base, opposing federal civil rights legislation, supporting the Landrum-Griffin bill to curb racketeering in organized labor, and backing the federal program to build the Toledo Bend dam and reservoir on the Sabine River, the boundary between Louisiana and Texas. As many other politicians had learned, no one could outpromise Earl Long, and the former governor's platform cleverly blended positions on national issues with specific promises to the district's voters. He would reopen Fort Polk; expand Esler Field, an air force base near Alexandria; use Kisatchie National Forest as the site for a massive community of federally funded homes for the poor; bring more industry into the district; provide free medical care for the elderly; lower the age for Social Security pensioners to sixty-three; and double the income tax exemption to $1,200.[11]

In blistering heat or driving rain, Ole Earl conducted his typical, vigorous campaign, making from five to seven speeches a day. As the campaign progressed he grew visibly weaker; at times, he felt so tired and feeble that aides had to lift him onto a platform or onto the tailgate of a pickup truck. But once on the stump, he seemed to draw strength from some mystical source as he put on another of his patented performances. Throughout June and July, he still made five to seven speeches daily in tours that lasted from early morning until late evening. Despite the oppressive summer heat, 95-degree temperatures and 90 percent humidity, he maintained that killing pace. At Moreauville, the sun was so hot that he had the crowd move into the shade to listen to him, and at Belledula, sudden afternoon thunderstorms interrupted his speech five times. But he persisted in his endless quest for votes, then headed for the next town, which might be a hundred miles away. One Earl Long campaign schedule gives an idea of the rigors of his daily routine: Boyce—7:00 A.M.; Lecompte—3:00 P.M.; Bunkie—5:00 P.M.; Marksville—7:00 P.M.; Simmesport—8:30 P.M.[12]

Earl's entourage consisted of his cousin and bagman, David Bell; his attorney, Joe Arthur Sims; his former executive secretary, State Senator A. A. Fredericks; state Board of Education member Estes Cole; and such politicians as Sixty Rayburn, Bill Dodd, and Sammy Downs. In the early part of the campaign, Earl reminded his audiences that he was the "poppa of the old age pension," the originator of the program that gave school-children hot lunches, the builder of schools for "spastics," and the poor man's friend. He told them that he had forgotten more about the needs of people in the Eighth District than both his opponents knew put to-gether. As he was chauffeured through the rural district, he never ne-glected an opportunity to capture votes. Learning of a farmer who op-posed him, Earl stopped at the man's house, introduced himself, and, after sipping some cool well water, sat down with the farmer and his wife. They talked about crops and animals. Twenty minutes later, Earl not only convinced the man to vote for him, but the farmer promised to get all his relatives in the area to vote for Earl, too. He repeated this scene many times, for nothing flatters voters more than personal attention, and Earl Long was the acknowledged master of that art.

With whites nearly 85 percent of the district's population, one would have expected to find a bulwark of racial bigotry, but in this campaign, Earl Long openly courted the black vote, and he publicly denounced the racists. While he did announce, as expected, his "one million percent" support for segregation, Earl also spoke about black concerns. Calling Willie Rainach a "radical," he told a crowd that while he favored segrega-tion, he hated the "Willie Rainach type of segregation, where he wants to boil the colored in oil." At a stump appearance in Alexandria, he declared his pleasure at seeing "white people and colored people mingling to-gether in the crowd," and he called on all of them, "white and colored, young and old," to come up and shake his hand. "I want the colored vote, the Catholic vote, the Jewish vote, and the Baptist vote," he told another audience. At night, Earl often slipped away from reporters to campaign in black churches, a tactic that won him almost every black vote in the election.[13]

In his career, Earl Long spiced his campaigns with giveaways, distrib-uting clothes, slabs of ham and bacon, cans of sardines, loaves of bread, and even live roosters and hens to the voters. In the 1960 campaign, he gave everything he could find to people he came into contact with: baskets of groceries, turkeys, watermelons, farm implements, and clothing. Carrying a pocketful of change, he threw quarters and half dollars to children, and at one rally, he tossed silver dollars to the crowd. Another trick of the trade was a hillbilly band, featuring singer Jay Chevalier of Lecompte, who entertained audiences with his rendition of "Bill Bailey" and his original composition, "The Ballad of Earl K. Long." Earl also advertised in newspapers to draw crowds. One ad for a rally in Boyce read: "Free Gifts: Cokes for the ladies, candy for the children, and cold drinks for everyone." One companion estimated that "Earl must have given away over one hundred thousand suckers, combs, and cokes." At a stump stop in Clarence, Linda Huffman, the daughter of Clem Huffman, who managed the pea patch farm, won a tub of lard. Earl pointed to her and shouted, "She don't need it!" and ordered her father to give the lard to a needy black man. To the child's great disappointment, Huffman took the tub from her and gave it to a black man standing next to them.[14]

During the initial part of the campaign, close observers of the Louisiana political scene recognized several salient characteristics of the Earl Long crusade. First, he appeared physically exhausted and was no longer able to hold audiences spellbound. Upon seeing Earl on the stump against McSween, many were shocked. Gaunt, pale, trembling, the Earl Long of 1960 seemed but a shadow of the old stumper. He looked years older, and, having lost full control of his bladder, he sometimes urinated in public. Second, people did not seem to turn out at campaign rallies as they once did, and Earl's audiences were usually sparse. Third, Long did not have the organized machine support that had proved so effective in his previous campaigns. Few local leaders backed him in this race, and he relied heavily on some old friends to accompany him on his speaking rounds. And fourth, even early in the campaign, many people seemed to know that this would be Earl Long's last hurrah in Louisiana politics.[15]

By the last week in June, Earl decided to inject some life into what had been a listless campaign by spicing it with his endless repertoire of name-calling. Although he had promised not to engage in personal attacks on his opponents, he started to denounce McSween with some of his choicest witticisms. To a disappointingly small crowd of fifty in Pineville on June 26, he roared in his gravelly voice, "If there ever was a full-fledged faker and anointed jackass, it is Harold McSween." By the beginning of

July, Earl used personal attacks on McSween as the focus of his speeches. Calling McSween "catfish mouth," he proclaimed that it would be good for "his wife, father and mother and everybody if he were to be given a severe political beating." "He's a hot-house plant," Earl yelled, "born with a silver spoon in his mouth, and you couldn't get it out with a crow-bar or a screwdriver!" At another appearance, Long charged McSween with hiring congressional aide Mary Helen Foster at $300 a month, and "she can't even type and hasn't ever been in his office!" McSween had refrained from name-calling, but when Earl started it, the congressman retaliated. Throughout the district, newspaper advertisements for McSween showed Earl Long with the pillowcase over his head as he emerged from the airplane in Fort Worth. He also charged Long with misrepresenting him as a rich man, but when Earl filed his financial statement, "he was worth more than a quarter of a million dollars." Turning to sarcasm, McSween said, "I've never pulled a pillow case over my head or bought a carload of watermelons or twenty-five horse collars." Earl had left himself wide open for another McSween barrage when he told a group of voters that a congressman should know a little bit about women and a little bit about a lot of other things. Seizing the opportunity, McSween said that "if knowledge of whiskey drinking, woman chasing, and the bug house are qualifications of a congressman, then he is more qualified than I." [16]

McSween had sewed up much of the organized machine support, and he had the backing of numerous well-heeled contributors. He could therefore conduct a lavishly financed campaign. One McSween organization, the Committee to Save Louisiana from National Embarrassment, resembled the citizens' committees that had given Sam Jones such effective support in the 1940 gubernatorial election. This McSween committee paid for full-page newspaper ads that depicted all the worst of Long's escapades during the previous year. Typically, the press also opposed Long. The Eighth District's leading newspaper, the Alexandria *Daily Town Talk,* lambasted Long almost every day. One anti-Long blast piously predicted that "the day when the politician who could cuss the loudest or use the greatest assortment of derogatory adjectives to describe his opponent would be the best vote-getter has long since passed out of the picture." [17]

The results of the first primary, held on July 23, 1960, indicated that the *Daily Town Talk* may have been accurate in its assessment of the political situation. Harold McSween came in first with 29,856 votes, and Earl

Long had 26,132. The third candidate, Ben Holt, finished a poor third with 10,278, a sufficiently high total to prevent McSween from having a majority. Thus, a second primary between McSween and Long would take place on August 27. Earl claimed that he had "run the shirttail off" McSween, but most political pros thought otherwise. McSween had run a very strong race in the first primary, and he had the solid backing of most of the district's office holders, the endorsement of virtually all the newspapers, and plenty of campaign funds. To defeat him in the runoff, Earl would have to capture three-quarters of Holt's voters. But then Holt endorsed McSween, and almost everyone was sure that Earl Long would lose. Now Long would have to wage a vigorous, come-from-behind campaign, and with no machine support and his usual sources of campaign funding dried up, his cause seemed hopeless. Nevertheless, Earl was confident of victory, and he borrowed $4,000 from his sister Lucille to add to the $4,000 he had already bet that he would win the runoff.[18]

The second primary witnessed both candidates going all out to win, but Long clearly outperformed McSween in taking his case directly to the people. To attract crowds to a rally in Alexandria, the Long campaign set up a "three-ring circus." Ole Earl himself served as "ringmaster" in one section, denouncing McSween as a "yellow-bellied sapsucker . . . he's a spoiled brat. They tell me he talks to his father like he would a bootblack—that little hypocrite." In another "ring," located in the city square, Edgar Coco of Marksville served as a "trumpeter," calling everyone to come get free drinks and bacon. In the third "ring," two vocal groups entertained the crowd with popular songs. Large numbers of people strolled through the "circus," availing themselves of all the free goodies and listening to the speeches and the music. One out-of-state woman commented that the rally "and 'My Fair Lady' are the most entertaining things I've seen since coming to Louisiana."[19]

Knowing that to win, he would have to get out a large vote in the rural areas, Earl Long ran a true "people's campaign." It went over the heads of the politicians and the press and carried his message straight to the voters. Although weakened by the labors of the first primary, Long drove himself relentlessly to reach as many people as he possibly could. When friends, concerned about his health, urged him to slow down, he replied, "No, this is my last campaign. I'm gonna die soon, and I want to go out a winner." So he maintained a furious, exhausting pace, wearing himself out in the process. Hardly able to sleep or eat, he dipped into his last reserves of energy for the final, critical weeks of the runoff. On the stump, shocked audiences saw the tired old man barely able to climb onto the platform. The physical strain showed also in the considerable amount of weight he lost, and his trousers hung below his waist. But when he spoke, flashes of the old sparkle again lighted his eyes, and he let McSween have many doses of his most effective personal attacks. In Colfax, he called McSween a "genuine, number one, eighteen carat smart alec." In Zwolle, he said that the only time in his life McSween ever stooped down was "to pick up a golf ball."[20]

Earl Long's final face-to-face confrontation with a political opponent came on August 5, in what reporters dubbed the "battle of Florien." Earl showed up, late as usual, for a stump appearance in the tiny community of Florien, and as he started speaking, he spotted McSween, who had arrived early for his stump speech. Earl invited McSween onto the platform to tell the people about the checks he had been issuing to Mrs. Foster, and McSween took up the challenge. Soon both combatants were yelling at each other, accusing each other of various misdeeds. McSween chided Earl for testifying against Huey in 1932, and Earl shot back that McSween had always opposed the things Huey stood for. During one tense moment, the foes were less than six feet apart and were shaking their fingers at each other, but then people on the platform separated them. Earl ended the confrontation by snapping his red suspenders, discoursing on Huey, and declaring that he would support the Democratic nominee for president. Then, before his temper flared up again, aides hustled him off the platform.[21]

While Long and McSween did not face each other directly again, the heated battle continued as they campaigned on their separate schedules. In Leesville, Earl promised to reopen Fort Polk and help secure federal financing for the Toledo Bend project. On Saturday, August 13, he traveled through Natchitoches, Winn, and LaSalle parishes. The following day, he crossed the expanses of Rapides and Avoyelles parishes, eventually reaching every town and city in the district. Down the home stretch of the campaign, Earl fired all the political guns he could muster. He had Jewell Long, the widow of his brother, George, appear on television, and he roped in Bill Dodd to appear with him on the stump. But Earl continued to steal the audiences' attention. Responding to McSween allegations that he was running around with strippers, he said, "I'm sixty-four years old and just had the worst operation a man could have. What would I do with a woman if I caught one?" On another occasion, he said, "I know one hundred things I need more than a woman." He told another crowd, "The day I think I'm one bit better than you good people and my head goes to swelling, damnit, I hope it will pop."[22]

On Friday, August 26, 1960, Earl Long celebrated his sixty-fifth birthday, and his cousin Ed Wingate advised him to take the day off, relax, and have a good time. But Earl refused. It was the day before the second primary, and he still had last-minute politicking to conduct. He told Wingate, "Ed, I've got a long time to rest. If I could beat him, I'd die happy." So he stumped the two pivotal parishes in the district, Rapides and Avoyelles, visiting country stores and calling on local farmers. Thus, Earl ended his political career the way he began it forty-four years earlier, hustling votes from the poor black and white farmers in rural Louisiana. The following day, Saturday, August 27, was the election, and as he awaited the returns in his room at the Bentley Hotel in Alexandria, Earl Long suffered a severe heart attack. Refusing his family's pleas to go to the hospital, he told reporters that he felt a little "puny" from eating "overripe pork," and he spent the day, as he did during every election, on the telephone contacting key people to ensure that they got out the vote. Only after the polls closed at 8:00 P.M. did he allow his family to have him taken to the hospital. In the election, Earl pulled off what many considered the most spectacular upset of his career by defeating McSween, 38,693 votes to 34,235. His incessant campaigning in the rural areas resulted in a huge country turnout, easily offsetting McSween's expected heavy vote in Alexandria and Marksville. By the thousands, poor black and white farmers, many of whom had never voted before, showed up at the polls to cast their ballots for their beloved Uncle Earl. One dedicated black supporter in Colfax proudly boasted that "I've been up 'til three o'clock every morning the past two weeks working for Uncle Earl. I have got him sixty votes, I bet." The country folk who gave him his last political victory did so out of appreciation for all the things he had done for them over the years, for they knew that this would be his last campaign.[23]

Jubilant over his upset victory, Earl Long waxed philosophical as he was carried in a stretcher from the hotel to a waiting ambulance. He told Lucille and State Senator Ralph King, "I've lived a full life, and I've done a lot of good things. So don't feel bad if I don't make it." In good spirits, he quipped and traded stories with reporters before the attendants put him in the ambulance. At Alexandria's Baptist Hospital, Earl seemed content to lie in bed and rest. He received a steady stream of visitors, including Blanche, who stayed in Alexandria and came regularly to his room. One acquaintance who tried to see him failed. Dressed in her usual eye-catching style, Blaze Starr entered the hospital and asked to see Uncle Earl. A hefty nurse on duty refused by responding, "Honey, the last person on earth he needs to see is you!" On September 3, Earl held his last press conference. Lying in bed, he appeared somewhat haggard but rested, and he displayed some of the spark that had made him such good copy. He stated that he looked forward to his new job, and that when he got to Washington, "I don't intend to keep my mouth shut." In his final comment to the press, Earl summed up his career: "I think I'm a kind of statesman-like politician. A politician is misunderstood. He is capable of doing something for the people. That is what I tried to do." To close friends who visited him in the hospital, Earl confided that he would not survive this attack, and his prediction was right. Death came to the congressman-elect early in the morning on September 5, 1960. According to Ellis "Easy Money" Littleton, his sound-truck driver who was in the room with him, Earl awakened about 6:30, sat up and drank a cup of coffee, then lay down and went back to sleep. At 7:10 A.M., he turned over in bed, coughed a couple of times, and stopped breathing. His nephew and the attending physician, Dr. Robert V. Parrott, made the official announcement. The night before Earl died, there had been an eclipse of the moon. Oddly enough, the same phenomenon occurred the night before Huey died almost exactly a quarter of a century earlier.[24]

14

The Last of the Red Hot Poppas

Twenty years after Earl Long died, a Lake Charles journalist wrote in his weekly column that "Louisiana politics have lost their glamour. I didn't realize how much of the old 'fire and brimstone' had faded until running across some Earl Long stories while doing research. . . . In the past, politicians never hesitated to let you know where they stood. Today, they often speak with forked tongues." Other commentators voiced similar sentiments. In late 1963, as a gubernatorial primary approached, a Long friend and supporter noticed an almost complete absence of political activity in Winn Parish, and he wistfully recalled that "when Ole Earl, hisself, was here directing political traffic, nobody was confused very long—he soon had the voters lined up for or against his man—not wobbling about like they are doing now." The death of Earl Long indeed removed one of the most colorful and controversial characters ever to grace the Louisiana political scene with his unique personality and style. He was, as he called himself, "the last of the red hot poppas." [1]

The Winnfield native was a complex human being, whose many-sided personality inspired a perceptive student of Louisiana politics to write: "When God made Earl Long, he threw away the mold with the assurance that he would never make another man so different from the masses of mankind." Everyone who knew him agreed that the only thing certain about Earl Long was his unpredictability, for no one, and probably not even Long himself, knew what he would say or do next. Yet, whatever he did or said, Long acted from political motives—he was a political animal through and through. "While the rest of 'em are sleeping," he once said of his rivals, "I'm politicking," a remark that accurately describes his total commitment to the political life. Friends and foes alike still marvel at his sheer physical stamina during political crises, when he could stay awake for days on end and could carry his campaign appeals to every village and hamlet in the state. Key members of the Long machine learned quickly to expect phone calls at three o'clock in the morning, when Earl wanted to discuss a subject. With an intense, consuming passion, he devoured every part of Louisiana politics, knowing in intimate detail even the most trivial information. His legendary wheeling and dealing became such an integral part of his life that he would often try to bargain when there was no need. Whether in the Governor's Mansion or in a hotel suite, when he discussed a political matter with someone, he seemed to emanate intensity: his eyes sparkled; his hands rubbed together gleefully; his whole being lit up, for he was doing what he loved best.[2]

Earl Long was one of the last of a dying breed of politicians, the old-fashioned stump orator who, through flamboyance and sheer force of personality, arouses the rural masses into a formidable political power. Near the end of his career, when television began to assume a critical role in electioneering, he recognized that his brand of politicking was doomed. "That television makes me look like a monkey on a stick," he told a friend, and he would hardly appreciate the modern trappings: pollsters, phone banks, professional fund-raisers, and the slick television commercials that proved so effective when Charles E. "Buddy" Roemer defeated Edwin Edwards in the 1987 gubernatorial election. To the end of his life, Earl clung to the intensely personal style of politicking. As state elections approached he grew eager to hit the campaign trail and carry his message to the people, and as Maggie Dixon wrote, he had "no equal when it comes to stumping Louisiana and telling the people what they want to hear." In Alexandria, in August of 1959, he gave one of his traditional denunciations of the privileged classes, a common theme in his stump oratory: "We got the finest roads, finest hospitals, finest schools in the country—yet there are rich men who complain. They are so tight you can hear 'em squeak when they walk. They wouldn't give a nickel to see a earthquake. They sit there swallowin' hundred dollar bills like a bullfrog swallows minners—if you chunked 'em as many as they wanted, they'd bust." The effectiveness of such appeals is amply demonstrated by Long's invariable heavy vote totals in the rural parishes. Some intimates maintain, however, that he was even more effective after he had finished speaking. For several hours after stump appearances, he would greet members of the audience and converse with them in plain, simple language. No one could make the common people feel a greater affinity with them than

Earl Long, for he knew and understood their needs and their desires. And he delivered on the promises he made to them. He gave them political entertainment on a grand scale, but he also gave them paved roads, hot school lunches, charity hospitals, and old-age pensions.[3]

A writer for the *American Mercury* observed that in 1956, the Long family "wields more power, effectively and collectively, than the Kingfish himself." The exaggeration nevertheless contained a great deal of truth. Earl Long held office as governor; his brother, George, was a congressman; and nephew Russell was becoming one of the powers in the U.S. Senate. Some commentators, in fact, bemoaned what appeared to be a permanent Long dynasty in Louisiana. Although founded by Huey, the dynasty was greatly enlarged under Earl. And during his administrations, the notorious Long political machine, which he had helped create, grew into one of America's most potent political organizations. He built a multilayered network of state, parish, and local officials, with precinct and ward leaders in every voting district in the state. Earl personally supervised the elaborate organization, and he knew personally every individual responsible for the machine's smooth functioning. His constant travels around the state, his incessant telephone calls to local leaders, and his unmatched knowledge of local problems gave him the steady flow of information he needed to keep a tight rein on the machine. According to Bill Dodd, Earl was hard to work for because "if you did too well, he cut you down. If you messed up, he was on you in a second. Nobody could get to be as big as Earl. He wouldn't even let department heads meet. When he was out of power, he wanted his friends out of power."[4]

For all his renown as a wheeler and dealer, Earl Long proved a surprisingly efficient and capable administrator of state government. In numerous interviews, political supporters and opponents alike praised Long as one of Louisiana's most able governors. State Representative Frank Fulco of Shreveport, an anti-Long leader, called Long "the most capable, qualified governor we have had in many, many years." One of Earl's most determined enemies, Senator Willie Rainach, admitted that "I had better relations with Governor Long than his own men did. Earl Long was not vindictive . . . like Huey. . . . One of Earl's good qualities was that he wanted everybody else in his administration to be honest. He didn't permit any level beneath himself taking money and he conducted a relatively honest administration." Dupree Litton, one of Earl's executive counsels, claimed that Earl "was frugal personally, and I believe he was frugal with the state's finances. We could use some more of that these days. There was less waste and corruption under Earl Long than any other governor since." Earl kept such tight control over the state bureaucracy that when politicians and private citizens went to him with problems, mostly of a trivial or a personal nature, Long invariably resolved them, with a minimum of red tape.[5]

Earl Long insisted that Louisiana adhere to sound fiscal policies; he kept state spending within reasonable limits and had balanced state budgets. Unlike most of his predecessors and successors, he refused to obligate future generations by financing state construction and other capital outlay projects through issuing state bonds. Instead, he pursued a "pay as you go" policy of annual appropriations. Long had no serious difficulty maintaining balanced budgets because his two full administrations as governor coincided with an era of enormous industrial expansion and economic prosperity. As a consequence, state revenues went up steadily throughout his two terms, and so did annual funding for his social programs. In his first administration, he did have massive tax increases enacted, but most of them had little impact on the ordinary citizen. He also administered his programs with a degree of efficiency that would astonish the most cost-conscious bureaucrat today. Although the available data do not permit an exact analysis, it appears likely that under Earl Long, more than 85 percent of state money went directly to the individuals or projects it was intended to fund, and less than 15 percent to administrative expenses. Earl expected his people to work hard for the state, and as the longtime president of the Lincoln Parish Police Jury, John A. Mitchell, recalled, "he wouldn't let any department head drive anything bigger than a Ford or a Chevrolet." Generally, he hired men with large families to feed and clothe because he believed that they would work harder for their wages. He also personally spot-checked state offices and construction projects, and when he found people loafing or neglecting their duties, he fired them.[6]

In analyzing the reasons for Earl Long's political successes, his archenemy Sam Jones declared that "Earl never made the same mistake twice. Earl had lots of friends, he had little friends, which was the secret of Earl Long. Earl knew people, he knew their weaknesses." Jones might have added that Earl also knew their strengths, and he had an uncanny knack for recognizing innate political talent. Among the many politicians Earl recruited into the Long machine were Robert Angelle, Allen Ellender,

John B. Fournet, Camille Gravel, Lucille May Grace, Russell Long, Gillis Long, Robert Maestri, John McKeithen, Mary Evelyn Parker, and Leander Perez. These and numerous other politicos learned their lessons from Earl Long, and he, in turn, learned many things from them. Once he spotted a talented politician, he would carefully teach him or her the most effective ways of getting results. Bob Angelle, speaker of the house during Earl's last gubernatorial term, vividly recalled one lesson Earl taught him: "Watch who you take money from. Some sons of bitches will feel like they own you if you take one dollar from them."[7]

A. J. Liebling, the New York reporter who spent several months in Louisiana in 1959, concluded that Earl Long was the only "true liberal in the South"—after observing Long fight for the right of his black constituents to vote. Long's political philosophy could indeed accurately be described as liberal, for he maintained a strong belief in government's responsibility to provide for the basic human needs of Louisiana's poor people, a philosophy he implemented throughout his career. In his 1955–56 campaign for governor, Earl promised to "sell the state capitol if I have to to pay the poor old folks a fitting pension." Although Earl knew that there was no serious chance of his having to resort to such an extreme measure, no one doubted his sincerity. Earl's campaign platforms have been widely criticized for their endless lists of pie-in-the-sky promises to the poor, yet his tangible record in office shows that he fulfilled more than 98 percent of his campaign promises, a record that few, if any, other governors could claim.[8]

Like Huey, Earl faced the opposition of Louisiana's leading metropolitan newspapers. Throughout his career, hundreds of editorials sharply criticized his policies, and the leading organs of the press invariably endorsed anti-Long candidates in elections. Earl Long made an easy target: the newspapers generally denounced his crude personal habits, such as spitting and scratching his rump, as unbecoming the Governor of Louisiana. Furthermore, Long's unethical political methods brought him constant press scrutiny. The owners of the leading papers—Douglas Manship of Baton Rouge and Alvin Howard and Leonard Nicholson of New Orleans—had fought many battles with Huey Long during his tumultuous career, and they continued the struggle with Earl. His neo-populist, liberal programs went against their conservative grain, and his active opposition to such press favorites as Sam Jones and Chep Morrison reinforced their anti-Long stance. Earl turned that opposition into a political asset, for in his campaigns, he reserved some of his most venomous diatribes and most scathing sarcasm for the press. In one of his classic stump remarks, Earl told the story of a *Times-Picayune* reporter who fell into a ditch with a hog. A prim and proper lady strolled by and said, "Well, you can tell some people by the company they keep!" According to Earl, "the hog got up and left." When the *Times-Picayune* endorsed Jimmie Davis for governor in 1959, Earl said, "I see where Perez and Davis and the *Times-Picayune* have gotten together. It reminds me of what the Bible says about the end of time, billy goats, tigers, rabbits, and house cats are gonna sleep together." Referring to the *Picayune* and the *States-Item,* both owned by the same company, he observed, "They've got two newspapers down there, but it's like taking crackers from a barrel—they all taste alike." Other papers also came in for their share of Long attacks. Of the one in Alexandria he pointed out: "The *Town Talk* prints just one side, or if they do print your side, it's way back on page sixty under the Lydia Pinkham ad," and his name for the paper was the Alexandria *Bladder.* He even criticized small-town papers. When a cub reporter for the Ruston *Daily Leader* came to him for an interview, Earl said, "That paper you work for, kid, you know I could hold that thing up just chest-high and drop it and before it hit the ground, I could read everything in it." [9]

Earl did get along very well with individual reporters. His favorite journalists included Maggie Dixon of the *Morning Advocate,* Ed Clinton of the *State-Times,* Jim McLean of the Associated Press, and Tom Kelly of the *Winn Parish Enterprise/News-American.* These and other reporters found Earl accessible and a source of choice news copy. He generally avoided formal press conferences, preferring instead personal interviews with individual reporters. With his customary frankness and wit, Earl gave them inside information about the political situation in Baton Rouge. He also made frequent telephone calls to reporters and publishers. A reporter for the *Picayune* discovered that Earl used to call the sports desk early each morning to get the latest race results and the odds on that day's horse races. He told the sports desk not to tell Earl anything until he granted a telephone interview with the news room. Walter Cowan, the editor of the *States,* remembers Earl calling several times a week to give him information or just to chat. Earl also became friends with John F. Tims, president of the Times-Picayune Publishing Company. Tims stated that Earl used to visit him in his office and telephone him regularly to receive his advice on state issues. [10]

Maggie Dixon called Earl Long "the most fascinating, funniest, wisest, best informed and thorough politician I have ever known. . . . Earl Long knew his politics and he knew his Louisiana." Unfortunately, Earl rarely recorded his thoughts on paper, but his few surviving letters provide insight into his personal views. Every politician must remember, he wrote, "every voter wants to see you and touch you be he man or woman and he wants you to ask him for his vote. You must never loose [*sic*] your temper as you would like to talk back. You never know how a person will vote when he gets alone in that booth." Once, he sat down at a typewriter and pecked out some homespun gems:

1. Our educational system is stimulating our youth to prey on us.
2. The keen business man is held up as a success regardless of which group of bandits he belongs to or the method he used to rob—the Jesse James or Al Capone???
3. We live in a predatory society, regardless of what the cummercial [*sic*] clubs preach. Money grabbing is still a high calling.
4. Make promises. Tell them that you are going to throw the polecats out. No one believes he is a polecat. He thinks [of] the fellow he does not like as a polecat.[11]

When asked to describe himself, Earl Long replied, "I'm just a common gazabo," an expression meaning that he was a plain, ordinary man, one of the common people. In his campaigns, he stressed his identification with his rural constituents, and nothing symbolized his attachment to his country roots more than his frequent visits to his pea patch farm. Located on the northeastern outskirts of Winnfield, the farm was bought from the Federal Home Loan Bank in 1937, and for the next twenty-three and a half years, it served as his home away from home, where he could relax, escape the bustle of city life, lick his wounds after a defeat, or savor victory. Most of all, the 320-acre homestead became a place where he could live the rural life he loved. Nothing gave him greater personal satisfaction than to arrive at the farm, shed his business suit and don a pair of faded coveralls, then mount a horse and ride into the woods to hunt hogs. The pea patch farm featured a dilapidated shack with a galvanized tin roof, linoleum floors, naked light bulbs hanging from the ceilings, and picture calendars pasted on the bare walls. It had two bedrooms, a storeroom, a kitchen, and a bath (the only "luxury" Earl added to the place). An oilcloth covered the kitchen table, and a dishtowel was draped unceremoniously over the bathroom window. Worn-out World War II bunk beds lined the bedroom walls. On the porch, a fifty-five-gallon urn constantly produced freshly brewed coffee whenever Earl stayed there. Scattered inside and out were the objects of his shopping sprees: sacks of potatoes; ten-gallon hats; strands of rope; dozens of hoes, rakes, and shovels; burlap sacks filled with seed; and a variety of other items. One person described his first and only visit to the pea patch farm: "Earl got me to sleep in that place just once, and believe me, never again. If I have to spend another night up there, I'll sleep on the ground outside; it's cleaner. The beds have filthy rags for blankets; the tin roof leaks; and you have to step hard on a plank to get the door shut." [12]

Three people tended the farm for Earl: his close friend Clem Huffman and two black cooks, Rosa Wells and "Miss Sadie" Caldwell. They kept the place up, took care of the animals, planted, watered, and harvested the crops. When Earl arrived at the farm, he changed into his country denims, then took off on a hog hunt. "I like to hunt wild hogs," he said. "You always come home with some meat." Neighboring farmers had trouble with Earl, who paid little attention to the hogs he hunted. When Earl suffered a heart attack in 1950 while he was hunting hogs, one local wag remarked that the reason was that he had accidentally killed one of his own hogs. On a hog-hunting jaunt through the woods, Earl and Public Service Commissioner Ernest S. Clements, one of his oldest friends, crossed a deep creek and got soaking wet. Clements recalled, "There I was, sitting next to the Governor of Louisiana, both of us sitting stark naked on the banks of a creek, waiting for our clothes to dry." At the pea patch farm, Earl always invited his Winn Parish neighbors and friends for visits, and many fondly remember his generosity. Every July 4, he held a watermelon party for the area's poor black residents. Earl enjoyed visiting with his neighbors, and he loved to play tricks on the children. One of his favorites was to hide in the woods and wait for local youths to steal watermelons from his patch. When he saw the teenage boys with watermelons in hand, he would fire his shotgun over their heads, and they would run home. [13]

Much of Earl's earthiness and crudeness derived from his attachment to his country heritage, and at times, he seemed to make deliberate efforts to shock people. He refused to allow social convention or personal inhibition to keep him from doing whatever he wanted. One morning, about four o'clock, he received a telephone call in his Roosevelt Hotel room, and he needed to make another call right away. Not wanting to disturb Blanche, who lay asleep next to him, Earl simply walked into the hall, ignoring the fact that he was not dressed. A couple returning to their room were shocked to see the governor, clad only in his underwear, screaming into a public phone. On another occasion, Governor and Mrs. Long were scheduled to entertain important guests in the Mansion, and Blanche had carefully planned an elaborate meal. When the guests arrived, Earl was resting in an upstairs bedroom and refused to come to dinner, so Blanche had to improvise. After dinner, Earl descended the stairs, stuffing his shirt into his pants. In the Mansion's exquisite East Room, Earl sat talking with the guests, a husband and wife and several children, then tried to spit into the fireplace, some fifteen feet away, but missed his target. Earl then ordered a state trooper to bring a hunting dog he owned into the room to show to the children. As soon as the animal entered the room, it defecated on the plush carpet, to Earl's great delight and to Blanche's utter embarrassment. Earl also never hesitated to employ his graphic vocabulary. In one classic Long story, Earl and a Roman Catholic priest were having a friendly, casual conversation in his office. Suddenly, a lobbyist walked in and dropped a wad of cash on Earl's desk. "Don't worry about a thing," Earl told the man. "I'll take care of you." A few minutes later, a lobbyist from the other side walked in and left an even bigger wad of cash on the desk. Earl said, "Don't worry about a thing. I'll take care of you." After the man left, Earl turned to the startled cleric and bellowed, "Who in the hell do those bastards think they are, trying to bribe the Governor of Louisiana? I'm not going to do a thing for either one of those sons of bitches!"[14]

Earl Long had the gift of gab and a sense of humor. In public and in private, he spiced his remarks with comic ad libs and hilarious anecdotes. A sampling provides only a glimpse of this important aspect of his personality. After Attorney General Jack Gremillion refused to endorse him for lieutenant governor in 1959, Earl told a crowd: "If you want to hide something from Jack Gremillion, put it in a law book." Campaigning against Jimmie Davis, he said that the former governor was "a liar, a thief, and he's got diabetes." Referring to Davis' laid-back political style, he said, "You couldn't wake him with an earthquake." On the stump against Francis Grevemberg, he said, "You're a fine boy. You're kind. You're decent. You're trustworthy. You've got good, God-fearing parents. You're just as smooth as a peeled onion." In his last campaign, Earl said of Ben Holt, "I'm going to get him so groggy, he's going to look like a muley bull coming out of a dripping vat." Of Harold McSween, Earl commented, "He's a confirmed alcoholic, a wife-beater." At the 1956 Democratic National Convention in Chicago, Earl was returning to his hotel after a day at the racetrack when he saw a shoe store advertising a sale, and, as usual, he bought several hundred pairs. The night before the balloting, Senator John F. Kennedy of Massachusetts, who was wooing southern support for his bid for the vice-presidential nomination, called on Earl in his hotel suite. Before Earl would discuss the balloting, he made Kennedy take off the expensive shoes he was wearing and put on a pair of the cheap shoes Earl had just bought. After Kennedy walked out of the room, still wearing Earl's shoes, Earl told a friend, "I'll bet that's the cheapest pair of shoes that young brat ever put on." (Kennedy's politicking failed. The Louisiana delegation voted for Estes Kefauver for vice-president.)[15]

Another characteristic of Earl Long was his personal eccentricity. Like his brother Huey, he had a restless streak, and he was constantly on the move, often taking spur-of-the-moment trips around the state. At any time of day, and frequently in the middle of the night, Earl would order his chauffeur, a state trooper, to drive him to a friend's house. About three o'clock in the morning, he developed a sudden urge to visit the attorney general, Bolivar Kemp. Arriving at Kemp's estate in Amite, Earl found the front gate locked, so he started banging on it. The ruckus awakened Kemp's gardener, who went to investigate. Earl ordered him to open the gate, but the gardener refused. Outraged, Earl screamed, "You goddamn nigger! Don't you know who I am! I'm the Governor of Louisiana! Now, you let me in right now!" The man would not, and a dejected Long finally left. One day Earl visited his friend Bill Dykes, who owned a country store in Montpelier, and he left with two live goats in the back seat. On another occasion, Earl offered a ham to a college president, but the man turned it down because he was about to leave on a trip. "I'll take it," a local labor leader said. "The hell you will," Earl replied. "I can buy you for a hamburger." Earl took the ham, and as he drove down the road, he spotted a local farmer and gave it to him.[16]

If Earl Long was quite an individual, he was also one of the most influential politicians in Louisiana history. An assessment of Long's political record begins, appropriately, with his accomplishments, for he could point to a longer list of genuine achievements than virtually every other governor in the state's history. When a reporter asked Earl Long what he was proudest of having done, he named the state old-age pension. Although the idea of an old-age pension funded by the state was Dudley LeBlanc's, Earl Long implemented it and expanded it into the nation's largest program for senior citizens. As lieutenant governor in 1936, he pushed the old-age pension bill through the legislature, and each year during his gubernatorial administrations, elderly Louisianians received increases in their pensions. By the time he left the governor's office for the last time, in 1960, the average monthly old-age pension amounted to $71.06, a substantial amount for people whose Social Security averaged between $20 and $40 a month. In health care, Earl Long built more charity hospitals than any other governor, providing free medical services to hundreds of thousands of citizens each year, and his "welfare prescriptions" program enabled them to obtain prescribed medication at no charge. Long also established a statewide network of free ambulance service and dental care, along with mobile medical clinics, which were particularly helpful for those in isolated rural areas. For poor people in general, he set up a variety of welfare programs, ranging from aid to families with dependent children to financial assistance to the blind. Under his administrations, Louisiana paid the highest welfare benefits in the South.[17]

In education, Earl Long presided over the construction of more than a thousand new public schools at the elementary and secondary levels, the establishment of several new college campuses and the expansion of existing ones, the building of dozens of new vocational-technical schools, and the funding of an adult education program that helped many become literate. Regularly during Earl Long's two full terms as governor, schoolteachers received salary increases, proportionally the highest teacher pay raises in state history, and for teachers, along with other state employees, there was significant growth in such fringe benefits as a lucrative retirement system. Throughout Long's governorships, Louisiana ranked first in the South in the amount of state funding for public education per students and in teachers' salaries. Long often attempted to interfere in the public schools by firing college presidents and principals, but he respected academic freedom in the classroom, and he was responsible for the enactment of Louisiana's teacher tenure law in 1936. In addition, Long built new institutions for the education of the mentally retarded and physically handicapped, vastly expanded the free school bus transportation system, and instituted free hot school lunches for all students. In transportation, he added tens of thousands of miles of paved roads and highways, constructed hundreds of new bridges, and cut many new gravel roads in remote rural areas. The list could be extended, but it can be stated with accuracy that no other governor could match his record.[18]

In the area of civil rights, Earl Long could justifiably claim real accomplishments for the time in which he served as governor. As the most deprived class of citizens, Louisiana's blacks received a significantly high proportion of the social, education, and health benefits he provided. Approximately 30 percent of the state's population, blacks received nearly 60 percent of the state funding for his programs. A staunch defender of racial segregation, Long nevertheless ensured that blacks obtained their fair share of his programs designed to assist the poor. More significant, Earl Long, virtually alone among southern politicians of his era, began to recognize the inevitability of the new age of racial equality, and he took certain preliminary steps to prepare Louisiana. In 1948, he established a pay scale for schoolteachers that gave white and black teachers equal pay, and during his administrations, he put it into practice. He expanded education opportunities for blacks through sharply increased funding for black colleges, the construction of hundreds of new grammar and high schools for blacks, the establishment of new vocational-technical schools for blacks, and the adult literacy program, aimed primarily at blacks. In 1958, when he fulfilled his campaign promise of opening a New Orleans branch of LSU, Long would not give in to the demands of the racist elements, and he enforced the opening of LSU-NO on a totally integrated basis. By granting and enforcing the right of over 150,000 black citizens to vote, he helped to give them the political leverage they would need for the future. His courageous defense of blacks' right to vote and his public denunciations of Leander Perez, Willie Rainach, and other segregationists stand in stark contrast to the performance of most of his southern political contemporaries. He steadfastly refused to surrender to the racial hatred infecting southern politics at the time, and despite the furious efforts of what he called the "grasseaters" to disfranchise his black supporters, in his last great political accomplishment, Earl Long successfully struggled to retain blacks on the voter registration rolls.

Long should also receive credit for his consistent loyalty to the national Democratic party. In 1948, he bucked the ground swell of popular support for the Dixiecrats by using his political muscle to have his friend Harry Truman placed on the ballot in Louisiana, and he covertly backed Truman in the presidential campaign. In 1952 and again in 1956, when many of Louisiana's political leaders supported Republican Dwight

Eisenhower for the presidency, Long openly endorsed the Democrat, Adlai Stevenson. In 1960, when the anti-Long and segregationist faction attempted to start a states' rights movement backing Senator Harry Byrd for president, Long again remained loyal to the national party, and just before he died, he publicly endorsed the Kennedy-Johnson ticket. Calling the Republicans the "party of the rich and greedy," he believed that the Democrats best served the interests of the common people. That is why he accepted the national party's increasing commitment to civil rights and remained faithful to its candidates. The national Democratic party reflected Earl Long's own personal principles, and it retained the electoral support of two of his strongest voting blocs, blacks and organized labor.[19]

If Earl Long made remarkable contributions, he also made great mistakes. Perhaps his greatest was his persistent advocacy of the notion that people can get something for nothing. "Free" became one of the most common words in his political lexicon. "Here in Louisiana," Earl would tell audiences, "we have free roads and bridges, free schools and free hot lunches, free charity hospitals." Like Huey before him, Earl based his political appeals on the lower classes' expectation that the state of Louisiana would provide certain services at no cost to them, and his campaign platforms contained an almost endless list of promises of state programs. Even though he doubled the total state tax burden in 1948, Long relied more and more on oil and gas revenues to fund his programs, and because those industries expanded enormously during his terms as governor, rising state revenues enabled him to fund annual increases in a myriad of state services. His successors in the governor's office followed his example by basing the major portion of state revenue on severance taxes, royalties, and mineral leases. In the 1970s, when the price of energy skyrocketed, the state actually reduced such traditional and essentially more stable revenue sources as sales and income taxes, and it abolished the property tax altogether, thereby increasing Louisiana's reliance on energy revenues. For Louisiana politicians, this happy situation enabled them to expand the programs Long established without levying the direct taxes necessary to pay for them. The average citizen of Louisiana grew accustomed to paying low taxes while simultaneously expecting a full range of state services. Naturally, the politicians took the easy way out, by having no state property tax, by having only a minimal state income tax, by enshrining the $3 annual automobile license plate fee in the state constitution. As long as the oil and gas industry continued to prosper and expand, the state's political leaders continued to foster the delusion, an enduring legacy of Longism, that the citizens of Louisiana could consume the proverbial free lunch.[20]

Not even the most determined of his opponents questioned Earl Long's sincerity in trying to assist the poor people of Louisiana, but the ultimately disastrous economic consequences of the policies he fostered came clear in the 1980s, when the decline of the oil and gas industry wreaked financial havoc, and the state had annual budget deficits of $250 million. Although Earl Long did balance the state budget during his administrations, he made no attempts to establish recurring stable sources of revenue. Instead, he pursued the politically acceptable—low taxes and high benefits. The sideshow emblazoned with his inimitable style gave the people of Louisiana entertainment on a grand scale, and his successors have followed his colorful, populist example of giving the voters the benefits of state government without the responsibility of paying for them. From the Longs to the present, not a single Louisiana governor has exhibited the political courage to educate the people to one of the fundamental dicta of economics: "You get what you pay for." And in Louisiana, they have chosen to pay for mediocrity.[21]

Ironically, the Longs are credited with reviving the spirit of democracy in Louisiana: they roused the poor masses from political lethargy and brought them to the polls in record numbers. At the same time, however, the Longs instilled an abiding lack of concern about politics in the average citizen. As John Maginnis observed, since the average citizen pays few taxes, he loses all interest in and concern with how government operates. If they received their monthly pension check, if the assessor valued their property below the homestead exemption, if their kids received a cheap lunch in school, most people in Louisiana under Long and even today exhibit a lack of interest in the political system. More than anyone, Earl Long helped to foster that pervasive, apathetic attitude. State government provided a sufficient variety of services to keep the people satisfied, but lacking a stable source of recurring revenue, it failed to maintain and extend those services as other states did. Today, Louisiana ranks among the lowest in health, education, transportation, and the other categories by which the standard of living is measured.[22]

Earl Long contributed to Louisiana's reputation as the most corrupt political system in the nation. Throughout his career, he displayed little respect for even the most elementary standards of honesty and ethics in politics. When he served as governor, money flowed freely in the executive mansion, in the aisles of the legislature, and in all levels of state government. Long once told a reporter that he had been offered a total of over $10 million in bribes during his career, but he refused to say how much he actually accepted. The very fact that, by Long's own admission, such a staggering sum of money would be offered to a single politician comments tellingly on the atmosphere that surrounded his administrations. Nurtured in state politics during the hegemony of the Kingfish, holding his first elective office during the uninhibited corruption of the Leche administration, Earl Long had little regard for honesty and integrity. Flagrantly contemptuous of political reform, he destroyed state civil service once and tried, unsuccessfully, to destroy it again. His criteria for hiring people to work in state government had loyalty, rather than qualifications, at the top of the list. He did not hesitate to profit from his political connections, readily accepting lucrative consulting contracts from state agencies and even selling foodstuffs to the state. The legislation he enacted all too often depended on the amount of campaign contributions its sponsors gave to the governor. Long even went so far as to try to corrupt the electoral process itself by running dummy candidates for office, spending huge sums of money to buy votes, and forcing state employees to "donate" part of their salaries to his campaign treasury and to campaign for his candidates.[23]

From the time Huey Long first entered into an arrangement with Frank Costello in 1935, until the end of his second full term as governor, Earl Long was closely connected with organized crime. According to documentary evidence from FBI records and from other sources, Long collaborated with such notorious mobsters and underworld bosses as Costello, "Dandy Phil" Kaistel, and Carlos Marcello in a network of gambling, prostitution, and other illegal activities. In return for a share of the profits, Long and other political leaders agreed to allow the syndicate to establish casinos, install slot machines, and operate horse racing handbooks and houses of prostitution throughout southern Louisiana. Such stalwarts of the Long political machine as Sheriffs Frank Clancy of Jefferson Parish, L. A. Meraux of St. Bernard Parish, and Cat Doucet of St. Landry Parish openly permitted the mob to conduct its illegal operations. Earl Long himself frequently met with Costello and Kaistel in his Roosevelt Hotel suite, and he accepted regular payoffs and enormous campaign contributions from them and others. As governor, he instructed the State Police not to enforce anti-gambling laws, and the casinos and slot and pinball machine operations flourished during his tenure. Long also granted pardons from the state penitentiary for individuals connected with underworld activities, and he made no secret of his own personal addiction to illegal gambling. He bet incessantly on horse races, and his bookies were in the state and across the nation.[24]

Despite the record of his long ties with organized crime, Earl Long did not allow these ties to alter his genuine commitment to improving the lives of the people of Louisiana. In numerous interviews, longtime political observers rank Long as the best governor in the state's history, an assessment that clearly stands verified by his record of concrete accomplishments. He never allowed political expediency or personal gain to detract from his concern for his people. His populist views, certainly shared by other Louisiana governors, contributed to the state's fiscal problems of the 1980s, and his disdain for political ethics, also shared by numerous other state politicians, contributed to the state's continuing reputation for political corruption. In the end, however, he was the true people's politician, living and dying in his ceaseless crusade for the poor. He was "the last great commoner of Louisiana politics," revered in life and in death by the masses whose causes he championed.[25]

For a day, Earl Long's body lay in state in the capitol rotunda, and thousands of Louisianians streamed past his coffin. A hearse carried the body to Winnfield for burial, and as the cortege traveled down the highway, black and white farmers stopped working their fields and stood silently, with heads bowed for their beloved champion. On September 8, 1960, Earl was buried in Winnfield, and politicians made the usual eulogistic remarks. A more fitting tribute came from J. A. Tisdale of Walker, an elderly pensioner who gave a reporter a ten-dollar bill for a floral wreath to lay next to the coffin as a gesture of appreciation for the things the great commoner had done for him. Earl would have appreciated that.

Notes

Introduction

1. For a fascinating account of the Edwards-Treen campaign, see John Maginnis, *The Last Hayride* (Baton Rouge, 1984). In October, 1987, Congressman Charles E. "Buddy" Roemer defeated Edwards in the gubernatorial election.

2. "Shaking the Money Tree: Old-Fashioned Vote-Selling in Louisiana," *Time*, December 25, 1978, p. 30; Bennett H. Wall (ed.), *Louisiana: A History* (Arlington Heights, Ill., 1984), 203.

3. For a journalistic account of Longism, see Stan Opotowsky, *The Longs of Louisiana* (New York, 1960).

4. William Ivy Hair, *Bourbonism and Agrarian Protest: Louisiana Politics, 1877–1900* (Baton Rouge, 1969), remains the best account of post-Reconstruction state politics. Also see Allan P. Sindler, *Huey Long's Louisiana: State Politics, 1920–1952* (Baltimore, 1956), 13–26; and Perry H. Howard, *Political Tendencies in Louisiana* (Rev. ed.; Baton Rouge, 1971), 153–210.

5. T. Harry Williams, *Huey Long* (New York, 1969), 187–88, 411, argues that the conservative oligarchy neglected the needs of the masses. For valuable critiques of this thesis, see Henry J. Dethloff, "The Longs: Revolution or Populist Retrenchment?" *Louisiana History,* XIX (1978), 401–12; Matthew J. Schott, "Huey Long: Progressive Backlash," *Louisiana History,* XXVII (1986), 133–45; and Glen Jeansonne, "Huey P. Long, Robin Hood or Tyrant? A Critique of *Huey Long,*" in "The Longs of Louisiana" special edition of *Regional Dimensions,* IV (1986), 22–37.

6. Williams, *Huey Long,* 409–14; Harnett T. Kane, *Louisiana Hayride: The American Rehearsal for Dictatorship, 1928–1940* (New York, 1941), 105–44; T. Harry Williams, "The Gentleman From Louisiana: Demagogue or Democrat?" *Journal of Southern History,* XXVI (1960), 1–20.

7. Kane, *Louisiana Hayride,* 60–84; Ed Reed, *Requiem for a Kingfish* (Baton Rouge, 1986), 55–62.

8. Reed, *Requiem for a Kingfish,* 58–59, 122–39.

9. Williams, *Huey Long,* 273–74, 303–11.

10. Edward F. Renwick, "The Longs' Legislative Lieutenants" (Ph.D. dissertation, University of Arizona, 1967), 92–124, 155–76, 202–73.

11. *Ibid.,* 106, 108.

12. Maginnis, *The Last Hayride,* 7–8; Kane, *Louisiana Hayride,* 60–69, 71–72, 96–97.

13. Maginnis, *The Last Hayride,* 7–8, 55–59, 60–62; Renwick, "The Longs' Legislative Lieutenants," 244–49; New Orleans *Times-Picayune,* September 25, 1951, hereinafter cited as *Times-Picayune.*

14. A. J. Liebling, *The Earl of Louisiana* (1961; rpr. Baton Rouge, 1971), 40.
15. James E. Comiskey; Robert S. Maestri; James A. Noe. All personal interviews are cited by the interviewee's full name. Places and years of interviews appear in the Bibliography.
16. Williams, *Huey Long*, 253–54, 621, 821.
17. Wall (ed.), *Louisiana: A History*, 286–89.
18. Sindler, *Huey Long's Louisiana*, 265–86; Howard, *Political Tendencies in Louisiana*, 251–94; V. O. Key, Jr., *Southern Politics in State and Nation* (New York, 1949), 168–79.
19. Sindler, *Huey Long's Louisiana*, 251–94.
20. Howard, *Political Tendencies in Louisiana*, 2, 292.
21. Liebling, *The Earl of Louisiana*, 85.
22. Williams, *Huey Long*, 253–54, 621, 821.
23. Maginnis, *The Last Hayride*, 6–10, 252–53.

Chapter 1

1. Clem Huffman; Ernest S. Clements.
2. Genealogical information on the Long family may be found in Williams, *Huey Long*, 10–19; Richard B. McCaughan, *Socks on a Rooster: Louisiana's Earl K. Long* (Baton Rouge, 1967), 6–7; J. Paul Leslie, "Earl K. Long: The Formative Years, 1895–1940" (Ph.D. dissertation, University of Missouri, 1974), 18–22; Lucille Long Hunt, "Louisiana Longs of Lincoln Parish," in *Lincoln Parish History* (N.p. [privately published], 1971), 121–34; Earl K. Long biographical data, Earl K. Long Papers, Department of Archives and Manuscripts, Hill Memorial Library, Louisiana State University, Baton Rouge, hereinafter cited as EKL Papers, LSU.
3. Williams, *Huey Long*, 10–15; Leslie, "Earl K. Long," 16–18; Earl K. Long, Address to the Legislature, May 26, 1959, tape in Michael L. Kurtz and Morgan D. Peoples, collection of Earl Long materials, hereinafter cited as Authors' Collection.
4. Williams, *Huey Long*, 15–17.
5. *Ibid.*; Lucille Long Hunt; Olive Long Cooper.
6. Williams, *Huey Long*, 19–20.
7. Leslie, "Earl K. Long," 24–26; Winn Parish Conveyance Records, Book A, pp. 24–28, in Parish Courthouse, Winnfield.
8. James Rorty, "Callie Long's Boy Huey," *Forum*, August, 1935, p. 78; Frederick W. Carr, "Huey Long's Father Relates the Story of the Senator's Boyhood," *Christian Science Monitor*, September 11, 1935, p. 8; Huey P. Long, Sr., "My Boy Huey," as told to George W. French, in John D. Klorer (ed.), *The New Louisiana* (New Orleans, 1936), 21–22.
9. Eck Bozeman.
10. Williams, *Huey Long*, 18; Leslie, "Earl K. Long," 26–28; Brooks Read and Bud Hebert (eds.), *Last of the Red Hot Poppas* (1961), a record album of Long speeches and interviews, with narration by the editors.
11. Williams, *Huey Long*, 21–22; Gerald L. K. Smith, *Huey P. Long: Summary of Greatness, Political Genius, American Martyr* (Eureka Springs, Ark., 1975), 3; Lucille Long Hunt; Olive Long Cooper; Clara Long Knott; Edgar A. Poe.
12. Leslie, "Earl K. Long," 26–27; Huey P. Long, Jr., *Every Man a King: The Autobiography of Huey P. Long* (New Orleans, 1933), 6–7; Lucille Long Hunt.
13. Morgan D. Peoples, "Earl Kemp Long: The Man From Pea Patch Farm," *Louisiana History*, XVII (1976), 365, 377, 384, 389, 390–92; Winnfield *News-American*, September 9, 1955.
14. Leslie, "Earl K. Long," 26–28; Read and Hebert (eds.), *Last of the Red Hot Poppas*; Lucille Long Hunt; Olive Long Cooper.
15. Williams, *Huey Long*, 28; Julius T. Long, "What I Know About My Brother United States Senator Huey P. Long," *Real America*, September 1933, p. 39; "The Wizard of Winnfield," WBRZ-TV, Baton Rouge, August 28, 1960; Lucille Long Hunt.

16. Williams, *Huey Long,* 28; Leslie, "Earl K. Long," 33; Earl K. Long, testimony before House Judiciary "B" Committee, May 25, 1959, tape in Authors' Collection.

17. Lucille Long Hunt; Harley Bozeman; Edgar A. Poe.

18. Williams, *Huey Long,* 65; McCaughan, *Socks on a Rooster,* 15; Leslie, "Earl K. Long," 32–33; Harley Bozeman.

19. Leslie, "Earl K. Long," 34–36. G. Dupree Litton, *The Wizard of Winnfield* (New York, 1982), 12, erroneously claims that Earl graduated from high school. Harley Bozeman; Dudley J. LeBlanc.

20. Ernest S. Clements. LSU has no record of Earl's attendance.

21. Williams, *Huey Long,* 80–81; Leslie, "Earl K. Long," 36–39.

22. Leslie, "Earl K. Long," 39, 218*n;* Lucille Long Hunt; Harley Bozeman; Dudley J. LeBlanc.

23. Peoples, "Earl Kemp Long," 377; Dudley J. LeBlanc; Shirley G. Jackson; Ernest S. Clements.

24. Leslie, "Earl K. Long," 49; Olive Long Cooper; Dudley J. LeBlanc.

25. Lucille Long Hunt; Dudley J. LeBlanc; Robert S. Maestri; Lionel Ott.

26. Liebling, *The Earl of Louisiana,* 105; Harley Bozeman; Ernest S. Clements; Clem Huffman; Gaston Ducote; James E. Comiskey; Edgar A. Poe; James T. Washington.

27. B. B. "Sixty" Rayburn, personal reminiscences of Earl Long, in "Remembering the Longs: Political Perspectives" session of "Longs of Louisiana" Symposium, Southeastern Louisiana University, Hammond, September 8–15, 1985, tapes on deposit in Special Collections, Linus A. Sims Memorial Library, Southeastern Louisiana University, Hammond (symposium hereinafter cited as "Longs of Louisiana"); Edgar A.Poe; James E. Comiskey; Seymour Weiss; Ralph Waldo Emerson Jones.

28. Eck Bozeman.

Chapter 2

1. Williams, *Huey Long,* 43–45; Leslie, "Earl K. Long," 40; Lucille Long Hunt; Clara Long Knott.

2. Williams, *Huey Long,* 122–25; Leslie, "Earl K. Long," 40–43.

3. Lucille Long Hunt; Olive Long Cooper; Clara Long Knott; Harley Bozeman; Eck Bozeman; Gillis W. Long.

4. Williams, *Huey Long,* 122–25; Leslie, "Earl K. Long," 40–43; Harley Bozeman.

5. Baton Rouge *State-Times,* January 23, 1940, hereinafter cited as *State-Times;* Baton Rouge *Morning Advocate,* May 9, 1948, hereinafter cited as *Morning Advocate;* Dudley J. LeBlanc; Harley Bozeman.

6. Williams, *Huey Long,* 191–213, omits Earl's role in the campaign. In an interview, T. Harry Williams acknowledged that Earl helped Huey in all his campaigns.

7. Leslie, "Earl K. Long," 49; Dudley J. LeBlanc.

8. Williams, *Huey Long,* 253; Leslie, "Earl K. Long," 51; Lucille Long Hunt; Robert S. Maestri; Allen J. Ellender.

9. Williams, *Huey Long,* 264–65; Robert S. Maestri; Seymour Weiss; Harley Bozeman; Dudley J. LeBlanc; Leander H. Perez, Sr.

10. Williams, *Huey Long,* 288–89; Leslie, "Earl K. Long," 55–59.

11. Williams, *Huey Long,* 315; Long, *Every Man a King,* 259–60; Leslie, "Earl K. Long," 59–61, 226*n;* Lucille Long Hunt; Olive Long Cooper; Clara Long Knott; Seymour Weiss.

12. Williams, *Huey Long,* 316; Dudley J. LeBlanc; Harley Bozeman; Allen J. Ellender; Seymour Weiss; Robert S. Maestri.

13. Williams, *Huey Long,* 303–305.

14. Dudley J. LeBlanc; Robert S. Maestri; Allen J. Ellender; James H. "Jimmy" Morrison; T. Hale Boggs; Seymour Weiss.

15. Seymour Weiss; Allen J. Ellender.

16. Williams, *Huey Long*, 347–409; Sindler, *Huey Long's Louisiana*, 61–67.

17. Williams, *Huey Long*, 354, 370; *Times-Picayune*, January 6, 1940; New Orleans *States-Item*, September 6, 1960, hereinafter cited as *States-Item*; Robert S. Maestri.

18. Williams, *Huey Long*, 354, 368–69; Renwick, "The Longs' Legislative Lieutenants," 221; Robert S. Maestri; Allen J. Ellender.

19. Williams, *Huey Long*, 385, 391, 399–400; Leslie, "Earl K. Long," 70–72.

20. Williams, *Huey Long*, 369; McCaughan, *Socks on a Rooster*, 33–36; Leslie, "Earl K. Long," 71; William C. Boone, *The Impeachment and Acquittal of Huey P. Long* (Shreveport, 1929); *Morning Advocate*, May 9, 1948; "The Wizard of Winnfield," WBRZ-TV; T. Harry Williams. Boone's title, however, is inaccurate: the trial having been averted, Huey was not acquitted.

21. "The Kingfish Swallowed the Pelican" is the title of Chapter 3 of Sindler, *Huey Long's Louisiana*, 67–97.

22. Huey P. Long, Jr., quoted in "The Career of Earl K. Long: From Farm Boy to Governor," *Louisiana Conservation Review*, Summer, 1939, p. 5; Robert S. Maestri; Seymour Weiss.

23. Leslie, "Earl K. Long," 64–66; Robert S. Maestri; Seymour Weiss; Allen J. Ellender; T. Harry Williams.

24. Robert S. Maestri; Seymour Weiss; Allen J. Ellender; Leander H. Perez; Harley Bozeman; James A. Noe; Harvey A. Peltier, Sr.

25. Robert S. Maestri; Seymour Weiss; Allen J. Ellender; Leander H. Perez; Harvey A. Peltier; James A. Noe; Richard W. Leche.

26. Williams, *Huey Long*, 481–83; Allen J. Ellender; Seymour Weiss; Harvey A. Peltier; Leander H. Perez.

27. Williams, *Huey Long*, 255–61, 464–65, 753–59; Harvey A. Peltier; Leander H. Perez; Robert S. Maestri; James A. Noe.

28. Sindler, *Huey Long's Louisiana*, 187–88, 196–97, 249–56, 265–73, 282–86; Paul Grosser, "Political Parties," and John Wildgen, "Voting Behavior in Gubernatorial Elections," both in James Bolner (ed.), *Louisiana Politics: Festival in a Labyrinth* (Baton Rouge, 1982), 262–64, 324–28, 331–34, 337–38.

29. Sindler, *Huey Long's Louisiana*, 248–49; Key, *Southern Politics*, 168–80; Howard, *Political Tendencies in Louisiana*, 223, 251–52; Mark T. Carleton, Perry H. Howard, and Joseph B. Parker (eds.), *Readings in Louisiana Politics* (2nd ed.; Baton Rouge, 1988), 359–61.

Chapter 3

1. Leslie, "Earl K. Long," 80–81.

2. *Ibid.*, 81; Williams, *Huey Long*, 485.

3. Williams, *Huey Long*, 473.

4. Long, *Every Man a King*, 260; McCaughan, *Socks on a Rooster*, 38; Long, "What I Know About My Brother," 178; Leslie, "Earl K. Long," 84–88.

5. Lucille Long Hunt; Olive Long Cooper; Clara Long Knott; Dudley J. LeBlanc; Harley Bozeman; Ernest S. Clements.

6. Williams, *Huey Long*, 527–29.

7. *Ibid.*, 529; Leslie, "Earl K. Long," 88.

8. Williams, *Huey Long*, 316, 529; New Orleans *States-Item*, September 6, 1960, hereinafter cited as *States*.

9. *Times-Picayune*, September 12, 1931; Clem H. Sehrt.

10. Long, *Every Man a King*, 260; *State-Times*, December 8, 1931.

11. Williams, *Huey Long*, 537–38.

12. Earl Long platform, 1931–32, in Authors' Collection.

13. *Ibid.*; Williams, *Huey Long*, 875–76.

14. Leslie, "Earl K. Long," 96–97; Elizabeth Mullener, "Stumping With Uncle Earl," *Dixie,* August 22, 1982, pp. 10–12; *Times-Picayune,* December 1, 1931.

15. Mullener, "Stumping With Uncle Earl," 10–12.

16. *Ibid.,* 17–18; Edgar A. Poe.

17. John B. Fournet.

18. Secretary of State, State of Louisiana, *Compilation of Primary Election Returns* (Baton Rouge, 1932), January 19, 1932, hereinafter cited as *Compilation of Primary Election Returns,* followed by the date of the primary. All local and state elections covered in this book were actually primaries of the Louisiana Democratic party. Since these primaries were tantamount to election, the terms *primary* and *election* shall be used interchangeably.

19. Leslie, "Earl K. Long," 101–106.

20. *Ibid.,* 106–107; McCaughan, *Socks on a Rooster,* 49–51; Earl Long biographical data in Earl K. Long Vertical File, Louisiana State Library, Baton Rouge, hereinafter cited as EKL Vertical File, LSL; Lewis M. Morris, Jr., and Brooks Read, interview with Blanche Revere Long (Typescript in Louisiana State Archives, Baton Rouge), 1, 3–4, 7.

21. Robert S. Maestri; Seymour Weiss; Lionel Ott.

22. U.S. Congress, Senate, Special Committee on Investigations of Campaign Expenditures, *United States Senate, Senatorial Campaign Expenditures (Louisiana), 1932–1933. Hearings Before Subcommittee. 72nd Congress, 2nd Session, on Senate Resolution 174.* 1933.

23. *Ibid.,* I, 794, 817–18, 835, 841, 953–54; *Times-Picayune,* February 4–18, 1933; New York *Times,* February 15, 1933.

24. Earl Long biographical data, in EKL Vertical File, LSL; Thomas A. "Tommy the Cork" Cochoran.

25. Williams, *Huey Long,* 665–69.

26. *Ibid.,* 712–15; Leslie, "Earl K. Long," 117–20; Herman B. Deutsch.

27. Williams, *Huey Long,* 690–91; Smith, *Huey P. Long,* 55–56; "The Career of Earl K. Long," 5; Lucille Long Hunt; Olive Long Cooper; Seymour Weiss; Robert S. Maestri; Gerald L. K. Smith; Allen J. Ellender; John B. Fournet; James A. Noe.

28. Allen J. Ellender.

29. Leslie, "Earl K. Long," 119–26. See Reed, *Requiem for a Kingfish,* for the most plausible account of Huey's assassination.

30. Among the most perceptive interpretations of Huey Long are Williams, *Huey Long,* 3–9, 315–16, 409–19; Sindler, *Huey Long's Louisiana,* 98–116; and Alan Brinkley, *Voices of Protest: Huey Long, Father Coughlin, and the Great Depression* (New York, 1982), 169–75, 179–86, 249–51.

31. Williams, *Huey Long,* 412–13, 417–18, 759–62.

32. *Ibid.,* 315–16; T. Harry Williams, Introduction to Liebling, *The Earl of Louisiana,* 1–4.

33. Liebling, *The Earl of Louisiana,* 16; Thomas P. Martin, *Dynasty: The Longs of Louisiana* (New York, 1960), 179. Valuable information on Earl's role in the politics of Huey's regime may be found in T. Harry Williams' interviews with Theophile Landry, Richard W. Leche, Harley Bozeman, David B. McConnell, Wilson J. Peck, Edgar G. Mouton, John B. Fournet, Robert Angelle, William Cleveland, and James T. Burns (Typescripts or summaries in T. Harry Williams Papers, Department of Archives and Manuscripts, Hill Memorial Library, Louisiana State University, Baton Rouge).

34. T. Harry Williams; Joe Gray Taylor.

Chapter 4

1. Legislator quoted in Sindler, *Huey Long's Louisiana,* 119.

2. *Ibid.,* 118–20; *State-Times,* September 19, 1935; *States,* September 11, 1935; New Orleans *Item,* September 21, 1935, hereinafter cited as *Item;* Allen J. Ellender; James A. Noe.

3. Leslie, "Earl K. Long," 126–30; *States*, September 23, 1935; Robert S. Maestri; Seymour Weiss; James A. Noe.

4. Robert S. Maestri; Seymour Weiss; James A. Noe.

5. Sindler, *Huey Long's Louisiana*, 121–22; *Compilation of Primary Election Returns*, January 21, 1936; *Times-Picayune*, December 21, 1935; Hammond *Daily Courier*, December 26, 1935; Leche campaign brochure, 1936, in Authors' Collection.

6. Leslie, "Earl K. Long," 141–42; James A. Noe.

7. Kane, *Louisiana Hayride*, 188–426, provides a comprehensive account of the scandals.

8. Robert S. Maestri; James E. Comiskey; William A. "Captain Billy" Bisso; Thomas A. Cochoran.

9. Clem H. Sehrt; James E. Comiskey; Robert S. Maestri; Seymour Weiss; Gerald L. K. Smith.

10. Earl Long biographical data, in EKL Vertical File, LSL.

11. *Ibid.*; Clem H. Sehrt; James E. Comiskey; Robert S. Maestri; Thomas A. Cochoran.

12. Williams, *Huey Long*, 851–54; Robert S. Maestri; Lionel Ott; Alvin Stumpf; James A. Noe.

13. Williams, *Huey Long*, 853–54; Robert S. Maestri; Seymour Weiss.

14. Kane, *Louisiana Hayride*, 203–204; Sindler, *Huey Long's Louisiana*, 123, 135; Edward F. Haas, *DeLesseps S. Morrison and the Image of Reform: New Orleans Politics, 1946–1961* (Baton Rouge, 1974), 13–14; Robert S. Maestri; Clem H. Sehrt.

15. Sindler, *Huey Long's Louisiana*, 136; Kane, *Louisiana Hayride*, 203–204. Edward F. Haas, "New Orleans on the Half-Shell: The Maestri Era, 1936–1946," *Louisiana History*, XIII (1972), 289–97, describes Maestri's first term as mayor.

16. Williams, *Huey Long*, 648–54, 824–25; Reed, *Requiem for a Kingfish*, 105–11; Michael L. Kurtz, "Organized Crime in Louisiana History: Myth and Reality," *Louisiana History*, XXIV (1983), 370–73.

17. FBI, New Orleans Field Office, Report of December 12, 1935, Serial No. 62–42396, Doc. No. 118, pp. 4–5, in FBI Files on Governor Earl Kemp Long, Special Collections, Linus A. Sims Memorial Library, Southeastern Louisiana University, Hammond, hereinafter cited as FBI Files, EKL.

18. New Orleans Field Office, Report of April 7, 1937, Serial No. 62–42396, Doc. No. 302, pp. 11–14, and B. E. Sackett, Special Agent in Charge, New Orleans Field Office, to J. Edgar Hoover, Report of May 27, 1939, entitled "Vice Conditions and Political Corruption in the State of Louisiana," both in FBI Files, EKL; testimony of Frank Costello, in U.S. Congress, Senate, Special Committee to Investigate Organized Crime in Interstate Commerce, *Investigation of Organized Crime in Interstate Commerce* (1950–51), Pt. 7, pp. 910–73.

19. Kane, *Louisiana Hayride*, 397–403.

20. Sindler, *Huey Long's Louisiana*, 204*n*; *Times-Picayune*, January 12, 1940, February 18, 1948; photocopy of check, in EKL Vertical File, LSL.

21. Sindler, *Huey Long's Louisiana*, 130–31; *State-Times*, September 7, 1937; *States*, August 12, 1937; *Item-Tribune*, July 1, 1937.

22. Stories from Douglas Fowler, collection of Earl Long humor, hereinafter cited as Fowler Collection.

23. Clem H. Sehrt; James A. Noe; Dudley J. LeBlanc; Leander H. Perez; Harvey A. Peltier; James E. Comiskey.

24. Leslie, "Earl K. Long," 158–63; Clem H. Sehrt; Margaret Dixon.

25. Davy C. Brooks, "A Turn of Events: Earl K. Long and the Louisiana Gubernatorial Elections of 1940 and 1948" (M.A. thesis, Southeastern Louisiana University, 1985), 61; *States*, June 9, 1939.

26. Drew Pearson and Robert S. Allen, "Washington Merry-Go-Round" column, June 17, 1939; *Item*, June 20, 1939; F. Edward Hebert.

27. Betty Marie Field, "The Politics of the New Deal in Louisiana: 1933–1939" (Ph.D. dissertation, Tulane University, 1974), 272–74; *Morning Advocate,* June 22, 1939; Robert S. Maestri; Seymour Weiss.

28. *Times-Picayune,* June 24–27, 1939; *Morning Advocate,* June 25–30, 1939; New York *Times,* June 27, 1939; Robert S. Maestri; Seymour Weiss; F. Edward Hebert; Richard W. Leche.

Chapter 5

1. B. E. Sackett to J. Edgar Hoover, May 22, 1939, Serial No. 62–54154, Doc. No. 1, pp. 1–3, in FBI Files, EKL.

2. B. E. Sackett to J. Edgar Hoover, June 26, 1939, Serial No. 62–54154, Doc. No. 23, p. 5, in FBI Files, EKL.

3. Robert S. Maestri; Richard W. Leche; Clem H. Sehrt.

4. *Morning Advocate,* June 27, 1939; *Progress,* June 23, 30, 1939; Clem H. Sehrt; Margaret Dixon; Robert S. Maestri; F. Edward Hebert; James E. Comiskey.

5. Leslie, "Earl K. Long," 172–77.

6. Kane, *Louisiana Hayride,* 207–10; Sindler, *Huey Long's Louisiana,* 133–34; Martin, *Dynasty,* 160–62.

7. Martin, *Dynasty,* 164–65.

8. Kane, *Louisiana Hayride,* 227–35, 253–59, 265–75, 341–55, 403–408.

9. Sindler, *Huey Long's Louisiana,* 134–40; *Times-Picayune,* September 7, 1940.

10. Leslie, "Earl K. Long," 176–84.

11. W. L. Atwood to J. Edgar Hoover, July 19, 1939, SAC (Special Agent in Charge), New Orleans Field Office, FBI (NO), to J. Edgar Hoover, October 16, 1939, B. E. Sackett to U.S. Attorney Rene A. Viosca, August 28, 1939, A. P. Kinchen to J. Edgar Hoover, February 27, 1940, Serial No. 62–54154, Doc. Nos. 138x, 314, 228x, 311, New Orleans Field Office, FBI, Report of March 13, 1940, all in FBI Files, EKL.

12. A. P. Kinchen to J. Edgar Hoover, April 6, 1940, Serial No. 62–54154, Doc. No. 287, a seven-page investigative report, in FBI Files, EKL; Field, "The Politics of the New Deal in Louisiana," 294–97.

13. David M. Ladd to E. A. Tamm, May 6, 1942, Serial No. 62–43818, Doc. No. 15, pp. 1–6, 8–13, and New Orleans Field Office, FBI, Report of December 12, 1939, Serial No. 62–42396, Doc. No. 884, pp. 5–8, both in FBI Files, EKL.

14. Kane, *Louisiana Hayride,* 317–24; *Progress,* n.d. [Fall, 1939].

15. Earl Long campaign circular, 1939, from Shelby M. Newman, collection of Earl Long materials, hereinafter cited as Newman Collection; Harvey A. Peltier.

16. Kane, *Louisiana Hayride,* 437; *Times-Picayune,* January 12, 1940.

17. McCaughan, *Socks on a Rooster,* 72; Brooks, "A Turn of Events," 60–68; James A. Noe; Sam H. Jones.

18. Brooks, "A Turn of Events," 67–69; *Morning Advocate,* October 26, 1939; Lionel Ott; Sam H. Jones.

19. Haas, *DeLesseps S. Morrison,* 19; Kurtz, "Organized Crime in Louisiana History," 370–71; DeLesseps S. Morrison, *Latin American Mission: An Adventure in Hemisphere Diplomacy,* edited and introduced by Gerold Frank (New York, 1965), 65; Robert S. Maestri; James A. Noe; F. Edward Hebert; John F. Tims; Sam H. Jones; T. Hale Boggs.

20. *Progress,* August 11, 1939; "The Career of Earl K. Long," 5; Robert S. Maestri, Seymour Weiss.

21. Sindler, *Huey Long's Louisiana,* 146; Kane, *Louisiana Hayride,* 434; Brooks, "A Turn of Events," 63–68; *Morning Advocate,* January 15, 1940; *State-Times,* January 9, 1940; *Item,* January 3, 1940; *Progress,* October 6, 1939; Winnfield *Enterprise,* September 7, 1949; Alexandria *Daily Town Talk,* September 7, 1939, hereinafter cited as *Daily Town Talk.*

22. *Times-Picayune,* January 14, 1940; Tensas *Gazette,* March 1, 1940; *Compilation of Primary Election Returns,* January 16, 1940.

23. James A. Noe; Sam H. Jones; James H. Morrison; Clem H. Sehrt.

24. Sindler, *Huey Long's Louisiana,* 148–49; Leslie, "Earl K. Long," 197–200; *Morning Advocate,* January 24, 1940.

25. Sindler, *Huey Long's Louisiana,* 149–50; *State-Times,* February 14, 1940; *Morning Advocate,* February 11, 1940; Robert S. Maestri.

26. Earl Long campaign leaflet, 1940, in Newman Collection.

27. Sindler, *Huey Long's Louisiana,* 146n; Sam Jones campaign circular, 1940, in EKL Vertical File, LSL; Sam H. Jones; James A. Noe; Robert S. Maestri; Harvey A. Peltier; Leander H. Perez.

28. *Compilation of Primary Election Returns,* February 20, 1940.

29. Sindler, *Huey Long's Louisiana,* 152; *Times-Picayune,* March 23, 1940; "Twelve Years," *Time,* March 4, 1940, p. 15.

Chapter 6

1. *States,* February 21, 1940; *Item,* February 21, 1940; *State-Times,* May 14, 1940.

2. Sidney J. Romero, *"My Fellow Citizens": The Inaugural Addresses of the Governors of Louisiana* (Lafayette, 1980), 317–23; James A. Bugea, Carlos E. Lazarus, and William T. Peague, "The Louisiana Legislation of 1940," *Louisiana Law Review,* III (1940–41), 98–199; Glen Jeansonne, "Sam Houston Jones and the Revolution of 1940," *Red River Valley Historical Review,* IV (1979), 73–87.

3. L. Vaughan Howard, *Civil Service Development in Louisiana* (New Orleans, 1956), 75–81; Charles S. Hyneman, "Political and Administrative Reform in the 1940 Legislature," *Louisiana Law Review,* III (1940–41), 1–54; Michael L. Kurtz, "The Struggle for Political Reform in Louisiana," *Papers of the Southeast Louisiana Historical Association,* VIII (1982), 4.

4. Floyd Martin Clay, *Coozan Dudley LeBlanc: From Huey Long to Hadacol* (Gretna, 1973), 133–40; James A. Noe; Sam H. Jones.

5. Howard, *Civil Service Development,* 80–81; Sindler, *Huey Long's Louisiana,* 157–58.

6. Sindler, *Huey Long's Louisiana,* 166–67; Morrison, *Latin American Mission,* 55n; Glen Jeansonne, *Leander Perez: Boss of the Delta* (Baton Rouge, 1977), 124–41; *Times-Picayune,* July 24, October 3, December 12, 1940; Clem H. Sehrt.

7. *Item,* March 28, 1943; Lucille Long Hunt.

8. Sindler, *Huey Long's Louisiana,* 185n; C. J. "Bobbie" Dugas, personal memorandum of 1943 meeting, in his collection of Earl Long materials, hereinafter cited as Dugas Collection; Robert S. Maestri; Clem H. Sehrt; Allen J. Ellender; C. J. "Bobbie" Dugas.

9. Haas, *DeLesseps S. Morrison,* 24–25; Clem H. Sehrt; Robert S. Maestri.

10. Sindler, *Huey Long's Louisiana,* 185n; Dugas memorandum, 3, in Dugas Collection, Robert S. Maestri; James E. Comiskey.

11. George M. Leppert, "Long Live the Kingfishes!" *American Mercury,* October, 1956, pp. 94–96; *Compilation of Primary Election Returns,* January 18, February 29, 1944.

12. Sindler, *Huey Long's Louisiana,* 186–89; *Compilation of Primary Election Returns,* January 18, February 29, 1944.

13. Sindler, *Huey Long's Louisiana,* 186–89; Clay, *Coozan Dudley LeBlanc,* 148; Robert S. Maestri.

14. Sindler, *Huey Long's Louisiana,* 190–97; Brooks, "A Turn of Events," 103–12, 115–16.

15. Haas, *DeLesseps S. Morrison,* 26–40; Michael L. Kurtz, "The 'Demagogue' and the 'Liberal': The Political Rivalry of Earl K. Long and DeLesseps S. Morrison" (Ph.D. dissertation, Tulane University, 1971), 38–46; David Lloyd Sigler, "Downfall of a Political Machine: The New Orleans Mayoralty Election of 1946" (Senior honors thesis, Tulane University, 1968).

16. Haas, *DeLesseps S. Morrison,* 41–66; Kurtz, "The 'Demagogue' and the 'Liberal,'"

45–48. For examples of Morrison's political maneuverings, see DeLesseps S. Morrison to Old Regular leaders Thomas Brahney, William Farrell, and Edward Haggerty, identical letters of June 11, 1946, all in Personal File III, DeLesseps S. Morrison Papers, Special Collections, Howard-Tilton Memorial Library, Tulane University, New Orleans, hereinafter cited as DSM Papers, TU.

17. Earl Long ticket and platform, 1948, in Newman Collection; James A. Noe; Dudley J. LeBlanc; Allen J. Ellender.

18. Sindler, *Huey Long's Louisiana*, 199–203; Brooks, "A Turn of Events," 117–20; Fowler Collection; Margaret Dixon.

19. Liebling, *The Earl of Louisiana*, 96–97; Brooks, "A Turn of Events," 120–23; Fowler Collection; Margaret Dixon.

20. McCaughan, *Socks on a Rooster*, 106; DeLesseps S. Morrison to Lawrence Eustis and Edward Haggerty, December 15, 1947, Elmer L. Irey to Morrison, December 21, 1947, all in Personal Correspondence File IV, DSM Papers, TU; DeLesseps S. Morrison to Sam H. Jones, December 18, 26, 1947, Jones to Morrison, December 6, 10, 12, 26, 1947, all in 1948 Gubernatorial Campaign File, DSM Papers, TU; DeLesseps S. Morrison to George Campbell, December 20, 1947, Morrison to Ashton Phelps, December 22, 1947, Morrison to Leonard K. Nicholson, December 26, 1947, all in Mayoral File III, DeLesseps S. Morrison Papers, Louisiana Room, New Orleans Public Library, hereinafter cited as DSM Papers, NOPL.

21. SAC, NO, to J. Edgar Hoover, December 17, 1947, Serial No. 62–75147–33, Doc. No. 33, pp. 2–3, New Orleans Field Office, "Crime Survey, New Orleans Division, December 15, 1947," Serial No. 62–75147–33, Doc. No. 36, pp. 6–9, 17–20, both in FBI Files, EKL; Haas, *DeLesseps S. Morrison*, 19, 26–40; U.S. Congress, Senate, Special Committee to Investigate Organized Crime in Interstate Commerce, *U.S. Senate, Kefauver Report: Third Interim Report* (1951), 77–83, 89–90.

22. Clay, *Coozan Dudley LeBlanc*, 159–60.

23. Opotowsky, *The Longs of Louisiana*, 197; F. Edward Hebert, with John McMillan, *Last of the Titans: The Life and Times of Congressman F. Edward Hebert of Louisiana*, ed. Glenn R. Conrad (Lafayette, 1976), 266.

24. Fowler Collection; Dugas Collection; William H. Talbot.

25. Robert S. Maestri; James E. Comiskey; William A. Bisso; William J. Dodd.

26. Secretary of State, State of Louisiana, *Report of the Secretary of State* (Baton Rouge, 1949), January 20, 1948, hereinafter cited as *Report of the Secretary of State*, followed by the date of the election; Sindler, *Huey Long's Louisiana*, 204n; McCaughan, *Socks on a Rooster*, 106–109.

27. *Report of the Secretary of State*, February 24, 1948; *Morning Advocate*, February 24, May 9, 1948.

Chapter 7

1. *Morning Advocate*, May 9–12, 1948; *State-Times*, May 11, 1948; Atlanta *Journal*, March 7, 1948; "Back in the Saddle Again," *Time*, May 24, 1948, p. 28; C. H. "Sammy" Downs.

2. Sindler, *Huey Long's Louisiana*, 208–10; Renwick, "The Longs' Legislative Lieutenants," 62–65, 200, 250–55; Student Board of the Louisiana Law Review, "Louisiana Legislation of 1948," *Louisiana Law Review*, IX (1948–49), 18–141; *Item*, September 25, 1951.

3. Clay, *Coozan Dudley LeBlanc*, 159–63; Margaret Dixon.

4. Sindler, *Huey Long's Louisiana*, 210–13; Public Affairs Research Council of Louisiana, *Louisiana Government in the News*, No. 11, September 15, 1951, p. 2. Hereinafter, all publications of the council shall be cited as PAR, followed by the appropriate information.

5. Sindler, *Huey Long's Louisiana*, 212–14; PAR, *Louisiana Government in the News*, No. 11, September 15, 1951, p. 2.

6. PAR, *Louisiana Government in the News,* 1951–52.

7. Howard, *Civil Service Development,* 105–109; Kurtz, "The 'Demagogue' and the 'Liberal,'" 94–97.

8. Governor's Office, State of Louisiana, *Special Message on Civil Service by Governor Earl K. Long to the Members of the Legislature, June 19, 1950* (Baton Rouge, 1950), 2; *States,* January 20, 1949; *Item,* February 4, 1948; Fowler Collection.

9. Sindler, *Huey Long's Louisiana,* 211–13; Renwick, "The Longs' Legislative Lieutenants," 100.

10. Renwick, "The Longs' Legislative Lieutenants," 63–64, 251–54.

11. Camille Gravel, fourth session, "Longs of Louisiana"; Robert A. Ainsworth, Jr.; James E. Comiskey; Seymour Weiss; Robert S. Maestri.

12. Renwick, "The Longs' Legislative Lieutenants," 244–48; Lois Nichols, "Legislative-Executive Relationships in the 1948 Session of the Louisiana Legislature" (M.A. thesis, Louisiana State University, 1954), 6; Robert A. Ainsworth; William M. "Willie" Rainach (Tape of interview in Oral History Collection, Louisiana State University, Shreveport, hereinafter cited as LSU-S).

13. Opotowsky, *The Longs of Louisiana,* 24; B. B. Rayburn, "Longs of Louisiana."

14. James E. Comiskey.

15. George D. Tessier; Dudley J. LeBlanc; Robert A. Ainsworth.

16. New Orleans Field Office, "Crime Survey, New Orleans Division, October 15, 1948," Serial No. 62–75147, Doc. No. 42, pp. 3–4, 10–13, 17–26, 43–45, "Crime Survey, New Orleans Division, October 15, 1949," Serial No. 62–75147, Doc. No. 61, pp. 19, 113–14, "Crime Survey, New Orleans Division, July 14, 1950," Serial No. 62–75147, Doc. No. 68, pp. 6, 26–27, "Crime Survey, New Orleans Division, December 16, 1955," Serial No. 62–75147, Doc. No. 86, p. 1, all in FBI Files, EKL; U.S. Senate, *Investigation of Organized Crime in Interstate Commerce,* Pt. 8, pp. 1–3, 5–31, 369–423; William Howard Moore, *The Kefauver Committee and the Politics of Crime: 1950–1952* (Columbia, Mo., 1974), 100.

17. New Orleans Field Office, "Crime Survey, New Orleans Division, April 15, 1948," Serial No. 62–75147, Doc. No. 37, pp. 6–9, 17–20, "Crime Survey, New Orleans Division, October 15, 1948," Serial No. 62–75147, Doc. No. 42, pp. 11–13, 19–24, 44–47, 56–62, both in FBI Files, EKL.

18. Reed, *Requiem for a Kingfish,* 138–39; Anna Mae Giacone; Frank Goodin.

19. Haas, *DeLesseps S. Morrison,* 121–22; Kurtz, "The 'Demagogue' and the 'Liberal,'" 71–73; Fowler Collection.

20. DeLesseps S. Morrison to Earl K. Long, February 25, 1948, in Mayoral File IV, DSM Papers, NOPL; Lennox Moak and Helen Moak, "The Rape of New Orleans," *National Municipal Review,* October, 1948, pp. 412–15.

21. Haas, *DeLesseps S. Morrison,* 125.

22. *Ibid.,* 125–26; *Times-Picayune,* July 2–4, 23, 24, 29, 1948.

23. Haas, *DeLesseps S. Morrison,* 126, 129.

24. Michael L. Kurtz, "Earl Long's Political Relations with the City of New Orleans, 1948–1960," *Louisiana History,* X (1969), 244–45.

25. House Bill 434, *Acts of the Legislature, 1948 Special Session,* 899–907.

26. DeLesseps S. Morrison to Kenneth L. Barringer and George D. Tessier, June 7, 1948, Morrison to Most Reverend Joseph F. Rummell, June 5, 1948, Morrison to Otto Passman, June 6, 1948, all in Mayoral File IV, DSM Papers, NOPL; *Times-Picayune,* June 3, 18, July 7, 20, 1948; *States,* June 7, 15, July 8, 1948; *Item,* July 9, 1948.

27. "The Winnfield Frog," *Time,* August 30, 1948, pp. 16–19; "Just Like Huey," *Time,* June 7, 1948, p. 24; "Scandals of 1948," *Newsweek,* March 1, 1948, pp. 22–23; "Happy Days," *Time,* March 8, 1948, p. 23; Cabell Phillips, "The Lengthening Shadow of Huey Long," *New York Times Magazine,* November 7, 1948, pp. 76–79; Brooks Read, Ann Price, Walter Cowan, Edgar A. Poe, all in third session, "Longs of Louisiana"; Herman B. Deutsch; Margaret Dixon.

28. Kurtz, "The 'Demagogue' and the 'Liberal,'" 93, 107–109.

29. Sindler, *Huey Long's Louisiana*, 214–15; Allen J. Ellender; T. Hale Boggs; Sam H. Jones.

30. *Report of the Secretary of State*, August 30, 1948, p. 23; Allen J. Ellender; T. Hale Boggs; James E. Comiskey; Seymour Weiss.

31. *Report of the Secretary of State*, August 30, 1948, p. 24; Leander H. Perez.

Chapter 8

1. Sindler, *Huey Long's Louisiana*, 218–20; L. Vaughan Howard and David R. Deener, *Presidential Politics in Louisiana, 1952* (New Orleans, 1954), 51–53.

2. Sindler, *Huey Long's Louisiana*, 179, 195–96, 202, 204; *Times-Picayune*, July 3, 1946; Sam H. Jones.

3. Howard and Deener, *Presidential Politics in Louisiana*, 52–53; Jeansonne, *Leander Perez*, 166–67, 173–75; Sam H. Jones, with James Aswell, "Will Dixie Bolt the New Deal?" *Saturday Evening Post*, March 6, 1943, pp. 20–26; *Morning Advocate*, July 19–22, 1944; Leander H. Perez; Sam H. Jones.

4. Sindler, *Huey Long's Louisiana*, 220–21; Jeansonne, *Leander Perez*, 174; Howard and Deener, *Presidential Politics in Louisiana*, 54–56.

5. Howard and Deener, *Presidential Politics in Louisiana*, 59–61; New York *Times*, July 18, 19, 1948.

6. Howard and Deener, *Presidential Politics in Louisiana*, 57–61; William H. Talbot.

7. Howard and Deener, *Presidential Politics in Louisiana*, 61–63; Sindler, *Huey Long's Louisiana*, 220–21; William H. Talbot; T. Hale Boggs; Sam H. Jones; Leander H. Perez; James E. Comiskey; Sam Jones campaign circular, 1940, in Newman Collection.

8. *Report of the Secretary of State*, annual reports, 1949–52, folding pages in back of each issue; John H. Fenton and Kenneth N. Vines, "Negro Voter Registration in Louisiana," *American Political Science Review*, LI (1957), 689–711.

9. Howard and Deener, *Presidential Politics in Louisiana*, 61–62; Sindler, *Huey Long's Louisiana*, 220–21.

10. Howard and Deener, *Presidential Politics in Louisiana*, 62–63; *Times-Picayune*, September 21, 1948.

11. *Report of the Secretary of State*, 1948, folding page in back; Howard, *Political Tendencies in Louisiana*, 315–316; James E. Comiskey.

12. Kurtz, "The 'Demagogue' and the 'Liberal,'" 110–14; *Item*, September 29, 1949; *Times-Picayune*, January 25, 1950; James E. Comiskey; Robert S. Maestri; Clem H. Sehrt.

13. Haas, *DeLesseps S. Morrison*, 142, 146; Sindler, *Huey Long's Louisiana*, 226–27; *States*, March 17, 18, April 5, 1950; Clem H. Sehrt.

14. Haas, *DeLesseps S. Morrison*, 145; Sindler, *Huey Long's Louisiana*, 226–27; Kurtz, "The 'Demagogue' and the 'Liberal,'" 119–20; *Times-Picayune*, June 27, 1950.

15. *Item*, July 11, 27, 28, 1950; Clem H. Sehrt.

16. Haas, *DeLesseps S. Morrison*, 144–46; Kurtz, "The 'Demagogue' and the 'Liberal,'" 122–24; Clem H. Sehrt; James E. Comiskey; Lionel Ott.

17. Sindler, *Huey Long's Louisiana*, 229–30; Secretary of State, State of Louisiana, *Report of the Secretary of State*, 1950, insert.

18. Sindler, *Huey Long's Louisiana*, 228; Robert A. Ainsworth; James E. Comiskey.

19. Kimbrough Owen, "The Need for Constitutional Revision in Louisiana," *Louisiana Law Review*, VIII (1947–48), 1–104; Louisiana Law Institute, *Projet of a Constitution for the State of Louisiana, With Notes and Studies* (Baton Rouge, 1950–54).

20. Sindler, *Huey Long's Louisiana*, 230–32; *State-Times*, August 7, 1950.

21. William C. Havard, "The Abortive Louisiana Constitutional Convention of 1951," *Journal of Politics*, XIII (1951), 708–17.

22. McCaughan, *Socks on a Rooster*, 129; "Louisiana Legends: William J. Dodd," WLPB-TV, Baton Rouge, November 8, 1985.

23. James E. Comiskey; Clem H. Sehrt; Robert A. Ainsworth; C. H. Downs; James A. Noe; Harvey A. Peltier.

24. Sindler, *Huey Long's Louisiana*, 234–35; Clay, *Coozan Dudley LeBlanc*, 190–94.

25. Jeansonne, *Leander Perez*, 152; Clay, *Coozan Dudley LeBlanc*, 192–93; Leander H. Perez; Dudley J. LeBlanc.

26. Sindler, *Huey Long's Louisiana*, 236–38; Jeansonne, *Leander Perez*, 152.

27. Jeansonne, *Leander Perez*, 152–54; Read and Hebert (eds.), *Last of the Red Hot Poppas*; *Item*, October 16, 21, 1951, January 5, 1952; *Morning Advocate*, January 5, 1952.

28. *Report of the Secretary of State*, 1952, pp. 28, 46; Read and Hebert (eds.), *Last of the Red Hot Poppas*.

Chapter 9

1. Wall (ed.), *Louisiana: A History*, 301–303.

2. Howard and Deener, *Presidential Politics in Louisiana*, 67–68; *Times-Picayune*, March 7, 1952.

3. James E. Comiskey; Clem H. Sehrt; Chester A. Wooten; C. J. "Cat" Doucet.

4. Earl Long campaign platform, 1955, in Newman Collection; B. B. Rayburn, fourth session, "Longs of Louisiana."

5. Kurtz, "The 'Demagogue' and the 'Liberal,'" 135–36.

6. Liebling, *The Earl of Louisiana*, 102; Maginnis, *The Last Hayride*, 11; "Uncle Earl," WLPB-TV, Baton Rouge, February 14, 1986; *Morning Advocate*, January 9, 1956.

7. Kurtz, "The 'Demagogue' and the 'Liberal,'" 137–39; Dudley J. LeBlanc to De-Lesseps S. Morrison, September 23, 1955, in 1955 Gubernatorial Campaign File, DSM Papers, TU.

8. New Orleans Field Office, "Crime Survey, New Orleans Division, December 16, 1955," Serial No. 62–75147, Doc. No. 86, pp. 1–2, General Investigative Report, November 15, 1956, Serial No. 62–75147, Doc. No. 151, pp. 16, 42–43, 57, SAC, NO, to J. Edgar Hoover, January 20, 1956, Serial No. 62–54154, Doc. No. 483, p. 1, and January 8, 1957, Serial No. 62–54154, Doc. No. 578, p. 3, all in FBI Files, EKL.

9. New Orleans Field Office, Report, May 10, 1956, Serial No. 139–343, Doc. No. 31, pp. 3–7, 21–25, in FBI Files, EKL; *Report of the Secretary of State*, 1956, p. 26; "Younger Brother," *Time*, January 30, 1948, p. 16.

10. *Report of the Secretary of State*, 1956, p. 26; *Item*, January 19, 1956; Clarence "Chink" Henry.

11. Renwick, "The Longs' Legislative Lieutenants," 261–65; C. H. Downs; Clarence Henry.

12. Renwick, "The Longs' Legislative Lieutenants," 265–66; *Morning Advocate*, June 17, 20, 1956.

13. PAR, *News Analysis*, No. 62, August 15, 1957, p. 3, No. 63, September 15, 1957, pp. 6–7, No. 68, February 15, 1958, p. 3, No. 76, February 15, 1959, pp. 2–3, No. 88, December, 1959, p. 7.

14. Renwick, "The Longs' Legislative Lieutenants," 200, 244–50, 258–59.

15. *Ibid.*, 246–48; "Uncle Earl," WLPB-TV.

16. Jeansonne, *Leander Perez*, 197–204; Fowler Collection; Leander H. Perez; Robert A. Ainsworth.

17. Renwick, "The Longs' Legislative Lieutenants," 100, 102, 106, 108–11; Secretary of State, State of Louisiana, *Roster of Officials, State of Louisiana* (Baton Rouge, 1957), January 18, 1957, pp. 55, 76.

18. Renwick, "The Longs' Legislative Lieutenants," 109–15; Edward F. LeBreton; Robert A. Ainsworth; C. H. Downs.

19. C. H. Downs; W. L. "Buddy" Napper; Robert Angelle; James E. Comiskey; Lionel Ott.

20. C. H. Downs; Theodore M. Hickey; B. B. Rayburn; James E. Comiskey; George D. Tessier; Edward F. LeBreton.

21. SAC, NO, to J. Edgar Hoover, January 8, 1957, Serial No. 62–54154, Doc. No. 578, p. 3, New Orleans Field Office, General Investigative Report, November 15, 1956, Serial No. 62–75147, Doc. No. 151, pp. 16, 42–46, 57–59, both in FBI Files, EKL.

22. SAC, NO, to J. Edgar Hoover, June 8, 1950, Serial No. 62–54154, Doc. No. 310, pp. 1–4, in FBI Files, EKL.

23. SAC, NO, to J. Edgar Hoover, August 28, 1956, Serial No. 62–75147, Doc. No. 149, J. Edgar Hoover to Commissioner, Internal Revenue Service, October 8, 1956, Serial No. 62–54154, Doc. No. 517), pp. 3–4, both in FBI Files, EKL.

24. SAC, NO, to J. Edgar Hoover, September 11, 1956, Serial No. 62–54154, Doc. No. 515, p. 2, William C. Sullivan to August H. Belmont, Internal FBI Headquarters Memorandum, April 10, 1959, Serial No. 62–54154, Doc. No. 618, SAC, NO, to J. Edgar Hoover, April 7, 1959, Serial No. 63–43296, Doc. No. 250, pp. 1–2, J. Edgar Hoover to Assistant Attorney General Malcolm R. Wilkey, September 11, 1956, Serial No. 63–53272, Doc. No. 551, p. 2, all in FBI Files, EKL; Clem Huffman; Ernest S. Clements.

25. J. Edgar Hoover, handwritten note at bottom of Hoover to Clyde W. Tolson, Memorandum, September 13, 1956, Serial No. 62–54154, Doc. No. 574, p. 2, Hoover to Attorney General William P. Rogers, September 20, 1956, Serial No. 62–54154, Doc. No. 585, 6 pages, both in FBI Files, EKL.

Chapter 10

1. Wall (ed.), *Louisiana: A History*, 304–11.

2. Old Regular campaign poster, 1946, in Mayoral File I, DSM Papers, NOPL; Earl K. Long, "Message to the White Voters of Louisiana," December, 1951, copy in EKL Vertical File, LSL; Earl Long campaign poster, 1955, in Authors' Collection.

3. Louisiana Legislative Council, *Resumé of Acts, Joint Resolutions, Vetoed Bills and Selected Resolutions at the Regular Session of the Louisiana Legislature* (Baton Rouge, 1958), 86–90.

4. Brooks Read, third session, "Longs of Louisiana"; Read and Hebert (eds.), *Last of the Red Hot Poppas*; Edgar A. Poe; Gaston Ducote; C. J. Doucet.

5. University of New Orleans, Division of Business and Economic Research, and Louisiana State Planning Office, *Statistical Abstract of Louisiana, 1981*, ed. Vincent Maruggi and Susanne Harth (New Orleans, 1981), 52, 60, 61, 219; PAR, "News Analysis," No. 62, August 15, 1957, p. 3, No. 88, December, 1959, p. 7; PAR, *PAR Legislative Bulletin*, June 9, 1956, p. 3, August 17, 1956, pp. 8, 13–14, May 10, 1957, pp. 1–11, August 7, 1957, p. 6.

6. *Report of the Secretary of State,* annual reports, 1949–60, folding pages at back of each issue; PAR, *Louisiana Government in the News*, No. 5, January 30, 1952, p. 1.

7. *Report of the Secretary of State,* annual reports, 1949–60. Folding pages at the back of each issue contain official voter registration statistics.

8. Morgan D. Peoples, "Ralph Waldo Emerson 'Prez' Jones: The Country Doctor of Higher Education in Louisiana, 1926–1977," *Louisiana History*, XXV (1984), 381–82; "Uncle Earl," WLPB-TV. Scholars of the post–World War II South give Earl Long virtually no credit for his pioneering efforts on behalf of Louisiana's blacks. See Thomas D. Clark and Albert D. Kirwan, *The South Since Appomattox: A Century of Regional Change* (New York, 1967), 356; Monroe Lee Billington, *The Political South in the Twentieth Century* (New York, 1975), 122; and Numan V. Bartley, *The Rise of Massive Resistance: Race and Politics in the South During the 1950s* (Baton Rouge, 1969), 280. In his lengthy study of black voting rights in the South, Stephen F. Lawson does not even mention Long and merely quotes the Bartley

work in an endnote (Lawson, *Black Ballots: Voting Rights in the South 1944–1969* [New York, 1976], 383*n*).

9. PAR, *PAR Legislative Bulletin,* May 26, 1956, p. 1, June 28, 1958, p. 3; *Times-Picayune,* November 6, 1957, May 1–30, 1958.

10. SAC, NO, to J. Edgar Hoover, July 14, 1958, Serial No. 62–10187–21, Doc. No. 16, G. H. Scatterday to August H. Belmont, Internal FBI Headquarters Memorandum, August 3, 1959, Serial No. 94–8–350, Doc. No. 1008, both in FBI Files, EKL.

11. Earl K. Long, "Farewell Address to the People of Louisiana," May 1, 1960 (Typescript in EKL Vertical File, LSL), 7–8. See *Times-Picayune,* May 1–September 30, 1958, for full coverage of the LSU-NO developments.

12. Homer L. Hitt to Blanche Revere Long, May 26, 1961, in EKL Papers, LSU; *Times-Picayune,* September 1–30, 1958.

13. See Morton Inger, *Politics and Reality in an American City: The New Orleans School Crisis of 1960* (New York, 1969), 233–34.

14. Jeansonne, *Leander Perez,* 213–14; Kurtz, "The 'Demagogue' and the 'Liberal,'" 157–58; *Morning Advocate,* May 4, 1956; *State-Times,* May 12, 1956.

15. Lionel Ott; Jimmie H. Davis; Leander H. Perez; Chester A. Wooten; William M. Rainach (LSU-S).

16. Haas, *DeLesseps S. Morrison,* 232, 247–48, 254–55; Homer L. Hitt to Blanche Revere Long, May 26, 1961, in EKL Papers, LSU; Lionel Ott; Scott Wilson.

17. *State-Times,* April 8, 1959; *Morning Advocate,* April 8, 22, 1959; *Daily Town Talk,* April 5, 14, 1959.

18. DeLesseps S. Morrison to John Charles "Charlie" Burden, April 9, 1959, Morrison to Leander H. Perez, Sr., William M. Rainach, and E. W. Gravolet, all of April 29, 1959, Morrison, personal memoranda of meetings of April 7, 21, 1959, all in 1959 Gubernatorial Campaign File I, DSM Papers, NOPL.

19. Haas, *DeLesseps S. Morrison,* 232; DeLesseps S. Morrison to Leander H. Perez, Sr., May 17, 1959, in Personal Correspondence File III, DSM Papers, TU; Scott Wilson; Chester A. Wooten; Margaret Dixon.

20. Glen Jeansonne, *Race, Religion, and Politics: The Louisiana Gubernatorial Elections of 1960* (Layfayette, 1977), 10–11.

21. SAC, NO, to J. Edgar Hoover, June 6, 1959, Serial No. 62–54154, Doc. No. NR2, pp. 2–7, G. H. Scatterday to August H. Belmont, Internal FBI Headquarters Memorandum, August 3, 1959, Serial No. 94–8–350, Doc. No. 1008, p. 2, Emmet L. Irwin to J. Edgar Hoover, June 14, 1959, Serial No. 62–54154, Doc. No. 752, pp. 1–5, all in FBI Files, EKL; *Report of the Secretary of State,* 1958, 1959, folding pages at back; *State-Times,* September 10, 1958.

22. Jeansonne, *Race, Religion, and Politics,* 11; *Morning Advocate,* May 27, 1959.

23. Earl K. Long, testimony before House Judiciary "B" Committee, May 26, 1959, tape in Authors' Collection.

24. T. Harry Williams, Introduction to Liebling, *The Earl of Louisiana,* 6–8.

25. *Ibid.,* T. Harry Williams; Joe Gray Taylor; J. D. Jimison.

Chapter 11

1. "Ole Earl," *Time,* June 15, 1959, p. 27; Shreveport, *Journal,* May 29, 1959; *Morning Advocate,* May 29, 1959.

2. *Times-Picayune,* May 26–July 29, 1959, and *Morning Advocate,* May 26–July 31, 1959, contain full coverage of these events.

3. For examples of the national news coverage, see "Louisiana Melee," *Newsweek,* July 6, 1959, pp. 15–16; "Strange Behavior," *Newsweek,* June 8, 1959, pp. 28–29; "His Worst Enemy," *Newsweek,* July 20, 1959, pp. 25–26; "Earl's Whirl," *Time,* May 18, 1959, p. 24; "Gover-

nor Goes Home," *Time*, June 29, 1959, pp. 13–14; "An Ill Governor—And Confusion in Louisiana," *U.S. News & World Report*, July 13, 1959, pp. 48–49; "A Portrait of Earl Long at the Peak of His Crack-Up," *Life*, June 15, 1959, pp. 32–36; Thomas Martin, "Still More Trouble for Ol' Earl Long," *Life*, July 13, 1959, pp. 30–31; William L. Rivers, "The Long Long Trail Awinding," *Reporter*, July 23, 1959, pp. 30–33; Harnett T. Kane, "Louisiana Story: End of a Chapter," *New York Times Magazine*, September 27, 1959, pp. 32–38; Gene Bylinsky and Dan Burnham, "Earl's Empire," *Wall Street Journal*, June 26, 1959, pp. 3–4; "The Weird World of Governor Long," New York *Journal American*, July 12, 1959.

4. Clem Huffman; Margaret Dixon; Gillis W. Long; Gaston Ducote; Lucille Long Hunt; John Hunt.

5. Opotowsky, *The Longs of Louisiana*, 186; Clem Huffman; David Bell; Gillis W. Long.

6. Jeansonne, *Race, Religion, and Politics*, 13; Opotowsky, *The Longs of Louisiana*, 186; McCaughan, *Socks on a Rooster*, 170–71; Clem Huffman; Gaston Ducote; David Bell; Gillis W. Long; Lucille Long Hunt; Blanche Revere Long.

7. Gaston Ducote; David Bell; Gillis W. Long; Lucille Long Hunt; Margaret Dixon; Morris and Read, Blanche Long interview, 76–84.

8. Opotowsky, *The Longs of Louisiana*, 186–87; McCaughan, *Socks on a Rooster*, 170; Phil Johnson, third session, "Longs of Louisiana"; Margaret Dixon; David Bell; Gaston Ducote; Seymour Weiss.

9. Gaston Ducote; David Bell; Robert Angelle; Margaret Dixon; Gillis W. Long; Harvey A. Peltier; Ben Holt, "Uncle Earl," WLPB-TV.

10. *Morning Advocate*, May 27, 1959; *Times-Picayune*, May 27, 1959; *States-Item*, May 27, 1959; authors' personal observations.

11. Lucille Long Hunt; John Hunt; Gaston Ducote; Morris and Read, Blanche Long interview, 83–86.

12. *Morning Advocate*, May 28, 29, 1959; *Times-Picayune*, May 30, 1959; Gillis W. Long.

13. A. R. Rosen to J. Edgar Hoover, Internal FBI Headquarters Memorandum, June 13, 1959, Serial No. 62–54154, Doc. No. 210, in FBI Files, EKL; *Morning Advocate*, May 31, 1959; *Times-Picayune*, May 31, 1959.

14. Jeansonne, *Race, Religion, and Politics*, 16–17; McCaughan, *Socks on a Rooster*, 174–76; Martin, *Dynasty*, 234–52; *Morning Advocate*, May 29–June 18, 1959.

15. Jeansonne, *Race, Religion, and Politics*, 17; McCaughan, *Socks on a Rooster*, 175–76; *Morning Advocate*, June 19, 1959.

16. Martin, *Dynasty*, 250; Liebling, *The Earl of Louisiana*, 100–101; Dugas Collection.

17. *States-Item*, June 19–21, 1959; New York *Times*, June 20, 1959; Gaston Ducote; C. J. Dugas; Mrs. Lether E. Frasar.

18. Liebling, *The Earl of Louisiana*, 35; Gaston Ducote.

19. *States-Item*, June 26, 1959; *Morning Advocate*, June 27, 1959.

20. *Morning Advocate*, June 27–29, 1959; *Times-Picayune*, June 27–29, 1959; New York *Times*, June 27, 1959.

21. Liebling, *The Earl of Louisiana*, 19–20; Morris and Read, Blanche Long interview, 89–90; "Uncle Earl," WLPB-TV, Baton Rouge, February 14, 1986.

22. McCaughan, *Socks on a Rooster*, 175; Martin, *Dynasty*, 250; *Morning Advocate*, June 18–July 2, 1959.

23. American Psychiatric Association, *Diagnostic and Statistical Manual of Mental Disorders* (3rd ed.; Washington, D.C., 1980), 209–13.

24. Joseph J. Roniger, a psychiatrist, reviewed this material on bipolar disorder.

25. American Psychiatric Association, *Diagnostic and Statistical Manual of Mental Disorders*, 208; Ronald R. Fieve, *Moodswing: The Third Revolution in Psychiatry* (Rev. ed.; New York, 1975), 22, 53–56, 77–78; Joseph J. Roniger.

26. Williams, *Huey Long*, 369–70; Fowler Collection.

27. *Morning Advocate*, June 27, 1959; tape recordings of Earl's legislative appearances, May 25, 26, 1959, in Authors' Collection; Joseph J. Roniger.

28. Fieve, *Moodswing*, 56; Liebling, *The Earl of Louisiana*, 35–36; B. B. Rayburn, fourth session, "Longs of Louisiana"; David Bell; Gaston Ducote; Joseph J. Roniger.

29. Fieve, *Moodswing*, 54–55; Liebling, *The Earl of Louisiana*, 178; Camille Gravel, fourth session, "Longs of Louisiana"; Dudley J. LeBlanc; Seymour Weiss; Joseph J. Roniger.

30. Fieve, *Moodswing*, 55; Robert Angelle; Allen J. Ellender.

31. Joseph J. Roniger; Fieve, *Moodswing*, 187.

32. A. R. Rosen to J. Edgar Hoover, Internal FBI Headquarters Memorandum, June 13, 1959, Serial No. 62–54154, Doc. No. 250, pp. 3–6, in FBI Files, EKL; Margaret Dixon; Gaston Ducote; Joseph J. Roniger.

33. Gaston Ducote; Lucille Long Hunt; Joseph J. Roniger.

34. Joseph J. Roniger.

Chapter 12

1. *Daily Town Talk*, July 5, 1959; *Morning Advocate*, July 2–5, 1959.

2. *Morning Advocate*, July 5, 1959; *States-Item*, July 5, 1959.

3. Gaston Ducote; C. J. Dugas; Clem Huffman.

4. *Morning Advocate*, July 13, 1959; Jerry McNeill; Ralph King.

5. McCaughan, *Socks on a Rooster*, 191–92; *Morning Advocate*, July 14, 1959; Russell Willie.

6. *Morning Advocate*, July 13–14, 1959; Jerry McNeill; Russell Willie.

7. Fort Worth *Star-Telegram*, July 14–16, 1959; *Morning Advocate*, July 15, 1959; Jerry McNeill.

8. Fort Worth *Star-Telegram*, July 17–18, 1959; *Morning Advocate*, July 15, 1959; Jerry McNeill.

9. El Paso *Times*, July 17, 1959; Jerry McNeill.

10. El Paso *Times*, July 17, 19, 1959; Jerry McNeill; James E. Comiskey.

11. Read and Hebert (eds.), *Last of the Red Hot Poppas*; Jerry McNeill; William Wisner.

12. McCaughan, *Socks on a Rooster*, 194–99; "I'll Shoot 'Em," *Newsweek*, July 27, 1959, p. 24.

13. Jerry McNeill; William Wisner; Gaston Ducote.

14. Jerry McNeill; William Wisner; Gaston Ducote.

15. *Morning Advocate*, July 22, 1959; Denver *Post*, July 24, 1959.

16. *Morning Advocate*, July 24, 1959.

17. *Ibid.*, July 26–27, 1959.

18. McCaughan, *Socks on a Rooster*, 206–208.

19. *Morning Advocate*, July 28, 1959.

20. *Ibid.*, July 28–29, 1959.

21. *Ibid.*, July 28–30, 1959; *Times-Picayune*, July 29, 1959.

22. *Morning Advocate*, July 29, 1959.

23. *Ibid.*, July 29–30, 1959.

24. *Ibid.*, July 30, 1959; Jerry McNeill to authors, October 25, 1987.

Chapter 13

1. *Morning Advocate*, August 1–2, 1959; "Uncle Earl," WLPB-TV.

2. *Times-Picayune*, August 11, 1959; *State-Times*, August 10, 1959.

3. *Morning Advocate*, August 10, September 1–2, 1959; New York *Times*, September 8, 1959.

4. Jeansonne, *Race, Religion, and Politics*, 28–34; C. J. Dugas, personal memorandum of meeting, in Dugas Collection; C. J. Dugas.

5. Martin, *Dynasty*, 294; Liebling, *The Earl of Louisiana*, 89–95; C. J. Dugas, personal memorandum of meeting, in Dugas Collection.

6. Liebling, *The Earl of Louisiana*, 89–103.

7. *Primary Election Returns*, 1959, p. 78; Jeansonne, *Race, Religion, and Politics*, 98–99; Leander H. Perez; Jimmie H. Davis.

8. SAC, NO, to J. Edgar Hoover, May 25, June 15, 1960, Serial No. 62–42396–33, Doc. No. 25, pp. 1–3, Doc. No. 370, pp. 1–4, both in FBI Files, EKL; Liebling, *The Earl of Louisiana*, 209; Jeansonne, *Race, Religion, and Politics*, 102–103; Gaston Ducote.

9. Linda Lou Ropp May, "A Rhetorical Study of the Public Speaking of Earl Kemp Long From 1955 to 1960" (M.A. thesis, Louisiana Tech University, 1964), 27; *Times-Picayune*, May 4, 1960; Jack McGuire; Gaston Ducote.

10. *State-Times*, May 25, June 1–3, 1960; New York *Times*, June 3, 1960.

11. McCaughan, *Socks on a Rooster*, 244–45; *Daily Town Talk*, June 4, 6, 1960; Earl Long platform, 1960, in Authors' Collection.

12. *Daily Town Talk*, June 13, July 24, August 22, 1960; Gaston Ducote; David Bell; A. A. Fredericks.

13. *Daily Town Talk*, July 2, 4, 22, 23, 1960; David Bell.

14. *Daily Town Talk*, June 6, July 2, August 1, 15, 1960; *Winn Parish Enterprise/News-American*, August 25, 1960; Clem Huffman.

15. "Uncle Earl," WLPB-TV; David Bell; A. A. Fredericks.

16. Read and Hebert (eds.), *Last of the Red Hot Poppas*; *Daily Town Talk*, July 29, 1960; Shreveport *Times*, August 19, 21, 1960.

17. *Daily Town Talk*, July 18, 25, 1960.

18. *Primary Election Returns*, July 23, 1960; David Bell; Lucille Long Hunt.

19. *Daily Town Talk*, August 1, 2, 8, 22, 1960; Lake Charles *American-Press*, August 16, 1960; "The Unquenchable Longs," *Newsweek*, August 8, 1960, p. 28.

20. *Daily Town Talk*, August 1, 6, 8, 1960; Shreveport *Times*, August 21, 1960.

21. McCaughan, *Socks on a Rooster*, 256; *State-Times*, August 6, 1960.

22. *Daily Town Talk*, August 6, 14, 22, 25, 1960; *State-Times*, August 26, 1960.

23. *Primary Election Returns*, August 26, 1960; McCaughan, *Socks on a Rooster*, 262; David Bell; Lucille Long Hunt; Gillis W. Long.

24. *Morning Advocate*, September 4–9, 1960; *Daily Town Talk*, September 1–9, 1960; Shreveport *Times*, August 26–September 9, 1960; *Times-Picayune*, September 4–9, 1960; David Bell.

Chapter 14

1. Lake Charles *American-Press*, January 24, 1980; Eck Bozeman.

2. Robert Angelle; Clem H. Sehrt; Robert S. Maestri; Gaston Ducote.

3. Margaret Dixon; Herman B. Deutsch; B. B. Rayburn; Clem H. Sehrt.

4. Leppert, "Long Live the Kingfishes!" 98; William J. Dodd.

5. Frank Fulco; William M. Rainach (both in LSU-S).

6. Robert Angelle; B. B. Rayburn; James H. Morrison; Allen J. Ellender; Robert S. Maestri; James E. Comiskey; Sam H. Jones.

7. Sam H. Jones; John B. Fournet; Gillis W. Long; Leander H. Perez; Robert Angelle.

8. Liebling, *The Earl of Louisiana*, 245; Margaret Dixon; Clem H. Sehrt.

9. Kurtz, "Earl Long's Political Relations With New Orleans," 247; Read and Hebert (eds.), *Last of the Red Hot Poppas*; Fowler Collection; Herman B. Deutsch; Edgar A. Poe; Margaret Dixon; John F. Tims.

10. Edgar A. Poe, Walter Cowan, both in third session, "Longs of Louisiana"; John F. Tims; Margaret Dixon.

11. Margaret Dixon; Martha L. Horton, "Master of the Pea Patch Farm" (Senior paper, Louisiana Tech University, 1964), 22–23.

12. Read and Hebert (eds.), *Last of the Red Hot Poppas*; Clem Huffman.

13. Clem Huffman; Ernest S. Clements; Lucille Long Hunt; Eck Bozeman; Harley Bozeman.

14. Opotowsky, *The Longs of Louisiana,* 134–37; Fowler Collection.

15. Read and Hebert (eds.), *Last of the Red Hot Poppas*; Fowler Collection; Camille Gravel, fourth session, "Longs of Louisiana."

16. Frank Anzalone; Thomas W. Gillen; James A. Noe.

17. See annual reports of the Departments of Education, Health, and Public Welfare for the budgetary amounts.

18. See *Acts of the Legislature,* annual volumes, regular and special sessions, 1948–52, 1956–59.

19. Allen J. Ellender; T. Hale Boggs; Thomas A. Cochoran; James H. Morrison; Sam H. Jones; James E. Comiskey.

20. See PAR, "News Analysis," 1952–60, for detailed discussions of state fiscal policies.

21. Sindler, *Huey Long's Louisiana,* 208–40; Key, *Southern Politics,* 156–82; PAR, "News Analysis," 1958.

22. See Maginnis, *The Last Hayride,* 3–9.

23. See Renwick, "The Longs' Legislative Lieutenants," 244–49; Key, *Southern Politics,* 156–82.

24. "Uncle Earl," WLPB-TV; C. J. Doucet.

25. Shreveport *Times,* May 8, 1989. For examples of the organized crime ties of other Louisiana governors and politicians, see John H. Davis, *Mafia Kingfish: Carlos Marcello and the Assassination of President Kennedy* (New York, 1988), 40, 307–15, 486.

Bibliography

Primary Sources

Manuscript Collections

Dodd, William J. Papers. Northwestern State University Library, Natchitoches.

Fredericks, A. A. Papers. Northwestern State University Library, Natchitoches.

Hester, Earl J. Papers. Louisiana Tech University Library, Ruston.

Jones, Sam H. Papers. Tulane University Special Collections, New Orleans.

Leche, Richard W. Papers. Department of Archives and Manuscripts, Hill Memorial Library, Louisiana State University, Baton Rouge.

Long, Earl K. File. Louisiana Tech University Library, Ruston.

———. Papers. Department of Archives and Manuscripts, Hill Memorial Library, Louisiana State University, Baton Rouge.

———. Vertical File. Louisiana Room, Louisiana State University Library, Baton Rouge.

———. Vertical File. Louisiana State Library, Baton Rouge.

Morrison, deLesseps S. Papers. Louisiana Room, New Orleans Public Library.

———. Papers. Special Collections, Howard-Tilton Memorial Library, Tulane University, New Orleans.

Morrison, James H. Papers. Special Collections, Linus A. Sims Memorial Library, Southeastern Louisiana University, Hammond.

Williams, T. Harry. Papers. Department of Archives and Manuscripts. Hill Memorial Library, Louisiana State University, Baton Rouge.

Wisdom, William B. Collection. Special Collections, Howard-Tilton Memorial Library, Tulane University, New Orleans.

State Government Documents and Publications

Acts of the Legislature. Baton Rouge, 1936–60.

Department of Education, State of Louisiana. *Annual Report.* Baton Rouge, 1948–60.

Department of Public Welfare, State of Louisiana. *Annual Report.* Baton Rouge, 1948–60.

Governor's Office, State of Louisiana. *Special Message on Civil Service by Governor Earl K. Long to the Members of the Legislature, June 19, 1950.* Baton Rouge, 1950.

Secretary of State, State of Louisiana. *Compilation of Primary Election Returns.* Baton Rouge, 1918–48.

————. *Primary Election Returns.* Baton Rouge, 1959–60.

————. *Report of the Secretary of State.* Baton Rouge, 1949–58.

————. *Roster of Officials, State of Louisiana.* Baton Rouge, 1948–60.

Parish Records

Winn Parish Conveyance Records, 1886–1960. Parish Courthouse, Winnfield.

United States Government Documents and Publications

U.S. Congress. Senate. Special Committee on Investigations of Campaign Expenditures. *United States Senate, Senatorial Campaign Expenditures (Louisiana), 1932–1933. Hearings Before Subcommittee. 72nd Congress, 2nd Session, on Senate Resolution 174.* 2 vols. 1933.

U.S. Congress. Senate. Special Committee to Investigate Organized Crime in Interstate Commerce. *Investigation of Organized Crime in Interstate Commerce.* 81st Cong., 2nd Sess., 82nd Cong., 1st Sess. 19 parts. 1950–51.

————. *U.S. Senate, Kefauver Report: Third Interim Report.* 82nd Cong., 1st Sess. 1951.

U.S. Department of Justice. Federal Bureau of Investigation. FBI Files on Governor Earl Kemp Long. Special Collections, Linus A. Sims Memorial Library, Southeastern Louisiana University, Hammond.

Private Research Publications

Bureau of Governmental Research. *Registration of Voters in Louisiana.* Baton Rouge, 1951.

George Peabody College for Teachers, Division of Surveys and Field Services. *Public Education in Louisiana: A Survey Report.* Nashville, 1954.

Louisiana Law Institute. *Projet of a Constitution for the State of Louisiana, With Notes and Studies.* 4 vols. Baton Rouge, 1950–54.

Louisiana Legislative Council. *Homestead Tax Exemption in Louisiana and Other States.* Baton Rouge, 1954.

————. *The Legislative Process in Louisiana.* Baton Rouge, 1953.

————. *Resumé of Acts, Joint Resolutions, Vetoed Bills and Selected Resolutions at the Regular Session of the Legislature.* Baton Rouge, 1956–59.

————. *The State Property Tax.* Baton Rouge, 1953.

Public Affairs Research Council of Louisiana. *Louisiana Government in the News.* Baton Rouge, 1951–53.

———. *Louisiana Lawmakers: A 25 Year Profile.* Baton Rouge, 1975.

———. *News Analysis.* Baton Rouge, 1954–56.

———. *PAR Analysis.* Baton Rouge, 1956–60.

———. *PAR Legislative Bulletin.* Baton Rouge, 1956–60.

———. *Twenty-five Years of Political Reform.* Baton Rouge, 1975.

———. *20 Years of Louisiana Politics: 1950–1970.* Baton Rouge, 1970.

University of New Orleans, Division of Business and Economic Research, and Louisiana State Planning Office. *Statistical Abstract of Louisiana, 1981.* Edited by Vincent Maruggi and Susanne Harth. New Orleans, 1981.

Audio-Visual Materials

Long, Earl K. Address to the Legislature, May 26, 27, 1959. Audio cassettes.

"Longs of Louisiana" Symposium. Hammond, La., September 8–15, 1985. Videotapes and audio cassettes of sessions in Southeastern Louisiana University Library, Hammond.

"Louisiana Legends: William J. Dodd." WLPB-TV, Baton Rouge, November 8, 1985.

Read, Brooks, and Bud Hebert, eds. *Last of the Red Hot Poppas.* Record album. 1961.

"Uncle Earl," WLPB-TV, Baton Rouge, February 14, 1986.

"The Wizard of Winnfield." WBRZ-TV, Baton Rouge, August 28, 1960.

Symposium Program

SESSION I: "The Longs: After Fifty Years."

Peoples, Morgan D. "The Last Campaign of Earl K. Long."

Reed, Ed. "The Assassination of Huey P. Long."

SESSION II: "The Huey Long Theme in Literature and the Arts."

Dowie, William. "The Huey Long Theme in Literature."

Parrill, William. "The Huey Long Theme in Film."

SESSION III: "Remembering the Longs: Journalists' Perspectives."

Moderator: Phil Johnson

Panelists: Walter Cowan; Edgar A. Poe; Ann Price; Brooks Read

SESSION IV: "Remembering the Longs: Political Perspectives."

Moderator: Michael L. Kurtz

Panelists: Jerry Fowler; Camille Gravel; B. B. Rayburn

SESSION V: "Huey Long in Historical Perspective."

Moderator: Roman J. Heleniak

Baiamonte, John V. "Charles Anzalone: A Political Profile of a Tangipahoa Parish Longite."

Hair, William Ivy. "The Kingfish."

Jeansonne, Glen. "Huey Long: Robin Hood or Tyrant?"

SESSION VI: "The Legacy of the Longs."

Moderator: Roman J. Heleniak

Panelists: Mark T. Carleton; Henry Dethloff; Edward F. Haas; Michael L. Kurtz; J. Paul Leslie; Edward F. Renwick

Private Collections

Dugas, C. J. Earl Long materials. Baton Rouge.

Fowler, Douglas. Earl Long humor. Baton Rouge.

Kurtz, Michael L., and Morgan D. Peoples. Earl Long materials. Hammond and Ruston.

Newman, Shelby M. Earl Long materials. Hammond.

Personal Interviews by Authors

Ainsworth, Robert A., Jr. New Orleans, 1971.

Angelle, Robert. Baton Rouge, 1969, 1973.

Anzalone, Frank. Independence, 1974.

Bell, David. Baton Rouge, 1969, 1970.

Bisso, William A. New Orleans, 1965.

Boggs, T. Hale. New Orleans, 1967.

Bozeman, Eck. Winnfield, 1978, 1982.

Bozeman, Harley. Winnfield, 1969, 1971.

Burns, James T. Covington, 1965.

Cefalu, Nicholas. Amite, 1966.

Clements, Ernest S. Baton Rouge, 1976.

Cochoran, Thomas A. Washington, D.C., 1978.

Coci, William S. Gretna, 1967.

Comiskey, James E. New Orleans, 1965, 1967.

Cooper, Olive Long. Natchitoches, 1967, 1969.

Davis, Jimmie H. Baton Rouge, 1984.

Deutsch, Herman B. New Orleans, 1966.

Dixon, Margaret. Baton Rouge, 1967, 1968.

Dodd, William J. Monroe, 1984.

Doucet, C. J. Opelousas, 1968.

Downs, C. H. Baton Rouge, 1981.

Ducote, Gaston. Baton Rouge, 1978, 1981.

Dugas, C. J. Baton Rouge, 1987.

Ellender, Allen J. New Orleans, 1969.

Fournet, John B. Baton Rouge, 1968; Jackson, Miss., 1979.

Fowler, Douglas. Baton Rouge, 1968.

Frasar, Mrs. Lether E. Lake Charles, 1975.
Fredericks, A. A. Baton Rouge, 1968.
Giacone, Anna Mae. New Orleans, 1965.
Gillen, Thomas W. Hammond, 1982.
Goodin, Frank. New Orleans, 1965.
Grace, Lucille May. Baton Rouge, 1966.
Gravolet, E. W., Jr. Baton Rouge, 1969.
Grosch, John J. New Orleans, 1967.
Haggerty, Edward A. New Orleans, 1967.
Hebert, F. Edward. New Orleans, 1967.
Henry, Clarence. New Orleans, 1965.
Hickey, Theodore M. New Orleans, 1968.
Howard, W. L. Monroe, 1966.
Huffman, Clem. Winnfield, 1976.
Hunt, John. Monroe, 1976, 1988.
Hunt, Lucille Long. Ruston, 1967, 1969, 1982, 1984.
Jack, Wellborn. Shreveport, 1968.
Jackson, Shirley G. Winnfield, 1974.
Jimison, J. D. Baton Rouge, 1983.
Jones, Ralph Waldo Emerson. Grambling, 1981.
Jones, Sam H. Lake Charles, 1969.
King, Ralph. Baton Rouge, 1966.
Knott, Clara Long. Many, 1966.
Larson, George. Baton Rouge, 1972.
LeBlanc, Dudley J. New Orleans, 1966, 1968.
LeBreton, Edward F. New Orleans, 1967.
Leche, Richard W. New Orleans, 1967.
Lockhart, Wilma. Baton Rouge, 1970.
Long, Blanche Revere. Baton Rouge, 1968.
Long, Gillis W. Washington, D.C., 1978.
Maestri, Robert S. New Orleans, 1966, 1969.
McGuire, Jack. Hammond, 1985.
McNeill, Jerry. Dallas, Tex., 1982.
Meraux, Claude. Arabi, 1966.
Monk, James. Natchitoches, 1977.
Morris, Henry. New Orleans, 1980.
Morrison, James H. Hammond, 1978.
Napper, W. L. Shreveport, 1979; Ruston, 1989.
Noe, James A. Monroe, 1966, 1967.
Ott, Lionel. New Orleans, 1983.
Peltier, Harvey A., Sr. Baton Rouge, 1969, 1977.

Perez, Leander H., Sr. New Orleans, 1965.
Poe, Edgar A. Hammond, 1985.
Rayburn, B. B. Hammond, 1982.
Read, Brooks. Hammond, 1985.
Roniger, Joseph J. New Orleans, 1988.
Sehrt, Clem H. New Orleans, 1965, 1967.
Smith, Gerald L. K. Eureka Springs, Ark., 1975.
Stumpf, Alvin. Gretna, 1967.
Talbot, William H. Baton Rouge, 1967.
Taylor, Joe Gray. Alexandria, 1980.
Tessier, George D. New Orleans, 1965.
Tims, John F. New Orleans, 1965.
Trist, Nicholas P. Arabi, 1965.
Washington, James T. Colfax, 1987.
Weiss, Seymour. New Orleans, 1965, 1966.
Williams, T. Harry. Baton Rouge, 1972.
Willie, Russell. Denham Springs, 1981.
Wilson, Scott. New Orleans, 1967.
Wisner, William. Baton Rouge, 1986.
Wooten, Chester A. New Orleans, 1965.

Personal Interviews by Others

Morris, Lewis M., Jr., and Brooks Read. Interview with Blanche Revere Long, Metairie, 1983. Transcript in Louisiana State Archives, Baton Rouge.
Oral History Collection, Louisiana State University, Shreveport. Tapes of interviews with Harney Bogan, Frank Fulco, Cecil Morgan, William M. Rainach, and Earl Williamson, Sr.
Williams, T. Harry. Interviews with Robert Angelle, Harley Bozeman, James T. Burns, William Cleveland, John B. Fournet, Theophile Landry, Richard W. Leche, David B. McConnell, Edgar G. Mouton, and Wilson J. Peck. Transcripts or summaries in T. Harry Williams Papers, Department of Archives and Manuscripts, Hill Memorial Library, Louisiana State University, Baton Rouge.

Newspapers

Alexandria *Daily Town Talk*, 1928–86.
American Progress, 1932–35.
Atlanta *Journal*, March 7, 1948.
Baton Rouge *Morning Advocate*, 1918–86.
Baton Rouge *State-Times*, 1918–86.
Denver *Post*, 1959.
El Paso *Times*, July 1–31, 1959.

Fort Worth *Star-Telegram,* July 1–31, 1959.
Hammond *Daily Courier,* 1932–35.
Lake Charles *American Press,* 1948–60.
Louisiana Progress, 1928–32.
Louisiana Watchman, 1944–48.
Louisiana Weekly, 1948–60.
New Orleans *Item,* 1939–58.
New Orleans *Item-Tribune,* 1928–39.
New Orleans *States,* 1928–58.
New Orleans *States-Item,* 1958–81.
New Orleans *Times-Picayune,* 1918–81.
New Orleans *Times-Picayune/States-Item,* 1981–86.
New York *Journal American,* 1959.
New York *Times,* 1928–86.
Progress, 1936–40.
Ruston *Daily Leader,* 1948–60.
Shreveport *Journal,* 1928–60.
Shreveport *Times,* 1928–86.
Tensas *Gazette,* 1940.
Winnfield *News-American,* 1940–60.
Winn Parish *Enterprise/News-American,* 1948–75.

Secondary Sources

Books

American Psychiatric Association. *Diagnostic and Statistical Manual of Mental Disorders.* 3rd ed. Washington, D.C., 1980.
Bartley, Numan V. *The Rise of Massive Resistance: Race and Politics in the South During the 1950s.* Baton Rouge, 1969.
Bass, Jack, and Walter DeVries. *The Transformation of Southern Politics: Social Change and Political Consequences Since 1945.* New York, 1976.
Billington, Monroe Lee. *The Political South in the Twentieth Century.* New York, 1975.
Bolner, James, ed. *Louisiana Politics: Festival in a Labyrinth.* Baton Rouge, 1982.
Boone, William C. *The Impeachment and Acquittal of Huey P. Long.* Shreveport, 1929.
Brinkley, Alan. *Voices of Protest: Huey Long, Father Coughlin, and the Great Depression.* New York, 1982.
Carleton, Mark T., Perry H. Howard, and Joseph B. Parker, eds. *Readings in Louisiana Politics.* 2nd ed. Baton Rouge, 1988.

Clark, Thomas D., and Albert D. Kirwan. *The South Since Appomattox: A Century of Regional Change.* New York, 1967.

Clay, Floyd Martin. *Coozan Dudley LeBlanc: From Huey Long to Hadacol.* Gretna, 1973.

Conrad, Glenn R., ed. *Readings in Louisiana History.* New Orleans, 1978.

Conway, James. *Judge: The Life and Times of Leander Perez.* New York, 1973.

Davis, John H. *Mafia Kingfish: Carlos Marcello and the Assassination of President Kennedy.* New York, 1988.

Fieve, Ronald R. *Moodswing: The Third Revolution in Psychiatry.* Rev. ed.; New York, 1975.

Haas, Edward F. *DeLesseps S. Morrison and the Image of Reform: New Orleans Politics, 1946–1961.* Baton Rouge, 1974.

Hair, William Ivy. *Bourbonism and Agrarian Protest: Louisiana Politics, 1877–1900.* Baton Rouge, 1969.

Havard, William C., ed. *The Changing Politics of the South.* Baton Rouge, 1972.

Havard, William C., Rudolph Herberle, and Perry H. Howard. *The Louisiana Elections of 1960.* Baton Rouge, 1963.

Hebert, F. Edward, with John McMillan. *Last of the Titans: The Life and Times of Congressman F. Edward Hebert of Louisiana.* Edited by Glenn R. Conrad. Lafayette, 1976.

Howard, L. Vaughan. *Civil Service Development in Louisiana.* New Orleans, 1956.

Howard, L. Vaughan, and David R. Deener. *Presidential Politics in Louisiana, 1952.* New Orleans, 1954.

Howard, Perry H. *Political Tendencies in Louisiana.* Rev. ed. Baton Rouge, 1971.

Inger, Morton. *Politics and Reality in an American City: The New Orleans School Crisis of 1960.* New York, 1969.

Jeansonne, Glen. *Leander Perez: Boss of the Delta.* Baton Rouge, 1977.

———. *Race, Religion, and Politics: The Louisiana Gubernatorial Elections of 1960.* Lafayette, 1977.

Kane, Harnett T. *Louisiana Hayride: The American Rehearsal for Dictatorship, 1928–1940.* New York, 1941.

Key, V. O., Jr. *Southern Politics in State and Nation.* New York, 1949.

Klorer, John D., ed. *The New Louisiana.* New Orleans, 1936.

Lawson, Stephen F. *Black Ballots: Voting Rights in the South 1944–1969.* New York, 1976.

Liebling, A. J. *The Earl of Louisiana.* 1961; rpr. Baton Rouge, 1971.

Lincoln Parish History. N.p., 1971.

Litton, G. Dupree. *The Wizard of Winnfield.* New York, 1982.

Long, Huey P., Jr. *Every Man a King: The Autobiography of Huey P. Long.* New Orleans, 1933.

Maginnis, John. *The Last Hayride.* Baton Rouge, 1984.

Martin, Thomas P. *Dynasty: The Longs of Louisiana*. New York, 1960.
McCaughan, Richard B. *Socks on a Rooster: Louisiana's Earl K. Long*. Baton Rouge, 1967.
Moore, William Howard. *The Kefauver Committee and the Politics of Crime: 1950 – 1952*. Columbia, Mo., 1974.
Morrison, DeLesseps S. *Latin American Mission: An Adventure in Hemisphere Diplomacy*. Edited and introduced by Gerold Frank. New York, 1965.
Opotowsky, Stan. *The Longs of Louisiana*. New York, 1960.
Reed, Ed. *Requiem for a Kingfish*. Baton Rouge, 1986.
Roller, David C., and Robert W. Twyman, eds. *The Encyclopedia of Southern History*. Baton Rouge, 1979.
Romero, Sidney J. *"My Fellow Citizens": The Inaugural Addresses of the Governors of Louisiana*. Lafayette, 1980.
Sindler, Allan P. *Huey Long's Louisiana: State Politics, 1920–1952*. Baltimore, 1956.
Smith, Gerald L. K. *Huey P. Long: Summary of Greatness, Political Genius, American Martyr*. Eureka Springs, Ark., 1975.
Wall, Bennett H., ed. *Louisiana: A History*. Arlington Heights, Ill., 1984.
Williams, T. Harry. *Huey Long*. New York, 1969.
———. *Romance and Realism in Southern Politics*. Athens, Ga., 1961.

Journal Articles

Baker, Riley. "Negro Voter Registration in Louisiana, 1879–1964." *Louisiana Studies*, IV (1965), 236–49.
Brooks, Davy. "A Turn of Events: Earl Long and the Gubernatorial Elections of 1940 and 1948." *Southern Historian*, V (1984), 38–45.
Bugea, James A., Carlos E. Lazarus, and William T. Peague. "The Louisiana Legislation of 1940." *Louisiana Law Review*, III (1940–41), 98–199.
Cosman, Bernard. "Religion and Race in Louisiana Politics, 1960." *Southwestern Social Science Quarterly*, LIII (1962), 235–41.
Desmare, Dudley. "History of the Old Regular Organization." *Louisiana Police Jury Review*, XI (1947), 99–126.
Dethloff, Henry J. "The Longs: Revolution or Populist Retrenchment?" *Louisiana History*, XIX (1978), 401–12.
Dur, Philip F., and Don M. Kurtz III. "North-South Changes in Louisiana Voting, 1948–1968." *Louisiana Studies*, X (1971), 28–44.
Fenton, John H., and Kenneth N. Vines. "Negro Voter Registration in Louisiana." *American Political Science Review*, LI (1957), 689–711.
Guste, William J., and Frederick W. Ellis. "Louisiana Tidelands: Past and Future." *Loyola Law Review*, XXI (1975), 817–34.
Haas, Edward F. "New Orleans on the Half-Shell: The Maestri Era, 1936–1946." *Louisiana History*, XIII (1972), 289–311.

Havard, William C. "The Abortive Louisiana Constitutional Convention of 1951." *Journal of Politics,* XIII (1951), 708–17.

Hebert, Paul M., and Carlos E. Lazarus. "The Louisiana Legislation of 1938." *Louisiana Law Review,* I (1938–39), 1–97.

Hyneman, Charles S. "Political and Administrative Reform in the 1940 Legislature." *Louisiana Law Review,* III (1940–41), 1–54.

Illig, Carl. "Tidelands—An Unsolved Problem." *Tulane Law Review,* XXIV (1949), 161–85.

Jeansonne, Glen. "Huey P. Long, Robin Hood or Tyrant? A Critique of *Huey Long.*" *Regional Dimensions,* IV (1986), 22–37.

———. "Sam Houston Jones and the Revolution of 1940." *Red River Valley Historical Review,* IV (1979), 73–87.

Kurtz, Michael L. "DeLesseps S. Morrison: Political Reformer." *Louisiana History,* XVII (1976), 19–39.

———. "Earl Long's Political Relations with the City of New Orleans, 1948–1960." *Louisiana History,* X (1969), 241–54.

———. "Government by the Civics Book: The Administration of Robert F. Kennon." *Journal of the North Louisiana Historical Association,* XII (1981), 52–61.

———. "Organized Crime in Louisiana History: Myth and Reality." *Louisiana History,* XXIV (1983), 355–76.

———. "Political Corruption and Organized Crime in Louisiana: The FBI Files on Earl Long." *Louisiana History,* XXIX (1988), 229–52.

———. "The Struggle for Political Reform in Louisiana." *Papers of the Southeast Louisiana Historical Association,* VIII (1982), 1–10.

Owen, Kimbrough. "The Need for Constitutional Revision in Louisiana." *Louisiana Law Review,* VIII (1947–48), 1–104.

Peoples, Morgan D. "Earl Kemp Long: The Man From Pea Patch Farm." *Louisiana History,* XVII (1976), 365–93.

———. "Ralph Waldo Emerson 'Prez' Jones: The Country Doctor of Higher Education in Louisiana, 1926–1977." *Louisiana History,* XXV (1984), 363–83.

Schott, Matthew J. "Huey Long: Progressive Backlash." *Louisiana History,* XXVII (1986), 133–45.

Student Board of the Louisiana Law Review. "Louisiana Legislation of 1948." *Louisiana Law Review,* IX (1948–49), 18–141.

Williams, T. Harry. "The Gentleman From Louisiana: Demagogue or Democrat?" *Journal of Southern History,* XXVI (1960), 1–20.

Signed Newspaper and Magazine Articles

Basso, Hamilton. "Huey's Louisiana Heritage." *New Republic,* August 30, 1959, p. 99.

Bylinsky, Gene, and Dan Burnham. "Earl's Empire." *Wall Street Journal,* June 26, 1959, pp. 3–4.

Carr, Frederick W. "Huey Long's Father Relates the Story of the Senator's Boyhood." *Christian Science Monitor,* September 11, 1935, p. 8.

Crown, James E. "Louisiana's David Who Slew the Giant That Was the Long Machine." *New York Times Magazine,* March 3, 1940, pp. 7–23.

Daniel, F. Raymond. "Huey's Heirs." *Saturday Evening Post,* February 12, 1938, pp. 5–7, 61–62.

Ferman, Irving. "Louisiana Side-Show." *New Republic,* January 21, 1952, pp. 13–14.

Fuller, Helen. "Huey's Brother Has a Problem." *New Republic,* October 4, 1956, pp. 5–6.

Irey, Elmer L., and William J. Slocum. "The End of the Kingfish." *Coronet,* January, 1948, pp. 47–58.

Johnston, Alva. "The Camera Trapped Them." *Saturday Evening Post,* June 15, 1940, pp. 22–26.

———. "Louisiana Revolution." *Saturday Evening Post,* May 11, 1940, pp. 16–21.

———. "They Sent a Letter." *Saturday Evening Post,* June 22, 1940, pp. 29–33.

Jones, Sam H., with James Aswell. "Will Dixie Bolt the New Deal?" *Saturday Evening Post,* March 6, 1943, pp. 20–29.

Kane, Harnett T. "Louisiana Story: End of a Chapter." *New York Times Magazine,* September 27, 1959, pp. 32–40.

Kurtz, Michael L. "The Last and Greatest of the Red Hot Poppas." *Gris Gris,* November 6, 1985, pp. 18–23.

Leavitt, Mel. "Let Us Now Think of Uncle Earl." *New Orleans Magazine,* April, 1971, pp. 33–36, 62–64.

Leppert, George M. "Long Live the Kingfishes!" *American Mercury,* October, 1956, pp. 93–100.

Long, Julius T. "What I Know About My Brother United States Senator Huey P. Long." *Real America,* September, 1933, pp. 39–41, 172–78.

Macmurdo, Bruce. "I Remember Earl." *Gris Gris,* June 15–21, 1976, pp. 11–15.

Martin, Thomas. "Still More Trouble for Ol' Earl Long." *Life,* July 13, 1959, pp. 30–31.

Moak, Lennox, and Helen Moak. "The Rape of New Orleans." *National Municipal Review,* October, 1948, pp. 412–15.

Moley, Raymond F. "Long Forever on the Throne." *Newsweek,* February 2, 1948, p. 76.

Mullener, Elizabeth. "Stumping With Uncle Earl." *Dixie,* August 22, 1982, pp. 10–18.

Muse, Orene. "Third Act in a Long Story." *Register,* May 19, 1956, pp. 2–3.

Parmentel, Noel. "Jambalaya in a Crawfish Bayou: Gone With the House of

Long, a Rambunctious Era in American Politics." *National Review,* May 21, 1960, pp. 331—32.

Pearson, Drew, and Robert S. Allen. "Washington Merry-Go-Round" column, June 17, 1939.

Phillips, Cabell. "The Lengthening Shadow of Huey Long." *New York Times Magazine,* November 7, 1948, pp. 76—92.

Rivers, William L. "The Long Long Trail Awinding." *Reporter,* July 23, 1959, pp. 30—33.

Rorty, James. "Callie Long's Boy Huey." *Forum,* August, 1935, p. 78.

Velie, Lester. "Louisiana's Long Long Dilemma." *Reader's Digest,* June, 1960, pp. 139—44.

Wool, Robert. "The Louisiana Story: Clowns, Complacency, Corruption." *Look,* December 8, 1959, pp. 42—55.

Unsigned Magazine Articles

"Back in the Saddle Again." *Time,* May 24, 1948, p. 28.

"Bitin' Man." *Time,* February 2, 1948, p. 13.

"Brother." *Time,* September 19, 1960, p. 25.

"The Career of Earl K. Long: From Farm Boy to Governor." *Louisiana Conservation Review,* Summer, 1939, p. 5.

"Earl's Whirl." *Time,* May 18, 1959, p. 24.

"Echoes in the Bayou." *Newsweek,* January 5, 1948, pp. 19—21.

"Gambling in Louisiana." *Gris Gris,* January 23, 1986, pp. 10—13.

"Governor Goes Home." *Time,* June 29, 1959, pp. 13—14.

"Happy Days." *Time,* March 8, 1948, p. 23.

"His Worst Enemy." *Newsweek,* July 20, 1959, pp. 25—26.

"Hustle Plus Elegance." *Business Week,* February 19, 1955, p. 121.

"An Ill Governor—And Confusion in Louisiana." *U.S. News & World Report,* July 13, 1959, pp. 48—49.

"I'll Shoot 'Em." *Newsweek,* July 27, 1959, p. 24.

"Invictus." *Time,* July 6, 1959, p. 17.

"Jambalaya." *Time,* January 18, 1960, p. 17.

"Just Like Huey." *Time,* June 7, 1948, p. 24.

"King of the Crescent City." *Time,* February 17, 1958, p. 27.

"Last of the Red Hot Poppas." *Time,* July 2, 1956, p. 15.

"Lonesome Man." *Time,* February 26, 1940, p. 19.

"The Long Count." *Time,* July 13, 1956, pp. 15—16.

"Long Hands." *Newsweek,* February 4, 1957, p. 25.

"Long Long Rule Comes to an End." *Life,* March 3, 1952, pp. 33—34.

"Louisiana Melee." *Newsweek,* July 6, 1959, pp. 15—16.

"Louisiana Ruckus." *Newsweek,* July 13, 1959, pp. 13–14.

"Old Girl's New Boy." *Time,* November 24, 1947,·pp. 29–31.

"Ole Earl." *Time,* June 15, 1959, p. 27.

"Ole Earl's Downfall." *Time,* December 14, 1959, p. 17.

"Out Again, In Again for Governor Long." *Life,* June 29, 1959, pp. 30–31.

"A Portrait of Earl Long at the Peak of His Crack-Up." *Life,* June 15, 1959, pp. 32–36.

"Ride on a Wild Steed." *Newsweek,* July 20, 1959, p. 19.

"Scandals of 1948." *Newsweek,* March 1, 1948, pp. 22–23.

"Second Look." *Time,* August 24, 1959, p. 16.

"Shaking the Money Tree: Old-Fashioned Vote-Selling in Louisiana." *Time,* December 25, 1978, p. 30.

"State in a Stew." *Newsweek,* June 29, 1959, pp. 25–26.

"Strange Behavior." *Newsweek,* June 8, 1959, pp. 28–29.

"Twelve Years." *Time,* March 4, 1940, p. 15.

"The Unquenchable Longs." *Newsweek,* August 8, 1960, p. 28.

"Up and Down." *Time,* December 13, 1948, p. 26.

"The Winnfield Frog." *Time,* August 30, 1948, pp. 16–19.

"With Long in Texas: I'll Shoot 'Em." *Newsweek,* July 27, 1959, pp. 25–26.

"Younger Brother." *Time,* January 30, 1948, p. 16.

Papers, Theses, and Dissertations

Baldwin, John T. "Election Strategy and Tactics of Earl Kemp Long as Seen in His Gubernatorial Campaigns." M.A. thesis, Louisiana Tech University, 1973.

Brooks, Davy C. "A Turn of Events: Earl K. Long and the Louisiana Gubernatorial Elections of 1940 and 1948." M.A. thesis, Southeastern Louisiana University, 1985.

Field, Betty Marie. "The Politics of the New Deal in Louisiana: 1933–1939." Ph.D. dissertation, Tulane University, 1974.

Horton, Martha L. "Master of the Pea Patch Farm." Senior paper, Louisiana Tech University, 1964.

Kurtz, Michael L. "The 'Demagogue' and the 'Liberal': The Political Rivalry of Earl K. Long and DeLesseps S. Morrison." Ph.D. dissertation, Tulane University, 1971.

Leslie, J. Paul. "Earl K. Long: The Formative Years, 1895–1940." Ph.D. dissertation, University of Missouri, 1974.

May, Linda Lou Ropp. "A Rhetorical Study of the Public Speaking of Earl Kemp Long from 1955 to 1960." M.A. thesis, Louisiana Tech University, 1964.

Nichols, Lois. "Legislative-Executive Relationships in the 1948 Session of the Louisiana Legislature." M.A. thesis, Louisiana State University, 1954.

Renwick, Edward F. "The Longs' Legislative Lieutenants." Ph.D. dissertation, University of Arizona, 1967.

Sigler, David Lloyd. "Downfall of a Political Machine: The New Orleans Mayoralty Election of 1946." Senior honors thesis, Tulane University, 1968.

Index

Agriculture Adjustment Act, 65
Albright's Prairie, La., 17
Alcoholic Beverage Control Board, 136, 188
Alexandria, La., 59, 117, 138, 205, 246, 253, 255–56
Alexandria *Daily Town Talk,* 246
Allen, Oscar K.: as assessor, 32, 36; as Highway Commissioner, 44–45; as candidate, 52–53, 56–57; as governor, 67, 78–80
Allen, Robert S., 93
American Mercury, 259
American Progress, 45
Amite, La., 222, 266
Anderson, James, 42
Angelle, Robert, 186, 260
Angola State Penitentiary, 137, 164, 193
Anti-Longs: described, 10–11, 47–48, 102–105, 113–17, 121–22, 134, 147–53, 209; as candidates, 11–12, 48–50, 58–59, 79–80, 103–105, 119–20, 121–24, 128, 144–45, 153–56, 159–63, 164, 179, 180–84, 186–87, 195, 230–31, 244–45, 247–49, 251–55; political tactics of, 40–41, 60–63, 106–109, 111, 115–17, 124–26, 134, 139, 142–43, 251–53; and reform measures, 113–15, 164, 179; racial policies of, 150–53, 179, 201–208
Arabi Club, 87, 137
Arizona, 21, 37
Arkansas Southern Railroad, 19
Arlington Race Track, 227
Assessors, 7–8, 32, 36, 85, 136
Atlanta, La., 17
Atlanta *Journal,* 129
Avoyelles Parish, 254–55

"Ballad of Earl K. Long," 251
Baltimore, Md., 247
Bankston, Jesse H., 212, 222
Baptist church, 16, 97, 213
Baptist Hospital, 255–56
Barkley, Alben, 152
Baronne Street, 29, 138
Baton Rouge, La., 22, 33, 37, 51, 52, 94–95, 97, 110, 117, 138, 142, 159, 191–92, 200, 203, 205, 212–13, 214–15, 220, 247
Baton Rouge *Morning Advocate,* 107, 143, 209, 211, 262
Baton Rouge *State-Times,* 113
Baynard, L. B., 103, 127
Belcher, Charles H., 212, 221
Bell, David, 250
Bentley Hotel, 205, 255
Benton, Ark., 242
"Better Government Group," 205
Beverly Club, 137
Bienville Hotel, 99
Big Spring, Tex., 234
Billings, Ann Scott, 241–42
Billings, Earl S., 192, 230
Bipolar disorder: described, 224–25; Earl afflicted with, 225–29
Birmingham, Ala., 150
Bisso, William A., 85, 153
Black Creek, 22
Blackman, Robert, 162
Blacks: Earl and, 12, 131, 151, 194–96, 198–200, 208–209, 239, 240, 246–47, 250, 268; civil rights of, 150–51, 194–96, 198–200, 208–209; voting rights of, 151, 184, 194, 197–98, 206–209. *See also* Long, Earl Kemp; Race Issue; Rainach, William M.